"If an institution were to commit itself fully to meeting the educational needs of women, what would it do?" A wealth of thought-provoking answers to that question is provided in this book.

Educating women involves more than simply admitting them to colleges and universities originally designed for men. It necessitates the reshaping of organizational structures, the questioning of institutional values, reexamination of policies and procedures, and the development of plans to meet the needs of women students, faculty, and administrators. This groundbreaking work begins with a commitment to and a belief in the notion that, after 300 years of higher education in America, institutions can be designed that fully respect and value women for themselves, as well as for their contributions to society.

Written by leaders in higher education, the 29 contributions contained in this volume discuss American women students in all their diversity—by race, age, class, learning styles, and levels of cognitive development. The book, which demonstrates the ways in which equity is a precondition for academic excellence, is divided into four sections:

- *Understanding Women's Diversity and Commonalities,* which focuses on women students in all their complexity and diversity, and deals with differences related to race, ethnicity, class, age, disabilities, sexual preference, learning style, and cognitive development.
- *Learning Environments Shaped by Women,* which explores historical and current programming designed for women, encompassing women's colleges, women's studies, women's athletics, and women's leadership, and which recognizes the rich legacy already available.
- *Reconceptualizing the Ways We Think and Teach,* which presents provocative arguments regarding the reconceptualizations of the ways women think and teach, and describes some early experiments in applying these new approaches.
- *Transforming the Institution,* which focuses on the process of change in academe, and addresses the questions: Where are we going? How can we get there? What is the societal context of this revolution in higher education?

Educating the Majority

Educating the Majority

Women Challenge Tradition in Higher Education

Carol S. Pearson
Donna L. Shavlik
Judith G. Touchton

American Council on Education ⋈ Macmillan Publishing Company
NEW YORK
Collier Macmillan Publishers
LONDON

Macmillan Publishing Company
866 Third Avenue, New York, N.Y. 10022

Collier Macmillan Canada, Inc.

Library of Congress Catalog Card Number: 88-31508

Printed in the United States of America

printing number
1   2   3   4   5   6   7   8   9   10

Library of Congress Cataloging-in-Publication Data

Educating the majority.

(The American Council on Education/Macmillan series
in higher education)
Includes index.
1. Women—Education (Higher)—United States.
2. Women in education—United States.   3. Minority
women—Education (Higher)—United States.   I. Pearson,
Carol, 1944-   .   II. Touchton, Judith G.
III. Shavlik, Donna L.   IV. Series.
LC1756.E38   1989   376'.973   88-31508
ISBN 0-02-924810-8

ACE Board of Directors

Class of 1990

Vera King Farris, President
Stockton State College

E. Gordon Gee, President
University of Colorado

James A. Hefner, President
Jackson State University

Anita Pampusch, President
College of St. Catherine

Donald G. Phelps, Chancellor
Los Angeles Community College
District

Hoke L. Smith, President
Towson State University

Cynthia H. Tyson, President
Mary Baldwin College

James J. Whalen, President
Ithaca College

Association Representatives

Lawrence W. Tyree, Chancellor
Dallas County Community College
*American Association of
Community and Junior Colleges*

Alice Chandler, President
State University College at New
Paltz
*American Association of State
Colleges and Universities*

James H. Daughdrill, Jr., President
Rhodes College
Association of American Colleges

Gene A. Budig, Chancellor
University of Kansas
*Association of American
Universities*

Francis J. Kerins, President
Carroll College (Montana)
*Association of Catholic Colleges
and Universities*

David M. Lascell, Esq.
Nixon, Hargrave, Devans & Doyle
*Association of Governing Boards
of Universities and Colleges*

Michael G. Morrison, SJ, President
Creighton University
*Association of Jesuit Colleges and
Universities*

David S. Sparks, Vice President for
Academic Affairs, Graduate
Studies, and Research
University of Maryland
Council of Graduate Schools

Charles H. Oestrich, President
Texas Lutheran College
Council of Independent Colleges

William P. Hytche, Chancellor
University of Maryland, Eastern
Shore
*National Association for Equal
Opportunity in Higher Education*

Joab M. Lesesne, Jr., President
Wofford College
*National Association of
Independent Colleges and
Universities*

John A. DiBiaggio, President
Michigan State University
*National Association of State
Universities and Land-Grant
Colleges*

Alice Gallin, OSU, Executive
Director
Association of Catholic Colleges
and Universities
*Washington Higher Education
Secretariat*

Contents

Foreword

Why a new book on educating women? Much has been said and written on this important subject. American campuses have been engaged with women's issues for years. But this book breaks new ground, pressing far beyond the familiar, and advancing more spacious claims for the education of women than colleges have addressed before. The leaders of campuses of all sorts will find in this book the fruits of decades of experience and also fresh thinking, brought together into a comprehensive view, directed toward major improvements in higher education for women and men as well.

We must pay attention. Women are the new majority among students in higher education, outnumbering men in nationwide enrollments and among the students on most coeducational campuses. Democratic majoritarianism now strengthens the challenges that women will continue to mount against traditional features of the academy. Yet the critiques and claims on behalf of women rest on more than head counts; they are grounded in the conviction that for women to be fully and properly served in higher education, they must be represented in every aspect of institutional life. The book confronts the need for women's full representation in all levels of higher education, in order to achieve their educational goals, and describes how these goals can be attained.

A major theme, explored in the first group of essays, is the great diversity among women, even though they share commonalities. Differences in age and maturity, race and ethnicity, sexuality and disability, and psychological type are all aspects of diversity that colleges must recognize and understand in order to serve different needs. A second focus in the work is how women shape the settings for their learning.

Women's colleges offer distinctive environments that still provide exceptional opportunity, incentive, and support for the development of high-achieving women. Women who teach and study on coeducational campuses have devised special settings and styles for learning and personal growth that have proved fruitful. But for all colleges and for the benefit of all faculty and students, male and female, the authors in the third portion of the book urge reconceptualization of the knowlege base that underpins teaching and learning. They draw on analysis of women's ways of knowing and learning to broaden our understanding of human knowledge and learning. Finally, this book proposes strategies and goals for the transformation of institutions, concluding with a clear and compelling program for change, a new agenda of women for higher education.

As editors and essayists and as theoreticians and practitioners of change in education, this collection of women's voices speaks from the perspective of women's distinctive experience. These critical and insistent voices speak to everyone in higher education. Their collective message is neither congratulatory nor comforting. They call for a comprehensive response to the new majority, beyond what has been achieved so far. This response requires changes affecting our institutions in every aspect from the core of knowledge to the surrounding values, culture, and structures. The arguments and urgings of this book merit our most serious and sympathetic attention. Taken together they will give us renewed energy and resolve to serve women properly, as students and colleagues, by full inclusion and representation in institutional life.

Through sponsorship and publication of another significant book the American Council on Education once again takes a leadership role in higher education. Donna Shavlik and Judith Touchton of the Office of Women in Higher Education, who joined with Carol Pearson in editing this volume, and the writers of all the essays have made a major contribution to American colleges and universities, to the women who will work and study on our campuses, and to their male fellow students and colleagues.

PHILIP H. JORDAN, JR.
September 1988

Preface

This book was originally conceived by Carol Pearson, who in 1985 recognized the need for a collection of essays addressing the demand for change in the education of women on college and university campuses. At that time, Carol was a consultant to the American Council on Education Office of Women in Higher Education. Carol's relationship with her friends and colleagues, Donna Shavlik and Judy Touchton, flowered into a stimulating and productive collaboration. This collaboration came at a critical time for the Office of Women, as it was beginning to expand its role beyond its primary focus on the advancement of women in administration to give more prominence to issues affecting the experience and success of female students and faculty as well. The Office was beginning to develop a new agenda, one that could effectively utilize the state and national networks created through the National Identification Program for the Advancement of Women in Higher Education Administration (ACE/NIP).

COLLECTIVE COMMENTS FROM THE EDITORS. As our work progressed we talked more and more about our vision for this collection of essays and how it might contribute to changing campuses to serve women better, especially those who are students. Somewhere along the way, it seemed logical to work on a book that could be used by all the people in the ACE/NIP networks, as well as others in higher education. We have expanded the initial concept into a book with contributions from thirty-six people, addressing the multiplicity of needs, concerns, and contributions of academic women. The three of us are grateful for the rich and rewarding experience this collaboration has afforded us.

We have many people to thank for their contributions to this project. We are especially grateful to the authors of the essays, all leaders in their fields, for both their pioneering work and their involvement in this endeavor. Several of the authors have been a part of the project from the start and have exhibited great patience as we continued to refine the focus of the book. Others were invited to make a particular contribution as the book evolved. We also appreciate the moral and intellectual support of our ACE colleagues and friends. We are especially grateful for the very able assistance, counsel, and advice of James Murray, Director of Publications, Advancement, and Membership at ACE. We also appreciate the guidance and support provided by Lloyd Chilton, Executive Editor at Macmillan, throughout the process, and the direction and patience of Michael Sander, our Managing Editor at Macmillan, who came to the project in the final, crucial months.

We give very special thanks to the staff of the Office of Women, who, in addition to proofreading and wordprocessing and offering helpful comments were a constant source of encouragement. These special people include Deborah Ingram-Peek, Lynne Davis, Dulie Kahn, and Ginger Gaines. Their involvement in and support of this project are deeply felt, and greatly appreciated.

We thank all those who have served as chairs and members of the American Council on Education's Commission on Women in Higher Education for their dedication to women's advancement and their willingness to address difficult issues. For their splendid leadership we especially thank Patricia Roberts Harris, the first chairperson, and Nannerl Keohane, Judith Sturnick, and Judith Ramaley, chairs of the Commission during the writing and production of the book. Robert H. Atwell, President of the American Council on Education, deserves special mention for his commitment to the goals of equity in higher education.

And finally, we thank the many women with whom we have worked over the years—especially women college and university presidents, ACE/NIP state coordinators and planning committee members, and others in the Office of Women in Higher Education leadership networks—who incorporate in their work a commitment to achieving equity for all women on campus. Their experiences and insights have continually informed our thinking concerning the condition of education for women, and what kinds of change are developing. We also appreciate the contributions and support of the many men involved in ACE/NIP, and are grateful that they share with their colleagues and constituencies their vision for a future that includes women at all levels and in all roles. We thank Bunny Sandler and her advisory group both for their review of the "New Agenda of Women for Higher Education," which became the last chapter of the book, and for their continuing work in behalf of equity for women in higher education.

In addition to our collective thoughts, each of us has some personal acknowledgments to make.

CAROL PEARSON. Too many people in the field of women's studies have greatly influenced my thinking to mention all of them here, but some individuals and institutions merit special attention. I am particularly grateful to those people who were associated with the University of Colorado Women's Studies Program during its formative years, such as Elizabeth Jameson, Kathi George, Suzanne Juhasz, Shirley Nuss, and the many "radical" young women whose thoughts influenced my own. I am also deeply indebted to the University of Maryland for the experience I had with the Women's Studies Program and with the Chancellor's Commission on the Status of Women. Among the *many* individuals who affected my thinking at Maryland, it is possible to mention only a few. Claire Moses, Laurie Lippin, Dorothy Franklin, Josephine Withers, Faith Gablenick, Mary Leonard, and Lee Knelfelkamp all made major contributions to the perspective that informs this book. At Goucher College, I give special thanks to the Maypole Committee and the Learning Assessment Committee for many beneficial discussions about women's education, and to Rhoda Dorsey for her encouragement and support of this project. Thanks most of all to David Merkowitz, whose personal support and deep commitment to the ideals of equity and excellence make it easier to remain optimistic about the possibilities for constructive change. And finally, thanks to Jeff, Steve, and Shanna for their ideas and encouragement, and for their personal integrity and liberation.

DONNA SHAVLIK. My professional career has been especially enriched by the opportunities I have had to work with and for strong women. Several of these women stand out in my mind as people who always believed that women and women's lives were and are of equal importance to men and men's lives. So I give very special thanks here—for the insight, strength, and values that they willingly shared with me—to my Mother, Sarah Healy, Helen Brush, Nancy Schlossberg, and Emily

Taylor. It would be impossible for me to recognize all the women scholars, faculty, and administrators who have influenced my thinking and intellectual development over the years. There are a few that I would especially like to mention, including Margaret Wilkerson, Ann Ida Gannon, Marjorie Downing Wagner, Rosemary Park, Elizabeth Minnich, Mary Rowe, Jessie Bernard, Mary Ellen Capek, Catherine Stimpson, and Cynthia Secor. My last and most personal thanks go to my husband, who is always there for me, always asks the hard questions, is always fair, and, most of all, always cares.

JUDY TOUCHTON.   My evolution from traditional southern woman to academic feminist has been an important one. It is clear to me that the seeds of my feminism were sewn early in life, but, as is true for many women, it took the fertile ground of adulthood and new experiences for them to flower. I feel fortunate that over the last twenty-five years I have had the opportunity to work with some exceptionally talented women and men with a strong social conscience. Their vision of society includes women in all occupational fields, at all levels, and in all major leadership positions, as well as the traditional familial, supportive, and nurturing roles. I am indebted to all of them and regret that I cannot name each one. Some people and settings merit special mention, however. I will always be grateful to Horace Busby for pointing the way to graduate school and cheering me on through two degrees. I greatly valued the opportunities, sense of community, and professional climate provided by those in the Department of Counseling and Personnel Services at the University of Maryland, College Park—especially Jan Birk, Janet Cornfeld, Lee Knefelkamp, Mary Leonard, Tom Magoon, George Marx, Loretta Wertheimer—where I spent rich and rewarding years in graduate school and working in student affairs. I am grateful to my colleagues at the American Council on Education for creating an environment that makes work a pleasure and a constant source of new learning. And I value the special and continuing friendship of three people: Beth Garraway, Judith Katz, and Eunice Shatz, who are always there for me. Finally, and most important, I am grateful to both Mary Leonard, whose life reflects her commitments in every way, and who is a constant source of support and encouragement, and to my daughter, Katie, now five years old, who is an endless source of energy, joy, and inspiration. May this book improve the future for her and all our children.

Educating the
Majority

Introduction

The purpose of *Educating the Majority* is to provide thought-provoking answers to the question, "If an institution were to commit itself fully to meeting the educational needs of women, what would it do?" Higher education scholars and administrators who have devoted time, study, and reflection to answering this question now agree that educating women well is a different matter from simply admitting women to colleges and universities designed for males. However, many educators do not yet know what to do to effectively educate this population—a population that already constitutes a majority of students in U.S. colleges and universities and represents a trend that is likely to continue.

Indeed, as with any major question in higher education, understanding is an evolving process. During the past fifteen years, a major body of scholarship on educating women has emerged, largely because of the development of women's studies during this period. The goal of this book is to engender dialogue and further study that will advance research and practice in this area and empower educators to make changes that will benefit women specifically and higher education generally. We hope this discourse addressing American higher education will encourage further thinking on how international dimensions could be included effectively.

The basic educational assumption that is the foundation for *Educating the Majority's* approach is that excellence in education requires educators to remain forever in the learning mode in order to be receptive to new information, to help evolve new paradigms incorporating new knowledge, and to continue to understand the learner.

1

In twentieth-century America, this also requires us to pay serious intellectual attention to the requirements of teaching in a pluralistic society—that is, to recognize the particular needs of students, with attention to such categories of diversity as gender, age, and race. It also requires the understanding that students do not all learn the same way. Responsible teaching requires not only expertise in our subject area, but understanding of the learning process and willingness to recognize the implications of what and how we teach in the society in which we live. With knowledge comes responsibility. Higher education has had a major influence during the crucial early adult years on the thinking of virtually all leaders in American politics, business, industry, and the media, as well as education. What we teach and how we teach shapes the world in which we live because it shapes the cognitive maps of people in it, defining what questions we ask, how we formulate them, and what questions will be out of bounds because they are seen as trivial, irrelevant, or unsophisticated.

Educating the Majority is designed to expand the territory of allowable questions and available answers by exploring the too-often invisible or silenced perspectives of women. As in many other cases, however, it is not possible to expand the existing boundaries of inquiry while leaving its system of thought intact. The process of orchestrating this book, and the long process of reflection that led up to it have convinced the editors that it is not possible to address the needs of women students and to honor women's perspectives without massive rethinking of the fundamental assumptions behind our scholarship and teaching, and even behind the ways we structure our institutions.

This book, then, is partly about educating the majority of students in higher education but, more than that, it is about a major paradigm shift that allows for greater equity and quality in education, a shift that, we believe, also will enable us to more effectively address the compelling societal issues of our time, from competitiveness to hunger and illiteracy to world peace.

The articles selected for inclusion are complex in their thinking, raise pertinent questions, reflect an awareness of the diversity of colleges and universities, demonstrate an understanding of how these institutions work, and show a keen sense of the great diversity of American women who attend higher education institutions. This diversity not only represents race, age, religion, sexual preference, and class, but also learning styles and levels of cognitive development. Finally, articles were selected because they provide fresh insights and/or workable models for real and effective change, as well as evidence of a positive attitude toward higher education and women, and the possibilities for appropriate responses to their needs and concerns. The articles are diverse in presentation as well as content. Some are scholarly, some are "think pieces," some reflect experience, and some are various combinations of the three

Selections were made to sample women's rich diversity of background and opinion, not to be exhaustive. Together, however, we believe they form a convincing argument—not so much about what precisely must be done to transform American higher education to meet the needs of the majority, but that *something* must be done. The overwhelming implication of the reflections of the authors is that the needs of women students are currently not well served by higher education.

What we hope from readers is serious attention to the perspectives in this book, leading first to reflection and dialogue and then to informed, expedited action. Addressing the needs of women students, who are the new majority of college students, should be a major agenda for higher education today. We hope that it will be a major agenda for you. We believe that if it is, you cannot help but be enriched by the process of thinking through these challenging and complex issues and then acting to make a positive difference in your own way.

NATIONAL CONTEXT

The history of higher education for women is replete with challenges by women for access to institutions, to particular academic disciplines, to programs. Some of these challenges have been met with positive change, some with indifference, and some with rejection, claiming women cannot succeed. The history of women in the academy has been one of pluses and minuses, pushes and pulls, but never has American higher education fully responded to women for themselves.

With the advent of the contemporary women's movement, the role of women in society was called into question in a more pervasive way than anytime in all of our societal history. This contemporary women's movement began, as described in Jessie Bernard's essay in Part IV of this book, with women sharing how they felt about themselves and learning in the process that they wanted more than second-class citizenship. Naturally, some women throughout history have always understood these concepts of self, which others among us had to discover along the way. These profound, shared learnings led to many changes that have affected all of society, including higher education.

These changes, especially during the 1960s and 1970s, forever altered the course of women's education. One of the most powerful of these changes in setting the stage for women to expand their participation and influence in higher education was the force of the law. Since 1972 a number of laws, regulations, and executive orders have been promulgated to advance the cause of equality for women in education. Some of the major ones include:

- Executive Order 11246 (as amended by Executive Order 11375), mandating the use of affirmative action;
- Title VII of the Civil Rights Act of 1964, as amended, prohibiting discrimination in employment on the basis of race, color, religion, sex, or national origin;
- Title IX of the Elementary/Secondary Act of 1972, the first law prohibiting discrimination against students on the basis of sex, and also including some aspects of employment;
- Title VI of the Civil Rights Act of 1964 (minority women included in 1964), prohibiting discrimination on the basis of race, color, or national origin;
- Section 503 of the Rehabilitation Act of 1973, prohibiting discrimination on the basis of handicap;
- Age Discrimination in Employment Act of 1967, as amended, prohibiting discrimination on the basis of age;
- Equal Pay Act of 1963, as amended, prohibiting differential pay rates for women and men doing the same work; and
- Pregnancy Discrimination Act of 1978, amending Title VII and asserting that pregnant women shall be treated the same for all employment-related purposes as other persons not so affected but similar in their ability or inability to work.

These legal mandates have been a powerful force in getting institutions to establish new policies and procedures, to open access to women students, faculty, and administrators, to assess the climate for all women, to undertake studies to remedy inequalities, and to examine other impediments to the full and equitable participation of women in the academy. The results have included elimination of quotas on admissions; establishment of special recruiting programs for disciplines not usually chosen by women; affirmative action procedures; more resources for women's programs, especially athletics; more open searches for faculty and administrators; and recognition of special problems, such as sexual harassment. These interventions, plus other governmental actions at the federal and state levels, placed women squarely on the national agenda, not an insignificant part of the advancement experienced by women over the last decade. Women's advocacy groups and organizations, national studies on the status of women, special task forces and commissions, federal enforcement of equal opportunity laws, and increased visibility of women at national meetings and in print and electronic media all contributed to an increased awareness of women as a vital force in society.

The increased awareness of women in all segments and at all levels of society has intensified the focus on women students. Along with making higher education, especially, more accessible to women, many concerned persons have sought to make it responsive to them in every possible way. Indeed, great progress has been made since the early 1970s. Women now constitute one half of all undergraduate and master's degree recipients, and receive 34 percent of all Ph.Ds. The number of women entering the professions of law, medicine, and dentistry has risen dramatically. Women now comprise 38 percent of new law school graduates, 30 percent of new medical school graduates, and 21 percent of new dental school graduates (*Digest of Educational Statistics*, 1987, Table 157). The number of women in senior administrative positions in higher education has doubled in the last decade; over three hundred women now serve as chief executive officers in colleges and universities. There is a steady increase in the total number of women faculty, with women now comprising 27 percent of all faculty. And women are being recognized for their scholarly achievements at greater rates. The number of women's-studies courses has mushroomed from 100 in 1970 to more than 30,000 today, and more than 300 academic programs have been established (Stimpson and Cobb, 1987).

But despite these gains, there are troubling signs. Salary discrepancies between men and women still exist at every level of the college and university hierarchy. Women hold only 10 percent of all college and university presidencies, and only a handful of those in research institutions. If all women administrators at the dean's level and above were equally distributed among all institutions, there would be only 1.1 per institution. Women faculty are tenured at about the same rate as a decade ago and continue to report difficulty breaking into the very system that produced them. Incidents of sexual harassment seem to be on the rise, perhaps due to increased reportage as women become more aware of their rights and opportunities, but possibly because of actual increases. Although women have made progress in nontraditional areas, they still find impediments to their acceptance and full participation in many fields. The vast majority of women students still major in a limited number of "traditional" fields. And, perhaps most telling of all, men (and some women) worry about the loss of prestige and influence as some fields approach or surpass fifty-fifty ratios of men and women or institutions begin to admit many more women than men.

As if these signs were not enough, the reports of the last few years on the quality of higher education were silent on the subject of women and minorities as well (Ernest L. Boyer, *College: The Undergraduate Experience in America,* 1987; *Involvement in Learning: Realizing the Potential of American Higher Education,* 1984; and *Intregrity in the College Curriculum: A Report to the Academic Community,* 1985). While these reports were important in guiding higher education in self-examination, they were seriously flawed in not addressing the issues articulated in this book. As Nannerl O. Keohane stated when discussing the deficiences in these reports, the "current zeal for reform should not blind us to the advances brought about by the study of women and minorities" (*The Chronicle of Higher Education,* April 2, 1986). Of course it is not only curriculum reform that should attend to women and minorities, but also the relationship of the faculty to students, the teaching/learning process, the atmosphere on campus, the relationships to the larger community. All of these concerns, raised collectively by these reports, would have been fuller, richer, and more complete with references to the increasingly important roles played by women and minorities on our campuses. It is unfortunate that these national efforts did not take advantage of the opportunity to assist institutions with the changes they need to make in order to better serve women and minorities.

Women have always been a major force in our society, yet their history, psychology, sociology, art, literature—and, indeed, women themselves—have for centuries been relegated to second-class status or ignored. This has been true in American society, in the world, and, as these reports demonstrate, in higher education. Countless theories and explanations have been proffered to explain and even justify this "condition of women." (See the chapters by Elizabeth Kamarck Minnich; Judith Harris, JoAnn Silverstein, and Dianne Andrews; Elizabeth Dodson Gray; Marilyn J. Boxer; and Beverly Guy-Sheftall and Patricia Bell-Scott in this book.) Most of these theories have been proven false through empirical observation or newer, more complete research, often done by women themselves. Others are based on false premises or world views that begin with the assumption that women are primarily child-bearers and have neither the desire nor the ability to count for much else in society. This point is not to downplay the privilege and importance of procreation, but rather to underscore the single unlimited focus of women's lives according to some theories. Perhaps it is not so surprising then that in 1988 we are still concerned with getting the institutions of our society—in our case, higher education—to conceive of women differently. We have become enlightened in comparison to the days when the early colleges declared that thinking was too much for the female brain. Still, much remains to be done before women are considered fully as important as men—just as true for minority as well as majority culture(s).

Since the early 1970s women have begun to be taken more seriously by higher education and many changes have occurred; still, institutions remain fundamentally, at the core, unchanged. Those who lead (including trustees) and teach are primarily the same, the knowledge base is basically unchanged, and the values governing the establishment of priorities and the making of difficult decisions often do not include women or the issues that they deem critical. Why?

Basically, our institutions of higher education were established as seminaries for young men from privileged families who could afford to send them to learn the classic traditions of our Western heritage and to prepare them for lives as teachers, ministers, leaders. The conventional wisdom of the time was that this type of learning was too strenuous for women and might result in severe malfunctioning of the individual female, not to mention her role in society.

Undergirding our attention to these institutional concerns is the recognition that even though women have made progress during the 1970s and 1980s, men still serve as the educational norm by which women are evaluated. Institutions have yet to really reflect the life experiences of women or to recognize their full humanity.

A 1984 article by Schuster and Van Dyne refers to "invisible paradigms" to describe how concentration on education for and about men has shaped the majority of our curriculum in higher education. They refer to these paradigms as "internalized assumptions, the network of unspoken agreements, the implicit contracts that all the participants in the process of higher education have agreed to, usually unconsciously, in order to bring about learning." They further point out that this infrastructure has worked long and well and therefore becomes so normative that it is no longer noticed (p. 417). This is but one example of how "right and proper" it can seem to continue discriminating by doing what has always been done and not questioning the assumption that there is only one way to be right.

These glimpses into history allow us to see clearly that the first institutions of higher learning in the United States, with the notable exception of the women's colleges, were never meant to provide appropriate education for women. Is it any wonder then that it has taken extraordinary measures to bring about the kind of changes necessary to provide high-quality education for women, free from the prejudices that have quite naturally resulted from history?

The nature of the changes, for the most part, has involved accommodation by women to study, teach, and engage in scholarship in the prescribed male tradition while institutions have made incremental, cosmetic, or minimal changes. Accommodation, as defined by Ogburn in his theory of social change, means that women learned to live by the values, structures, and systems created by men. Clearly, women have effectively made these "accommodations," but neither they nor the institutions have yet realized the full magnitude of the changes that lie before us if women are to be part of the institutions and also fully themselves. What we are calling for in *Educating the Majority* is the recognition that it is now institutions, structures, systems, and organizations that need to change. As we discovered for ourselves, the only way that women may be fully who they are is if institutions are fundamentally changed to allow for women's perspectives to emerge.

It is no longer enough to make progress toward greater equality for women. *Now* is the time for our institutions of higher education to reshape organizational structures, question institutional values, reexamine policies and procedures, and develop plans to sincerely meet the needs of women faculty, administrators, staff, and *students*.

STRUCTURE OF THE BOOK

The structure of this book follows from its philosophy. *Educating the Majority* begins with students. Part One, then, focuses on women students in all their complexity and diversity as well as their commonalities. This section is not exhaustive in its diversity. For example, although racial diversity is addressed, not all races or ethnic groups are represented, and although we have tried to represent many different kinds of diversity from sexual orientation and disability to learning style, we could not recognize them all. Conspicuously absent, for example, is any consideration of the impact of different religious backgrounds and affiliations and the special problems of low-income women.

We are hoping that, by providing a representative look at diversity, this section can serve as a touchstone for all of us designing programs, services, and curriculum offerings for students. It should remind us to ask, "Does this program, service, or curriculum meet the needs of women as well as men? Does it meet the needs of minority as well as majority students? Have we considered the needs of disabled students and students of different personality types and learning styles? Have we thought through the needs of homosexual as well as heterosexual students? Have we considered variable needs by the age and economic status of our students? Have we respected the different religious orientation of our students?" And so on.

Part Two, "Learning Environments Shaped by Women," is an exploration of historical and current programming designed for women—from women's colleges, to women's centers, women's studies and women's athletics. This important section recognizes the rich legacy already available to us. Becoming educated about this rich heritage allows us not to reinvent the wheel, but to build upon the foundation of wisdom coming from the successes of colleges and programs created for, and often also by, women.

Part Three, "Reconceptualizing the Ways We Think and Teach," grew naturally out of the programming discussed in Part Two. People involved in designing programs to meet the needs of women students almost always come to recognize that it is not possible to do so without radically reconceptualizing the ways we think and teach. This section, then, presents thought-provoking arguments about the nature of that reconceptualization and some early experiments in translating these new approaches into practice.

Finally, Part Four, "Transforming the Institution," focuses on the change process. Where are we headed? How can we get there? What is the societal context for this revolution in academe? And, where do we begin? Its mission is to be both utopian in vision and pragmatic in approach. The issues of how to begin an orderly and inclusive process that not only improves higher education for women, but makes it better for everyone, are complex and challenging ones. Essays included here reflect an understanding of the immensity of the task before us, while also staying grounded in the realities of how current institutions function and how institutional change occurs.

WHAT CAN YOU DO?

As you read this book we hope you will be sufficiently inspired to think seriously and deeply about the issues and how you, personally, can be a part of making change occur on behalf of women. Some of you will naturally want to explore these ideas in more depth, and perhaps deepen your understanding of this new majority of college students through additional reading and through discussions on your campus or at national or regional conferences and workshops. Others among you already may be well versed in these ideas and will be ready to take direct action. What kind of action you can take depends in great measure on who you are and what you do. But it is vital to realize that each person, no matter what role he or she plays with regard to the institution, can make an important and necessary contribution to the process of change.

We have tailored our recommendations to the many different constituencies of higher education. However, there are a few generalities that apply to all groups. The concepts, values, programs, ideas, theories, and strategies suggested in this book need to be woven into the very fabric of the institution—they need to be "mainstreamed." As the institution through its various constituent groups plans for the future, women's issues and perspectives need to be considered and included. And there needs to be a mechanism whereby institutions can effectively plan for continuing enlightenment in all these areas.

To Trustees: Ask that works such as *Educating the Majority* be discussed at trustee meetings to educate yourselves about women. Consider the implications for your institution and what needs to happen to meet the needs of *all* students. Be sure that as your institution plans for the future, the needs of women students—majority and minority—are considered. Implement these new plans in a timely, efficient fashion in all areas. When hiring a new president, ask questions about her or his level of understanding about what is required to responsibly educate a pluralistic student body and to provide the leadership to follow through on needed changes.

To Presidents and Chancellors: No one is more important in this effort than you are. It is you who can inspire, cajole, and educate others within the college and university community to begin the planning and educational process that makes change happen. You also are the one who can apply sanctions when actions are not taken. Because institutional transformation requires a change of heart and mind for many people, as well as change in policies and procedures, it is advisable to begin with an educational process but to move quickly into devising a workable plan for institutional change. Because we are talking here about major transformations of ways we think and teach, the planning cannot effectively be separated from other planning processes—certainly it must not be separated from the reward structure. If meeting the needs of the new majority of students becomes an institutional priority, then the reward system needs to reflect it—in considerations affecting salary, retention, reappointment, promotion, tenure, and departmental budgets.

To Faculty: You are in the enviable position of being able to reconceptualize the way you think and teach and immediately reflect this new knowledge and these new perspectives in your teaching, research, and other student contacts, such as advising. You are also in the position, especially is some fields, to introduce students to perspectives which help them "name" their own realities and experiences. Those of you who are involved or who are willing to become involved in service to your department, campus, or professional association can call for discussion of the needs of women students. You also contribute to our ongoing understanding of the teaching/learning process through constant attention to improving your own knowledge and practice by doing primary or applied research in the areas of gender and sex. Some of you are furthering knowledge by making your classes laboratories where students can study the teaching/learning process with attention to questions of gender/sex and other kinds of diversity. Moreover, you can support each other in the process of learning and discovery in what may be very new areas of thought and exploration.

To Administrators (other than presidents): You, too, are in a position to begin a planning and educational process within your unit and to ask for such action at the campus level. Develop the habit of considering implications for gender and other kinds of diversity when contemplating both new initiatives and current practice. Ask questions frequently of those who report to you about their efforts in programming for diversity to signal them about your seriousness regarding this issue. And most important, hold them accountable for being competent and professional with regard to it. Certainly, their contribution, or lack thereof, could be profitably discussed in evaluation sessions.

To Students: As students you may initially feel powerless, but you are far from powerless. Begin where you are. Become as educated as you can about gender issues and sex discrimination. Encourage student organizations to sponsor speakers, workshops, and other events which help educate others. In your interactions with professors, administrators, counselors, and advisers, ask questions: What were women doing during this historical period? Why is there no sexual harassment policy? What is the process to adopt one? Would you give me this same advice if I were male or female? If there is no campus initiative about "educating the majority," ask that a commission be appointed to study the issue and volunteer to serve on it. Get involved in your own education.

To Parents: Whether you have daughters or sons, your knowledge of the changing expectations and roles of women can help your child become better educated and able to succeed in work and personal life alike. You, too, can challenge the institutions on these important issues. After all, you do pay a large share of the costs! You can ask about the curriculum, the campus climate, the faculty, the leadership, and so on. It is important to this entire change process we are advocating that you as parents become involved and educated.

To Alumni: As you experience life day by day, you no doubt have and will continue to confront gender differences and sex discrimination that complicate your lives at work and at home. You can help by encouraging your alma mater to write about, plan alumni programs around, and generally educate you in these areas. Your support is particularly important because you know the institution and you now know what would have helped you when you were there. Your willingness to be educated about women's roles and lives will not only help you, but also will help your institution to be more effective.

To Associations and National Education Leaders: In spite of the revolution in thinking about women's education, during the 1970s and 1980s no major national education report has addressed the needs of this new majority of students. It is as if women did not exist. The time has come to make women and their involvement in higher education a major agenda item, through your annual conventions of associations, ongoing discussions in educational journals, higher education reports, and future planning of national priorities. You can sponsor dialogues, issue guidelines, and, in general, promote timely consideration of issues. As individual educational leaders, you can consider these questions in your own work and include issues of gender and diversity in reports, research, policy statements, and public speeches. Above all, you can serve as role models, as individuals of stature who set the tone for a national dialogue and debate about the most effective way to promote excellence through appropriate recognition of diversity.

Educating the Majority begins with a commitment to and a belief in the notion that finally, after three hundred years of higher education in the United States, we can design institutions that fully respect and value women for themselves as well as for their contributions to society. And, furthermore, that men and women will all be better off in these "new" institutions. You can play a major role in this rebirth. Won't you join us in meeting this exciting challenge?

REFERENCES

BENNETT, WILLIAM J. *To Reclaim a Legacy: A Report on the Humanities in Higher Education.* Washington, D.C.: National Endowment for the Humanities, 1984.

BOYER, ERNEST L. *College: The Undergraduate Experience in America.* New York: Harper and Row, 1987.

Digest of Educational Statistics, 1987. Table 157, First Professional Degrees Conferred by Institutions of Higher Education by Sex of Student, Control of Institution, and Field of Study, 1981–82 to 1984–85. Washington, D.C.: Center for Education Statistics, Office of Educational Research and Improvement, U.S. Department of Education.

Integrity in the College Curriculum: A Report to the Academic Community. Washington, D.C.: Association of American Colleges, 1818 R Street, 1985.

Involvement in Learning: Realizing the Potential of American Higher Education. Washington, D.C.: National Institute of Education, 1984.

KEOHANE, NANNERL O. "Our Mission Should Not Be Merely to 'Reclaim' a Legacy of Scholarship—We Must Expand on It." *The Chronicle of Higher Education*, Washington, D.C., April 2, 1986.

SCHUSTER, MARILYN and VAN DYNE, SUSAN. "Placing Women in the Liberal Arts Curriculum," *Harvard Educational Review*, November, 1984, No. 4, Volume 54, pp. 413–428.

STIMPSON, CATHERINE, and COBB, NINA KRESSNER. "Women's Studies in the United States," The Ford Foundation, P.O. Box 559, Naugatuck, Conn., 1987.

PART ONE

Understanding Women's Diversity and Commonalities

A look at American higher education as we approach the 1990s reveals a degree of pluralism never before witnessed in the history of our nation. To focus on women students in that context is to become aware of a richness in background, experience, talent, and potential that is impressive. Women have rarely been the focus of higher education observers, except as related to women's colleges or as a special case in colleges and universities dominated by men. Now that women students constitute a numerical majority of all students, however, it is time that their issues be addressed. It makes no sense to continue to design education environments and experiences without a thorough and ongoing analysis of women students. As educators, parents, and concerned citizens, we need to know who our women students are, and how colleges and universities can foster their full development and prepare them for full participation in society.

15

Questions of gender sameness and difference are complex. In some ways, women's educational needs are the same as men's, but in other ways they differ. Similarly, women share many commonalities that emerge out of the shared experience of femaleness and societal definitions and treatment of women. But women also differ in important ways—in background, attitudes, and experience. Women students today vary widely by age, race, ethnic group, and sexual preference. They come from all socioeconomic classes. They include able-bodied women and women with disabilities. And they vary in styles of learning, leading, and being. On the whole, differences among women are as important and as great as comparative differences among men. Yet, neither set of differences should be ignored by educators seeking to fit the educational experience to the needs of the students.

We are well past the era in which women college students could be easily characterized, if indeed they ever could. As Barbara Miller Solomon has shown in her 1985 work, *In the Company of Educated Women*, women's experiences in higher education since the mid-nineteenth century are far richer and more complex than most people know or imagine.

Who were the early collegiate women? Although women represented a sizable proportion of all college students in the latter part of the nineteenth century, the fact that so few of the total population of either sex went to college made description and generalization much easier than it is today. Women collegians in the late 1800s "came from a range of families within the broad and expanding middle class. Heads of these families included those in the professions (doctors, ministers, lawyers, professors, and teachers), those in business (manufacturers, professors, and teachers), and still others in agriculture" (Solomon, 1985, pp. 64–65). Many families made sacrifices so that their daughters could attend college, and many young women worked, especially in teaching roles, to provide some of their own support. As the new century began, the expanding college population included many women, some of whom were from ethnically and racially diverse groups. In 1900 approximately 85,000 women were enrolled in college, and they represented 36.8 percent of all students enrolled (ibid., p. 63, Table 2). To put this in context, however, it is important to note that the women collegians in the same year represented only 2.8 percent of all women in the eighteen-to-twenty-one-year-old age group. Women collegians were, along with their male counterparts, a rarity (ibid., p. 63, Table 3).

By 1920 women constituted almost half (47 percent) of all collegians, the highest proportion they were to represent for another 50 years. Although the number of women attending colleges would continue to grow steadily, along with the numbers of men seeking higher education, women as a percentage of all students dropped significantly in the middle of this century, notably after World War II. Dramatic changes were to come, however, in the decade of the 1960s, an unprecedented period of rapid growth in higher education that was to have major impact on the education of women, minorities, and other underserved groups. For the first time since the GI Bill opened higher education to returning World War II veterans, the federal government began pouring enormous sums of money into every aspect of higher education. One of the major new policies of the era was the provision of federal financial aid, which made it possible for students (who were not veterans) from working class families to begin entering higher education in great numbers.

It has been more than twenty years since the doors of colleges and universities widened to admit any student desiring to pursue higher education, regardless of economic circumstances. The "new student" was one who in an earlier era could not even have aspired to college—first-generation collegians, often from working class backgrounds, representing diverse racial and ethnic populations, and older than what was considered the "traditional" age (eighteen to twenty-two years old) for college students. Many women were among these students, and not only did their numbers increase greatly in the 1960s and 1970s, they also grew in comparison to male students. By the mid-1980s more women than men were attending colleges and universities as undergraduates, and half of all students obtaining master's degrees are women.

Women presently constitute 52 percent of all persons enrolled in college. They are, in fact, a majority. This "new majority" is a diverse majority, rich in complexity, background, and talent. Today's women collegians include, in addition to traditional-age students, a high proportion of what are called "returning women," those returning to school after interrupting their education for work, family, or other responsibilities. These returning women include the "new students" described above as well as those from more privileged groups, middle- and upper-middle-class women who could and can afford college, but who did not attend or finish at an earlier age because of lack of interest or encouragement. Collectively, today's women collegians are diverse in terms of age, social class, race, ethnic group and religion, each one bringing with her life experience and cultural heritages which enrich, and sometimes challenge, the prevailing culture.

Even with the wide spectrum of diversity represented by this collection of articles, we have not addressed the critical area of religious preference and spirituality. The complex web of beliefs, customs, values, and interconnections of the spiritual with everything we do made us realize that to address this subject cryptically would be a disservice. We determined instead to take note of how important this dimension of life is to what we are discussing here and suggest that colleges and universities seek ways to develop the fullness of campus life for women and men students and recognize the religious and spiritual dimension to their lives.

The differences among the women described above are ones that are usually, at least to some extent, visible to observers. If one looks at a group of women, one can note many differences having to do with age, race, ethnic identity, and physical disability. But there are other differences that are not outwardly observable but that are just as significant from an educational viewpoint. These factors have to do with differences in learning style, personality type, leadership style, and sexual preference. Such attributes have a powerful influence on the nature and quality of learning that takes place inside and outside the classroom. Differential perceptions of these characteristics also affect the learning process. Whether these differences are visible or invisible, to take women students seriously is to respect and be sensitive to them.

The eleven articles in Part One describe and reflect the great diversity in women students described above. The articles focus on women students—who they are, where they are, and what they need in a learning environment. Some authors identify ways in which women's needs differ from those of men, others focus on how women's needs differ from each other, and some do both. The articles vary somewhat in style and tone, reflecting to some extent the subject being presented. The editors have chosen to respect the uniqueness of each piece to ensure that the differences are part of the message. It is hard to imagine anyone reading the section as a whole without being impressed by the collective talent, the range of differences, the uniqueness, the special contributions, the breadth of spirit, and the essential commonalities among the women. Their voices are many, yet their voices are one. Most of all, they deserve to be heard.

In the first essay, "Majority, Minority, and the Numbers Game," Margaret Wilkerson speaks eloquently of the value of cultural pluralism and knowingly of the majority culture's game of "trick mirrors," as it defines and redefines majority and minority at will. Wilkerson implores college decision-makers to take account of the changes that have occurred in their student populace. "With women as the new majority," she writes, "educational institutions should see this development as a unique opportunity to rethink their assumptions and to reformulate their academic programs and students activities. A fundamental error is to ignore the differences among this numerically dominant minority. Merely recognizing the differences among the 'other,' as if it were a monolithic mass, is inadequate."

The next five essays focus respectively on white, Black, Hispanic, Asian Pacific, and Indian women—their diverse values, cultures, history, and demography. Each was written by a person or persons who are personally knowledgeable about their own group or expanded group, but are also thoughtful and reflective about their particular cultures. They shared their perspectives eloquently and uniquely. Without exception, each of the authors emphasized the diversity within the groups as much as the contrast or commonalities with women of other races or ethnic identities.

In "The 'Traditional' Undergraduate Woman in the Mid-1980s: A Changing Profile," Anne Hafner provides a quantitatively rich and detailed description of what is still called the "traditional" undergraduate student. Hafner describes the characteristics of these college women, including background variables, trends over time in degree and career aspirations, self-concept, values, and life goals, and discusses the general implications of this changing profile for higher education institutions. Ms. Hafner's data was drawn from the twenty years of data collected by UCLA's Higher Education Research Institute, based on its annual national surveys of college freshmen. Only full-time, first-time college students are included in this survey, and most of the students are white. Among Hafner's many findings is that, although the gap narrowed between men and women students in educational and career aspirations, there was a continuance of the gap in self-confidence and self-rating of academic ability. In fact, according to "women's self-rating of academic ability . . . declined by 7 percent between 1966 and 1985. Although college women have a higher general self concept than in the past," she continues, "they still lag behind men in many subareas of self-concept, including academic ability, intellectual self-confidence, math ability and public-speaking ability, and in physical and mental health." Other studies have also documented women's decline in self-confidence during the college years, in contrast to the gains made by men. What, indeed, does this say about differential effects of college environments on men and women?

Beverly Guy-Sheftall and Patricia Bell-Scott, in "Finding a Way: Black Women Students and the Academy," provide enlightening glimpses into the education of Black women over the years in single-sex, coeducational, and white-dominated institutions. They address historical issues such as separate education, curriculum, and the special needs of Black women due to race and sex, as well as emerging issues related to affirmative action, campus climate, and women's studies. They offer several educational priorities for Black women during the remainder of the century—for example, the need to keep access at the top of the list of equity issues, the need to devise creative strategies for financing higher education, the need to support scholarship on Black women, and the need for more women of color as faculty, administrators, and policymakers in all educational settings. "It is imperative," they conclude, "that all of us commit ourselves to building educational institutions and experiences that promote the self-empowerment of women generally and especially Black women. Historically Black and predominantly white institutions must engage in this struggle."

Sara E. Meléndez and Janice Petrovich, in "Hispanic Women Students in Higher Education: Meeting the Challenge of Diversity," present a thoughtful and complex portrait of the great diversity among Hispanic women. Their essay focuses on the sociocultural commonalities that make the needs, concerns, contributions, and problems of Hispanic women distinct from those of other ethnic groups. They also discuss the participation of Hispanic women in higher education, identify some specific behaviors that can be at odds with campus cultures, and make recommendations for creating a more hospitable campus culture for Hispanic women. "Hispanic women," they conclude, "and cultural minorities in general, can be a valuable asset to colleges and universities. Hispanic cultural values of cooperation, respect for people's feelings, intrinsic motivation, interdependence, and zest for life can contribute to a more humane and caring campus environment for all."

Joanne Sanae Yamauchi and Tin-Mala, in "Undercurrents, Maelstroms, or the Mainstream? A Profile of Asian Pacific American Female Students in Higher Education," discuss the great diversity of Asian Pacific American (APA) women as well as the dual influence of ethnic and gender-based factors in their evolution in American higher education. The authors discuss their status, interpersonal needs and concerns, achievement, and aspirations, and explore all of these in relation to enhancing higher education for APA female students. Yamauchi and Tin-Mala share the view that there is a strong commitment by both Asians and other ethnic group memebers to correct misconceptions about Asian Pacific Americans and to educate both Asians and non-Asians about the needs and concerns of APA women students. "The enhancement of their higher education," say the author, "will enable Asian Pacific American women to develop their unique blend of multicultural identities and ensure the equity of their participation in the American mainstream."

In "American Indian Women in Higher Education: Common Threads and Diverse Experiences," Robbi Ferron writes sensitively and personally of the needs and concerns of American Indian women in higher education. American Indian women represent a very small percentage of students in our colleges and universities, all the more reason to be thoughtful about who they are and what they need. Ferron identifies and describes a number of problems facing Indian women students, such as paying for college, dealing with the influence of tribal culture and tradition, special issues of child care, implications of right-brain dominance (a frequent occurrence among American Indian students), and conflict between traditional female roles and leadership roles for women. She also offers recommendations on how to deal with these challenges. Ferron describes some of the unique contributions Indian women can make to higher education. Indian women "have an honesty that is gentle yet incisive," she says. "They are clear about their interpretation of what they perceive. An older Indian woman will expose that perception gently, often through stories or humor, whereas a younger woman may speak directly. The contribution is a response to an inquiry or situation that is unfettered by game-playing and which can be threatening or refreshing.

In the next three essays the authors write about other kinds of differences among women students. Unlike the preceding five essays, which essentially divide women students into mutually exclusive categories primarily on the basis of race, the following three essays describe types and characteristics of women irrespective of race and ethnic identity. We turn our attention now to returning women, lesbians, and women with disabilities.

Returning women, or reentry women as they are also called, constitute one of the largest new contingents of women students today. Lesbians constitute a significant minority, comprising about 10 percent of all women students. And women with disabilities constitute about 6 percent of freshmen women students. Women in all three of these groups have some differences that, if ignored, constitute forms of discrimination as limiting and prejudicial as racism.

Jean F. O'Barr writes about returning women today in "Reentry Women in the Academy: The Contributions of a Feminist Perspective." Reentry women are an important constituency in higher education in numbers, quality, and diversity. Given the decline of traditional-age college students in recent years, many colleges and universities would have experienced sharp cutbacks in enrollments, or actually closed, had it not been for the influx of reentry women. But O'Barr suggests that their contributions have been even more profound. She makes an important connection between the continuing education movement and the development of women's studies, an approach which relates directly to Part Two of this book. "The results of the continuing education movement, modified policies, and more older students have contributed, albeit indirectly, to the development of women's studies," she writes. "And the new scholarship on women has grown and been appreciated in part as a result of people having worked on parallel questions for nontraditional students. I have not argued the two efforts were informed by one another, except indirectly. Nonetheless, both seek a similar campus climate, one that values diversity over homogeneity, applauds a larger picture instead of a narrower one, and affirms the contributions of all learners to the collective enterprise."

Toni A. H. McNaron, in "Mapping a Country: What Lesbian Students Want," provides insight into the lives and wishes of lesbian students. "Like all women in our colleges and universities," she observes, "lesbians want more visible attention paid to the lives and works of all women within whatever culture or time period a given course claims for its province. In addition, they want the support services of their campus to be more responsive to their particular needs. Generally speaking, this means addressing heterosexist language and heterosexist presumptions." Examples of areas in which attention is needed include health services, counseling services, use of campus facilities, allowance and respect for lesbian-feminist research and writing, more courses devoted to or including lesbian culture and history, and the simple ability to "feel safe" as a lesbian on campus. McNaron offers many suggestions for improving institutional climates, the most important of which is to break the silence around lesbianism. "To have a college or university president or dean make a simple statement in which the words lesbian research and culture occurred would do more toward giving students what they need than almost any other single act."

Yvonne Duffy, in "Enhancing the Effectiveness of Postsecondary Education for Women with Disabilities," writes of the special needs and challenges of women students with disabilities. She offers a firm reminder that for such women the disability is but one characteristic of their total identity, along with curly hair, career ambitions, math fears, personality type. "For students with disabilities to gain maximum value from their college education," she writes, "there must be full recognition on the part of administrators that they are persons *first*, with the same needs as nondisabled students, and therefore deserve access to all the same academic, counseling, housing, health, financial, social, and recreational services." Speaking of the particular needs of women with disabilities, she reminds us that in order to compete for jobs, such women "need all the same support services the university provides nondisabled women—assertiveness training, exercises to increase self-esteem, and sexual health care, including family planning, but they may need them to be in a slightly different form."

Explorations of differences among women students so far have focused on factors such as race, age, social class, sexual preference, and physical ability/disability. Another kind of difference has to do with ways of perceiving and acting in the world. Although there are demonstrable differences, as Gilligan (1982) argues, between male and female "voices," women do not all see the world the same way, any more than all men do. The next essay provides a model for recognizing the diversity of psychological type among women and suggests ways of fostering women's development while recognizing and respecting such pluralism.

In "Recognizing the Diversity of Women's Voices by Psychological Type," Faith Gabelnick and Carol S. Pearson discuss women students' personality types in terms of the Myers-Briggs Type Indicator (MBTI). "To address adequately the diversity we find among women," they claim, "it is necessary not only to explore differences by race, class, age, and sexual orientation, but also to recognize that women differ by psychological temperament." The authors briefly describe the MBTI, offer some basic generalizations about typical women students of each temperament, and suggest some teaching strategies designed to foster their success. According to Gabelnick and Pearson, "Working with women in the classroom involves supporting the variety of perspectives or voices that women represent. Too often women have been pressured into conforming to one image, whether it be the traditional nurturing housewife or the more modernized superwoman, performing competently in a variety of ways and thus also suppressing their individuality. One of the educational tasks that confronts educators during the last decade of the twentieth century will be to enable women to articulate and strengthen their individual perspectives and identities."

In spite of all this diversity among women, there appear to be shared values, experiences, and perspectives among them. In the final essay of this introductory section, "The Meaning of Gilligan's Concept of 'Different Voice' for the Learning Environment," Carolyn Des-Jardins focuses on the work of Carol Gilligan, whose research and publications (best known is *In a Different Voice*, 1982) provide some of the most important new insights on women and women's development today. The work of Gilligan and her associates has powerful implications for the educational environment, and DesJardins' experience as a member of Gilligan's research team in 1986 provided valuable perspective for this article. Gilligan does not believe that it is possible to measure women's moral and human development with the present standards, since the present standards are based on studies of male development. When male development is used as the standard, and females are found to be different, the most common result has been to interpret the difference in terms of female deficiency. Gilligan's unique and much-heralded contribution has been to present a persuasive account of female moral development and the female life cycle and to call attention to women's perceptions and experiences of self. "The task for women," says Gilligan, "is to realize that they have a perspective and that the way they see things is valued and that there is truth in what they know."

REFERENCES

GILLIGAN, CAROL. *In a Different Voice*. Cambridge, Mass.: Harvard University Press, 1982.

SOLOMON, BARBARA MILLER. *In the Company of Educated Women: A History of Women and Higher Education*. New Haven: Yale University Press, 1985.

1

Majority, Minority, and the Numbers Game

MARGARET B. WILKERSON

When a colleague heard that I was preparing an anthology of plays by black women playwrights, she exclaimed, "Why divide women into such minute groups? How can you break them up into small, special interests?" I have pondered her statement now for some time. Her surprise at the "specialness" or "minuteness" of my project was matched only by my surprise at her reaction. On reflection, it is an all-too-common assumption that to recognize differences, particularly those of race and gender, is to foster division and to mitigate against the universality that we presume to be the ideal. Perhaps it is a legacy of the historical effort by Americans to "tame" such an expansive land as the continental United States by homogenization and the imposition of conformity at the expense of diversity.

The "melting pot" has long been a popular metaphor among many Americans. The idea that the different races, creeds, and nationalities represented by the many immigrants from throughout the world could be absorbed and shaped into one formidable, new being— the American—was attractive testimony to the vision of the New World and a denunciation of a Europe severely divided along class, ethnic, religious, and other lines. However, in recent decades that concept has been challenged as this nation has divided itself along seemingly endless lines—racial groups, gender differences, religious affiliations, physical abilities and limitations, sexual preferences, and on and on. Some claim that the metaphor has shifted from "melting pot" to "stew," in which the individuality of each entity is retained yet contributes to a delectable whole. At the moment, however, the perfect balance between diversity and unity implied by that metaphor seems an impossibility, and the only available evidence of that ideal "stew" is that we are in it.

Educational institutions were built in part on the expectation that they would play a primary role in socializing the diverse population of new Americans who came from various parts of Europe, forging them into a unified populace with common goals and values and preparing them to govern the land—either as officials or as informed citizens, with higher educational institutions reserved for those who would lead the nation in fields of government, education, science, the arts, and technology. A simple language was required, a school system that not only taught fundamentals of the constitutional government but also subtly promoted common values and cultivated beliefs based on the notion that sameness ensured unity. This idea of the melting pot persisted, fueled by immigrant efforts to conform by changing or anglicizing their foreign-sounding names or by adopting various "Americanisms"; the sacrifice of one's ethnic or national differences was extracted and often willingly given as the price for full citizenship.

The fact that education was expected to change behavior reinforced the structuring of institutional settings to serve the needs and interests of the potential power brokers—privileged white men. Thus, when small numbers of women and other groups entered the hallowed halls of ivy, they were expected to conform (and often did and do) to the norms already set by the male-dominated institution. One group, however, was "unmeltable"—its particular difference being so entrenched in the symbolism, mythology, politics, and economics of the society that even their best efforts to "integrate" met with sharp and sometimes violent resistance. At the same time, their efforts at separatism were declared "un-American." This vocal minority, distinguished from others by their color, their forced passage from Africa to the Americas and the legacy of the slavery they endured, forced this nation and its educational institutions to grapple continually with the evidence of "difference" in its midst. Giving a new formulation and presence to the term "minority," this group insisted that the rights guaranteed to American citizens be extended to them. Ultimately their fight inspired women to reexamine their own status and to claim citizenship rights and full educational privileges. And now, in a surprising twist of history, this "minority"—women—has become a major force both in politics and education. Regarded in recent decades as a special interest group, women now constitute more than 50 percent of the student population in colleges and universities, many of which are still administered under assumptions attendant to a predominantly male student body. Thus on one hand, colleges and universities, unprepared for this radical change, have felt beleaguered by a staggering range of new demands, from curricular reform to child care, while on the other hand, women—claiming a subtle form of gender apartheid—often find themselves treated as a minority, despite their greater numbers.

Majority—minority—sometimes it seems to be a mere game of numbers with trick mirrors. Women students are a numerical majority in higher education, yet their needs and interests are often a low priority. At the same time, white males may be in the minority in a college or university, but may in fact have more power to define the college's goals and values. People of color are referred to, in all instances, as minorities when, in fact, they are fast becoming the majority in certain areas of the United States and when they are increasingly identifying with the majority of the world's population. The locus of power may shift when a significant minority—college alumni, for example—takes a strong position. The census has become one of the most politicized government activities as individuals argue over group designations and challenge the accuracy of the final count. Majority and minority are political designations that shift depending on the intent of the individual or group using the term. The numbers game can be both advantage and disadvantage: it can be the basis for acquiring a greater share of resources, and it can also obscure genuine institutional problems.

Rosabeth M. Kanter's (1979) study of women in corporations documented the effect of majority and minority status on human behavior. "Majority" is as much a state of mind as a numerical reality: it is the locus of power that defines, enforces, and thereby controls—not merely by the force of numbers, but by dint of historical legacy. The "majority mentality" generally assumes superiority in knowledge. Its experiences and values are defined as the norm, and everything different from those are considered deviant and perhaps even inferior. Recognition of differences is an interim phenomenon, a temporary adjustment that an institution with this mentality makes, biding time until the regular, "important" business can be resumed. This mind-set results in a cycle of regression and advocacy that saps the strength of an institution and the patience of all involved.

In the 1960s and early 1970s, some believed that the entry of Blacks into higher education in record numbers was a temporary affair; that they would soon adjust themselves to the norm of institutions and settle in like "other students." The demands for Black studies programs, new student services, minority faculty, and for a less Eurocentric curriculum caught many by surprise. The same phenomenon has occurred with women as the entry of large numbers of women students has brought women's studies, revisionist/feminist research, demands for new services and for more women faculty. Neither administrators nor faculty with "majority mentalities" had nor have expected that the institution itself had to learn, to change its behavior.

A minority mentality, on the other hand, emanates from the effect of being defined as "other," something opposite or different from the majority—"not this" or "not that." The term "minority" indicates what one is not, rarely connoting what one is. Thus, whole groups of individuals are labeled "nontraditional" or "alternative." The person being defined finds herself designated as a negative, a minus, and always conceptualized in relation to a dominant majority. This difference then becomes negative, not just different. It is not unlike the unaccommodating public accommodations in the pre-1960's South. There was often a rest room for "white ladies," "white men' " and then, almost as an afterthought, located around the back of the building, one for "colored." None of the finer distinctions, even that of men and women, were recognized for that particular group which was defined as "other." Minorities experience the world differently. W.E.B. Du Bois described this phenomenon as "double-consciousness," the contradiction between one's perception of self and society's reflection of oneself. The two images, according to Du Bois, engage in a continuous war for supremacy, creating a constant, internal tension.

But what happens when the minority becomes the majority, when the minority consciousness becomes too compelling to be ignored or subordinated. What happens when the premises of college decision-makers do not take account of the changes which have occurred in their student populace? With women as the new majority, educational institutions should see this development as a unique opportunity to rethink their assumptions and to reformulate their academic programs and student activities. A fundamental error is to ignore the differences among this numerically dominant minority. Merely recognizing the existence of the "other," as if it were a monolithic mass, is inadequate. For although women students are a majority, many have had the minority experience of being defined as outside the norm. Women vary by age, race, class, sexual preference, disability, and other factors, each of which forms a nexus of experiences, attitudes, and in some cases culture. Thus, the framework within which a single mother over thirty operates may be radically different from that of an eighteen-year-old straight out of high school, and greater still when either is Black, poor, lesbian, or disabled.

But, administrators ask, isn't it enough to provide a special service for women? Must we respond also to all the subdivisions—minority women, disabled women, lesbian women, women over thirty? Where does it end? We cannot accommodate an unending demand for resources. If we respond to Black women, won't the Chicanas also want something? And the lesbians? And who knows who else? Such questions are the stuff of administrative nightmares because the majority mentality views these groups as less important to the institution's ultimate goals. Where does the relentless subdividing of the human family end? The more important question is where and why did it begin? What conditions exist in the institution that create the need for "special groups"? It began with the failure of colleges and universities to recognize cultural diversity, and to conceptualize themselves as microcosms of American society and as culturally pluralistic institutions. For all the arguments framed around "majority" and "minority" interests, both terms are problematic because they allude to monolithic, often adversarial positions that ultimately obscure the range of educational interests and needs. To understand the implications of educating women—this new majority—is to shift one's mind-set, to avoid the mentality that frames matters in terms of numbers, majority and minority, us and them. But rather to cultivate a mind-set that recognizes diversity—the condition of being different—with no pejorative connotations attached. This mental attitude evolves from a fundamental respect and acceptance of the varied voices and experiences within the human family, and from a belief that an educational institution (to be worthy of the name) must create an environment that will nurture, stimulate, and challenge the many members of this family. Inevitably, the institution will reap extraordinary benefits from this rich diversity.

In order to create a supportive and stimulating environment, institutions must first reexamine goals and recognize the nature of the present state of affairs. "Integration" into a melting pot, in the old sense of amalgamation and an implicit loss of group identity, is no longer a viable goal. The persistent differential treatment of women, racial groups, and others in this society has created experiences of discrimination that cannot easily be overcome. The point of discrimination has become the definer of these groups: thus the nonracial aspects of the Black woman, the nonsexual aspects of the lesbian, or the nonparenting concerns of the student mother may go unrecognized except possibly among her very closest colleagues who share her particular experience of discrimination. Educational institutions need to organize the curricular and extracurricular learning environment around the ideal of diversity and cultural pluralism. Specific groups for Hispanic (Latina, Chicana, Puerto Rican, Cuban), Black, lesbian, and married women as well as single mothers and others should be permitted and, in fact, encouraged. At the same time, the college environment should encourage interaction among these and other more traditional organizations, such as sororities, on equal terms. And, of course, the formal learning environment should provide an appropriate intellectual context by making related cultural issues an integral part of the knowledge base and, therefore, the curriculum.

Some college administrators may be uncomfortable with the coexistence of these levels and confused by the seeming contradiction. If cultural interaction is an end goal, then why encourage diversity? Are not the two ideals mutually exclusive? Certainly, if women's history were taught as an integral part of American history, there might be no need for "special" or separate courses on women. However, respect for diversity demands more than simply infusing a few thoughts or facts about women into what has become known as American history. The concept requires a refocusing of subject matter, a transformation shaped by the full presence of those previously excluded. Thus, the diary of an eighteenth-century housewife or nineteenth-century female slave may reveal as much about the events and sensibilities of an era as the papers of a nation's president. Such presumptions may indeed seem to shake the very foundations of an institution as it ventures into new and uncharted territories. But in the arena of cultural diversity, all are novices, and institutions are in a state of becoming. Simultaneous efforts to define, understand, and express differences, to foster interaction and exchange, and to confront fully the implications of recognizing diversity must continue.

The recognition of diversity should pervade college policies, procedures, and personnel selection in order to ensure that the presence of women is felt—not just "any" female, but women who themselves bring to the institution the richness and diversity of female experience. The tendency to hire women who are most "like ourselves" or who "will fit in easily" robs an institution of an essential resource. The same intellectual challenge that we claim to cherish in an excellent faculty should inform our choices for administrative positions. The diverse voices of women must be heard in the dialogue over policy issues. The same care and attention must be given to faculty selection. Perhaps the faculty should be given even greater attention, since these are the people who shape the curriculum, interact directly with both women and men students, and set the tone for their future decisions. Faculties and professional associations must seek solutions to field discrimination that ignore or punish those who have ventured into newer areas informed, in part, by a reexamination of "women's place" in history, literature, and other disciplines.

It is not a matter of offering academic palliatives for this new population, but rather of preparing all students for a world in which differences are crucial and a blindness to diversity can be fatal. The new majority with all the sensibility of a minority respects and cherishes its differences and rightfully expects institutions to learn from its presence. This new majority will be here for the foreseeable future; therefore, institutional response should not be characterized as a temporary arrangement but rather as embodying fundamental changes that will benefit the institution and its community. In order to meet the challenge of educating the "majority," colleges and universities must become true communities of learners, in which the most sacrosanct assumptions of cultural arrogance must be examined and a new basis for learning established—one that includes the entire human family.

REFERENCE

KANTER, ROSABETH M. *Men and Women of the Corporation.* New York: Basic Books, 1979.

2

The "Traditional" Undergraduate Woman in the Mid-1980s:

A Changing Profile

ANNE L. HAFNER

Today's "traditional" college freshman woman (that is, first-time, full-time) is slightly older than her counterpart was in the late 1970s. She is more likely to be from a lower- to middle-income family, or from a family in which her parents have a lower level of education than was previously the case. Freshman women are still more likely than men to attend four-year colleges, two-year colleges, Black colleges, and institutions of low selectivity levels. Full-time female students today maintain slightly higher grades than males. They have a higher level of academic preparation in high school subjects than in the past, but have slightly weaker academic backgrounds in math and the physical sciences than males.

College females today are more materialistic and status-oriented, and less altruistic than in the past. Females' career and degree aspirations have changed dramatically in the past eighteen years, and now they look a lot like male college students, although males still domi-

Data for the study were drawn from UCLA/HERI national surveys of freshmen from 1966 to 1985. The author would like to thank Helen S. Astin for her help in formulating and writing the paper.

nate in engineering and physical sciences and females still dominate in teaching and nursing.

Although college women have made great strides in many areas in the 1970s and 1980s, their self-concept level has not kept pace with that of men. Data suggest, however, that if present trends continue, by the 1990s women may "catch up to" or surpass men in this area. To encourage this trend, education of women in psychosocial development and in leadership/achievement skills is needed. Lack of attention to such matters could result in changing these positive trends for women.

This essay is divided into three parts. The first section describes the characteristics of college women, including background variables, trends over time in degree and career aspirations, self-concept, values, and life goals. The second section contains a brief discussion of the self-concept of college women in this study and how a college education can serve their needs. The final section discusses major points and the general implications of this changing profile for higher education institutions, along with possible future trends.

DATA SOURCES

The primary source of data for this analysis is the Cooperative Institutional Research Program (CIRP), which every year since 1966 has surveyed freshman classes from a representative sample of about six hundred colleges and universities. The entire first-time, full-time cohort of freshmen at each institution is surveyed. Because the population surveyed includes only first-time, full-time women students, older women who may be returning to college or part-time students may not be included. The freshman questionnaire asks students about their family background, high school preparation, future plans and aspirations, self-concept, attitudes, and values. By comparing successive freshmen classes, one is able to ascertain the ways in which college students today differ from students in earlier cohorts.

CHARACTERISTICS OF FIRST-TIME FULL-TIME WOMEN COLLEGE STUDENTS—YESTERDAY AND TODAY

What are the characteristics, aspirations, and values of full-time undergraduate freshmen college women today? And how do they differ from freshman women students of the early 1970s? The decade of the 1970s according to Astin and Kent (1983), saw many changes in our society, especially with respect to womens' roles. Women took jobs outside the home in ever-increasing rates; they began to marry later and to defer childbearing. Womens' rights became an important political issue, as more people of both sexes became aware of sex-role stereotypes. Economic forces were also influential as inflation soared, the job market tightened, and a general trend was seen which placed more emphasis on practical and materialistic values over the idealistic. Astin and Kent believe that these forces appear to have affected the aspirations, level of self-esteem, and values of college students, especially women.

Background Variables

TYPE OF INSTITUTION ATTENDED.   Women now make up over one half of U.S. college students (in 1985, about 52 percent). In the first year of CIRP's freshman survey (1966), males made up 54 percent of the sample. As in 1966, women are still overrepresented in Black colleges, four-year colleges, two-year private colleges, Protestant and Catholic colleges, and at institutions with low selectivity rankings.

AGE.   The average U.S. full-time entering college woman is young, although increasing numbers of older, nontraditional women are now attending college; 79 percent of first-time full-time freshmen women in 1985 were seventeen or eighteen years old. Although 21 percent were nineteen or over, only 5 percent were twenty or over. In the first year of this national survey (1966), 85 percent of all women were eighteen or under. Thus, from 1966 to 1985, there has been a small increase in the percentage of freshman women nineteen or over.

RACE.   The vast majority of female college freshman are white (86 percent in 1985): 9.1 percent are Black, 1 percent American Indian, 2 percent Asian-American, 1 percent Chicano, 0.6 percent Puerto Rican, and 1.5 percent other. In contrast, in 1966, 91 percent of freshman women were white, 5.6 percent were Black, 0.6 percent were American Indian, 0.7 percent were Asian-American, and 3 percent were "other." While fewer whites among college-going women were enrolled in 1985, they still are a large majority. While Black women have increased their enrollments substantially since 1966, from 6 percent to 9 percent, the percentage enrolling in college for the first time peaked around 1984 (at almost 11 percent) and has dropped since to the current 9 percent level.

PARENTAL INCOME.   The average U.S. student's parental income in 1985 was about $30,000. There was a greater number of females with parents who had lower incomes than males, however, and a greater number of male students from families with higher incomes (over $30,000). In 1985, 43 percent of women and 39 percent of men had parents with incomes below $30,000 and 18 percent of women and 14 percent of men had parents with incomes below $15,000. In 1966, about the same proportion of males and females fell into these family income categories. Thus, we conclude that a greater proportion of females from lower-income families are now attending college than previously.

PARENTAL EDUCATION.   The proportion of freshmen who are first-generation college students continues to be substantial. In 1985, almost half of all college freshmen had fathers who had a high school diploma or less. However, in 1966, 54 percent of college freshmen had fathers who had a high school diploma or less. It is evident that today's college students are coming from increasingly better-educated family backgrounds.

In 1985, a larger percentage of females than males came from families in which the father had a high school diploma or less (49 percent for females vs. 40 percent for males). By contrast, a much larger population of females in 1966 came from families in which the father had a college degree or higher degree (28.6 percent for females vs. 17 percent for males). Thus, in 1966, female college students tended to come from families with higher incomes and educations, whereas today's female college student is more likely than today's male college student to be from a family with lower income and/or lower educational background.

HIGH SCHOOL PREPARATION.   It is instructive to examine the high school preparation of college freshmen. In Table 2.1 we see the percentage of males and females who have met or exceeded the generally recommended number of years of study in high school in 1985. Both males and females have taken about the same number of years of English (four years), history (one year) and social studies (two years). Females have taken more foreign language classes (69 percent females vs. 62 percent males have taken two years), slightly more biological science classes (37 percent females vs. 33 percent males have

TABLE 2.1 *Proportion of Male and Female Students Who Have Met or Exceeded Recommended Years of Study (All Institutions, 1985)*

	MALE	FEMALE
English (4 years)	91.6	93.1
Math (3 years)	87.7	83.1
Foreign language (2 years)	61.7	68.9
Physical science (2 years)	60.9	48.6
Biological science (2 years)	33.1	36.7
History/Government (1 year)	99.0	99.1
Other social studies (2 years)	32.5	30.3
Computer science (1/2 year)	62.1	53.4
Art/Music (1 year)	54.9	66.9

Source: Cooperative Institutional Research Program, 1985 norms

taken two years). Females also have tended to take more classes in art and music (66 percent females vs. 58 percent males have taken one year). Males, however, have taken more physical science courses (61 percent males vs. 49 percent females have taken two years), slightly more math courses (88 percent males vs. 83 percent females have taken three years) and more computer science courses (62 percent males vs. 53 percent females have taken one-half year). These results are similar to those obtained by the College Board in its national sample.

The Department of Education's 1982 High School and Beyond survey found that while nationwide the average high school student took about 2.5 years of math, about 75 percent of males and 67 percent of females took three or more math courses. Females had higher average math GPA's (females 2.35 vs. males' 2.18) and had higher grades in Algebra 1, Algebra 2, and Geometry. Males received slightly higher grades than females in trigonometry and calculus (Carroll, 1984).

In a 1972 survey (Sells, 1978) of University of California at Berkeley freshmen, 57 percent of the entering men and only 8 percent of entering women had the second year of high school algebra and year of trigonometry required to prepare for freshman calculus (i.e., four years of high school math). Thus, 92 percent of the women in this freshman class were relegated to five fields: the humanities, music, social work, elementary education, and guidance and counseling. Although UC Berkeley is not representative of all U.S. colleges (being relatively selective), it is instructive to note that even in this selective university, virtually all the entering freshman women were unqualified for most undergraduate majors in math, the biological and physical sciences, business, architecture, computer science, and many other fields.

As compared with the early 1970s, female college students today are very well prepared for college. Females have substantially increased the number of years of math, physical science, and biological science taken. Because of this change, women today have strengthened their position and are prepared to enter most major fields or careers. This has been a major change in the makeup of female college students. Although some believe there is still a discrepancy between womens' and mens' math and science preparation in high school, it is probably that this is true largely for students in two-year colleges or four-year low-selectivity colleges. In 1985, only 75 percent of women in two-year colleges took the recommended three years of high school math, while 96 percent of women in universities and 85 percent of those in four-year colleges took three years of math. Women in universities and selective four-year colleges are competing quite well in this area with men.

ACADEMIC PERFORMANCE.   Research in general shows that women get higher gradees than men in both high school and college. Astin (1978) found that college women with high grades far outnumbered men with high grades.

Even though women enter college with better records of high school performance, they do not have as high expectations of performing well in college. For example, in 1985 while 40 percent of females enter college with HSGPAs of B+ or better (compared with only 35 percent of men), only 11 percent of women compared with 13 percent of men expect to graduate from college with honors.

STUDENT SELF-RATINGS.   Self-concept beliefs can be ascertained by examining a student's self ratings on a number of personal traits. Students are asked on CIRP's Student Information Form to rate themselves on various traits as compared with the average person their age. They can choose from four choices: highest 10 percent, above average, average, or below average. Ratings on these traits are shown in Table 2.2 for the years 1966, 1976, and 1985, along with the percentage of change. College women have shown gains on a number of traits: social self-confidence, intellectual self-confidence, general

TABLE 2.2 *Trends in Self-concept, 1966-1985, College Females (in %)*[a]

TRAIT	1966	1976	1985	CHANGE
Academic ability	59	51	52	−7
Athletic ability	24	26	b	+2
Artistic ability	22	23	21	−1
Drive to achieve	58	62	61	+3
Leadership ability	35	39	46	+11
Math ability	26	27	32	+6
Originality	36	38	b	+2
General popularity	29	27	38	+9
Popularity with opposite sex	25	25	b	+10
Public-speaking ability	21	19	b	+3
Intellectual self-confidence	31	38	47	+16
Social self-confidence	26	33	44	+18
Understanding others	66	72	b	+6
Writing ability	29	35	40	+11

[a]Percentage rating themselves as "above average" or "in the top 10%".
[b]Item was not asked in that year.
Source: HERI CIRP data

popularity and popularity with the opposite sex, leadership ability, writing ability, drive to achieve, math ability, and understanding others. Paradoxically, women declined 8 percent in their self-ratings of academic ability between 1966 and 1976. Between 1976 and 1985, women's self-rating of academic ability increased by only 1 percent, but between 1983 and 1985, there was a 3 percent decline, for an overall decline of 7 percent from 1966. Overall, women rate themselves lower than men on academic and math abilities.

However, since 1976, an increase of 5 percent among women has occurred with respect to self-rating of math ability, although they still rank themselves lower on average than men. For example, in 1985, 32 percent of women and 46 percent of men ranked themselves as above average in math ability. This is hard to understand in light of the fact that females have higher math grades than males, and have almost equal high school math preparation. Although college women have a higher general self-concept than in the past, they still lag behind men in many subareas of self-concept, especially academic ability, intellectual self-confidence, math ability, and public-speaking ability.

In the most recent survey (Fall 1985), students were asked to rate themselves as compared with others of their age on two additional items: emotional health and physical health, and to note how often they felt depressed or overwhelmed by all they had to do. Males rated themselves higher than females on physical health (72 percent of males reported their health as above average or higher, compared to only 52 percent of females) and on emotional health (65 percent of men reported their health as above average or higher compared to 56 percent of females). In addition, only 6 percent of men reported feeling depressed frequently, while 10 percent of women reported feeling depressed frequently; furthermore, 12 percent of the men felt overwhelmed frequently, while 20 percent of the women indicated such feelings. This is somewhat distressing with regard to emotional and physical health.

VALUES AND LIFE GOALS.   The freshman survey includes a section with statements about students' values or life goals. Students are asked to rate the importance of a variety of goals. Table 2.3 summarizes some of the responses of 1966, 1976, and 1985 freshman women to certain selected items.

The items are grouped in five categories: interest in business, need for status, altruism/social concern, interest in art, and marriage and the family (using Astin's 1978 categories). The major focus here is change over time. Freshman women have shown the greatest positive changes in the areas of business interest and status need and the greatest losses in altruism and social concern. Women show a 35 percent increase in the percentage endorsing "being well off financially," from 32 percent in 1966 to 67 percent in 1985. Although the percentage of women who want to be successful in businesses of their own declined from 1966 to 1976, it has increased by 12 percent since 1976. The number of women who want to be experts in finance has also increased, from 6 percent to 22 percent since 1966. In addition, the percentage of women who think it important to have administrative responsibility for others has doubled (21 percent to 41 percent), and large increases are also seen in obtaining recognition (from 36 percent to 59 percent) and in being an authority in one's field (from 61 percent to 69 percent). From 1966 to 1985, women declined in their belief that it is important to develop a meaningful philosophy of life (down 21 percent from 1976). Declines are also observed in women's belief that it is important to help others in difficulty (down 10 percent) and in participation in community action programs (down 8 percent from 1976).

TABLE 2.3 *Changes in Life Goals of Full-time Freshman Women, Percentage Endorsing "Essential or Very Important," 1966–1985*

CHANGE LIFE GOAL	1966	1976	1985	1966–1985
Business Interest				
Be well off financially	32	45	67	+35
Be successful in business of own	40	35	47	+7
Be expert in finance	6	10	22	+16
Status Need				
Have administrative responsibility over others	21	29	41	+20
Obtain recognition for contributions	36	42	54	+18
Be authority in one's field	61	67	69	+8
Altruism/Social Concern				
Develop meaningful philosophy	a	64	43	−21
Help others in difficulty	80	72	70	−10
Participate in community programs	a	32	24	−8
Influence social values	a	32	35	+3
Artistic Interest				
Create artistic work	21	18	12	−9
Write original works	17	14	12	−5
Be accomplished in performing arts	13	13	12	−1
Marriage and Family				
Raise a family	78	57	70	−8

[a]Item not asked that year
Source: CIRP norms, 1966, 1976, 1985

The percentage of women believing that it is very important to raise a family declined by 21 percent from 1966 to 1976; however, it increased by 13 percent between 1976 and 1985. Since 1971, freshman students have shown a gradual movement from a liberal position to the political center. While there is a trend toward greater conservatism, students readily endorse some very liberal issues, such as pollution control and less funding for defense.

EDUCATIONAL/CAREER ASPIRATIONS. The traditional gap between women's and men's educational aspirations in the freshman year has almost been eliminated in recent years. As we can see in Table 2.4,

TABLE 2.4 *Highest Degree Planned Changes in Educational Aspirations of Full-time Freshmen Women and Men 1966–1985 (in %)*

	WOMEN		MEN	
	1966	1985	1966	1985
Less than master's	58	48	43	47
Masters	32	32	31	32
Ph.D. or Ed.D.	5	9	14	10
M.D., D.D.S.	2	6	7	6
L.L.B., J.D.	0.3	4	3	4

[a] *Source:* CIRP Norms, 1966, 1985

in 1985 full-time, first-year women college students have degree aspirations virtually identical to men's. At present, about one-half of entering college freshmen surveyed in the CIRP norms plan to get a bachelor's degree or less and about one-half plan to get a master's or higher degree. Women college students have changed dramatically in this respect since 1966, when almost 60 percent of college women aimed at less than a master's degree and 90 percent aimed at master's level or less. Today, 19 percent of college women plan to obtain a Ph.D., Ed.D., M.D., D.D.S., LL.B., or J.D. degree, compared with only 7 percent in 1966. These figures should be considered with some caution, however, since data on degree aspirations collected in the freshman year do not always reflect college outcomes.

In a recent study, Hafner (1985) found that variables that were important predictors of level of educational aspiration for women and men in 1971 and 1983 included fathers' and mothers' level of education, high school GPA, intellectual self-confidence, and attending college to prepare for graduate school. Males and females had similar variables predicting degree level, with several exceptions. For females, being Black or of "other" ethnic group predicted a higher aspiration level (1971 and 1983), but this was not so for males. For females only, the number of years of math taken, self-estimate of intellectual self-confidence (in 1971 only) and self-estimate of academic ability (in 1983 only) predicted higher aspirations. Again, we see that self-estimate of academic ability and intellectual self-confidence are important determinants of womens' educational plans.

Dramatic changes have been seen in women's career choices since 1970. In the freshman year, female and male career choices are more similar today than at any other time in the past. In the early 1970s, the modal career plans for females were the traditionally female occupations: elementary and secondary teacher, nurse, social worker. On the other hand, the modal career aspirations for males were the traditionally male careers: business management, engineer, lawyer, M.D., and dentist. By 1985, females' career choices had changed dramatically, while males had remained about the same. In 1985, the most common careers for women were business manager, followed by nurse, lawyer, M.D., dentist, and computer programmer.

Astin believes that these dramatic changes in career preferences of college women have a profound effect on the labor force and on these professions (that is, the quality of professional practice in the professions may improve). With the exception of law and medicine, careers that have shown increased popularity do not require education beyond the bachelor's degree and are generally higher-paying (that is, engineering, business). Careers that declined the most are low-paying ones, or ones that require extensive postgraduate work (such as college teaching or social work) (Astin, 1982).

THE SELF-CONCEPT OF TODAY'S COLLEGE WOMAN

Although most educational practitioners today would agree that the main purpose of a college education is intellectual development, other goals are also important. These include the development of general job skills and psychosocial development. Women seem to be competing with men quite well in the intellectual arena, but are lagging behind in the psychosocial and self-concept area.

As self-concept is such an overwhelming influence on womens' college choices and achievement, it may be the most important arena in which colleges can best serve women students. Women students can compete very well academically with men students, earn higher grades, win more scholarships, and so forth, in spite of the fact that they rate their academic ability, intellectual self-confidence, and math ability as lower than men's. Although high school academic preparation has greatly improved for women, and college performance and future aspirations are as high as men's in general, the traditional female college student still has a lower overall level of self-concept. This may be a real handicap, as one's self-concept is intimately related to one's sense of competence and performance in college and on the job.

According to Shavelson and Bolus (1982), one's self-concept is organized, multifaceted, and hierarchical. Particular facets reflect different important categories (that is, general self-concept, academic-self concept, social self-concept, emotional and physical self-concept). Self-concept has been theoretically differentiated from academic achievement. Although previous research (Shavelson and Stuart, 1981, Calsyn and Kenny, 1977) found that achievement is the primary determinant of self-concept, Shavelson and Bolus (1982) found in a more recent study of junior high school students that self-concept is probably causally predominant over achievement within specific subject matter areas (English, math, and science). This indicates that self-concept may have a larger influence on school achievement than past achievement has on self-concept.

Perhaps partly because of these research findings, performance in math and science courses and on achievement tests in these areas has been the focus of much research in recent years. Although females generally score lower than males on common math achievement tests, they do as well in class grades, when math background is controlled. A 1985 study by Boli, Allen, and Payne found that women did as well as men in college math and chemistry courses when math background was controlled. Although gender had no direct effect on course performance, it had a large indirect effect on performance via math background (SAT-math score). In addition, women who had had female math teachers in high school did somewhat better than those who had not (this was not true for males), and confidence in one's own sex's ability was positively related to math ability score. Although in this study women enrolled in these undergraduate courses in numbers proportionate to their enrollment in the school, and were as likely as men to complete the course sequence, many more men still chose to major in technical fields like engineering, chemistry, and physics. Women who chose "technical" fields tended to major in the life sciences. A major reason for this seems to be women's slightly weaker math background in high school and not their poor academic performance.

Although it appears that math background is important, it is likely that self-concept with respect to math ability has a larger influence on math achievement than past achievement has on self-concept. It would be instructive to carry out this analysis controlling not for math background but for level of math self-concept. Reasons for low math self-concept should be investigated, in addition to which groups may be particularly prone to low self-concepts.

It is evident that, although the average college woman has a lower self-concept in most areas than the average college man, if one considers only particular groups (such as females attending high-selectivity private universities), conclusions are somewhat different. College females from highly selective private universities have self-ratings about equal to men from similar institutions in self-estimate of academic ability, leadership ability, popularity, social self-confidence and writing ability, self-ratings higher than men in artistic ability and drive to achieve, and self-ratings lower than men in math ability, emotional and physical health (1985 only), and intellectual self-confidence. The largest difference in this group is in math ability (71 percent females vs. 84 percent males rated themselves above average). This group of women had self-estimates of math ability higher than the vast majority of college men (excluding only men in highly selective private universities).

Interestingly, if one considers only freshman women at universities, this group in 1985 rated themselves as above average in almost every category in greater numbers than the average freshman man (from all institutions). Women students from two-year colleges and Black colleges, however, tend to have lower-than-average self-ratings. These findings indicate a need for further studies on college women's self-concept and its relationship to achievement.

CONCLUSION

It is imperative that programs be developed to help female faculty, counselors, and students became aware of these trends and influences and understand that women are competing well with men academically and in the job market. Characteristics of women students who score high and low on academic/math self-concept and on social self-confidence/leadership ability should be investigated. What background/attitudinal variables determine high self-concept? Why do women in highly selective institutions have such high self-ratings? Which are the variables that best discriminate between low and high academic self-concept and between low and high leadership ability? These are some of the questions which should be pursued by researchers in the field of higher education.

The traditional goals of a college education (that is, intellectual development, job skill development, and psychosocial development) can probably be used to serve many women students. But we have seen that in several crucial characteristics, specifically self-concept and leadership skills, college women differ from men significantly. In these areas, the traditional goals of a college education are not being met for many women students. Research and practitioner focus on the determinants of high self-esteem and leadership ability is indicated.

REFERENCES

ASTIN, A. W. "The Undergraduate Woman." In *The Higher Education of Women* (edited by H. S. Astin and W. Hinsford). New York: Praeger, 1978.

ASTIN, A. W. The American Freshman: 1966–1981: Some Implications for Educational Policy and Practice. Paper prepared for the National Commission on Excellence in Education, May 1982.

ASTIN, A. W., GREEN, K. C., KORN, W., and MAIER M. J. *The American Freshman National Norms for Fall 1983.* UCLA: American Council on Education, 1983.

ASTIN, A. W., GREEN, K. C., KORN, W., and MAIER, M. J. *The American Freshman National Norms for Fall 1984.* UCLA: American Council on Education, 1984.

ASTIN, A. W., GREEN, K. C., KORN, W., and SHALIT, M. *The American Freshman National Norms for Fall 1985.* UCLA: American Council on Education, 1985.

ASTIN, A. W., KING, M., and RICHARDSON, G. *The American Freshman. National Norms for Fall 1976.* UCLA: American Council on Education, 1976.

ASTIN, A. W., PANOS, R., and CREAGER, J. *National Norms for Entering College Freshmen—Fall 1966.* Washington, D.C.: American Council on Education, 1966.

ASTIN, H., and KENT, L. "Gender Roles in Transition." *Journal and Higher Education* 54, 3 (May/June 1983): 309–324.

BOLI, J., ALLEN, M., and PAYNE, A. "High Ability Women and Men in Undergraduate Mathematics and Chemistry Courses." *American Educational Research Journal* 22 4 (1985): 605–627.

BOWEN, H. R., et al. *Investment in Learning: The Individual and Social Value of American Higher Education.* San Francisco: Jossey-Bass, 1977.

CALSYN, R. J., and KENNY, D. A. "Self Concept of Ability and Perceived Evaluation of Others: Cause or Effect of Academic Achievement?" *Journal of Educational Psychology* 69 (1977): 136–145.

CARROLL, C. DENNIS. *High School and Beyond Tabulation: Mathematics Course Taking by 1980 High School Sophomores Who Graduated in 1982.* Washington, D.C.: U.S. Department of Education, 1984.

HAFNER, A. L. Gender Differences in College Student's Educational and Occupational Aspirations: 1971–1983. Paper presented at the annual meeting of the American Education Research Association, 1985.

SELLS, L. W. "Mathematics—A Critical Filter." *The Science Teacher* February 1978: 28–29.

SHAVELSON, R. J., and BOLUS, R. "Self Concept: The Interplay of Theory and Methods." *Journal of Educational Psychology* 74 (1982): 3–17.

SHAVELSON, R. J., and STUART, K. R. "Application of Causal Modeling to the Validation of Self Concept Interpretations of Test Scores." In M. D. Lynch, K. Gregen, and A. Norem-Hebelson (eds), *Self Concept: Advances in Theory and research.* Boston: Ballinger Press, 1981.

3

Finding a Way:
Black Women Students
and the Academy

BEVERLY GUY-SHEFTALL
AND PATRICIA BELL-SCOTT

African-Americans have sustained a deep faith in the power of education to improve the status of the race and the conditions affecting their personal lives. However, attempts by Blacks to obtain quality education have been thwarted by American mores and values, prejudice against women, and racial discrimination.[1] Despite long-standing interest on the part of some scholars in the subject of higher education for Blacks, the history of Black women's higher education has been neglected by educational historians, as well as women's and Black studies scholars. A special issue of *The Journal of Negro Education* (Summer 1982) and the premier issue of *SAGE: A Scholarly Journal on Black Women* (Spring 1984) are recent exceptions to this generalization and contain the most comprehensive discussion of Black women's higher education. Despite their significant contributions to this sorely neglected topic, however, much of the history of higher education for Black women remains elusive. For example, while it is easy to ascertain enrollment figures, it is still difficult to determine the status of Black women in coeducational schools over the past century. Questions remain unanswered about whether Black women were subjected to different admission requirements than Black men or white women, whether they were encouraged to pursue certain courses, or whether they were victimized by sexist and/or racist attitudes on the part of both Black and white administrators, faculty, and male students.

Three questions have been central to the historical development of formal, higher educational opportunities for Black women: (a) Should the higher education of Black women be separate or coeducational? (b) Should the educational curriculum for Black women be different from or similar to the curriculum in institutions that are predominantly male and/or white? (c) Do Black women students have special psychosocial needs that must be considered by educational planners? Though these are certainly not the only questions that have emerged over time in the higher education of Black women, they represent some of the most debated and enduring ones.

THE FORMAL BEGINNINGS

The history of formal, higher education for Black women has its origins in the efforts of Myrtilla Miner, a young white woman from New York. She led the first organized effort to provide higher education for Black women in the 1850s in Washington, D.C. She received help from the Quakers and Harriet Beecher Stowe in establishing the seminary that came to be called The Miner Normal School for Colored Girls. This school resembled the typical seminary of the 1850s in its curriculum, library holdings, and lectures. Years later, the school became Miner Teachers College (O'Connor, 1969).

By the late 1860s several white institutions were admitting Black women and men. Of these, Oberlin College was a forerunner, being the first institution of higher learning in the United States to open its doors to women and men of all races. The first circular issued by the college listed "the elevation of female character" as one of its major priorities. As a result of its commitment to women's education, Oberlin produced the first Black female college graduate in America in 1862—Mary Jane Patterson. Patterson taught for seven years at the Institute for Colored Youths in Philadelphia after graduation from Oberlin and later became the first Black principal of the Preparatory High School for Negroes in Washington, D.C., in 1871.

Between 1865 and 1900, a number of Black colleges were established in the South, largely as a result of the desire of religious groups to increase the number of Black teachers and ministers. With the growth of Black colleges, a small number of Black women received a college education. Most, like Patterson, were trained to join the ranks of grammar school teachers.

Because the development of Black colleges came about at the same time that the idea of women's colleges achieved some measure of social acceptance, a few attempts were made to establish Black women's seminaries. Of those attempts, the experiments in Atlanta, Georgia, and Greensboro, North Carolina, had an enduring impact upon the history of Black women's higher education.

In 1881 in Atlanta, Georgia, Sophia B. Packard and Harriet E. Giles—two missionaries of strong, traditional New England background—founded Spelman College. Packard and Giles believed strongly that higher education for Black women should be separate and in the liberal arts tradition, though considerable attention should be devoted to practical skills. Unlike Spelman College, Bennett College was established initially as a coeducational institution in 1873 in Greensboro, North Carolina. Newly emancipated slaves provided the land upon which the college now stands, and Lyman Bennett provided ten thousand dollars for the construction of one of the earliest, large buildings on the campus. In the early years, Bennett College trained men and women for careers in the ministry and education, respectively. In 1926, Bennet was reorganized into a four-year liberal arts college for Black women, largely as a result of the decision of the Women's Home Mission Society to make a contribution to higher education.

THE ISSUE OF SPECIAL NEEDS

The question of whether Black women have special psychosocial needs has been central to the historical development of Black women's higher education. Implicit in the design of the curriculum and institutional policy of Spelman and Bennett colleges are assumptions about the motivation and needs of Black women, for example. The charter for Spelman describes this institution as one concerned with "learning for young colored women in which special attention is to be given to the formation of industrial habits and of Christian characters." The Spelman charter was in many respects similar to the charters of other predominantly Black and women's colleges, most of which were founded as a result of a concern for the development of skills and character among Blacks and women—the underlying assumption being that these qualities were lacking.

In 1937, Lucy Slowe, who was Dean of Women at Howard Univer-

sity, asserted that "Black women come to college with several problems: (a) inexperience in civic life affairs; (b) a conservative background which fosters traditional attitudes toward women; and (c) a
debilitating psychological approach to life (Slowe, 1939, pp. 276–279).
Slowe further described the impact of these problems upon the psychological outlook of the Black coed in the following manner: "Under these conditions, it is inevitable, therefore that the psychology of
most of the women who come to college is the psychology of accepting what is taught without much question; the psychology of inaction
rather than that of active curiosity." Some attention has been given to
the special needs of Black women, as outlined by Slowe, at Spelman
and Bennett. For example, in 1944, Spelman hosted a conference on
"The Current Problems and Programs in the Higher Education of Negro Women." The purpose of this historic conference was to explore
those psychological and socioeconomic factors related to the academic success and failure of Black women students. More recently,
women's studies curricula have been developed at both Bennett and
Spelman to promote self-empowerment and the desire of their students to discover themselves in the curriculum. Historically, because
of the need to train Black women for potential leadership roles, both
Spelman and Bennett placed considerable emphasis upon the participation of students in community life and civic affairs. This kind of
participation was institutionalized in the extracurricular activities of
the colleges via the development of the YWCA on campus, women's
choral societies, and service-oriented clubs, for example.

Participation in activities outside the classroom (sometimes referred to as the informal curriculum) was strongly encouraged by
administration and faculty and was carefully designed to promote
the moral, social, intellectual, and physical development of Black
women students. Such activities included daily chapel services, lectures, literary society meetings, concerts, debates, and the social and
philanthropic events of sororities. Dances, which eventually became
popular, were in the early years prohibited as inappropriate social
activity.

Other predominantly Black coeducational institutions of higher
learning attempted to meet the special needs of Black women
through the development of rigid and puritanical curricula and behavior codes (Noble, 1956). Female students found almost every aspect of their lives regulated, including what they should and should
not bring to college. For example, as early as 1896 the Knoxville College Catalogue carried a section entitled "What to Bring Along" for
the female students which stated:

Each girl will be expected to have two calico dresses, one satine or gingham for wear during the warm months, and three long sleeved aprons. Each girl will be permitted to have three dark worsted dresses, without trimming other than the material itself, and each should have two work dresses, two dark skirts, and plain underwear. These should last the student the entire year. Light and fancy clothing should not be brought. If brought, it will be taken charge of until the student leaves. (*Catalogue of Officers and Students of Knoxville College . . .* , 1896)

Black women at single-sex institutions, however, experienced the most intense concern for their "special" moral needs. At Spelman, for example, while there was a definite emphasis on training for jobs (mainly teaching and missionary work), the building of Christian character, which was reflected in the school's motto, "Our Whole School for Christ," was of paramount importance. This emphasis on developing strong moral character must be seen as a reflection of prevailing societal attitudes about Black women during the late nineteenth and early twentieth centuries. According to Jeanne Noble in her pioneering study of the historical development of collegiate education for Black women, the emphasis on moral education was directly related to perceptions about Black women that persisted during slavery and lingered for generations afterward:

> . . . the one role of her past that did come up in discussions concerning the Negro woman's education related to her foremother's role as concubine. The Negro woman's *new* role carried not only the stigma of being a Negro but also a new sense of inferiority in being a woman. . . . Authorities prescribed a rigid moralistic curriculum . . . many of the Negro women's rules and regulations may possibly have been predicated on reasons relating to her foremother's sex role as a slave. Overnight she was to so live that by her ideal behavior, the sins of her foremothers might be blotted out. Her education in many instances appears to have been based on a philosophy which implied that she was weak and immoral and that at best she should be made fit to rear her children and keep house for her husband. (Noble, 1956, p. 24)

THE CONTEMPORARY SCENE

Though the issues of separate education, the curriculum, and the special needs of Black women students have been important historically, there are many other issues that must be explored in a consideration of Black women's higher education over the past twenty-five years. They include (a) the impact of Black and women's studies upon the design of curricula and extracurricular activities for Black women on historically Black and predominantly white college campuses; (b) the importance of role models and campus climate to the development of positive self-concepts among Black women. This is a critical issue to explore, since Black females compose less than 2 percent of faculty in all colleges and universities and half of these are clustered in historically Black colleges; (c) the impact of affirmative action/equal opportunity policy on Black women's access to and performance in institutions of higher learning; (d) the impact of current trends in education (such as the shift away from liberal arts to more professionally oriented education) on Black women's career choices and; (e) the importance of critical life events to Black women's achievement in college.

Some attention to demographic data as they relate to Black women students and higher education is important at this point. First of all, despite the expansion of opportunities for Blacks and women over the past several decades as far as higher education is concerned, Black females constitute only 5 percent of the total student enrollment in American colleges and universities, and many of these are enrolled in two-year institutions.

One of the most important differences in where Blacks attended college over the past two decades has been the striking decrease in their enrollment at historically Black institutions (HBIs). To illustrate, according to economist Margaret Simms, 50 percent of the Blacks enrolled in colleges in 1964 were in HBIs but by 1980 the numbers had dropped to 20 percent. Moreover, though HBIs awarded nearly 38 percent of the B.A.s received by Blacks in 1980 (they enrolled only 19 percent of all students attending college), Black women received only 3.9 percent of all B.A. degress conferred in 1980, 3.7 percent of all M.A. degrees, and 1.7 percent of Ph.Ds. (Simms, 1985, pp. 7–9). It should be pointed out, however, that Black women have experienced considerable increases (as much as 50 percent) in the numbers of degrees they have received from graduate and professional schools between 1976 and 1981.

Because Black women are attending predominantly white institutions in greater numbers, the issue of the "chilly" classroom environment (Hall and Sandler, 1982) (a serious issue for women students generally) is even more critical for them. Since there are so few Black female faculty, Black female students who attend white colleges and universities are in serious need of appropriate role models and too often experience a chilly and unreceptive classroom environment. One of the authors of this article (Patricia Bell-Scott) will never forget her first year as a college student at a large, predominantly white university in 1968. She was part of "an experiment" that year; about one hundred Black freshman students entered a university community of thirty thousand white students. She will remember always her excitement at meeting her lab partner, a white male destined to be a doctor, so he said. She was astonished at how average he was. And yet, she remembered how much encouragement he received from the professor, and how much surprise her A grades on tests elicited from the same professor. She received no reinforcement for her excellent performance. This experience was made more difficult by the fact that she had no one with whom to share these discoveries and anxieties. She eventually learned to accept rejection and not to expect encouragement from anyone except parents for good work. She came to believe that academic success was something she had to achieve in spite of the classroom environment. Needless to say, she could have been a better, more creative student had the reinforcements been there.

Though Black women students who attend HBIs find the chilly classroom environment less of an issue, the problem of being educated "away from themselves" remains. One of the authors of this article (Beverly Guy-Sheftall) experienced a supportive and reinforcing environment at Spelman College when she arrived in 1962, but she can still remember having left in 1966 with no understanding of patriarchy or colonialism or apartheid. She did not know the conditions under which the majority of the world's women lived. She did not know what female circumcision or foot-binding or purdah or suttee was, though she did know about the horrors of the Middle Passage, lynching, and the Holocaust. Though she knew the particular burdens of Black women as a result of her own family history and what she had observed growing up in Memphis, Tennessee, before integration, she did not fully understand the concept of "double jeopardy" as it related to women of color, and she was ill-equipped to handle a class analysis of the plight of Black women. She did not know many of our important Black foremothers—Frances E.W. Harper, Anna J. Cooper, Selena Sloan Butler (a Spelman alumna), Josephine St. Pierre Ruffin, or even Zora Neale Hurston (an unfortunate circumstance that Alice Walker, a fellow student, also bemoans but fortunately has corrected for others). She had not read Sojourner Truth's now famous "Ain't I a Woman" speech or W. E. B. Du Bois' moving account of the tragedy of Black womanhood in "The Damnation of Women" from *Darkwater* (1920), though she had read his more familiar *The Souls of Black Folk* (1903). She was unaware of the strong Black feminist tradition in the intellectual history of African-Americans that had been bequeathed by Sojourner Truth, Frederick Douglass, William E. B. Du Bois, and Mary Church Terrell, to name only a few.

Despite the phenomenal growth of women's studies in certain colleges and universities during the 1970s and 1980s, Black women's studies was not included, for the most part, in this movement. Moreover, women's studies (and Black women's studies) or a gender-balanced curriculum have not penetrated HBIs in general and, except for projects at the two Black women's colleges and colleges involved with the Atlanta University Center Africana Women's Studies project, too many Black women students still leave colleges and universities with similar gaps in their knowledge, as was the case when Guy-Sheftall left college in 1966.

CONCLUSION

Our history and the contemporary scene suggests the following educational priorities for Black women during the remainder of this century: (a) a need to keep access at the top of the list of educational equity issues; (b) a need for diverse and creative strategies for financing our education, since our economic plight precludes our entering and frequently completing college; (c) a need to support scholarship on women of color—scholarship, that will change the knowledge base of the traditional curriculum; (d) a need for career counseling, mentoring relationships, networks, and role models that will enhance our educational experiences; (e) a need for skill-development programs designed to prepare us for the workplace of the future; and (f) a need for more women of color as faculty, adminstrators, and policymakers in all educational settings. Obviously, the struggle against economic discrimination and race and sex prejudice is central to the achievement of these goals.

In summary, the educational needs of Black women have not changed substantially over the past century. Access to formal schooling is still a problem, racist and sexist attitudes still persist about us, and the quality and appropriateness of our educational experiences are often of questionable nature. We must still struggle to "find a way" to achieve educational equity. It is imperative that all of us commit ourselves to building educational institutions and experiences that promote the self-empowerment of women generally and especially Black women. Historically Black and predominantly white institutions must engage in this struggle. It is imperative that white and Black students (male and female) leave colleges and universities committed to improving the lives of women, no matter where they live in the world. They must be exposed to an environment and a curriculum that sensitizes students to the plight of adolescent mothers with inadequate prenatal care and limited resources; they must be concerned about rural women in Kenya and elsewhere who walk miles every day in search of firewood in order to feed their families; they must be concerned about women in South Africa who are virtually imprisoned in "homelands" far away from their husbands, who must seek work in urban areas. The needs and concerns of Black women students are ultimately the needs of all of us.

NOTE

1. Atlanta University, founded in 1867 in Atlanta, Georgia, chose as its motto "I'll Find A Way or Make One," which speaks to the miracle of Black education in the nineteenth century. The Black community, through self-help and the contributions of Northern philanthropies, founded and supported a variety of private schools to educate children and adults during the last half of the nineteenth century. The Atlanta University motto has provided the impetus for the title and tone of this chapter.

REFERENCES

BENDER, ELEANOR M., ed. *All of Us Are Present, The Stephens College Symposium, Women's Education: The Future.* Columbia, Missouri: James Madison Wood Research Institute, 1984.

BOND, HORACE M. *The Education of the Negro in the American Social Order.* New York: Prentice-Hall, 1934.

Catalogue of Officers and Students of Knoxville College, Knoxville, Tennessee for the Year Ending June, 1896. Knoxville: Knoxville College, 1896.

CHAMBERS, FREDERICK. *Black Higher Education in the United States, A Selected Bibliography on Negro Higher Education and Historically Black Colleges and Universities.* Westport, Conn.: Greenwood Press, 1978.

DU BOIS, WILLIAM E. B. *The College-bred Negro.* Atlanta: Atlanta University Press, 1907.

FLETCHER, R. A. *A History of Oberlin College.* Volume II. Oberlin, Ohio: Oberlin College, 1943.

GUY-SHEFTALL, BEVERLY, and JO MOORE STEWART. *Spelman: A Centennial Celebration.* Atlanta: Spelman College, 1981.

HALL, ROBERTA M., and SANDLER, BERNICE R. *The Classroom Climate: A Chilly One for Women?* Project on the Education and Status of Women. Washington, D.C.: Association of American Colleges, 1982.

Journal of Negro Education 51(Summer 1982). The Impact of Black Women in Education.

NOBLE, JEANNE L. *The Negro Woman's College Education.* New York: Columbia University, 1956.

O'CONNOR E. *Myrtilla Miner: A Memoir.* Miami: Menemosyne, 1979.

OFFICE OF MINORITY CONCERNS. *Minorities in Higher Education.* American Council on Education, 1984.

READ, FLORENCE M. *The Story of Spelman College.* Princeton: Princeton University Press, 1961.

SAGE: A Scholarly Journal on Black Women 1 (Spring 1984). Black Women's Education.

SIMMS, MARGARET C. *Minority Women in Higher Education.* Washington, D.C.: Urban Institute, 1985.

SLOWE, LUCY D. "Higher Education of Negro Women." *Journal of Negro Education* 2 (July 1933).

————. "The Colored Girl Enters College: What Shall She Expect?" *Opportunity* 15 (September 1937).

STRINGER, PATRICIA, and THOMPSON, IRENE. *Stepping off the Pedastal: Academic Women in the South.* New York: Modern Language Association of American, 1982.

WILKERSON, MARGARET B. "A Report on the Educational Status of Black Women During the UN Decade of Women, 1976–85. In *Slipping Through the Cracks, The Status of Black Women,* eds. Margaret C. Simms and Julianne M. Malveaux. New York: Transaction Books, 1986.

4

Hispanic Women Students in Higher Education:
Meeting the Challenge of Diversity

SARA E. MELÉNDEZ AND JANICE PETROVICH

Hispanics on the U.S. mainland comprise one of the most seriously underrepresented groups in higher education. Despite improvement in their participation rates fostered by social and educational programs initiated in the 1960s, many of the same problems remain: poverty, insufficient financial aid, ineffective recruitment practices, exclusionary admissions requirements, shortage of Hispanic faculty and administrators, irrelevant curricula, and culturally illiterate campuses. Programs to increase minority and Hispanic participation have traditionally concentrated on doing something for or to the students to make them more competitive, to help them adapt to campus life, or to provide them with financial resources. Often the efforts to assist students adapt to the campus have amounted to encouraging students to behave like white, middle-class Anglos. The motivation for such programs has been a concern for equity and, sometimes, the need to comply with federal and state laws. Very little attention has been paid to the benefits of diversity to the campus and to society.

Educators need to develop greater awareness of what minorities can contribute. The American middle class and the wealthy have traditionally sent their sons and daughters to travel and/or study abroad in an attempt to broaden their cultural perspectives and make them more well-rounded persons. Today we are missing an opportunity to learn from minority students right on our own campuses. Hispanic students on our campuses represent a possibility for us to learn about the world vision of the Hispanic peoples with whom the United States deals daily, often unsuccessfully. We can learn their cognitive style, their analytic style, and their problem-solving strategies. We can learn about their values, beliefs, traditions, and motivations. Preparing some of these students themselves to go into the fields of government, diplomacy, and international commerce could give us an edge in dealing with these countries. In addition, our traditional students could learn much from these students.

Unfortunately, our campuses have often been less than welcoming and friendly to students from other linguistic and cultural backgrounds. Campus environments can be made more friendly to Hispanics in general and to Hispanic women, in particular. It is hoped that the following discussion can help increase awareness of how campus policies, practices, and general atmosphere can help or hinder the success of Hispanic women students. The growing population of Hispanic college-age youth and the decline of the Anglo cohort now makes campus action to address issues of access and retention particularly pertinent.

Hispanic women students in the United States are a broadly diverse group. They differ in color and physiognomy, degree of adaptation to the dominant culture and ties to their native culture, proficiency in English, social class background, and financial need. Recognizing this diversity, this chapter will focus on those sociocultural commonalities that make their needs, concerns, contributions, and problems distinct from those of other ethnic groups. We will discuss the participation of Hispanic women in higher education, identify some of their specific behaviors that can be at odds with campus cultures, and make recommendations for creating a more hospitable campus environment to help improve the individual and collective experience of Hispanic women.

One researcher describes these shared characteristics:

> What are the commonalities among Hispanic women in the United States that manifest themselves in spite of enormous differences among them? Historical influences have left their mark in cultural processes and in class and race differentiation. Other commonalities have to do with the cognitive and affective effects of sharing common language and with experience of *oppression*. (Espin, 1986).

THE LIMITS TO ACCESS

Despite years of programs with varying degrees of success to increase minority access to higher education, when Hispanic participation is compared to that of other ethnic groups, large disparities are still evident. While 46 percent of whites and 36 percent of blacks had one year or more of college education in 1982, only 24 percent of Hispanics had attained the same level of education. The disparity in college degree attainment is even greater: 25 percent for whites, 13 percent for blacks, and 10 percent for Hispanics (U. S. Bureau of the Census, 1983).

Hispanic women have achieved greater gains in academia than their male counterparts. Hispanic male bachelor's degree attainment remained stable between 1976 and 1981, while that of women increased by 42 percent. Furthermore, Hispanic women increased from 43 percent of Hispanic bachelor's degrees earned in 1975 to 51 percent in 1981 (Hispanic Higher Education Coalition, 1984). A similar pattern occurred in master's and doctoral degrees: Hispanic women's share of master's degrees increased from 46 percent in 1976 to 52 percent in 1981, while doctoral degrees increased from 27 percent to 40 percent (Hispanic Higher Education Coalition, 1984).

However, Hispanic women remain the poorest, least-educated major population in the country. Furthermore, Hispanic family income was three-fourths that of whites ($15,178 for Hispanics compared to $20,171 for whites) in 1982. For the 23 percent of Hispanic households headed by women, the median income was only one-third that of whites ($7,602). The median years of schooling for Hispanic females in 1981 was 10.5 years, compared to 12.1 for black females and 12.6 for white females. In 1979, 34 percent of Hispanic women aged 16 to 24 were high school dropouts, compared to 13 percent of white females and 20 percent of black females (Escutia, 1985).

Thus, the increases in Hispanic higher educational attainment fueled by the programs instituted during the late sixties and early seventies (Upward Bound, Talent Search, federal financial aid programs, and open enrollment) have not been sufficient for Hispanics to approach parity with whites or blacks in higher educational attainment.

CULTURE AND COMMUNICATION

In addition to Hispanic women's shared experience of low educational and economic attainment, they share a common cultural, historical, and religious heritage. These shared experiences, however, do not produce a homogeneous group. U.S. mainland Hispanics run the gamut of adaptation to the dominant culture, from residents of the Southwest who have inhabited the area for four hundred years or more and consider themselves Spanish-Americans, to Chicanos born and brought up in "barrios" as monolingual Spanish speakers until they enter school. Puerto Ricans, who are citizens by birth, may be born on the mainland or the island of Puerto Rico and migrate back and forth several times in their life. Cubans represent the third largest group, with the first wave coming from middle-class backgrounds. Recent arrivals come from every country in Latin America. Hispanics also differ broadly in their proficiency in the English language; from monolingual Spanish speakers (mostly recent arrivals or pre-school-age children born to monolingual Spanish speakers) to monolingual English speakers, and varying degrees of bilinguals in between.

All of these types may be present in college and university campuses, complicating the task of educators. If we think about diversity as enriching, however, the task can be a rewarding one for all, the educator, the student, and the campus.

Hispanics have a mixed Indian/European/African ancestry. Their skin and culture reflect this mix, which has engendered attitudes and behaviors that differ in subtle and signficiant ways from those of the dominant culture. Many attitudes and values of the university culture are at odds with the character of Hispanic interpersonal relationships, forms of communication, and sex-role expectations.

Some culturally determined behaviors of Hispanics, such as ways of dealing with authority figures, expressing unwillingness or disagreement, the role of friendship, sources of motivation, cooperation versus competition, communication styles (verbal and nonverbal), and the relationship with time and physical space, may be in conflict with the counterpart behaviors in the dominant culture. These culturally determined behaviors and beliefs are most often unconscious, but can create difficulties for Hispanic women students in the classroom and in individual interchanges with peers, faculty, and staff.

Authority Figures

University professors and administrators are authority figures of high status in Hispanic culture. Hispanic students often keep a respectful distance between themselves and their professors. They do not expect to be friends with authority figures (Nine-Curt, 1983). The use of first names does not occur in Hispanic culture, except among persons of equal age and status. Thus, calling professors by their first names tends to make Hispanic students, particularly recent arrivals, feel extremely awkward.

Expressing Disagreement

Hispanic students may feel that openly disagreeing with an authority figure is a sign of disrespect (ibid.). This behavior may lead to academic problems if professors interpret their silence as lack of interest or independent thinking, and not as a sign of politeness.

Dealing with Conflict

Hispanic culture promotes tolerance of differences of opinion (Grossman, 1984). It would be a sign of disrespect to try to change someone's beliefs. Debating issues or questioning the opinions of others in public, therefore, makes Hispanics feel uncomfortable. Again, professors may misinterpret this reluctance as lack of interest or concern.

Friendship

For Hispanics, friendship and informality are linked. The informality (use of first names and the blurred lines of hierarchy) of the dominant culture is confusing to Hispanics because it is common among casual acquaintances. Furthermore, friendship among Hispanics develops mainly between people of the same sex and status groups. Friendships are deep and involve loyalty and sacrifice for one's friends (Nine-Curt, 1983). Hispanics tend to spend time getting to know people, building relationships, and, even with a hectic schedule, finding time to be with friends. Cancelling engagements at the last minute because of more pressing concerns will usually cause offense unless the excuse is accompanied by extensive explanations and apologies.

Culturally different expectations of friendship may complicate the task of making friends and aggravate the feelings of isolation which can, in turn, impair academic success. The presence of more Hispanics on campus can help overcome these adaptation problems.

Motivation

Research shows that, while majority culture students are effectively motivated by external impersonal rewards—grades, status, potential economic benefits—Hispanic students can be more effectively motivated on a more personal level (Grossman, 1984). Enjoying the course, identifying with the content, and relating well to the professor are generally important to Hispanic students. Despite the respectful distance from their professors that Hispanic students maintain, a professor who takes personal interest in their needs and problems is a powerful motivating force. They are usually put off by the businesslike, cool manner of majority culture professors and admininstrators and see it as unfriendly, curt, and distant.

Anglo professors on U.S. campuses are often task-oriented and get right to the point in conferences with students. Hispanic students are used to professors asking about their families, vacations, hobbies, and so forth, before discussing business. The immediate discussion of the business at hand without an exchange of pleasantries is considered indifferent and cold, and students have been alienated to the point of losing interest in a course and not doing as well as they might.

Cooperation vs. Competition

Competition and individual achievement are highly regarded values in the dominant U.S. culture. For Hispanics, group belongingness and cooperation are more important values. Hispanics have been found to do better than Anglos on tasks requiring cooperation and less well on tasks requiring competitiveness and individual effort.

While Hispanics need to learn to survive and thrive in a competitive environment, they may well need a period of transition before they can tackle individual and competitive projects. Professors can help by permitting students to do some group projects. Non-Hispanic students could also benefit from opportunities to develop cooperation skills.

Independence

Anglo Americans, particularly those from the middle class, foster independent decision-making and self-sufficiency in their children. Hispanic parents, however, are very protective of their children, particularly their daughters. By majority culture standards, Hispanics overprotect their daughters. They are certainly not encouraged to take risks, to move out and away from the family, or to make decisions that run contrary to their parents' wishes. In fact, for many Hispanic females, their freshman year at college is the first time they have ever been away from their families and homes. For these young women, coping with being away from home and learning to make decisions independently in a place they may feel is cold and uncaring may cause the freshman year to be extremely difficult.

Verbal and Nonverbal Patterns

Hispanics who have recently immigrated (or migrated, in the case of Puerto Ricans), or who were brought up in predominantly Spanish-speaking neighborhoods, may have understandably limited oral competence in the English language. Most Hispanics experience communication difficulties relating to verbal interactions as well as nonverbal patterns (touching, eye movement, interpersonal space, and body movement).

Just as the native language often has a discernible effect on the pronunciation of a second language, so do the nonverbal patterns of the native culture remain as integral parts of the communication process. Often the nonverbal patterns are at odds with those of the new culture; that is, they can lead to errors of interpretation.

In the Hispanic culture it is considered good manners, when talking to someone, to acknowledge any newcomer into the conversation. This occurs both verbally (proceeding with introductions) and nonverbally (smiling and nodding at the newcomer and opening the circle to include her until a break in the conversation allows for introductions to proceed). Not acknowledging an approaching person is considered rude, and will be likely to make her feel snubbed and hurt.

Nine-Curt (1983) observes that in the Anglo culture, looking directly ("tunnel" gazing) at a person to whom one is speaking is an appropriate and expected behavior connoting assertiveness and honesty. For Hispanics, continuous eye-to-eye contact is a sign of challenge or, if between members of the opposite sex, seduction. The intent gaze of an Anglo male professor may be embarrassing and unsettling to a Hispanic female student. On the other hand, the Anglo teacher may get the impression that the Hispanic student who does not maintain eye contact is not paying attention or is uninterested in the discussion.

The interpersonal space necessary for people to feel comfortable also varies across cultures. Hall (1959) noted that the interaction distance for Hispanics is less than for Anglos. What is comfortable distance to a Hispanic can evoke either sexual or hostile feelings in an Anglo. Interpersonal space that is comfortable for an Anglo will probably be perceived by a Hispanic as distant and cold.

The variation in the interpersonal space between people of the same or opposite sex is also influenced by culture. Studies have also documented these Anglo-Hispanic differences (Levine and Adelman, 1982). Hispanics of the same sex stand very close together, while members of the opposite sex stand farther apart than the Anglos do. Hispanic friends of the same sex touch each other quite frequently, whereas those of the opposite sex do not touch each other at all. Anglos on campuses may misinterpret the closeness, hugging, and kissing among Hispanic female friends.

Professors, counselors, and others on campus can help Hispanic students feel more comfortable by being aware of their need for more proximity and by controlling their reaction to the "invasion" of their personal space. If professors feel uncomfortable with the diminished physical distance, they can turn the situation into a learning experience by discussing with the students how different cultures handle physical space.

In summary, Hispanics are less likely than Anglos to exhibit the styles of communication and behavior that are highly valued in academia in the United States: openly expressing disagreement, actively participating in classroom discussions, working independently, maintaining eye contact, and speaking assertively. Hispanics, particularly women, are more likely to exhibit less assertive and more "personal" styles: avoiding differences of opinion, working cooperatively, averting eye contact, and qualifying their statements. The academic consequences to Hispanic women students of undervaluing these cultural patterns can be serious miscommunication between them and their professors, which can lead to performance on the part of the students of less quality than that of which they are capable. Their social lives may also suffer, as they feel isolated and misunderstood.

INSTITUTIONAL BARRIERS

Certainly, a need basic to the successful retention and graduation of non-Anglo students is an awareness, understanding, and acceptance of cross-cultural differences by themselves and by the academic community. But increasing the numbers of Hispanic women in U.S. colleges and universities requires culturally-sensitive recruitment and admissions procedures and a culturally-supportive academic environment.

Traditional recruitment methods appear to be less effective with Hispanics that with the non-Hispanic population. This may be particularly true for Hispanic females, whose families are often reluctant to allow them to go to college too far from home. One Hispanic dean of students tells of personally reassuring Mexican-American parents that he will keep an eye on their daughters, the tacit understanding being that he will look after their virtue.

Hispanics are largely urban dwellers and institutions in rural settings are at a disadvantage in attracting Hispanic students, as are those institutions that do not have Hispanic communities nearby. Those institutions need, perhaps more than usual, to have a "critical mass" of Hispanic students, some Hispanic faculty, and attractive curricular offerings.

Many Hispanics still find campuses unfriendly, uncaring, and often hostile. These perceptions are sometimes due to cultural differences that make adjustment to campus life difficult. Other times, they are due to lack of sensitivity, if not overt racism, on the part of faculty, administration, and other students.

Overcoming Barriers

Higher education institutions can be made more hospitable to Hispanic women students. But increasing the success rates of Hispanic women (and men) in the United States colleges and universities entails essential changes in attitudes and practices. While much of the discrimination that Hispanic women students face today goes far beyond what can be changed by laws or policies, official statements of commitment and practices can go a long way towards reducing overt discrimination. Important changes in higher education should occur in areas of recruitment and admissions practices, personnel, curriculum, support services, and attitudes.

RECRUITMENT. Institutions with few Hispanic students need to develop a "critical" mass and provide the necessary resources to help them feel comfortable. While it is important for Hispanic students to have every opportunity to become integrated into the mainstream campus life, for many it is also important that they have opportunities to express and share their culture, speak Spanish, and socialize with others who understand their cultural experience. Hispanic students who have been successfully integrated into the campus and feel comfortable that their culture is accepted on campus can be the best recruiters for colleges. They will be enthusiastic in talking to prospective students about their experience on campus.

Recruitment efforts also need to stress financial aid availability. Many first-generation college-going Hispanics do not know how to get the information they need. For many Hispanics financial-aid packages need to cover the total cost of education through scholarships and grants, given their low-income status and, often, their inability to obtain credit.

ADMISSIONS.   Standardized tests have been shown to discriminate against Hispanics and other minorities. Campuses should rely less on scores from such tests and more on interviews and personal references in judging the potential of Hispanic women to benefit from college. The academic community in general should encourage the development of culturally fair tests.

PERSONNEL.   Hispanic women (and men) are extremely underrepresented among faculty and administrators in higher education. Their hiring has lagged far behind their enrollments, thereby denying students access to role models, mentors, and sponsors. The paucity of Hispanic staff at all levels tends to preserve a primarily Anglo perspective, thus hampering improvements that would make postsecondary institutions more hospitable to culturally diverse populations. Hispanic faculty and administrators could play a significant role in recruiting other Hispanics. It is important, however, that they be convinced that there is a real commitment to diversity and not merely lip service to affirmative action.

CURRICULUM.   Disparaging students' interests in ethnic studies is an all too common occurrence in academia that contradicts the view that "involvement" in learning is crucial to academic success. Topics that are of vital interest to students and can serve to motivate them to excel are often considered "too narrow," "not objective enough," or "too personal." But building on what a student knows provides a far more exciting and efficient learning experience. The incorporation of women's studies and ethnic studies into college curricula has helped scholars examine new angles and develop new methodologies.

Campuses should recognize the contributions and knowledge-expanding benefits of diversity. The academic community needs to become more literate regarding other cultures. Cultural literacy contributes to self-knowledge and to the critical assessment of individual and collective values that should be a major focus of higher learning. College administrators should promote and support core curricula with a multicultural perspective. The development of a culturally literate academic community is essential to the retention of non-Anglo students and to the vitality of our nation's campuses.

SUPPORT SERVICES. Low income levels, limited access to quality schooling, and cultural and language differences make the adaptation of Hispanic women students to college a difficult process. The availability of support networks, of academic and personal counseling, and of information on available financial resources can increase their opportunities for academic success.

ATTITUDES. The unquestioning acceptance of the values and behaviors of any culture may be unhealthy at best, and at worst may lead to intolerance and bigotry. While greater competitiveness, individualism, materialism, self-motivation, and orientation toward the future may help Hispanics become more successful in this society, Anglos might benefit from developing a group orientation and a cooperative style. The Anglo celebration of effort and the Hispanic celebration of life are not necessarily antagonistic but can, indeed, be complementary.

CONCLUSION

Hispanic women, and cultural minorities in general, can be a valuable asset to colleges and universities. Hispanic cultural values of cooperation, respect for people's feelings, intrinsic motivation, interdependence, and zest for life can contribute to a more humane and caring campus environment for all. The institutional adaptations that need to occur for dealing with culturally diverse populations promote a greater concern for the individual student. A more caring campus environment benefits the entire academic community and fosters involvement, excitement, and success.

Perhaps the greatest contribution that Hispanic women students, and students from other cultural minorities, can make to the nation's campuses is that they can help us learn useful and enlightening things about ourselves. As Hall (1959) points out:

... taking seriously the culture of others ... forces you to pay attention to those details of life which differentiate them from you. (p. 40)

Such diversity is an energy-giving experience. It allows us to see diversity not as a problem to be solved or tolerated but as an asset to be appreciated and celebrated.

REFERENCES

ESCUTIA, MARTA. *Labor Market Status of Hispanic Women.* Washington, D.C.: National Council of La Raza, 1985.

ESPIN, OLIVA M. "Cultural and Historical Influences on Sexuality in Hispanic/Latin Women." In *All American Women,* ed. Johnnetta Cole. New York: Free Press, 1986, p. 273.

GROSSMAN, HERBERT. *Educating Hispanic Students.* Springfield, Ill.: Charles C. Thomas, 1984.

HALL, EDWARD T. *The Silent Language.* New York: Fawcett World Library, 1959.

HISPANIC HIGHER EDUCATION COALITION. Special Tabulation on Bachelor's Degrees Conferred by Institutions of Higher Education in the 50 States and D.C., by Racial/Ethnic Group and Sex, 1975–76, 1976–77, 1978–79, 1980–81, in Second Annual Status Report on Minorities in Higher Education, eds., Reginald Wilson and Sarah E. Melendez. Washington, D.C.: American Council on Education, 1984, p. 12.

LEVINE, DEENA R. and ADELMAN, MALA B. *Beyond Language.* Englewood Cliffs, N.J.: Prentice-Hall, 1982.

NATIONAL COMMISSION ON SECONDARY EDUCATION FOR HISPANICS. *Make Something Happen: Hispanics and Urban School Reform.* Washington, D.C.: Hispanic Policy Development Project, 1984, p. 24.

NINE-CURT, CARMEN JUDITH. *Intercultural Interaction in the Hispanic-Anglo ESL Classroom from a Non-verbal Perspective.* Rio Piedras, Puerto Rico: University of Puerto Rico, 1983.

U.S. Bureau of the Census. Current Population Reports, Series P-23, No. 130, "Population Profile of the United States: 1982." Washington, D.C.: U.S. Government Printing Office, 1983, p. 20.

5

Undercurrents, Maelstroms, or the Mainstream?

A Profile of Asian Pacific American Female Students in Higher Education

JOANNE SANAE YAMAUCHI AND TIN-MALA

The status of Asian Pacific American (APA) female students reflects a dual influence of ethnic and gender-based factors in their academic evolution in institutions of higher education. APA students must face the influences of value orientations of their particular ethnic group, their gender role of generally being secondary in status to their male counterparts, and societal stereotyping and institutional discrimination. Their complex status, encompassing interpersonal needs and concerns as well as achievements and aspirations, will be explored in relation to enhancing higher education for APA female students.

BACKGROUND

Asian Pacific American female students reflect a diversity of sixty subgroups, ranging from the four largest groups of Chinese, Japanese, Koreans, and Filipinos to the Guamanians, Samoans, and Asian

*The authors wish to acknowledge the aid of research assistants Cheryl Guzzardo and Dawn Hackley, graduates, Public Communication program, American University.

69

Indians. Demographers estimate the Asian-American population at 5.1 million as of 1985, comprising 2.1 percent of the nation's population. The gain of almost 50 percent in the five-and-a-half years since the 1980 census highlights the status of Asian Pacific Americans as the fastest growing minority in America (Gardner, Robey, and Smith, 1985).

For years, Asian Pacific Americans have been associated with academic success in the media. Figures from the 1980 census indicate that 35 percent of adults aged twenty-five and older in the six major Asian-American groups were college graduates, more than double the 17 percent of white adults (U.S. Bureau of the Census, 1984).

These figures, at first glance, might be interpreted as an indication of the successful academic achievement of Asians who reside in the United States. Further analyses reveal, however, a more complex set of issues that challenge such a relatively simplistic perspective. Recent census data also indicate that roughly two-thirds or more of the APA population—with the exception of 28 percent for the Japanese—is composed of immigrants. Furthermore, a substantial majority of these immigrants came to the United States with relatively high levels of education. Selected immigration laws reflecting an anti-Asian sentiment forbade Chinese and other Asian groups from entering the United States and limited selected immigrants to individuals who had professional skills and or high levels of education (Gardner, Robey, and Smith, 1985).

In addition, recent analyses from the National Center for Education Statistics (1984) reveal that APA women constitute 46 percent of the total APA population in colleges and universities, in contrast to the national average of 50 percent of all woman enrolled in institutions of higher education.

In response to the large representation of educated APAs, some of the top universities have reportedly adopted unofficial admissions quotas for APA students, regardless of country or origin, to reduce their high representation in university student bodies. Such a practice has been viewed by many educators and researchers as a type of academic anti-Asian discrimination. Bell (1985) noted the irony of the situation because "charges of discrimination today arise most frequently in the universities, the setting generally cited as the best evidence of Asian American achievement" (p. 28).

Additional criticism of the selective use of census data to form a gross overgeneralization of the educational advantages of APAs was addressed by Nishi (1981). Negligence of major demographic factors in misinterpreting the census data included the use of median and percentage of levels of schooling completed that masks the great variability that exists among the APA groups—for example, omission of the low levels of education of Indochinese refugees, who constituted the second wave of less-educated immigrants after the mid-1970s. Recent U.S. Census statistics also indicate that a disproportionate number of APA women are underemployed, indicating that education has not resulted in comparable occupational status nor an income that is equal to that of white Americans with the same level of education (U.S. Bureau of the Census, 1973; McBee, 1982).

In addition, a rather skewed picture of college performance by APA students has emerged. A national study of Asian-American student SAT performance indicated that while APA students tended to score higher than the national average in the mathematical section, 47 percent of Asian-Americans scored below the national average in the verbal section. These scores were attributed to limited English reading and writing skills, which often restrict success (Lee, 1985).

Moreover, Sue and Zane (1985) reported that some university students compensate for their limited English-speaking abilities by taking ligher course loads, studying longer, and limiting their majors to more technical fields.

A survey conducted at the University of California at Davis revealed that 59 percent of Asian-Americans were majoring in the physical and natural sciences while only 22 percent opted to major in the humanities or social sciences. A similar study conducted for the American Council on Education stated that only 8 percent of Asian-American students were pursuing degrees in the social sciences while 52 percent of Asian-American students opted for degrees in mathematics, engineering, the health professions, and the physical scienes. As a result, many APA students are tracked into fields that utilize more technical and mathematical skills as opposed to utilizing English skills (Endo, 1974).

Another factor related to the academic achievement of Asian Pacific American students is the accumulation of stress as a result of pressure to succeed academically—strong influence administered from either the community or the family. Competitiveness is emphasized and often inbred in the students at an early age (ibid.).

The dual influence of societal myths and discrimination that has affected Asian Pacific Americans in general and APA women in particular in higher education is connected with the relationship between their value orientations and development of their identities.

VALUE ORIENTATIONS

Asian Pacific American female students are influenced by ethnic values, sex roles, and stereotypes of APA women held by other cultural groups. Many Asian females have been raised in a social context of filial piety. Individual obligation to and unquestioning respect for parental and older male sibling authority are more important than personal goals and aspirations (Ogawa, 1975). Associated with this concept is the cultural value of shame control. Any inappropriate social behavior displayed by an individual is perceived as the fault of her entire Asian ethnic group. There is a collective blame shared by others in contrast to individual guilt and embarrassment (Chung and Rieckelman, 1974).

In addition, there is the reluctance to call attention to oneself in any social situation for fear of ridicule or criticism of not only her status but that of her family, community, and entire ethnic group (Ogawa, 1975).

The general subordination of the individual's self to that of the group is underscored by the value of fatalism, a calm acceptance of one's situation. Adapting to existing situations rather than attempting to change them is seen as a virtue, reflecting the strength to survive.

In addition to ethnic influences, several researchers have found that in terms of gender differences, more traditional Chinese, Japanese, and Korean families tend to exhibit more subservience to males in contrast to their Caucasian female counterparts (Blane and Yamamoto, 1970; Chung and Rieckelman, 1974; Fujitomi and Wong, 1973; Hsu, 1971; Kim, 1975; Yun, 1976). According to Payton-Miyazaki (1971):

> Asian women are placed in a worse condition that Western women, since their socialization has never allowed them to be as achievement oriented as that of Asian men and Westerners. Asian women are less encouraged than Western women to seek occupational, educational or social activities other than familial relations. Still, in spite of higher educational opportunities, familial pressures are on Asian women to marry, raise children, and become housewives before becoming active in society at large. (p. 117)

The exception of this secondary role relationship seems to be the case of Filipino women who, for the most part, come from a social context in which males and females share similar or equal loads in family planning and in work relations (Ponce, 1974; Stoodley, 1957).

Moreover, Asian-American women must contend with a third

source of societal influence: stereotypes held by members of the dominant society, like the "mixture of the docile, submissive Oriental doll who will cater to the whims of any man; the Suzie Wong sexpot; the efficient secretary, sexy stewardess, good housekeeper and domestic; and the girl any guy would like to marry" (Kuramoto, 1976, p. 218).

Such interracial biases have also had a detrimental effect on the education of Asian-American women. Yoshioka (1974) claims that stereotypes play a negative role in the counseling process by reflecting biases of both counselor and institution. In California, for example, Asian-American women graduated from high school and college annually but relatively few continued on to graduate or professional schools. Most of these women become secretaries, clerks, or technicians. Those who did advance appeared most frequently in the health sciences and technical research areas. This suggests that Asian-American women may have been subjected to biased academic tracking that resulted in their disproportionately larger numbers in occupations placing minimal emphasis on assertive, verbal behavior.

In addition, the multiple influences of ethnic, sexual, and interracial factors are related to the patterns of communication that have been displayed during their process of cultural adjustment. Asian-American women have been reported to be more indirect, less expressive, and minimizing of conflict in their communication behavior in comparison to their Caucasian counterparts (Hutchinson, Arkoff, and Weaver, 1966; Johnson, Marsella, and Johnson, 1974). Additional findings indicate a continuing pattern of less-assertive communication behavior exhibited by Asian students in university settings (Fukuyama and Greenfield, 1983).

This relatively less-assertive communication style, based on an Asian value of respect for authority, has oftentimes been interpreted differently by members of the dominant, Westernized culture, which values more spontaneous, direct communication. Asians, therefore, are seen as having less credibility and showing a lack of leadership ability (Yamauchi, 1981).

In conjunction with the women's movement for liberation there were reports of the related efforts by selected Asian women's organizations toward more visible leadership. In attempting to be effective, they had to be more assertive, contrary to Asian values of deference. In becoming more effective, they become visible publicly, in contrast to Asian values of moderation and modesty (Fujitomi and Wong, 1973; Meade, 1970).

A survey of APA women in male-dominated, nontraditional occupations indicated that they were more assertive and better able to deal with negative stereotypes than their counterparts in female-dominated occupations. On the other hand, they were also able to retain the use of a more indirect and sensitive communication style when situationally appropriate, reflective of the leadership style that values the enhancement of human relations in management. In sum, these Asian women displayed a situational style of communication strategies that reflected both Asian-based values and more Westernized values in a variety of intercultural situations (Yamauchi, 1983).

On selected university campuses as well, more Asian American female students have also taken the reins of leadership to effect changes in curriculum development.

CURRENT EDUCATIONAL INITIATIVES

A recent exploratory national survey of APA female students of representative American universities identified some mutual academic concerns (Yamauchi and Tin-Mala, 1986). Societal and personal problems related to being victims of both racism and sexism were pinpointed by the students as major forces still to be addressed in the 1980s. The students agreed that there were still the same stereotypes of past vintage—including those of "quiet, passive, submissive, short, and cute"—being applied to their respective Asian female groups. Although a good number of the respondents also saw themselves as exhibiting quiet and passive behavior at times, those students who were in positions of leadership saw themselves as eschewing these stereotyped molds and instead being more assertive and more self-confident.

In addition, the values that the APA female students saw as most influential were those of honesty, compassion, and education. These values were seen as important in relation to their identified accomplishments and contributions of obtaining a good education as well as organizing other Asian students to be more involved in university activities and helping their respective Asian communities.

The student leaders, moreover, saw themselves as (a) seeking a greater degreee of self-development to balance their bicultural and gender-influenced identities, (b) learning from Asian female role models in the community and serving local Asian communities, and (c) pursuing some type of career. These female students in leadership positions also saw themselves as sources of influence to promote academic reforms within the university system.

A corollary event was a grant in 1985 from the Women's Educational Equity Act Program of the U.S. Department of Education to fund a modular educational package on APA women's courses for universities, secondary schools, and community organizations. A significant aspect of the project included the creation of experimental, pilot courses on Asian Pacific American women. In order to increase significantly the number of courses dealing with APA history and culture beyond the few at UCLA and UC Berkeley in the early 1970s, APA women's courses were included in the experimental curricula of Brown, Duke, Oberlin, Smith, Stanford, Wellesley, Wesleyan, and Yale (Tin-Mala, 1986).

Feedback from both Asian and non-Asian participants in the courses reflected the significant impact of the venture together with strong endorsements to institutionalize the courses. Representative views about identity were captured by Shin (1986), a Korean-American student at Wesleyan University:

> I was unaware of the what Asian Americans were going through . . . as a whole, aside from some of the problems I faced. . . . I realize now . . . that I should be proud of my heritage and try to acculturate yet at the same time not lose my Asian identity. (p. 2)

Another insight offered by Chin (1986), a Chinese-American student at Wesleyan, focused on APA women in general:

> I feel that I have become more knowledgeable about the plight of Asians in American history. . . . I've read about more strong and persevering women than I've ever believed existed. (p. 2)

Roummel (1986) from Brown University expressed a non-Asian view of her broadened intercultural sensitivity:

> This course has gotten me in touch with the unique brand of racism which is used against Asian Americans. . . . I am working through my own racism and jealousy of Asian American women. . . . After taking this course I feel convinced that I must fight for all women to be free. I am white and can use that "privilege." (p. 1)

IMPLICATIONS FOR INSTITUTIONAL CHANGE

In 1979, a national conference of Asian Pacific leaders in education and APA national and local organizations met to identify resolutions to major educational problems of APAs and to specify strategies for the 1980s to enhance the education of Asian Pacific Americans in the United States.

The recommendations presented by the APA educational leaders and those of the APA female students of the national project on Asian-American women's courses are strikingly parallel and reflect the collective thinking of administrators, faculty, students, and community leaders (Asian/Pacific American Concerns Staff and The National Asian/Pacific American Education Alliance, 1980; Tin-Mala, 1986). Yamashiro (1985), a Japanese-American student at Yale, summarized the thoughts of many of her peers:

> As an immediate goal . . . we need clear, specific protection in our university regulations as racial and sexual minorities. If we are to effectively implement social change at the university level, we must first ensure that our respective universities will protect us from harassment, intimidation or assault. . . . we students must be active participants and empower ourselves, because no one else will look out for our interests. We must take the responsibility to correct the structure where we find flaws in it. (p. 3)

Other recommendations made by educators, students, and community leaders are as follows:

- implementation of courses in multicultural education to focus on the interrelationship of minority groups at all levels of the educational system;
- recognition of Asian/Pacific American studies as a relevant and legitimate field of study in higher education institutions and as a source of providing individuals with a better cultural understanding of APAs;
- provision for adequate funding of programs to meet the needs of APAs in institutions of higher education, specifically support service programs like counseling programs to address the needs of non-English and limited English-speaking APA students;
- inclusion of APA representation in administrative positions and faculty positions to provide adequate role models and sensitivity to the needs of APA students;
- continuation of specific courses on APA women in more universities to promote the education of both APA women and others;
- reassessment of university admissions policies that currently discriminate against APA students;

- promotion of more active Asian student organizations and support groups to promote better dialogue among APAs and other non-APA students;
- encouragement of more visibility of APA students to amend their status of "invisibility" by raising their levels of activism and self-awareness as individuals and as an ethnic group;
- sponsorship of more research on APA student needs and concerns, including comparisons along gender lines;
- initiation of improved communication lines among minority student groups to combat institutional racism and more immediately eliminate discriminatory admissions policies; and
- more student involvement with local communities, whose female leaders can provide role models and a support system for the students.

There is a strong commitment by both Asians and other ethnic group members to correct misperceptions about Asian Pacific Americans and to educate both Asians and non-Asians about the needs and concerns of APA female students. Appropriate actions by committed administrators, faculty, counselors, students, and community leaders can protect the rights of APA female students to attain the best education possible. The enhancement of their higher education will enable Asian Pacific American women to develop their unique blend of multicultural identities and ensure the equity of their participation in the American mainstream.

REFERENCES

ASIAN/PACIFIC AMERICAN CONCERNS STAFF and THE NATIONAL ASIAN/PACIFIC AMERICAN EDUCATION ALLIANCE. "Asian/Pacific American Education Agenda for the 1980's." Washington, D.C.: U.S. Department of Education, 1980, pp. 13–19.

BELL, DAVID A. "The Triumph of Asian Americans." *The New Republic*, July 15 and July 22, 1985:26–30.

BLANE, H., and YAMAMOTO, K. "Sexual Role Identity Among Japanese and Japanese-American High School Students." *Journal of Cross-cultural Psychology* 1 (1970):345–354.

CHIN, JEAN. Survey data from the project "From the Curriculum to the Mainstream." Middletown, Conn.: Wesleyan University. May 6, 1986.

CHUNG, SOON-HYUNG, and RIECKELMAN, A. P. "The Koreans of Hawaii." *People and Cultures of Hawaii: An Introduction for Mental Health Workers* (eds. Wen-Shing Tseng, J. F. McDermott, Jr., and T. W. Maretzki). Honolulu: Department of Psychiatry, University of Hawaii School of Medicine, 1974.

ENDO, RUSSELL. Asian Americans and Higher Education. Paper presented at annual meeting, Southwestern Sociological Association, March 1974:1–22.

FUJITOMI, I., and WONG, D. "The New Asian Women." *Asian Americans Psychological Perspectives* (eds. Stanley Sue and Nathaniel Wagner). Palo Alto, Calif.: Science and Behavior Books, 1973.

FUKUYAMA, M. A., and GREENFIELD, T. K. "Dimensions of Assertiveness in an Asian-American Student Population." *Journal of Counseling Psychology* 30 (1983):429–432.

GARDNER, ROBERT W., ROBEY, BRYANT, and SMITH, PETER C. "Asian Americans: Growth, Change, and Diversity." *Population Bulletin* 40, October 1985:1–44.

GIVENS, RON, et al. "Asian Americans: The Drive to Excel." *Newsweek on Campus*, April 1984:4–7.

HSU, F. L. K. *The Challenge of the American Dream: The Chinese in the United States.* Belmont, Calif.: Wadsworth, 1971.

HUTCHINSON, S., ARKOFF, A., and WEAVER, H B. "Ethnic and Sex Factors in Classroom Responsiveness. *Journal of Social Psychology* 69 (1966):321–325.

JOHNSON, F. S., MARSELLA, J. A., and JOHNSON, C. L. "Social and Psychological Aspects of Verbal Behavior in Japanese Americans." *American Journal of Psychiatry* 5 (1974):580–583.

KIM, S. D. "Demonstration Project for Asian Americans: An Analysis of Problems of Asian Wives of U.S. Servicemen." Seattle: Demonstration Project for Asian Americans, 1975.

KURAMOTO, FORD H. "Lessons Learned in the Federal Funding Game." *Social Casework* 57 (1976):208–218.

LEE, JANET. "National Study Launched on Asians' Verbal Skills." *Asian Week*, August 1985.

McBEE, SUSANNA. "Asian Americans—Are They Making the Grade?" *U.S. News and World Report*, April 2, 1982:41–47.

MEADE, ROBERT D. "Leadership Studies of Chinese and Chinese-Americans." *Journal of Cross-cultural Psychology* 1 (1970):325–332.

NATIONAL CENTER for EDUCATION STATISTICS. *Preliminary Statistics on Students in Higher Education.* Washington, D.C.: NCES, 1984.

NISHI, SETSUKA MATSUNAGA. The Negative Implication of Misinterpreting the Educational Attainment Levels of Asian Pacific Americans. Paper presented at the Asian Pacific American Research seminar, National Association of Asian and Pacific American Education, Los Angeles, Calif.: UCLA Asian American Studies Center, 1981.

OGAWA, DENNIS M. Identity, Dissonance and Bilingualism: Communication Problems of Asian American Assimilation. Paper presented at Speech Communication Association convention, Houston, Texas, 1975.

PAYTON-MIYAZAKI, Y. "Three Steps Behind and Three Steps Ahead." *Asian Women.* Berkeley, Calif.: University of California, 1971.

PONCE, D. E. "The Filipinos of Hawaii." *Peoples and Cultures in Hawaii: An*

Introduction for Mental Health Workers (eds. Wen-Shing Tseng, J. F. McDermott, Jr., and T. W. Maretzki). Honolulu: Department of Psychiatry, University of Hawaii School of Medicine, 1974.

ROUMMEL, KIKI. Class journal from the project "From the Curriculum to the Mainstream." Providence, R.I.: Brown University, February 4, 1986.

SHIN, JAE EUN. Survey data from the project "From the Curriculum to the Mainstream." Middletown, Conn.: Wesleyan University, May 6, 1986.

STOODLEY, B. M. "Some Aspects of Tagalog Family Structure." *American Anthropologist* 2 (1957):236–249.

SUE, S., and ZANE, N. W. S. "Academic Achievement and Socio-emotional Adjustment Among Chinese University Students." *Journal of Counseling Psychology* 32 (1985):570–579.

TIN-MALA. "From the Curriculum to the Mainstream: An Educational Equity Package for Asian American Women." Bethesda, Md.: National Network of Asian and Pacific Women, 1986.

U.S. BUREAU OF THE CENSUS. "1980 Census of the Population: General Social and Economic Characteristics." Washington, D.C.: U.S. Government Printing Office, 1984.

U.S. BUREAU OF THE CENSUS. "1970 Subjects Reports Japanese, Chinese, and Filipinos in the United States." Washington, D.C.: U.S. Government Printing Office, 1973.

YAMASHIRO, AMY. Speech in Asian-American women pilot course. New Haven, Conn.: Yale University, November 2, 1985:3.

YAMAUCHI, JOANNE S. *The Cultural Integration of Asian American Women: Issues of Identity and Communication Behavior.* Washington, D.C.: National Institute of Education, 1981.

YAMAUCHI, JOANNE S. *The Interrelationship Between Socially Attributed and Personally Applied Stereotypes by Asian American Women in Nontraditional and Traditional Occupations.* Washington, D.C.: The American University, 1983.

YAMAUCHI, JOANNE S., and TIN-MALA. *National Survey of Asian Pacific American University Students.* Washington, D.C.: American University, 1986.

YOSHIOKA, ROBERT B. "Stereotyping Asian Women." *Civil Rights Digest* 9 (1974):45.

YUN, H. "The Korean Personality and Treatment Considerations." *Social Casework* 57 (1976):173–178.

6

American Indian Women in Higher Education:
Common Threads and
Diverse Experiences

ROBBI FERRON

American Indian women are often asked to comment on being Indian. They may be willing to do so, may even want to, but are uneasy about it. And for good reason. The reasons are rooted in a sense of respect for those people who are being written about as well as those being addressed. Those unfamiliar with American Indian cultures may not understand this reluctance to comment on the experience of being "Indian."

The uneasiness stems from trying to share information about an illusion. There is no "Indian," no "Indian experience." There are Navajos, Siouxs, Creeks, Arikaras—and more than two hundred other distinct tribal groups. The term "Indian" lumps together all the aboriginal tribal groups of what is now the United States. The uneasiness arises also from the recognition of the very grandiosity of the task, that is, dealing with the diversity of the tribes while presenting observations that have integrity.

A closer examination of the diversity may help to clarify the discomfort. The Sioux have a four-day Sundance, during which the dancer is attached by skin, and in some cases muscle, to a rope that is attached to a central pole. This is called "piercing." The dance culminates when the dancer breaks free from the pole. The Kiowa, who once sundanced, no longer do; instead, men who have been accepted into the Kiowa Gourd Clan participate in the Gourd Dance. It is a men's society dance in which movements and steps are repeated, with very subtle changes being made as the dance progresses. By contrast, the Cherokees do the Stomp Dance.

A member of one tribe can speak of her Cherokee experience, but not of the Sioux experience—much less of the "Indian" experience.

And finally the uneasiness, for many, has roots in the inappropriateness of speaking about a tribe or its customs. Respected tribal spokespersons are not self-appointed or self-anointed. They are chosen. Many contemporary Indian women remember their elders commenting humorously on white people's fondness for palaver. Whites would talk without being chosen, without considering the importance of what they said, even without knowing what they were talking about. The effects of this are still audible. An Indian person may be comfortable with silence, but white people are often less comfortable with it and tend to fill the silence with noise.

Nevertheless, this essay will try to give voice to the needs and concerns of American Indian women in higher education. The hope is that these comments will diminish the harmful effects of people's ignorance and misinformation about the subject.

True to an "Indian way" of addressing a topic, the first requirement is to recognize the topic's place in the scheme of things. Despite the rich diversity of Indian experiences, some common threads bind together the experiences since the early 1800s. Neighboring tribes have borrowed from each other in the last century, and the sharp cultural distinctions between them have faded. And Indian culture generally has been traumatized greatly by white culture throughout the 1800s, and to the present 1980s.

The effects of that trauma, however, are quite varied. Some contemporary Indians have identified heavily with white culture, while others reject it. The degree of acculturation varies widely among tribes, within tribes, even within families. An Indian woman may speak her native language in addition to English, practice Indian religion, date Indian men, seek an Indian spouse, perhaps even restrict her choice to a tribal member. Another student from the same tribe may speak only English, be ignorant of tribal religious practices, and prefer to date non-Indians.

Often the rural or urban area the women come from is an important factor in the degree of acculturation. The Navajo, who have the largest Indian reservation, have only peripheral exposure to non-Indians. They have maintained a tribal language and traditional family system, whereas the Indian woman raised in Washington, D.C., is more non-Indian in culture.

As aspects of the cultures are being described, the word "traditional" hovers near and often permeates the explanation. To understand "traditional" requires accurate knowledge of the history of the tribe. A tribe's history will demonstrate that the traditions of 1886 differ starkly from those of 1986. The following two examples will illustrate.

Photographs in the archives of the Smithsonian Institution show an Assiniboine woman cooking dog in a kettle over an open pit. Today this is rare. Some Assinibonine women have never tasted dog, may even be repelled by the thought. They may be ignorant of the ceremonies that once attached to this practice.

Traditionally, Sioux women did not pierce at the Sundance. Today some do. To an elderly Sioux, today's women who pierce are not traditional. However, to young Sioux women, few of whom Sundance or pierce, the woman who does may be perceived as traditional.

Given that Indian women represent diverse tribes and a wide range of acculturation in the scheme of things, they may face common problems and issues when they enter or work in higher education. It is important to face those as straightforwardly as possible. In the text that follows, problems are identified, solutions suggested, and concerns articulated.

PROBLEM. Paying for an education is made problematic both by a declining federal commitment to financial assistance and by financial burdens that may be unique to Indian women. The status of educational funding for Indian students is widely misunderstood. Myths run the gamut, from a belief that every Indian has a free ride through college (treaties, it is imaged, guaranteed a free education to every Indian) to the notion that Indian students are unlikely candidates for academic scholarships. These myths are often linked. Guidance counselors often do not encourage Indian students to seek academic or other scholarships. This happens because the counselor does not believe the Indian student can compete academically or erroneously believes the student has a free ride. The student will not be aware of the scholarships unless the counselor guides the Indian student through those applications, as they do for white students.

The Bureau of Indian Affairs (BIA) is implicated in the financial status of most Indian students. In the early 1800s the BIA was lodged in the Department of Defense. Later, it was moved to the Department of the Interior, where it has remained. More's the pity; if it were still in Defense, it might benefit from defense-budget increases.

The Bureau's education office distributes funds allocated by Congress for Indian education. Two problems arise from this. First, the bureaucracy, like most bureaucracies, is unresponsive, in this case to Indian educational needs. Second, the BIA has faced continual budget cuts. Fewer and fewer Indians are receiving BIA financial assistance. Meanwhile, though the Department of Education has earmarked some money for Indian education, this too has diminished in recent years.

Other financial problems unique to Indian women derive from their culture. The family organization within many tribes is an extended family system. This is a bloodline system that is focused not on a nuclear family of mother, father, and child but on grandparents, parents, uncles and aunts, cousins, and children. In some tribes, as with the Crow, this is further expanded to include deceased ancestors, resulting in a clan system. In some tribes a first and even second cousin is called "sister" or "brother."

In the extended family system several nuclear families may share shelter and food. This may cause discrimination against the Indian woman when she is seeking housing. Landlords want to rent to a nuclear family and resist the wear and tear an extended family may have on property. It has been easier not to rent to Indians than to face the problems posed if the extended family should appear. The Indian woman cannot afford to rent a facility that would give all members their own bedroom and private space.

The Indian woman may find her finances strained if her extended family visits often. Within some tribal groups, when the family arrives, protocol requires that a meal be prepared and a long visit follow. Besides the time expenditure, the actual cost of feeding the family can be formidable.

The "giveaway" system that may tribes practice to commemorate significant events—births, graduations, entry into military service, or death, for example—may also impose a financial burden on a student who is trying to skimp. Well in advance of such milestone events, family members make and gather goods for the ceremony. Handmade beadwork, baskets, shawls, and quilts are highly valued. Though Tupperware and polyester blankets are common today, the expense of time and money preparing for these special events is significant for a population—Indian women students—trying to live within a fixed budget.

SOLUTION. Students need conscientious help from high school guidance counselors in obtaining financial aid or scholarships for higher education. Knowledgeable and sensitive financial aid officers in higher education are also required. Orientation programs for beginning students can address the matter of budgeting of time and resources in a way that is sensitive to their cultures.

PROBLEM. An Indian woman's visible, physical difference from others may become amplified into a dizzying—and destructive—self-consciousness. Indian women are often asked to explain, in some fashion, what it means to be Indian. The questions may be well-meaning enough, but they burden the student and the woman employed in higher education—a burden that non-Indian women are not required to shoulder. The Indian student is no more prepared to answer the question than, say, a different student might be is asked to describe a white bourgeois experience in Muncie, Indiana.

Rather than explain "Indianness" to a group that might be supportive, Indian women may choose to isolate themselves. But without a supportive environment, educational and employment success come harder. For the student the college experience is now always the joyous time that reunion movies emphasize.

SOLUTION. The Indian woman needs to be free from having to explain or justify her Indianness to non-Indians. People who work with Indian women need to find other topics to converse about with Indian women.

PROBLEM. The Indian woman may be different in invisible ways from other students and employees, and unless that is acknowledged, the differences may work to her detriment. Within her tribe, the Indian woman has responsibilities and obligations. She may have to absent herself from school in order to go home and cook for a ceremony. A professor, administrator, or co-worker may think it foolish, but her acceptance as a tribal member may rest on her participation in such activity. The social pressures she faces may be invisible to academicians.

So may be the psychological demands. There are strong indications that Indian students are right-brain dominant. In such individuals, the right hemisphere of the brain, the source of intuitive and creative though, is dominant, rather than the left brain, source of logical and systematic though. Researchers at Brigham Young University (BYU), which enrolls many Indian students, determined that most of the Indian students participating in a study dealing with learning styles were right-brain dominant. BYU is tackling the challenge of adjusting teaching methods to accommodate right-brain-dominant students. BYU is an exception. Most educational institutions key on left-brain dominant students and will continue to do so.

Even the content of the student's education may, ultimately, pit her against her own culture. In speech classes, students are encouraged to look into the eyes of the audience, to make attention-getting movements, and to use words of power to impress. Such lessons may cut against the grain of the Indian student. For the Indian woman, there may be cultural rules about looking into the eyes of persons older than herself, of men, and of children. The Indian woman employed in higher education is at a disadvantage if she carries these cultural prohibitions into the workplace.

The Indian woman soon realizes that, in a sense, she has left one culture but not yet arrived in another. Her journey is painful, she risks being ostracized by the culture that is her root. In more ways than one, the cost of education or of working in higher education is dear.

SOLUTION. The Indian woman in higher education still needs contact with tribal practices and with her extended family. She needs a support system to help her bridge the cultural gap and to help her hang on to her traditional values. The Indian student needs instructors sensitive to her right-brain-oriented learning style, to her hesitancy to comply with certain instruction—such as that she might receive in speech class. She needs educational materials free of subtle racism or white-majority ethnocentrism.

PROBLEM. Peer pressure and infighting among Indians mar the educational process and the Indian woman's effectiveness. Since the early 1970s, a pan-Indian movement has flourished among Indian people. More Indians have received formal education and have learned for the first time the shameful history of the federal government's treatment of the American Indian. For example, few treaties between the United States and tribes have been fully honored. Such knowledge may breed a population of angry, cynical students and graduates. Reacting to disturbing knowledge, they may call upon all "real" Indians to join them, while attempting to establish criteria for being Indian, such as blood quantum or dress. The pressure they exert on younger, less experienced Indian students and Indian women comes in many forms and can be compelling. The less-traditional Indian woman trying to find her Indian identity may be particularly vulnerable to pressure to prove her Indianness.

Infighting develops. Within a diverse Indian community, intertribal politics and allegiance to bloodline systems affect relationships. For example, the Sioux and the Crow are historic enemies. This was demonstrated during Custer's Last Stand, against the Sioux, at the battle of Little Big Horn. Crow scouts served Custer's Seventh Cavalry. Today there may be some hesitancy among Sioux and Crow to support each other in higher education activities.

Currently, some Navajo and Hopi are pitted against each other because the Hopi have been recognized by the federal government as owners of land that some Navajo families have lived on since the 1880s. Tribal allegiance may prevent cooperative support of each other on a distant higher education campus.

If two students are bloodline-related they will be expected to support each other in all circumstances. This causes conflicts in all kinds of social interchanges.

An Indian woman may fall prey to any or all of these diversions, which sap the energy and concentration that would otherwise go into her education tasks. Her allegiance to her bloodline or tribe may prevent her from actively supporting other Indian women.

SOLUTION. The Indian woman may opt to resist pressure to prove her allegiance and Indianness by concocted standards. She needs to understand the causes of the dynamics within the higher education Indian community so she is comfortable with the degree of activism she chooses.

PROBLEM.   Adequate and culturally sensitive child care for the children of Indian women is often lacking. Many, if not a majority, of women college students and professionals are mothers. Most of those mothers are probably single parents. Traditionalists in many tribes have opposed abortion, and being an unwed mother carries no stigma. All newborns are embraced. But such support will not pay the bills or overcome the logistical difficulties the mother faces when she leaves home to study or to work.

The Indian student may lack the knowledge, connections, or resources to place her children in the better day-care centers. The Indian woman employees faces the same problems all working mothers and single parents face—a comfortable social life and adequate child care facilities. She must face the likelihood of her child being drawn into the mainstream and losing exposure to the Indian culture.

SOLUTION. The Indian mother needs equal access to appropriate child care, which includes sensitivity to the mother and child's root culture.

PROBLEM. Indian people have drinking problems. U.S. culture is generally troubled by the problem of alcoholism, but the Indian person's skin color lends greater visibility to the problem among Indian peoples. Arrests of whites for alcohol possession and intoxication in towns near reservations are few compared to the arrests of Indians. Nevertheless, the majority of persons in expensive in-patient treatment centers are white.

An Indian woman may not recognize her alcohol abuse as a problem. What might be considered abuse drinking in a white community may be only social drinking in an Indian community.

When alcohol abuse in the community is part of a larger problem affecting the woman's spirit, elders or medicine people are available to effect a cure. On campus, alcoholism is recognized as a disability to be treated through counseling programs. Given her tribal background, the Indian woman may eschew the unfamiliar psychological approaches offered by a counselor—especially if the counselor is not an Indian. And oftentimes, Indian students are unaware of the scope of counseling services that are available to them.

A related problem is that of inadequate health care. At home the Indian woman probably has had access to doctors, nurses, often a hospital, provided by the Indian Health Service. When a campus does not have full medical services, the Indian woman must rely on near-campus facilities for herself and her family. Too often the reimbursement process for health care expenses is cumbersome or impossible to implement. Here again, bureaucracy is a problem.

SOLUTION. Diversion programs that include good in-patient treatment should be provided to Indian people as an alternative to incarceration in prosecution processes. Counseling programs that use elders or medicine people should be provided for the Indian population in higher education. Student affairs offices should provide programs that assist Indian students with health care reimbursement procedures.

PROBLEM. Indian women have to determine the place that concepts, issues and expectations of the feminist movement have in their lives. When the Indian woman moves into higher education culture she inevitably encounters, often for the first time, some aspect of the feminist movement.

The feminist movement of the 1970s was a white, middle-class woman's movement. Equal opportunity, equal pay, abortion rights, lesbian, and political power issues fueled the movement. While white women were banging the podiums demeaning women who had "fetus fetishes," Indian women were concerned about infant mortality and clandestine sterilization by the Indian Health Service. Indian women, even those who tried, could not relate to the feminist movement.

The women's movement has slowed and many of the structures it created—women's centers, women's studies programs, support groups for older women, displaced homemakers and lesbians, and women's speciality caucuses—often are not minority-culture sensitive.

The Indian woman has never been called upon to cognitively appraise what it means to be a Navajo, Sioux, Creek, or Arikara woman, nor the benefits she experiences because of the feminist movement. She must look at her degree of acculturation and her posture regarding tribal cultural preservation. All of this may lead her to an identity crisis.

SOLUTION.   Indian women must not allow themselves to be swept into a women's movement without first appraising the potential conflict with their tribal culture.

CONCLUSION

The problems faced by Indian women in higher education have solutions, although they may be difficult ones. Indian women have concerns that defy solution, because of the diversity of tribal cultures and the state of affairs in Indian country. Some examples:

Indian women in leadership roles find the relationship of the sexes troubling. Nearly all the Indian women who are nationally prominent are single. Some of these women choose this, but most do not. Compatible partners for Indian women leaders are scarce. Most Indian men leaders already have partners, often white women— much to the chagrin of Indian women. When Indian men leaders are available, they are often not considered suitable by Indian women. The situation is exacerbated by the discrepancy of educational levels of Indian women and available Indian men.

A deeper concern for Indian women leaders is the survival of Indian tribes and cultures. Cultural preservation is dependent upon marriage and propagation. An Arikara marrying a Navajo dilutes both cultures. At best, the offspring can be raised in one culture, but this is highly unlikely.

The political survival of tribes requires the maintenance of federal recognition. This requires relentless effort—an effort that often becomes a primary effort. Indian women leaders make efforts to support Indian men and their Indian sisters, many of whom face poverty and discrimination every day. It is difficult to keep a culture alive in the face of the far more elemental needs of everyday survival.

With concerns such as these, little time is left for mating, play, or involvement in feminist concerns.

The price the Indian woman leader pays is dear. Willingly or unwillingly, she sacrifices her personal life. In a society that is lacking heroes, these heroines can be seen in action at Eastern Montana, Big Horn Community, and Dull Knife Community colleges; Montana State, Arizona State, and Northeastern State universities; Stanford, Dartmouth, and the universities of Arizona, California at San Diego, Kansas, and New Mexico; and many other institutions of higher education nationwide. These heroines and others are named in *OHOYO 1,000*, a listing of Indian women leaders throughout the country. The contributions to higher education these and other Indian women make are unique. They have an honesty that is gentle yet incisive. They are clear about their interpretation of what they perceive. An older Indian woman will expose that perception gently, often through stories or humor, whereas a younger woman may speak directly. The contribution is a response to an inquiry or situation that is unfettered by game-playing and can be threatening or refreshing.

A subtle contribution Indian women make is the recognition of a unifying spirit, that is, the human spirit respecting nature and that which is natural. This manifests itself in intuitive questioning of situations; "What is the nature of the spirit here and how is that spirit operating in this situation."

Most poignant is the contribution of personal sacrifices that the Indian woman has made for the survival of her people and culture. These are sacrifices few others are called upon to make and even fewer are capable of making. The survival of Indian people in this eleventh hour is dependent upon their women.

7

Reentry Women in the Academy:

The Contributions of a Feminist Perspective

JEAN F. O'BARR

From 1970 until 1982, I served as Director of Continuing Education at Duke University. After a year's leave of absence, I returned to the same institution to create a Women's Studies Program. Twelve years of working with reentry women combine with my present involvement in women's studies for college-age students to provide a particular perspective on continuing education that forms the basis of the discussion in this chapter.

I often muse on whether or not it might have been done "the other way around"—what would it have been like to work with women returning to higher education in the 1970s if women's studies had been more fully in place and the curriculum transformed to reflect women's experiences, expressions and expectations. I submit that it could not have been done without the knowledge gained by hammering away at institutions to accept and assist nontraditional students, we would not have had the angle of vision required to see how limited the educational enterprise is on gender-based questions. But I know that it should have been done, that the obstacles returning women students faced would have been minimal if feminist scholarship had been integrated into the curriculum they recieved when they arrived on campus.

This chapter begins with a brief overview of the recent literature on returning women students that illustrates what has been learned in two decades of incorporating older women on the campuses through continuing education programs. It then goes on to describe the process by which one administrator, myself, came to see the contradictions between the contributions older women were making in the academy and the nature of the institutions they were entering. Finally, this chapter analyzes how the questions posed by returning women students illustrate the "problems" of higher education with reference to gender as much as the "problems" of a group of learners.

RETURNING WOMEN STUDENTS: NUMBERS, NEEDS, CONCERNS

The fact that large numbers of older women students return to U.S. campuses is an increasingly familiar theme in our society. And not only those of us directly involved in reentry programs know this. College administrators note the changing age and gender composition of their applicant pools in every school and division. Households and families adjust their life-styles as the women in them reenter training and education at all levels to better their economic prospects as well as to enlarge their personal horizons. Schools, churches, and communities acknowledge that the stay-at-home mother has become the going-back-to-school person and is no longer automatically available to form the core of their volunteer work force. Employers depend increasingly on women's recent course work and degrees to maintain the skill level of the labor force and to guarantee a competitive advantage in changing labor markets.

Who are returning women? While no technical definition is widely used, returning women are generally thought of as over twenty-five years of age and with a history of delay or interruption in their educations. They are drawn from every racial, ethnic, and regional group. Age and educational history combine in a variety of ways to create "returning women."

When continuing education for women programs first began in the 1960s, at schools, colleges, and universities of all kinds, the most frequent client was likely to be a woman in her late thirties or forties who was married, who had children now in school full time, and who was either completing an associate or baccalaureate degree or going for an advanced degree. With each decade of continuing education the returning woman got younger and had greater variation in her personal and educational background. By the 1980s, the returning woman category also included single women in their twenties who were dissatisfied with the direction of their first college work as well as relatively well-educated women, often with young children, who were switching fields for employment purposes.

In the beginning of the continuing education movement, returning women often evidenced doubt about the legitimacy of undertaking their plans. Women raised in the 1930s and 1940s felt doubtful about putting their own aspirations up front, accustomed as they were to putting the needs of others ahead of their own and failing to see the interrelationship between their welfare and the family's well-being. Three decades later, reflecting changing cultural norms about women, returning women were living more diverse life-styles and more ready to see that without their own development the happiness and well being of those around them was stymied.

Divorce played an important part in encouraging some women to return to education. When marriages break up, one strategy women frequently follow is to seek the education necessary to enter employment or to gain better employment. Many continuing education counselors, working with returning women, report that educational-counseling sessions often seemed more like marriage-counseling sessions as returning women struggled to develop their own identities through education in the process of redefining their marital status.

The evolution and diversification of continuing education programs, running the gambit from liberal education programs for masters' degrees in elite institutions to in-house half-day training programs at places of employment, meant that returning women came to understand education more as a process than as a onetime acquisition. The earlier idea that women return to the campus to get "prepared for life" gave way to the contemporary approach that learning opportunities are ongoing and that women will enter and reenter for a long time period in response to their evolving personal and professional needs. Thus, women of many backgrounds gained access to a wider variety of educational programs at any one point in time and did so more than once in their lives, viewing it as an ongoing process of self-development by the 1980s.

The figures on returning women students are impressive and growing[1]:

- Women are the majority of students in higher education in the 1980s.
- By 1986 women over 25 constituted 24 percent of all postsecondary students.
- Returning women students are found in every type of institution, pursuing every kind of degree, while continuing to confront patterns of discrimination in some areas of study and in classroom expectations generally.
- Part-time study and enrollment in community colleges are particularly strong, both because they are more accessible to larger numbers of women and because of the hesitancy on the part of the more traditional and prestigious institutions to fully welcome and integrate returning women students.
- Programs of continuing education for women vary considerably in their focus, scope, and energy, yet almost every institution of higher learning makes some accommodations for older students and many have been highly successful in recruiting and educating large numbers of women.
- Women who have been reentry students and are now in the work force are enthusiastic advocates in their positions as co-workers, employers, and college personnel.

In short, women return to education because they want to for personal reasons and because they have to for economic reasons, as we shall see below. What are the needs and concerns of the students, on the one hand, and of the institutions in which they matriculate, on the other, as the two meet?

The research literature on reentry women has grown so that we now have a base from which to study returning women students and on which to design and implement the programs that will meet the needs they have identified. Two publications of the last year review the previous research literature and demonstrate what twenty years of service and research have established. Ekstrom and Marvel[2] describe the educational barriers facing adult women as *institutional*, the formal parts of the college process that begin with admissions credentials and run to financial aid limitations, course regulations, and lack of women-centered counseling; *situational* factors such as class and ethnic background, family responsibilities, time conflicts and lack of mobility; and *personal* or *psychological* concerns stemming from weak self-concepts, derived in turn from the position of women in American culture and society generally. The authors go on to describe in some detail the many programs for reentry women that work. The programs "work," in the authors' view, because they start with women's strengths as students (while acknowledging their relative lack of resources and skills in certain areas) and readjust the institutional policies to make them flexible enough to give reentry women a chance to succeed.

Holliday[3] describes the specific policies of institutions of higher learning that demand alteration if reentry women are to be welcomed, citing the research literature supporting various recommendations. She highlights changes in recruitment policy, admissions procedures, orientation programs, financial aid restrictions, staff attitudes, child care availability, and counseling to facilitate women's successful reentry.

The voices of reentry women themselves have begun to be heard. The Modern Language Association[4] compiled a rich collection of women's experiences in *The Road Retaken.* Twenty-five women, writing from diverse perspectives, describe their eventual successes in resuming their educations. A second portion of the book documents the place of women as employees of higher education, all written by women who took less than a direct path to their present positions. The final section puts forth the view of women who struggle on the perimeters of the academy and how the academy's mores resist change. Taken together, the essays give a clear portrait of the women served by reentry programs and their reactions to the processes they have undergone. While no single pattern can summarize the reentry process, all twenty-five women exhibit courage in the face of obstacles, asking of the academy that it focus on their potential and not be bound by an evaluation of their particular current characteristics nor discriminatory attitudes toward women's achievement in general.

The title of McLaren's discussion of working-class women in adult education in Britain, *Ambitions and Realizations,*[5] speaks directly to the need to conceptualize broadly when describing as well as planning for reentry women. McLaren surveys the growth of adult education and then explores in depth a group of students from working class backgrounds. The women she interviews see reentry programs as enabling them to change their social position, to provide them with improved job qualifications, and to assist them in finding more rewarding work. While ever cognizant of the obstacles in realizing their ambitions, her study suggests that with a solid matching of individual learners and institutional needs, the goals of both can and have been met.

THE PERSONAL AS POLITICAL: EXCERPTS FROM AN ADMINISTRATOR'S JOURNAL

The demographic trend is clear: reentry women are an important constituency in higher education. The experiences of continuing education personnel who serve adult women are equally clear: adult women students possess characteristics that are both strengths and liabilities when they embark on a reentry process. Generally, they do very well as students if their liabilities can be addressed and their strengths allowed to flourish. The lessons of twenty-five years of program development substantiate these claims: with requisite leadership and support, the academy can and does modify itself and exhibit the flexibility needed to incorporate older women as students. And the academy is rewarded: reentry students tend to do well and to show appreciation to the institutions that welcome them. And yet, after two decades of working with reentry women, a piece of the puzzle has been missing.

Clues about the characteristics of the missing piece are found in these episodes drawn from my administrative memory.

Episode #1

A biochemist by doctoral training, this reentry woman came to me through a continuing education course on life-planning, explaining that the research laboratory was too demanding now and that she had come to feel she had made a career mistake. Her interest in human interaction, fostered by her work as a mother and as a civic leader, was now the more decisive; she wanted to do a postdoctoral sequence of courses in child development. Arrangements were made and some faculty in the psychology department were eager to utilize her talents and interests. After several courses, the enthusiasm on the department's side slackened. She was too persistent in her questioning, I was told. She doubted the assumptions and methods behind much of the research she was being asked to replicate. Based on her experiences as a mother and as a female leader, she asked for a fundamental rethinking on what was being studied; her new colleagues resisted.

Episode #2

I discouraged another reentry woman from taking an American politics course from her neighbor. I felt that, for the woman's first course, she ought to try something that she entered with no previous history that might entangle things. No, she insisted, if she was going to go back for her B.A. she might as well start with her friend and neighbor, for he had promised to look out for her and set her straight on political science. She took the course, and the problem was not the one I had anticipated. She handled the friendship and personal relationships with maturity. What she could not handle was the subject matter. American politics as she understood it dealt with people, even women people, and issues; she had after all been a League of Women Voters chapter president. But the course as presented to eighteen-year-olds never mentioned women, the issues she thought were on the political agenda, and the relationship between the women's movement and the changing face of politics. Not only could she never get an answer for why the material she valued was absent, she could not get the faculty member to value the question itself. Women, according to the party line, were not active in politics and little more needed to be said.

Episode #3

This reentry woman's love of literature was staggering. Mention a character, a plot, a poem and she could tell you something about it, how she had reacted when she read it, and what the critics said about it. I thought she would sail through her English literature courses and was already making mental plans for encouraging her to go on to graduate school. As she resumed her college work, reading more and being required to read it from a more structured perspective, her frustrations grew rather than diminished. One day, after a long talk, she said things were a bit better. She was reading Virginia Woolf and Simone deBeauvoir and Doris Lessing regularly now on the side—they were making the reading of *real* literature possible. By *real* literature, of course, she was referring to the *canon*, the writing of white males and an occasional female that constitutes the literature major. Confronted with the question of why what spoke to her was not considered literature, she explained that she would think about that problem when she finished. When indeed I feared she would be finished as the predetermined product of a process that denied legitimacy to her own, a female voice, imposing another in its place.

Thinking back to these three students and many others like them, I realize that, as the Director of Continuing Education during the 1970s, I sensed something was wrong although I lacked a coherent explanation at the time. I urged older women students to speak up, to refuse accommodation in the classroom as their political mode, to believe in and pursue the values of rationale disclosure, the very values espoused by the settings in which they found themselves.

Occasionally, confrontation between reentry women and faculty led to understanding and understanding led to modification in what was taught. But more often, questioning led to silence. The older students made do with two worlds, the world of the classroom and the world of their experiences. The faculty and staff claimed that as soon as older women got accustomed to the campus they would settle in, questions would disappear, and acceptance of the-way-we-do-things would emerge. The silence persisted through the granting of degrees, for power lay on one side, confusion on the other, and no explanatory system was readily available to say "Now, look here. . . ."

It is at this point in my experience as a program director that the new scholarship on women pointed to the missing piece of the puzzle. The early discussion on Title IX, first brought up by the American Council on Education's Commission on Women, linked the question of *who* was studying *what.* As I became more familiar with the feminist scholarship in my own field, African politics and development studies, and the interdisciplinary discourse that was sweeping the social sciences and humanities, I came to see that many of the obstacles to reentry were as rooted in the curriculum as in policies of the academy and that changes needed to address both content and structure. Continuing education and women's studies are often linked, spoken of as parallel movements in higher education, but the way one informs the other is rarely examined in detail. This is what I propose to do in the final section of this chapter.[6]

MOVING ON TWO FRONTS: CONTINUING EDUCATION AND WOMEN'S STUDIES

The research literature on reentry women, the experiences of program administrators, and the testimonies of older students themselves agree with each other about what the obstacles are and the successful strategies for overcoming them. Prescriptions urge institutions out of their inertia and individuals out of their hesitancies, asking each to assume a risk-taking stance. Success stories for programs and people underscore the appropriateness of such advice.

What would this process of matching nontraditional students with traditional colleges and universities have been like if feminist scholarship had been a central force in the day-to-day workings of the schools? If the understandings derived from a study of gender systems had informed our thinking about causes and consequences? Quite different, I would argue. Consider the following examples.

A primary institutional obstacle to reentry women has been their lack of preparation and their lack of comparability to the younger students who form the majority of their class cohort. Through two decades of continuing education, programs have helped these older women get up to speed through courses, individual counseling, and general support. The women's studies perspective on this problem of the lack of fit between person and place gives us another angle of vision. It suggests that there may be less wrong with the *person* than the *place*, and that the problem in making a match between the two should be conceptualized as a problem of "What constitutes a student?" rather then as "We know a student when we see one, now let's work on making this person more studentlike."

Developments in women's history spring to mind to illustrate how the issue might be recast. As social historians began to investigate women's lives—What did they do on the western frontier? How did they experience industrialization? What did they think about the moral climate of their communities? and so forth—they began to argue that American history as it was conceptualized was only a partial history of the American people's experience. They pointed out that understanding any of the standard topics would be both improved and corrected by an expanded definition of the topic, expansion that focused on what was happening to women and how men's and women's experiences came together to form the whole historical picture. In the process of incorporating women, historians are redefining what constitutes the study of history. Similarly, by incorporating older women students, colleges and universities have had to confront questions about what constitutes a student.

In fact, of course, both the development of women's history and the evolution of incorporating nontraditional students were going on simultaneously in higher education during the 1970s. But as reform movements they only rarely informed one another. Hindsight allows us to see how much easier it would have been to conduct the continuing education debate if the historical debate had been more fully developed and more widely disseminated outside the profession. Older women students would have been seen as new students more frequently than as deficient students, just as women's history is coming to be seen as a new perspective on all history as opposed to a specialized development in a corner of the discipline. Having argued the case for older students, those students and their mentors were among the first advocates of women's history central place in the curriculum. Sensitive to what exclusion meant in a personal domain, they welcomed inclusion in the political domain of the profession.

Another obstacle for women returning to college has been articulated as the tension between their present and anticipated situations. How can a mother take courses as opposed to helping her kids with their homework? How can a wife put priority on her goals and yet keep a marriage and her husband's career in central focus? How can women of diverse backgrounds utilize institutions designed for elite white men? Situational factors, said to prevent women's reentry and to limit their educational success, take on a different cast if seen from the perspective of feminist scholarship.

Feminist scholarship in the social sciences, particularly sociology and anthropology, has argued that women's private lives as mothers, wives, workers, carriers of culture, are not only a matter of personal choices and circumstances but the result of societal arrangements created by social and historical forces and reinforced by the expectations and the training that accompany such arrangements. Feminist sociologists and anthropologists have been looking closely at the way in which economic, political, and social relationships shape the options open to individuals and showing that individual women are the recipients of a cultural system that defines and shapes women's expectations of themselves as well as the culture's view of their place. Seen from the perspective of feminist scholarship, the situational obstacles that women face in returning to college are as much social as personal. Addressing those obstacles takes on a more informed and effective cast when the woman ceases to blame circumstances and begins to address policies. While a feminist analysis of the situational obstacles by no means eliminates them, it does provide the framework of redressing them that is lacking when an individual woman reentry flounders over the reasons for her difficulties. Having seen how linked the personal and professional lives of reentry women were, advocates of continuing education found in the scholarly debates about the private-public linkages in women's lives a powerful analytic tool for addressing individual needs and institutional policies.

A third example, drawn from the final set of reasons said to prohibit older women's easy reentry, again illustrates the contribution of a feminist analysis. Conventional wisdom has it that older women students lack confidence, rely on others for validation, have relatively weakly developed self-concepts. While the literature and the experiences of those continuing education are replete with instances of women who grow into their own as a result of returning to school, there is consensus on the fact that many women began with few psychological resources. Why? Again the new scholarship on women suggests answers to that question.

In the acts of eliminating errors of fact about women, of adding knowledge about them and of creating new theories about the way gender systems work, the new scholarship on women directly attacked the basis on which women's views of themselves as inferior beings rests. Feminist literacy criticism tells us women did write, even if their writing is not anthologized. It goes on to analyze women's writing on the basis of what was said, how it was said, and to whom, rather than holding it up against male-defined standards of excellence. Art history and music composition, slow to include and value the works of women, are beginning to study pre-twentieth-century painters and the musical compositions of women over the centuries. Philosophers have started to deal with feminist questions such as rape and abortion, to explore gender perspectives on moral reasoning, and to critique the ancient thinkers for their gender-based constructions of the world. All of these endeavors mean that women's experiences, expressions, and expectations are becoming part of transmitted knowledge. Through being exposed to that knowledge, women, especially older returning women, validate their own sense of self and are empowered to see that women's contributions have a place in systems of meaning. Once women's creative activities are in focus, teachers, researchers, and students can explore the question of why they have not been spotlighted, what it means to women and men to keep them invisible, and how making them visible alters peoples' perceptions of men and women's capabilities. Having worked so very hard for twenty years to get returning students recognized as visible citizens of the campus community, continuing education people readily appreciate the personal and psychological contributions that studying women makes to the individual women doing the studying.

The results of the continuing education movement, modified policies, and more older students have contributed, albeit indirectly, to the development of women's studies. And the new scholarship on women has grown and been appreciated in part as a result of people having worked on parallel questions for nontraditional students. I have not argued the two efforts were informed by one another, except indirectly. Nonetheless, both seek a similar campus climate, one that values diversity over homogeneity, applauds a larger picture instead of a narrower one, and affirms the contributions of all learners to the collective enterprise. Just as it would have been easier for continuing education if a feminist curriculum were in place, the curriculum transformation sought by women's studies will be made somewhat easier by the presence of reentry women on both sides of the lectern. And reentry women themselves, having borne the brunt of much of the experimentation in continuing education and the absence of the records of their lives in the classroom textbooks, will benefit by the success of both developments. For access to education for women is the first goal and access to the curriculum is the second—without which the first will be a hollow victory.

NOTES

1. An excellent summary is found in two papers by the Project on the Status and Education of Women at the American Association of Colleges, 1818 R. Street, NW, Washington, D.C., 20009, *Re-entry Women: Special Programs for Special Populations* (1981, 19 pages) and *Re-entry Women: Relevant Statistics* (1981, 4 pages).

2. Ruth B. Ekstrom and Majory G. Marvel, "Educational Programs for Adult Women," in Susan S. Klein, ed., *Handbook for Achieving Sex Equity Through Education* (Baltimore: Johns Hopkins Press, 1985), pp. 431–454.

3. Gay Holliday, "Addressing the Concerns of Returning Women Students," in Nancy J. Evans, ed., *Facilitating the Development of Women* (San Francisco: Jossey-Bass, 1985), pp. 61–74.

4. Irene Thompson and Audrey Roberts, eds., *The Road Retaken: Women Reenter the Academy* (New York: Modern Language Association of America, 1985).

5. Arlene T. McLaren, *Ambitions and Realization: Women in Adult Education* (Washington, D.C.: Peter Owen, 1985).

6. Florence Howe, in *The Myth of Coeducation* (Bloomington: Indiana University Press, 1984), examines the way in which feminist scholarship was necessary to fully realize the education for civil rights workers and draws similar links.

8

Mapping a Country:
What Lesbian Students Want

TONI A. H. McNARON

Adrienne Rich began one of her *Twenty-One Love Poems* with moving and provocative words about what it feels like to be out in a country where "the maps they gave us were out of date by years...."[1] So many lesbian students feel as they progress through their collegiate years. Ironically, this group of students (at least one-tenth of the total population, and a much higher proportion of those students involved in women's studies or feminist work) has two distinct groups from whom they want various things not usually present: first, the larger administration and faculty; second, those faculty and administrators who are also feminists and lesbians.

Like all women in our colleges and universities, lesbians want more visible attention paid to the lives and works of all women within whatever culture or time period a given course claims for its province. In addition, they want the support services of their campus to be more responsive to their particular needs. Generally speaking, this means addressing heterosexist language and heterosexist presumptions.[2] For instance, when a lesbian is asked to fill out any one of numerous necessary forms, she is often faced with a question about whether she is married, single, or divorced. If she is currently in a committed relationship, responding to such a seemingly routine question can fill her with confusion and anger. If she says that she is married, which may most nearly express the reality she lives, the university or college can accuse her of distortion or lying. If she says that she is single, knowing that is how the administration will see her, she most certainly accuses herself of lying even as she contributes to her own invisibility.

One of the more often cited instances of mistreatment and insensitivity turns around a lesbian's visit to her campus health service. Physicians, especially gynecologists, treat women students as if they were heterosexual all too often. "If I go in for a routine exam, why am I asked if I'm on birth control and if I'm sexually active with men?" This question, asked by numerous lesbian students, suggests the insensitivity at many health services. This line of questioning is particularly stressful for lesbians, since their options are to lie in order to fit the doctor's assumptions or to tell the truth and risk being reported as "deviant." Surely a sensitive staff, open to multiple modes of sexual expression, could find a more neutral phrase to ascertain necessary information about a woman's sexual activity or lack thereof. It goes without saying that lesbians, like most women students today, would prefer women doctors, so a simple way any institution could ease tensions would be to hire more female physicians, particularly gynecologists.

To the extent that a campus maintains counseling facilities, they need to ensure that present staff can accept lesbian life choices as valid rather than a cause for alarm. Campuses have in recent years conducted successful sensitivity-training sessions in other areas effecting women students, most notably sessions with police focusing on how best to respond to a rape charge. Similar sessions could be required for all so-called helping professionals on a campus to demystify and educate them about emotional patterns and difficulties likely to surface for lesbian students who may seek their help. Scenes of counselors instigating proceedings leading to expulsion or mandatory curative therapy have occurred sufficiently often to cause many lesbian students to refuse help they are entitled to as a part of a college or university community. If such offices could bring themselves to hire a few women who, either as lesbians themselves or as feminists who have worked on their own homophobia, state openly that they welcome women whose lives reflect alternative choices, many lesbians would feel more comfortable seeking emotional help.

After speaking with numerous lesbian students, I believe that one major desire, phrased as a "dream" by my respondents, is to feel safe as a lesbian on their campuses. Such students deserve a clause in their institution's antidiscrimination policy openly affirming their university's or college's intention not to discriminate on the basis of sexual identification. In order for an institution of higher education to add such a clause, its administrators and faculty would have to come to view lesbians (and gay men) as another minority deserving the same considerations currently extended to Blacks, students of color, older or returning students, handicapped students. If an institution adopted such a statement, then faculty and students alike would have grounds for complaining about language, jokes at their expense (so-called "queer jokes," which still go unchallenged), and the more serious omissions of lesbian and gay history and culture from the curriculum.

Lesbians want their campus administrators to support their right to hold meetings using campus facilities, as long as their groups conform to regulations asked of any organization. Since this has been distinctly lacking in many locations, it ranks high on students' lists of needs. When a campus denies meeting space to any group, it delivers a message to members of that group that their issues and indeed their very selves do not quite measure up to standards. As more and more lesbians decide to come out of their hiding, to break silence around this central aspect of their personalities, they naturally seek validation from those individuals and institutions that claim their time, money, and energy. Many lesbian students experience genuine shock when their union boards bar them from having weekly meetings or an occasional dance. They have been led to believe from the words in bulletins that their campus is at least tolerant of diversity if not actively seeking it. The hypocrisy hurts and often angers such women, causing them to question other espousals to humanitarian values or high-minded goals.

At the graduate level, lesbians need their faculty in seminars and most especially on examining committees and dissertation panels to allow lesbian-feminist research and writing. This is perhaps the most pressing need, and not having it met is perhaps cause for the most acute damage to the students involved. After all, the fundamental tenet of virtually any institution of higher learning is the right of students to think independently and to conduct research on any subject of vital interest to them and the society. For an increasing number of lesbian graduate students, those thoughts and that work turns around lesbian history and culture. No longer content to write non-feminist papers and theses on exclusively white male subjects, these students first focused their lenses on female material. But the more they delved into such material, the more frustrated they became at having to mute any information they found that cut against preconceptions that "women" meant white, middle-class, heterosexual. And the more voice they gained from their feminist consciousness, the more determined they became to write about that portion of female life and work closest to their own daily lives.

So they now approach their professors not only asking to write about Willa Cather rather than Frank Norris or to reexamine the history of the westward movement placing wives and mothers within it. They want to say outright that Cather's emotional and psychological focus was always on other women and that her life attachments to two or three women sustained her both as woman and writer. Or they wish to include in their reexamination of westward development those women who refused roles intended for them in order to perform crucial functions as teachers, farmers/ranchers/miners, even outlaws and renegades. These students want faculty to be able to hear the academic and scholarly merit behind such requests and to take them seriously by giving them encouragement.

Among those graduate students with whom I spoke, many have felt deep rejection of their research designs by advisers, usually male professors, who never say outright "No, you can't conduct lesbian research," but who make themselves patently clear through such rhetorical devices as trivialization, offhand humor, and sidestepping. Consequently, too many such students end up writing dissertations to which they feel only halfhearted commitment and about which they feel a fundamental ambivalence. If the Ph.D. thesis constitutes a scholar's first major research effort, such responses have serious repercussions for future work. The point cannot be made forcefully enough: graduate advisers must be alerted to the growing interest in lesbian and lesbian-feminist research perspectives; such professors owe it to their prospective students to familiarize themselves with the growing body of such research published in books and articles; finally, they need to be encouraged if not urged by their administrations to allow such work to proceed not with a mumbled tolerance but with the same degree of intellectual curiosity and rigor they would extend to a more traditional proposal. Without this fundamental shift in mood and level of knowledge and acceptance, lesbian students wishing to begin their research at the usual time will continue to be set back if not diverted entirely from their original theories and goals.

EXAMINING WHAT AND HOW WE TEACH

"False history gets written every day/and by some who should know better: the lesbian archaeologist watches herself/sifting her own life out of the shards she's piecing, asking the clay all questions but her own." Again I look to Adrienne Rich for words to begin to articulate the more difficult part of this essay.[3] Lesbian students exist in a posture which gives them two levels of needs. The first, about which I have been speaking, is by far the easier to define, since it has to do with the woman student's interactions with the larger university or college structure. In other words, it represents a familiar adversarial stance that feminists of all stripes have come to expect to assume vis-à-vis the institution and many of its male-identified members. The second level is less easily broached, precisely because it involves internecine questions. Lesbians making their way through institutions of higher education are naturally drawn to any identifiable women's studies presence, or, lacking that, to those faculty and courses treating women's lives and work. The ratio of lesbian students to total numbers of women taking such courses is very high.

For many younger women in particular, women's studies is seen as a potential threat to their personal plans and to their assumptions about life and reality. However, for many lesbians, courses in women's studies offer an oasis or haven. Consequently, their presence is noticeable and their expectations sharp. Having broken through the culture's heterosexist plans for them on a personal level, many such students have also begun to read books by and about women since they crave alternative stories and actors.

Too often, lesbian students are tacitly silenced by perfectly well-meaning teachers who themselves have not yet examined their own assumptions about what the word "woman" encompasses or who still teach only those women included in someone's list of the "greats." Though many such figures managed to live quietly lesbian-feminist lives, the received information about them blots that out. If teachers of women's studies courses, then, depend upon such sources, they continue the myths already circulating. For instance, many women's studies faculty perpetuate stories about Emily Dickinson's supposed love affair with some mysterious older man; or they support the view that Leonard Woolf saved Virginia from herself, keeping her going enough to allow her to write the fine works she did; or they omit references to Willa Cather's intense attachments to women, thereby neutering her to her own and the students' disservice.

In an essay that might well become basic reading for feminist faculty of all persuasions, Adrienne Rich speaks about the systematic manner in which the culture separates women from each other in order to achieve the necessary heterosexual balance.[4] She is most concerned about the result: a body of unexamined assumptions in women who become feminists at some point in their lives. Since any female has the ability to be a lesbian, all of us need to look rather closely at our sexual histories, or more importantly, at our erotic histories, to see if and when and how we were turned away from intense bondings with other women and told that the higher, more mature path lay in being intimate with men and eventually with a man.

Lesbian students desperately need women faculty to read this and similar essays, consider their own personal life-styles (whether lesbian or heterosexual), and, most centrally, map the connections between those life-styles, the cultural message attendant upon each, and the resultant emphases in their courses, research, and writing. If I am a teacher of women's studies and happen to be a lesbian but have not processed my own ways of coping with cultural disapprobation, I may be of even less service to students eager to find and study lesbian culture and history than a self-conscious, self-accepting heterosexual feminist teaching such a course. My own homophobia, internalized hence more elusive to identify and root out, keeps me from introducing pertinent readings and background material if I do not truly believe that such intellectual work is valid. Similarly, if I am a teacher of women's studies and happen to be heterosexual but have not processed the cultural privileges and blindness surrounding that fact, I will also be of less than maximum service to my lesbian students. I will duplicate the very invisibility against which I rebel as a feminist; I will teach as if women were all heterosexual (or failures at being so), just as some of my less-enlightened colleagues continue to teach as if everyone were male (or failures at being so). This irony, which exists on campuses at the present time, would be more likely to be detected and corrected if lesbian history and culture were prominent in curricular and service decisions.

Many women's studies programs in America have held fruitful meetings among faculty and students to articulate precisely this irony. I believe that at many colleges and universities faculty within such programs (whether formal and identified as such or more loosely aggregated) have come genuinely to accept the life-style of lesbian students (and faculty) as part of the spectrum called women's control of their own bodies. What has not happened in nearly as many cases if for the same individuals and groups to take that personal understanding into their classroom planning and into their own research. More syllabi need to reflect the diversity among the women being studied in terms of their erotic or emotional preferences. Survey courses in which various feminist issues are included need to do more than spend a day or two with a guest lecturer or visiting panel of lesbians speaking about something relevant. Just as it was not enough for general feminists a decade ago to have book publishers add paragraphs or sections to existing texts, so it is not enough for lesbians to have faculty tack on something about culture or daily life. In every unit or course concept, lesbian reality and existence need to be interleaved. If families are the topic, lesbian groupings need to be brought in, not as an interesting curiosity or deviation from the norm but as one of several equally viable patterns for intimacy and child-rearing. If mothering is the subject, lesbian mothers need to be discussed at every stage of the course rather than being treated as a special topic at the end of the overall consideration of this central experience and institution in society. If Black women writers are being read, lesbian voices need to be a genuine part of the course, not magically "covered" by introducing students to Audre Lorde.

This need of lesbian students will involve serious attention and perhaps painful self-searching on the part of faculty, inside and outside women's studies. But without so radical an overhaul in the notion of curricular design and research potential, students will continue to feel like appendages to the real matter at hand, tolerated or even romanticized for what they do at home or within their larger community, but still invisible within the scholarly world in which they find themselves for at least the years of college or graduate school. For those planning academic careers, such slighting is even more damaging, since it teaches such women implicitly to bury their truest subject and blunt or distort their truest voices as scholars and teachers.

In conversations with both undergraduate and graduate students for whom lesbianism figures centrally in their pursuit of education, I found several patterns emerging about what is most important to them. As one student put it, "I want teachers to provide avenues or networks which will allow me both to find other lesbian students in my classes and then to incorporate work we do into regular classroom activity." When asked to elaborate on such how such networks might be formed, the student suggested affinity groups organized under various headings. Students could elect which one(s) they wished to join. I find this idea particularly creative, since it would do more than connect lesbians; it would allow any students having ethnic or cultural identifiers to meet and work with similarly inclined class members. The most obvious groups might be lesbian students, working class students, older or returning students, black or other minority groups of students, and handicapped students. Other ideas for groups would occur to faculty, depending on their particular locations or populations, but the idea deserves serious consideration. Such "caucuses" would strengthen the clarity of many students, which would in turn enliven class discussion of texts and issues. The teacher allowing this to happen in her or his classroom would satisfy a need of many students while improving the level and intensity of participation. Everyone would benefit.

The most poignant need expressed by students can be summed up by this comment: "I want my teachers, particularly at the graduate level, to use examples that include me." As I have spun out what this eloquent request might entail, the possibilities become limitless. So, for instance, in a class in family systems approach to current problems, the professor would talk routinely about single-parent families and about families with two mothers or fathers and about extended families. When these alternative groups are mentioned, furthermore, they would simply illustrate one of the ways adults and possibly children choose to live together. In a course in women's health issues, material would be introduced specific to lesbian health, some of which is particular to women choosing to be sexual with other women, to women aging without having had children, and the like. A seminar on The Mother needs to incorporate recent work on nonbiological mothering historically and currently often done by lesbians, work on the mythic role of the lesbian woman in the relationship of the mother to the daughter, work on women choosing intimate partners who resemble their own mothers not only in intangible ways but in actual anatomy. In speaking of research on incest or alcoholism or any of the pressing social issues affecting girls and women, serious attention needs to be paid by the teacher to similarities and differences in how such realities impact the lives of lesbians or how lesbians cope with such realities.

Courses on literature or history of Black American women need to devote class time and syllabus weight to those examples of lesbians within their numbers. Acknowledging the compelling nature of the cultural bias against lesbianism in Black communities,[5] professors nonetheless run the risk of silencing students whose experience does not conform to the heterosexual requirement, and they certainly lie to all their students about the complexity of Black female reality.

Within the many kinds of literature courses currently offered, certain courses emerge as crucial to lesbian students as they face their cultural obliteration historically and attempt to change that for the present and future. I think of the increasingly popular emphasis on courses in Women's Autobiographies. To teach such a course without including works by both explicitly open lesbians and by women we now know to have lived lesbian lives or nurtured a lesbian consciousness is to continue to falsify women's history. All women suffer from this falsification: lesbian women are rendered invisible within a context that has the potentiality to help them most directly in their struggle to find and shape their voice; heterosexual women are deluded about their foremothers. Since such courses also often provide an option of writing an autobiographical essay, it behooves any teacher to make lesbian life stories an integral part of the reading and discussion. Otherwise, the teacher unwittingly continues the social ban against airing and indeed celebrating such stories. Anyone teaching such a course need not worry about having explicit autobiographies to include, since several collections of essays now exist,[6] and a few full-length works are in print.[7] If we are to have the rapid appearance and publication of more such books, then such courses must make that dream a reality within the context of required work for which credit is awarded.

An often-named need, again especially felt by graduate students, is for more courses devoted expressly to lesbian culture and history. The problems attendant upon realizing this legitimate request are worth enumerating, since they open the whole question of what lesbian faculty need from university and college administrations. While such a question lies outside the immediate purview of this book, it remains central to the limited ability of some of the best-qualified faculty to give students what they need and want. When any faculty member expresses a desire to teach a course with the word "lesbian" in the title or description, she or he immediately encounters individual and institutional homophobia. Years ago, when the women's studies program at my university was in its fledgling days and in need of collegiate approval, I wished to teach a senior seminar on The Woman as Other. I included in my course description a paragraph about The Lesbian as Other Woman. Several of my colleagues, while eager for me to offer the course, urged me to omit the sensitive paragraph, since the college review committee might not approve such a course and since some prospective students might shy away from taking it. The fact that such voices were accurate in no way lessens the complexity of such decisions.

If a faculty member wishing to teach a course focusing on lesbian issues does not have tenure and if the institution has no clause protecting lesbians scholars from discrimination, she runs a very basic risk of being fired—almost never for being a lesbian, but for reasons that read very much like smoke screens behind which liberal academics hide their own unexamined homophobia. But if faculty are not allowed to propose and teach such courses as routinely as they may do others, then the message to students and faculty alike is to stay in one's closet or to sneak in research and reading without announcing it to anyone before hand. Either choice is debilitating. One thing lesbian students need, then, is for administrators and other faculty to determine the extent of their own prejudice against research and teaching which deals openly with lesbian culture and history. It will not be the first or last time such an examination has had to be conducted. Many disciplines have split over the validity of certain "schools" within their practicing scholars. In most cases, such processes, albeit painful for persons on all sides of the issue, have resulted in richer scholarship and teaching.

If I consider my own field, literary studies, the evidence is clearly in favor of calling lesbian consciousness by its proper name. For example, Willa Cather becomes a more interesting person to study if the facts are laid bare. Rather than being seen as a sexless creature writing lovely novels about prairie life, she becomes the passionate woman she was, whose love for women not only taught her to describe female characters with sensuous particularity but also complicated her life as writer and human being. Her struggle to keep her identity hidden or at least private meant choices about narrators and degrees of exposure of feelings that sometimes marred her work. Jim Burden is unreliable not because Cather could not create good narrators; he is unreliable because he is not the true narrative voice of Antonia' story—Willa Cather is, but she remained afraid to speak in a woman's voice about a woman's body and psyche. To keep her life buried means we continue to find her literary faults attributable to false causes. Certainly this instance is duplicable in most other fields of study.

Lesbian students want what all students deserve and should demand of all of us who teach and serve them: the fullest, truest presentation of the case that we know. To give them anything less is to shortchange them and to lie. We who teach, therefore, must acquaint ourselves as fully as we can about the material we teach. As new information becomes available from feminist researchers and other revisionists within or without academe, we must take it in, sift it through the filter of our previous knowledge, and incorporate it into our presentations and syllabus formation. And our administrators must make this growth process easier by funding leaves to allow faculty to read and assimilate new areas of expertise concerning lesbian and gay culture and history, by publicly stating a commitment to diversity of approaches to knowledge and to living life, and by meaning it.

To have a college or university president or dean make a simple statement in which the words lesbian research and culture occurred would do more toward giving students what they need than almost any other single act. Such a sentence would signal to faculty that their own efforts and the efforts of colleagues along lesbian research lines would be taken seriously and not used as probable cause. Such a sentence would signal to students that their personal choices were understood to affect their academic work, and that their institution was ready to allow that connection to thrive in its midst.

CONCLUSION

Lesbian scholars have been at the forefront of research on women's lives and culture from the beginning days of women's studies and feminist academic work. Adrienne Rich, Audre Lorde, Mary Daly, Susan Griffin—household words in most feminist intellectual circles, all women writing from a conscious articulation of lesbianism's being at the very heart of their theory, art, and politics. Lesbian students and faculty similarly have taken leadership positions within women's studies and their own disciplinary programs. The sad fact remains, however, that on local levels especially, such leaders' identities as lesbians has often been muted for fear of reprisals from administrators and faculty. A more responsive administration could facilitate students and faculty in making it clear that their excellence is not in spite of their lesbianism but rather deeply connected to it.

NOTES

1. Adrienne Rich, *Twenty-One Love Poems*. Emeryville, CA: Effie's Press, 1976.
2. Heterosexism means the assumption by portions of the culture that being heterosexual is not only the norm but also the only acceptable mode of intimacy and bonding.
3. From the poem, "Turning the Wheel," in *The Fact of a Doorframe*, W. W. Norton and Co., New York, 1984.

4. *Compulsory Heterosexuality and Lesbian Existence*, Onlywomen Press Ltd., London, 1981.

5. For a clear explanation of this point, see Cheryl Clarke, "Lesbianism: An Act of Resistance," in *This Bridge Called My Back: Writings by Radical Women of Color*, edited by Cherrie Moraga and Gloria Anzaldua, Persephone Press, Watertown, Massachusetts, 1981, pp. 128–137.

6. The fullest collections are *The Coming Out Stories*, edited by Julia Penelope Stanley and Susan J. Wolfe, Persephone Press, Watertown, Massachusetts, 1980, and *The Lesbian Path*, edited by Margaret Cruikshank, Angel Press, Monterey, California, 1980.

7. Two easily available such books are *Zami*, by Audre Lorde, W. W. Norton and Co., 1983, and *The Notebooks Emma Gave Me*, by Kady Van Deurs, distributed by Naiad Press, Tallahassee, Florida, 1978.

9

Enhancing the Effectiveness of Postsecondary Education for Women with Disabilities

YVONNE DUFFY

"First and foremost, I want people to know that I am a person regardless of whether I have a disability. I have wants and needs and fears. I'm not immune to feelings and because I do have feelings I am a person. . . .

Secondly, I'm a woman. I do consider myself liberated—if not physically liberated, legally liberated . . . spiritually liberated. . . .

Last and by no means least, I am a disabled woman. That also brings with it a few added concerns, but my disability is not the biggest, most important thing in my life." (Duffy, 1981)

This quote from a college junior with the disabling condition of spina bifida was chosen to introduce the chapter on specific service needs of female students with disabilities because it represents scores of similar comments received from women participating in this study and at workshops and conferences around the country.

Shaping everyone's view of persons with disabilities has been the traditional media portrayal of long-suffering, heroic individuals happy to be the objects of others' charity, miraculously free of all worldly desires, and, above all, *separate* from the rest of humanity. Terms such as "victim," "confined to," "wheelchair-bound" accurately express these perceptions and, despite sporadic efforts to find less pejorative terms, their usage has not changed significantly.

A few words on the language used in this chapter are appropriate here. Although the phrase "disabled women" would be less cumbersome, the term "women with disabilities" will be used because it indicates that this is but one characteristic of their total identity, along with curly hair, jobs, math fears, fat thighs, and so forth.

All reliable population statistics indicate that the proportion of Americans with disabilities has risen sharply in the past few decades. According to the Health Interview Survey conducted by the U.S. Bureau of the Census, the number of persons with significant activity limitations rose 37.3 percent from 1966 to 1976 in contrast to a 10 percent increase in the size of the general population during the same period (DeJong and Litchez, 1983). A Louis Harris poll conducted at the end of 1985 concluded that there were 27 million Americans over the age of sixteen with disabilities that significantly limited their participation in school, work, and/or social life.

Largely responsible for this increase has been the advancement of medical technology, which now saves many who would have died in earlier times but who may be left with severe physical limitations. Technology has also greatly extended the lifespan of those already living with a disability. For example, the young woman quoted at the beginning of this chapter, had she been born fifty years ago, would have died at birth or in early childhood. Now she can anticipate becoming a senior citizen.

As the numbers increase, however, society will become less able to support this minority. Disability-related expenditures in 1977 were estimated to be $61.5 billion (DeJong and Litchez, 1983) and will continue to escalate with higher health care costs and additional recipients.

The obvious answer to this dilemma is to adapt the environment so that more persons with disabilities are able to live independently and support themselves. Eager to work, most persons with disabilities are not preoccupied with their limitations but regard them as inconveniences or, at most, obstacles to be overcome in the achievement of individual life goals.

To render employable this segment of the population, quality postsecondary education is vital for many persons with significant disabilities who are unable to perform less-skilled jobs that usually require physical strength and/or mobility. Although more than half of all American women of working age are employed, fewer than one out of five women with disabilities have jobs (Bowe, 1984). Because there are fewer skilled occupations open to women than men, providing good postsecondary preparation is, therefore, even more crucial for women with disabilities.

For students with disabilities to gain maximum value from their college education, there must be full recognition on the part of administrators that they are persons *first*, with the same needs as nondisabled students, and therefore deserve access to all the same academic, counseling, housing, health, financial, social, and recreational services. Providing equal access to the many departments that meet these needs may require not only the physical modification of facilities but also the sensitization of faculty and staff members to meet the needs of students with disabilities coming to their offices.

In addition, students with disabilities may need specific disability-related services such as door-to-door transportation, attendants to aid with personal care, interpreters, readers, and so forth. Sometimes advocates are necessary to assist the students in communicating their needs to university personnel. At most major postsecondary institutions, specifically designated offices for disabled students furnish these services with varying degrees of success.

Even though most of these colleges and universities also have programs offering support services designed to equalize educational opportunities for women, few attempts have been made in either type of setting to initiate programming to meet the unique needs of women with disabilities.

In order to successfully compete for jobs, women with disabilities need all the same support services the university provides nondisabled women—assertiveness training, exercises to increase self-esteem, and sexual health care, including family planning, but they may need them to be in a slightly different form. For a hearing-impaired student to participate effectively in an assertiveness workshop, an interpreter may be needed, for example.

All women have been hurt by society's emphasis on sexual attachment to a man, preferably through marriage, as the only valid measure of self-worth; to women with disabilities whose sexual identity has been systematically invalidated by society, this is particularly devastating (Duffy, 1981; Saxton, 1981).

Being female and disabled in a culture obsessed with beauty and athleticism is a cause for double oppression or even triple should the woman also belong to a racial or ethnic minority.[1] The economic effects of this oppression are dramatically underscored by the earnings figures released by the Disability Rights Education and Defense Fund, Inc., which show that for every dollar earned by a nondisabled white male, a white woman with a disability earns 24 cents and her black sister earns 12 cents (Newmark, 1984).

Since their bodies have also been devalued, often from an early age, women with disabilities frequently lag far behind nondisabled peers in their basic knowledge of sexuality. Whether because of this ignorance, embarrassment over the appearance of their bodies, or simply the inaccessibility of facilities, many neglect their sexual health care. Of 121 women seen at a gynecology clinic sponsored by United Cerebral Palsy of New York, only a few had previously received routine gynecological health care. The results were similar in a study done at the Dallas (Texas) Rehabilitation Center (Ziff, 1984; Hennig, 1984).

Since the objective of providing any special service is the eventual mainstreaming of the recipients, a liaison between offices serving students with disabilities and those providing support services for women in order to develop, and adapt where necessary, services accessible to all women would be beneficial. In the process of formulating plans and integrating them into scheduled activities, the staff members involved will gain a sensitivity to the needs of this population that will be likely to ensure that future programming is accessible to women with all types of limitations. Being included in services offered to nondisabled women students can provide women with disabilities with an affirmation of womanhood denied in most other areas of their lives.

The Office for Disabled Students at Barnard College in New York City is proving that such liaisons do work. Financed by a three-year grant from the U.S. Department of Education's Women's Educational Equity Act, the Office has developed programs for integrating female students with disabilities into all areas of campus life, such as dormitory residence and health care. The programs, designed to be implemented by the departments providing the services to all students, are threefold, utilizing awareness exercises, support materials, and specific resources. Now entering the final phase of this grant, the plans are now being field tested at five university sites in New York State.

Women with diabilities, either students or community members, should be actively involved in every stage of program planning and used as trainers and group leaders whenever possible. Knowing what is needed from personal experience, they will help target approaches more effectively while also acting as role models, the value of which cannot be overestimated.

Assertiveness training will be a most important aspect of any co-sponsored program. The ability to make changes and exercise control over their own lives may be a new concept to women whose disability occurred at birth or in early childhood. Especially difficult for women whose disability happened later in life may be learning to ask for help, for women have been socialized early to be the caregivers. That independence is a state of mind and not related to physical ability should be emphasized, and ample time should be scheduled for the sharing of feelings and role-playing new ways of relating to others.

Some women may require one-on-one counseling before true integration into campus life can become a reality. Whenever possible, a peer counselor should be utilized. A woman with a disability who has successfully made the transition from living in an institution or with family to living independently is in a unique position to provide "resource information, support, understanding, and direction to another disabled person who desires to make a similar transition" (Schatzlein, 1978).

For the same reasons, facilities should be made available to women with disabilities who wish to organize a peer support group. Because many have felt isolated due to their disabilities, being able to come together and discover a mutuality of feelings and experience can be very empowering. For those who often view themselves as perpetual receivers of aid, the benefits accrued from being able to help others can be very valuable.

Equally essential is access to reproductive health care. Depending on facilities available to nondisabled female students, this may mean building a ramp, widening doorways, rearranging or enlarging an examining room, or installing an adjustable examining table. Brailling or taping printed material routinely disseminated, although a less extensive change, is nevertheless an important method of extending access to students with visual disabilities, just as is arranging for interpreters for women with impaired hearing.

Almost certainly, true access to health care for female students with disabilities will require changing attitudes, for, despite the anatomical knowledge possessed by medical professionals, many still share society's discomfort with sexuality in general and more specifically in relation to disability. Effective methods to foster the necessary changes are sexual attitude reassessment seminars, sensitivity training workshops, and media presentations. Again, women with disabilities should be visible and involved at every stage of the planning and implementation.

The extension of already established services to women with disabilities is likely to cost far less than might be anticipated. Since the modification of physical facilities to extend accessiblity to all students has been mandated by Section 504 of the 1973 Rehabilitation Act, most of the buildings housing these services may be barrier-free already or soon will be. Therefore, making programs responsive to the particular needs of women with disabilities may only require the sensitization of staff members in these areas and/or the hiring of one or two part-time peer support persons as advisers/trainers/counselors. Trained peer counselors are often available through local centers for independent living. Joint sponsorship of some programs with one or more colleges or community organizations might be another creative approach.

Not all women students with disabilities will need all of these services, any more than their nondisabled sisters will; some have learned to survive very well in an environment fraught with physical and attitudinal barriers. Nonetheless, opening up support services to the women with disabilities who can flourish and become successful because of them is absolutely vital. The time is fast approaching in our social evolution when we can no longer afford to underutilize the talents and abilities of this fast-growing segment of our population.

NOTE

1. The definition of "oppression" used here is "the systematic invalidation of one social group by another" (Saxton, 1981).

REFERENCES

BOWE, FRANK. *Demography and Disability: A Chartbook for Rehabilitation.* Fayetteville: Arkansas Rehabilitation, Research and Training Center, University of Arkansas, 1984.

DeJONG, GERBEN, and LITCHEZ, RAYMOND. "Physical Disability and Public Policy." *Scientific American,* Vol. 248, No. 6, June 1983.

DUFFY, YVONNE. *All Things Are Possible.* Ann Arbor, Mich.: A. J. Garvin and Associates, 1981, p. 172.

HARRIS, LOUIS, and ASSOCIATES. *ICD Survey of Disabled Americans: Bringing Disabled Americans into the Mainstream.* New York: Louis Harris and Associates, 1986, p. iii.

HENNIG, LINDA M. Unpublished paper cited in personal correspondence, December 16, 1983.

NEWMARK, JUDY J. "Disabled Americans: A Question of Rights." *PD* Magazine, *St. Louis Post Dispatch,* January 29, 1984, pp. 6-11.

RICHMAN, LYNN C., and HARPER, DENNIS C. "Personality Profiles of Physically

Impaired Young Adults." *Journal of Clinical Psychology,* Vol. 36, No. 3, 1980, pp. 668–671.

SAXTON, MARSHA. "A Peer Counseling Training for Disabled Women." *Journal of Sociology and Social Welfare,* Vol. 8, No. 2, 1981, pp. 334–345.

SCHATZLEIN, J. E. "Spinal Cord Injury and Peer Counseling Education." Unpublished paper. Minneapolis: Regional Spinal Cord Injury Center, Department of Physical Medicine and Rehabilitation, University of Minnesota Hospitals, 1978.

ZIFF, SUSAN FOX. Personal correspondence, January 19, 1984.

10

Recognizing the Diversity of Women's Voices by Psychological Type

FAITH GABELNICK AND CAROL S. PEARSON

The effort to articulate and legitimate a female voice, as important as that effort is, can be reductive if, in an attempt to distinguish women's reality from men's, we ignore women's plurality. To address adequately the diversity we find among women, it is necessary not only to explore differences by race, class, age, disability and sexual orientation but also to recognize that women differ by psychological temperament.

When women students become educated about learning styles, it has the effect of helping them to move beyond dualistic, hierarchial formulations about reality. Learning to appreciate and hear the contributions of women who understand the world in different ways enriches their own learning and provides a critical recognition of diversity as strength. The students are then more able to talk about sex, race, or class differences without immediately assuming that difference means one group must be superior and the other inferior.

In order to see whether there were diverse learning approaches among women, the authors tested over three hundred students in two semesters using the Myers-Briggs Type Indicator (MBTI). The course selected was a women's studies course that was at once representative of women's studies courses and was also fairly typical of university courses in that it was a large lecture/survey course attended by students from a variety of class years. About 50 percent were sophomores, 20 percent each were freshmen and juniors, and 10 percent were seniors. About 10 percent were minority students. A large percentage of the students worked full- or part-time and most were women.

Of the several instruments available to assess learning styles, the authors chose the MBTI because it has long-established validity. The Myers-Briggs is now used widely in the United States and throughout the world to help people understand and appreciate one another: in education, business, psychology, and religion.

The MBTI, which has philosophical roots in Jungian psychology, is an indicator that gives us insight into how people gather information about the world and how they make decisions. Unlike an IQ test, it does not tell us how able someone is. Rather, it tells us their preferences: how they prefer to take in information and to make judgments. In that sense, learning style is analogous to right- or left-handedness. A person starts with a preference that is heightened by practice. The more we use our right or left hand, the better we get at it. However, if we choose to develop (or are forced to develop, for example, because of injury) the other hand, we can. So, too, with learning style preference. An indicator of preference only, the MBTI should never be used to label anyone, nor should it be used as a predictor of ability level.

Key concepts in the MBTI are often combined and abbreviated for convenience into four paired letters: Extrovert/Introvert (EI), Intuiter/Sensor (NS), Thinker/Feeler (TF), Perceiver/Judger (PJ). In each of the four categories, we will have a preference for one quality over another. In perceiving, or gathering information about the world, some of us prefer to use our senses (S) to collect specific information and details about what is actually occurring. Others of us prefer to use our intuition (N) to perceive in more general terms that which may not be directly accessible to our senses. In judging or making decisions about what we have perceived, we may prefer to make decisions based on a narrative feeling mode of cognition (F) or on an analytical thinking mode of cognition (T). We use all of these processes, but in each pair we *prefer* S or N, T or F.

In considering in what environment or context we prefer to exercise these preferences, we may like to act in the outer world of people and things, and thus our preference would be for extroversion (E). Others of us prefer to operate in the inner world of ideas and introspection. Our preference then would be for introversion (I). The last preference pair points to a liking for decision-making and closure (Judging) or a liking for generating and collecting information, ideas or possibilities (Perceiving). This last pair influences life-style. A judging type values orderliness and predictability, while a perceiving type opts for spontaneity and openness to change. These four pairs combine to form sixteen four-letter types. Each type has its own characteristics and becomes more than a sum of its elements. Importantly, these types are neutral: no type is more advanced or better than another, but many of the types differ markedly from each other.

While each student was assigned a four-letter type, we used two-letter temperament designations to analyze the preferences. These "temperaments" identified by Marilyn Bates and David Keirsey in their book *Please Understand Me* are the Sensing Perceiving (SP), the Sensing Judging (SJ), Intuitive Thinking (NT), and Intuitive Feeling (NF). According to Bates and Keirsey, SPs (38 percent of the population) are active, impulsive, and lighthearted, making excellent athletes, performers, and troubleshooters. SJs (39 percent of the population) care about duty, usefulness, belonging, and the work ethic. Their dedication to established norms and institutions makes them likely to choose professions such as banking, schoolteaching, nursing, or middle management. NTs (12 percent of the population) love intelligence, competence, objectivity, and work. Highly critical and self-critical, they excel in science, engineering, research and development, or business management. NFs (12 percent of the population) are questors, who value integrity, meaning, and caring for others. They often are effective as counselors, psychologists, ministers, and teachers.

The E/I, S/N, and J/P preference scales show no significant variation by gender, with 50 percent of males and females, respectively, choosing each. On the F/T scales, however, some difference is evident, with more than 60 percent of women preferring the F function over the T function. (These percentages are about the same for males, except in reverse). It is not clear yet to what degree this difference reflects socialization patterns, but the net result is a difference between the dominant decision-making preferences for the genders which may shed some light on ways males and females prefer to learn and act. This difference also reminds us that a sizable minority find typical generalizations about their gender inadequate and possibly misleading.

Any temperament will succeed best in an environment that is congruent, by and large, with its preferences. However, the experience of working or learning in a culture where another type represents a norm for that culture can enhance adaptability and flexibility so long as the atypical type receives support and even instruction in how to operate in this other environment. With this in mind, it is important to remember that K–12 education is usually an SJ culture, while higher education is usually dominated by NTs. SPs and NFs will each have their time to shine: NFs will usually do reasonably well in either environment because of their desire to please teachers and peers, but SPs will eventually find the academic scene to be too alienating for their preferences and will find another environment, such as the performing arts or sports, to be more rewarding.

The following are some basic generalizations about typical women students of each temperament and some teaching strategies designed to foster their success. The authors hope that these brief sketches will spark in our readers additional creativity in finding ways to develop the full capacity of women of differing temperaments.

NT: INTUITIVE THINKING TEMPERAMENT

Intuitive thinkers are characterized by their dispassionate, scientific assessment of a situation. They are reflective, analytical, inventive, and skeptical. "Intelligence" is the key word for NTs. They prefer to view the world in terms of systems, theories, and models, not values and relationships. They enjoy debates and controversial topics, respect competent presentation of academic material, and will work hard if they think that the task is meritworthy. Writes an NT: "I feel better when people respond negatively as opposed to nothing at all; at least it proves they're listening."

The private aspect of this outwardly calm and reasonable presence is a persistent self-examination and self-criticism. "My inner voice is always busy," confesses the NT. "It's hard to talk or write about yourself because there is so much that you already know." While the NT may be quite accepting of other's foibles, she is mercilessly scrupulous about her own imperfections. This quality impels her to be a very hard worker, conscientious, and sometimes unaware that other people don't prefer to work as hard and long as she does. Work is play to the NT, the play of the mind in the world. As one NT put it, "I'm a deep thinker and enjoy talking about serious topics. . . . I like people with strong opinions like myself."

In the classroom, NTs will ask direct, penetrating questions. They will pay less attention to liking an instructor and pay much more attention to assessing the rigor and thoroughness of the presentation. They appreciate rigorous, analytical theory and are good at theorizing. They will also participate with curiosity and initial openness in a variety of classroom teaching strategies, but may become closed down and obstinate to further experimentation if they judge these activities are conducted incompetently. Assignments that involve analysis, synthesis, model building will intrigue the NT. Assignments that call for creative or utopian writing, expression of personal values, or continuous physical practice will not appeal to the NT unless a good *reason* for their inclusion in the course material is presented along with the assignment.

This independent, problem-solving, clear-minded, competitive type of woman is at home in academia, but may be misunderstood by some women who value community above confrontation or by anyone expecting stereotypical female nurturing and care-taking behavior. It is important that classroom instructors do not expect stereotypical NF behavior from the NT woman, nor conversely impose the NT model on other types. NTs need to be affirmed for their assertiveness and keen powers of observation, qualities that make them excellent process observers. If something is going awry in classroom dynamics, NTs will often be able to articulate the problem and the process that is contributing to it.

SJ: SENSING JUDGING TEMPERAMENTS

The pillars of the commuity are the responsible, dutiful SJs. These women look at the world in a matter-of-fact, goal-oriented way. They may use this pragmatism to run a business or form new organizations, but in general SJs will be at home in a well-organized world of community action. Many SJs are class officers. Writes one student: "I have always been a role model for my community and my friends."

Unlike the NT student, the SJs will have little patience with vague, abstract theories, which they will consider useless unless connected very quickly with a practical extension. They will also tend to shy away from hypothetical arguments and analytic writing assignments. Because SJs enjoy detail, they will be able to amass a great deal of information about a project but may be less skilled in assembling the information in a thematic way. SJ writing may seem episodic, fragmented, or even superficial.

Because of their devotion to "the System" or community in which they live, SJs may be overly compliant "good girls" in class. However, since the mode of teaching in college depends a great deal on the presentation of theories or models for understanding human problems, the SJ sometimes works very hard to stay afloat. A typical SJ wrote: "School has always been a positive journey to me. In fact, I never had negative feelings toward school until I attended college." It is for this reason that a variety of learning strategies, especially experiential or hands-on learning, are useful. The SJ can then make meaning of the more abstract material in a concrete, realistic context. Writing assignments that ask a student to retrieve information are also enjoyable and interesting to the SJ because they will result in a practical outcome. SJs also want and need a structure, rules, and a clear sense of what is expected of them and how they will be evaluated.

Since SJs are our society's conservers, they feel uncomfortable in environments that are very different from the norm (or what they judge is the norm), and they also tend by preference to uphold established institutions, values, and, by implication, gender roles. They enjoy inventiveness, surprise, and new ideas *within the context of the known and accepted.* Teachers of SJ students will be very helpful if they can assist students in making traditional connections with nontraditional ideas.

The primary resistance of these conventional students to feminist material or any other material that challenges traditional ways of thinking, is a fear about its explosive effect on their communities. However, once SJs do accept new perspectives, they are gifted at integrating these ideas into their lives so pragmatically and tactfully that they barely cause a ripple in the quiet pond of community life. SJs can teach the other types about effecting orderly institutional change—that is, if the typically more radical NFs and NTs do not dismiss them as too conventional. It is not surprising, therefore, that the SJs are community builders, forming the bedrock of members for many student organizations.

When comparing the major groups found in college (NT, NF, and SJ), some differences are immediately apparent. Both NTs and NFs may be so enamored of their analytical systems or future visions that they are oblivious to present realities. SJs—and SPs, for that matter— are much more fully engaged in the present and more observant about the actual world around them. While the intuitive types focus on identifying the forest, the sensing types see the trees. In class, SJs will keep discussion grounded in the actual and will point out facts or issues that are not accounted for in any system. Again, in contrast to the intuitives who like to reach beyond any system or community and thus enjoy challenging concepts or ideals in class, the SJs relish the expected, uphold the authority of the teacher, complete assignments and help create a cooperative working atmosphere.

NF: INTUITIVE FEELING TEMPERAMENTS

The women in search of the perfect relationship or community are the NFs. Harmony, balance, relationships, congruence: these concepts motivate the NF. If the NT women seek models, and the SJs order, the NFs strive for emotional cooperation. Says an NF woman: "The realization that the problems I go through are the same as the problems someone else goes through made all the difference." First she must feel connected with others and then she can do her work. To the NFs, the world is personal and immediate, urging them toward concerns with aesthetics and values.

This preference thus places a different pressure on the teacher, for in order to respond fully in a classroom, the NF students must feel connected to the teacher and feel comfortable in the learning environment. NFs want classes in which they can discuss their feelings and values as well as their ideas. They strive for a totality of experience, integrating the affective with the intellectual. As one student wrote in describing her criteria for friendship: a friend is "there to cry with, laugh with, and really share everything. . . . She knows me inside and out. Anything I've done or felt, she knows about." The enormous expectations around relationships that these students bring to class affect their class performance in several ways. If they do not like a teacher, they may not be willing to do their work in a timely fashion; they may cut classes; they may put out minimal effort; they may withdraw from active classroom participation. On the other hand, if they like the teacher and feel appreciated, they will be devoted, enthusiastic students and will participate energetically in all types of projects. NFs particularly enjoy cooperative enterprises with other students and journals that allow them to process their feelings about the material. While the NT may be settled back in her chair speculating on the pros and cons of a particular issue, and the SJ may be wondering how to translate the topic into a practical project, the NF will be making friends and will be highly attuned to the emotional climate and then will be setting down in her notes a narrative of the teacher's remarks.

NFs are questors and love to imagine better (and often more feminist) futures. They also are drawn to theories that celebrate women's intuitive, emotional and relational abilities—abilities they possess in abundance and which they rightly find undervalued by the culture. They greatly appreciate teachers who also recognize the importance of these traits. The NT may complain of not being able to fill up the writing assignment because she has condensed her thoughts into a few pithy statements; the SJ may become overwhelmed with too much information which she cannot sort and categorize, but the NF is rarely at a loss for words. Narrative thinkers, they enjoy writing stories. While her papers will often benefit from editing, they will also contain penetrating insights and a good "feel" for the material. Giving the NF a chance to exercise her imagination will produce magical and creative assignments, whereas assigning her concrete, information-gathering projects will often produce an uninspired and vague response.

The NF questor mentality means that as soon as NFs begin to understand new ideas, they will begin changing their lives—drastically. This inevitably puts a strain on their relationships, and since NFs find their sense of identity in relationships, a crisis may develop, especially since NFs have a propensity for high drama. Hence, the responsible teacher will insure that NFs in particular, have emotional support. Their contribution to the class comes in their ability to inspire with visions of the future, their sensitivity to the emotional tone of the group, and a quality of passion and intensity that enlivens the classroom. "It has taken a lot of time to become the person I am today. It is still not perfect—but many of the flaws that were there just two years ago are gone."

SP: SENSING PERCEIVING TEMPERAMENT

When Shelley wrote "Hail to thee: Blythe Spirit," he might have been describing the SP temperament. Playful, whimsical, ethereal, the SP lives for each moment, her attention flitting from one action or person to the other. As one SP wrote: "I am most myself where I can just do and say what comes." Because the sensing function is combined with the perceiving mode, the SP is at once very down-to-earth and literal-minded while being spontaneous and ready for action. SPs are among the great artistic performers of the world. Their approach to their lives is decidedly nonintellectual, and they prefer activities in which they can manipulate their bodies or concrete objects.

As a group, they have the smallest representation in higher education. Their interests, like the SJs, draw them to the world of action, but unlike the SJs they are not organizationally bound. They require movement and change and can be greatly misunderstood or labeled as being frivolous or uninterested in class. Since teachers tend to want a class that sits, listens, and occasionally interacts, the restless SPs may not be a favorite. They may also be labeled "dumb" or "dizzy" because their questions may seem literal or obvious. They may also be disruptive.

Involving the SP, is a rewarding challenge to any teacher. Used to being ignored or having to work in an unpreferred mode, the SP may respond enthusiastically to any effort to devise appropriate assignments for her. She will happily do research if it is accompanied by experiments or other activity. Since her writing will tend to be descriptive, literal, and concrete, she will prefer short, specific assignments. Like the SJ, she will enjoy experiential learning, and hands-on activities, but more than other types, she will be willing to do repetitive activities, in other words, to practice. She will happily repeat an activity if its goal is to perfect the quality of the presentation. Practice is effortless to the SP, which is why this group constitutes our great pianists, dancers, and gymnasts.

SPs may have little apparent interest in feminist ideas or in joining in a social movement. However, they put a high premium on independence and may live very liberated lives, avoiding situations that tie them down to a particular role or expected pattern of behavior.

SPs excel at practical applications of ideas—often skipping the stage of articulating theory altogether. SPs know how to respond to the action needs of the moment and how to negotiate on the spot. They are excellent in the front lines. If they are not bored in a class, their vitality gives it sparkle. If they are, they may drop the class without ever telling you why because their preferred mode of communication is through action, not words.

IMPLICATIONS

When teachers pay attention to their students' learning styles and the way they use them as learners in a classroom, the tasks in the classroom take on different meaning and importance. Even recognizing that the learners may differ in their approach to the material is important. While the attention span of the NT and NF will usually endure through a long lecture, that of the SP and SJ will not. Therefore, different delivery systems, such as using films, small-group work, or hands-on projects will be necessary to support the learning styles of these two groups. Similarly, home assignments will need to be varied.

Papers that require careful analysis will delight the NTs and frustrate the SPs. Assignments that ask students to imagine an ideal landscape will enthrall the NFs and baffle the SJs. Often when students come in for assistance, they will be indicating some trouble with the style of the assignment. Teachers who are familiar with type and temperament may be able to "translate" such an assignment from one type to another. Or, they may give a variety of possible assignments so that students may choose one which is "in type" and therefore is relatively accessible to them. Especially in upper-level courses, students should also be encouraged to branch out and develop some new skills. Briefly, NTs excel at analyses and critiques; NFs shine in journals, creative or imaginative projects, and (if extroverted) in discussion groups. SJs like fact-based research papers and respond best to a great deal of structure in assignments, while SPs most enjoy experiential learning and projects which call for practical applications of knowledge.

Not only can assignments be adapted to different learners; the actual enterprises of educational exchange can be enhanced through better communication and more open acceptance of difference as students come to understand that their learning style is but one of many. Students, ever intent on finding people who agree with them, can learn to respect different views or approaches to the material. And this perception can also lead to deeper self-respect and confidence. Table 10.1 is offered both as a summary of the types discussed and as a way to think about the behavior differences the types produce.

As adults students will develop their voices—and they will differ from each other. They will frame their arguments in different ways even though they may be making the same point. The following quotations from mature voices clearly illustrate the plurality of women's voices. Each presents her experience of the world in a different mode, although each is clearly committed to the development of women. For Gilligan, who writes in an NF style, the experience of being a woman implies relationship, connection, community. On the other hand, DeBeauvoir, an NT, praises the very detachment Gilligan would decry. She conceptualizes the experience of being a woman in phenomenological terms, affirming women's ability to talk from their own experience but seeing this ability in terms of knowledge and objectivity.

Kay Lindsey, an SJ, sees her identity through her senses and the actual physical aspects of her life. Being a woman involves community connection but also specific concrete perceptions about one's re-

TABLE 10.1 *Different Voices for Women*

	NF	NT	SJ	SP
In a dialogue or conversation, she is	empathic and concerned	sorting out; challenging	being agreeable	telling everything; taking in all the information
She is most comfortable sharing	feelings	opinions	practical information in a context	facts and experiences
Her affect is	dramatic and concerned	cool; reasonable	affable and helpful	lively and alert
As a learner, she prefers assignments which involve	creativity, values, a chance to relate to others	analysis, logic, model building	structure, data-based research or theory with practical application	experience and practical application of knowledge
In a teacher, she appreciates	caring, vision, a concern for values	well-organized intellectual stimulation	structure, practical examples, down-to-earth approach	variety of teaching modes, activity and engagement

lationships. Emma Goldman, on the other hand, talks like an SP when she emphasizes independence and spontaneity expressed through physical action.

> Among the most pressing items on the agenda for research on adult development is the need to delineate *in women's own terms* the experience of their adult life. . . .The concept of identity expands to include the experience of interconnection, [and the] moral domain is similarly enlarged by the inclusion of responsibility and care in relationships. (Gilligan, 1982)

Many problems appear to us [women] to be more pressing than those which concern us in particular, and this detachment even allows us to hope that our attitude will be objective. Still, we do know the feminine world more intimately than do the men because we have our roots in it, we grasp more immediately than do men what it means to a human being to be feminine, and we are more concerned with such knowledge. (DeBeauvoir, 1974)

To be a Black woman, therefore, is not just to be a Black who happens to be a woman. . . . For it is immediately within the bosom of one's family that one learns to be a female and all that the term implies. . . . Our first perception of ourselves is of our physical bodies, which we are then forced to compare with the bodies of those with whom we live, mothers, fathers, grandmothers, aunts, uncles, and whomever. Our clothing and the kinds of play activity we engage in are reflections of the lives of those with whom we live. Treatment at school reinforces our sexuality, so that by the time we reach adolescence, we as Black women have perceived our role, all too clearly. (Lindsey, 1974)

If I can't dance. . . . I don't want to be part of your revolution.
—Slogan popularly attributed to Emma Goldman

Working with women in the classroom involves supporting the variety of perspectives or voices that women represent. Too often women have been pressured into conforming to one image, whether it be the traditional nurturing housewife or the more modernized superwoman, performing competently in a variety of ways and thus also suppressing their individuality. One of the educational tasks that confronts educators during the last decade of the twentieth century will be to enable women to articulate and strengthen their individual perspectives and identities. These final quotations underscore this point: we need *all* of these perspectives in the classroom, in the world, and we need to help young women to stay in touch with their own special views, so that they can continue to represent the diversity of women's voices for the future.

REFERENCES

The Association for Psychological Type, 414 Southwest 7th Terrace, Gainesville, Florida 32601.

BATES, MARILYN, and KEIRSEY, DAVID. *Please Understand Me*, and BRIGGS-MYERS, ISABEL, *Gifts Differing.* Available from Consulting Psychologists Press, Inc., 577 College Avenue, Palo Alto, California 94306.

DEBEAUVOIR, SIMONE. *The Second Sex.* New York: Random House, 1974, p xxvii.

GABELNICK, FAITH, and PEARSON, CAROL. "Using the Myers-Briggs Type Indicator to Identify and Understand Women's Voices." *Feminist Teacher* V, 1985, pp. 11-17 and 30.

GILLIGAN, CAROL. *In a Different Voice.* Cambridge, Mass.: Harvard University Press, 1982, p. 173.

LINDSEY, KAY. "The Black Woman as Woman." In Cade, Toni (ed.), *Black Woman: An Anthology.* New York: NY, NAL Penguin Inc., 1974, p. 87.

11

The Meaning of Gilligan's Concept of "Different Voice" for the Learning Environment

CAROLYN DESJARDINS

Too often psychologists as well as other researchers have listened to and studied men and then merely extrapolated from their findings to generalize about women. This limitation has led them to assume that women are, or should be, identical the men or that they are men's opposites. Neither approach is adequate because neither studies women on their own terms.

Lawrence Kohlberg, for example, who has written the classic work on moral development and advanced Piaget's classic concept of morality as justice into a major theory of moral development, constructed and validated his stages as did Piaget on an exclusively male sample: adolescent boys. To determine stages of moral development, Kohlberg developed hypothetical moral dilemmas in which males were asked whether a particular response was right or wrong and the reason for their decision. From the resulting data, he hypothesized six stages of moral development; lower stages deal with issues regarding punishment for stealing, concerns with being a "good person" occur in the middle stages, and consideration of life over property marks the highest levels of moral development. Kohlberg's schema, then, defines morality as justice or fairness reasoning with an emphasis on movement toward objectivity and universality as the ideal or highest stage of development (Kohlberg, 1969).

In the early 1970s, Carol Gilligan, a psychologist also working in the area of moral development at Harvard University, made several discoveries that significantly changed commonly held concepts in the areas of moral development, psychology and philosophy. Her work has important implications for education and for the learning environment.

Gilligan's process of discovery began with the observation of a discrepancy between theory and data while selecting students to participate in a study of moral development. These students were college seniors who had as sophomores taken a class with Kohlberg concerning moral choice. Gilligan found that a majority of the students who had dropped the class were women. When she contacted these students to interview them concerning their moral conflicts, she found that their descriptions of the moral problems they faced did not fit with existing theories of moral development. Instead, their dilemmas appeared to be related to problems with personal relationships (Gilligan, 1986).

Gilligan's findings, however did not lead her to think in terms of gender differences, nor was that thinking a part of her next study. In collaboration with Kohlberg, she became interested in the relationship between people's moral reasoning versus what they actually did when faced with real moral dilemmas: the divergence between judgment and action. This research—which initially included male decisions about the draft and later was extended to include women's decisions regarding abortion—was markedly different from Kohlberg's in that subjects were not asked to think through or judge hypothetical dilemma's but rather were asked to explain their moral thinking and consequent action when faced with a real life dilemma.

In listening to these women discussing their real life problems and how they made decisions about what to do, Gilligan heard a voice that did not fit into the patterns of Kohlberg's model of moral development. This different voice focused on care for others' needs and on the value of and concern for connections and attachments between people (Gilligan, 1982). According to Gilligan,

> When one begins with the study of women and derives developmental constructs from their lives, the outline of a moral conception different

from that described by Freud, Piaget, or Kohlberg begins to emerge and informs a different description of development. In this conception, the moral problem arises from conflicting responsibilities rather than from competing rights and requires for its resolution a mode of thinking that is contextual and narrative rather than formal and abstract. This concept of morality is concerned with moral development around the understanding of responsibility and relationships, just as the conception of morality as fairness ties moral development to the understanding of rights and rules. (ibid., p. 19)

Gilligan has described the discovery of a morality of care and responsibility in *In A Different Voice* (1982) but does not limit this voice by gender because this voice is identified by the theme—not by virtue or by gender. The contrast between male and female voices is presented to "highlight a distinction between two modes of thought and to focus on a problem of interpretation rather than to represent a generalization by either sex." Gilligan cautions the reader that "the association is not absolute" (ibid., p. 2). She notes, however, that gender differences do exist, and she often gives the example that men are clearly responsible for more violent crimes than women. This does not mean, however, that all men are violent or that women cannot be.

Men and women are fully capable of using both voices to solve moral problems. One voice, articulated by Kohlberg, predominates in men and values justice, fairness, and objectivity as the primary bases for moral decisions. This voice places relationships on a continuum of inequality-equality, and its goals are autonomy and reciprocity in interactions with others. Treating others fairly and not interfering with their rights are the moral injunctions of this voice, so a moral person then becomes one who steps back from situations in an attempt to be objective and fair. The other voice, as articulated by Gilligan, predominates in women. It values attachment, care, and engagement as the primary bases for moral decisions. The moral injunction is concern with the needs of others. This voice places relationships along a continuum of attachment-detachment and values intimacy and nurturing in interactions with others.

Nona Lyons, in her doctoral research, presented empirical evidence which documents that *both* women and men were able to use *both* justice and care reasoning. However, gender differences existed in the predominant use of each reasoning mode, with more men using justice reasoning and more women using care reasoning. Lyons also found that when people described themselves in relation to others it was through two distinct orientations: separate/objective or connected. These descriptions also indicated gender-related differences, with more males using "separate" descriptions and more women using "connected" (Lyons, 1983).

Another researcher, Kay Johnson, found that when sixty female and male adolescents were presented with dilemmas posed in two of Aesop's Fables, fifty-four initially responded to the problem in either the justice or care perspective. When asked if there was another way to think about each dilemma, over half were able to respond from a different mode and to express a preference for one mode or the other (Johnson, 1985).

The research of Gilligan, and others, continues to show that moral voice is sex-related but not sex-determined. The research indicates that most people asked to describe the moral conflicts in their lives introduce at least one or more considerations related to care and one or more related to justice. Most, however, tend to focus their attention in one mode, with focus defined as 75 percent or more of their considerations in one mode (Gilligan, 1986).

Gilligan further illuminates this point in reporting that in a sample of eighty educationally advantaged adults and adolescents, with various ethnic and geographical backgrounds, it was found that fifty-seven, or two-thirds, demonstrated high focus in one mode and one-third demonstrated equal numbers of care and justice considerations. Additionally, sex differences occurred in the direction of focus. Of the two-thirds of men with a focused orientation, all but one chose justice. Women with a focused orientation were nearly equally divided between care and justice. In this study, as in others, it is clear that if women were not included in the research, not only would the importance of the care perspective be lost, but also women's experience would be virtually excluded (ibid.).

WHY WE NEED TO HEAR BOTH VOICES

Women so resonated to the accuracy of Gilligan's description of the female voice and to the importance of a sense of "interdependence" in the world that in 1984 *Ms* magazine recognized Gilligan as "Woman of the Year." In making this tribute, the journal's editors stated their belief that her recognition of the care perspective as a major moral value could hold the key to the future survival of the planet earth. Adding to her powerful presentation of the care perspective, Gilligan has further asserted that dispassion has been valued as the essence of impartiality in the justice mode of reasoning, and that reliance on others has been devalued as a weakness to be avoided. The inability to recognize or respond to the needs of others, and to fail in establishing connections with oneself and others, are the results of dispassion—indeed, another crucial realization affecting the future of our planet. While Kohlberg has argued that boys' competitive play develops more moral lessons than girls', Gillian believes that girls' play does develop moral lessons but that the values may be different: namely that "competition between persons is not as important as relationships between persons." Lindsy Van Gelder, in writing the *Ms.* article about Gilligan, has us "imagine a world that would listen to little girls who've been saying all along that they don't like to play games where people win or lose." "In many ways," she adds, "they are Gilligan's key to the future" (Van Gelder, 1984, p. 38).

Michele Dumont, a philosopher studying Gilligan's work in relation to the field of philosophy, also stresses the importance of an awareness of *both* moral modes:

> In terms of morality, the ability to see along both lines is a serious requirement since the reduction of one to the other leaves open the possibilities of oppression on one side and abandonment or isolation on the other. Without the ability to see both, survival is endangered. (Dumont, 1986, p. 9)

> The focus on justice to the exclusion of care endangers interdependence and connection while the focus on care to the exclusion of justice endangers the rights of the parties involved. (Dumont, 1986, p. 9)

Gaining an awareness of both moral orientations can be difficult. Gilligan describes them as similar to the Gestalt perception image of the vase and two faces, in which only one image can be seen at a time, although both exist simultaneously. Alone, each picture is a flat, stable, understandable reality, void of motion, void of connection, void of expansion. Neither perception is better or more real. Each, then, has a truth and reality in itself, but the greater truth and reality lies in the awareness that *both* images are interdependent; the same lines are used to define both figures that in reality coexist. This coexistence of two images dependent on each other implies a magical dimension that expands awareness of perception as well as knowledge about relationships holistically rather than in a linear process far beyond what either image can accomplish by itself. How much greater, then, the magic can become, when human beings rather than the images are involved.

IMPLICATIONS FOR HUMAN DEVELOPMENT, THEORY, AND PRACTICE

In a speech given at Harvard in the summer of 1985, Gilligan discussed what she termed the female paradox: "that in searching for connections, women often find themselves isolated" because they live in a male-defined world which values separation. Women are also culturally defined as care-givers in a society which too often equates care with self-sacrifice. The task for a woman is to learn to put herself and her needs in the equation and on her own agenda—to care for herself as well as others. Furthermore, "the exclusion of self, like the exclusion of others, renders relationships lifeless by desolving the fabric of connection" (Gilligan, 1985).

The overemphasis on individuation and separation in men's development leads to loneliness and emotional deprivation in men. Paradoxically, while women's developmental task is to learn to assert their needs—even if doing so leaves them alone—the male task is to risk vulnerability and interdependence with other people.

Earlier linear concepts of development emphasized the severing of parental and other bonds as a natural part of developing autonomy and/or adulthood. Gilligan's model views development rather in a cyclical way, in which attachments with parents, children, friends, teachers may assume varying importance at various times, but tend to circle in and out of our lives. Dependence is not seen as the opposite but the complement of independence, and the holistic focus on what holds people together is greater than the unitary focus on freedom and independence. This model not only deserves attention as a viable different theory but also as a true challenge to the theories based on assumptions about human behavior that are derived primarily from studying males.

IMPLICATIONS FOR THE EDUCATIONAL ENVIRONMENT

The work of Gilligan and Lyons and their associates has major implications for the educational environment.

Early in the women's movement assimilation of male, societally defined attitudes, values, and behaviors, and denial or rejection, not always conscious, of what have been traditionally assigned female attitudes, values, and behaviors, were viewed as the path to equality.

It was asserted that if differences did not exist, then the equity would result. Assimilation was the goal, sometimes accompanied by the view that if enough women were assimilated the attitudes, values, and behavioral characteristics of the institution would reflect their presence. The danger of acknowledging difference was that such arguments can be used to relegate women to particular roles and functions, to reinforce a "woman's place."

Assimilation became the answer to the equity question for institutions under legal and social pressures to provide equal opportunity. Concern for assimilation naturally led to higher education's emphasis on moving women into nontraditional or male-dominated career areas. Efforts were made to encourage women to take more math and science classes, and women's athletics programs that emulated men's received more support. In this process women have been encouraged to become autonomous, separate, and competitive so they will succeed in these endeavors, since success is equated with male behavior and because it now has been assumed that it is better to act like a male than like a female. Gilligan's theories, however, have stressed that femininity and competence are not contradictory virtues and that the competence of caring is as important as that of justice, leaving the door open to the recognition that other values previously consigned to women should also be given greater prominence and appreciated in men as well as in women. With this new thinking, assimilation at the expense of femaleness becomes not only undesirable but a kind of death. In denying an important part of themselves—that is, the caring, intuitive feminine part, and trying to become like men—women may instead develop a kind of hollowness that comes from being half a person which may, in fact, feel like a kind of personal death. It is therefore of great importance for successful women to think of themselves as women rather than as "honorary males."

There is a kind of death for society in general when the care perspective is not recognized as essential to bringing wholeness to the justice perspective. Everyone loses when the care perspective is not part of the workplace, part of institutions, part of both personal and professional relationships, and part of the efforts toward world understanding and peace. Education is the key to developing the two distinct moral voices in both sexes, to allowing the full use of these voices by both sexes, and to more accurately and fully mapping human growth and development. Since the educational system has been built primarily on knowledge of men's development, men's development must now be rethought in terms of its interaction with and relationship to women's development. This would imply, as Gilligan has suggested, "relinquishing the comfort of a single right answer and the clarity of a single road in life" (Gilligan, 1984, p. 22).

Carol Shakeshaft, in the article "A Gender at Risk," describes the need for women's educational equity as a major crisis in education. She believes that it is a myth that the culture of schools is female. Schools began, she asserts, "in response to what males needed to know in order to become public people." Thus, "schools were created to serve the public purposes of men's lives not the private purposes of women's" (Shakeshaft, 1986, p. 500). Perhaps the concept of education can now be expanded to better serve both public and private lives of both genders, as well as to better serve a variety of cultures and races. The rigidity of distinction between public and private life needs to be softened to better educate whole persons.

All areas of education must be reconsidered, beginning, perhaps, with measures of educational aptitude and human development that, according to Gilligan, have been used to judge people's psychological health through psychological theories and interpretive schemes that are affected by their moral beliefs (Gilligan, 1985). Perhaps the universality of invariant, irreversible stage sequences in cognitive development must also be challenged to determine gender and racial variations. Shakeshaft believes that many areas of the educational system need to be changed to better meet the needs of women and other minority groups. She believes that, "the interactions of teachers with students reinforce the societal message that females are inferior." This comes in part, she says, from boys talking and interacting more and being told that they have ability. She feels also that the use of competition as a learning style is a teaching technique that may be less effective for many women. "The failure to integrate female experience into the general curriculum," Shakeshaft says, "drives home the message that women and their experiences are somehow 'other'" (Shakeshaft, 1986, p. 501).

Evidence of valuing the female experience occurs, according to Shakeshaft, in such things as male exclusive language, bias, and stereotyping in books and movies, and both the invisibility of strong female character and being told that women's identities and experiences are not the stuff of literature or of history (ibid., p. 501). It is interesting to imagine here a "her-story" class in which the major study would be the attachments between people and the motivations of care that influenced the expansion and settlement of countries, as well as the creation of industries and more humane political systems. Perhaps this knowledge could then be integrated with concepts of justice and fairness into a new course, "our-story."

The educational environment, it appears, must provide for women, as well as other minorities, a safe place in which to come to know themselves and allow others to better understand them. It is a possibility, also, that whole cultures, such as some Native American, Asian, or other "minority" groups, may be more adequately described from the care than the justice perspective. Or, more importantly, by defining their unique voices these groups can expand still more our understanding of the full range of human voice with its many octaves and harmonies.

Carolyn Heilbrun, in *Reinventing Womanhood*, says that "it is the mark of a caste that it internalizes the judgements of the oppressor, particularly the judgements upon itself." In commenting on women's literature, she believes that "women, like children, have told stories in which the details are more important than the plot, in which their own action was not possible." She believes that while women have been participants in this culture, they have been without a history. She encourages women to expand and learn to speak from their own experience to "bring their collective memory up from darkness." Women must create a language out of what they know, out of their own experience, and no longer be content to feel, judge and act according to standards set by a patriarchal culture (Heilbrun, 1979).

Ann Wilson Schaef, in *Women's Reality*, expresses how difficult it can be for women to develop a language that enables them to communicate their experiences. This difficulty comes, she believes, from being educationally trained in a reality that is not women's own. Schaef fears that many women believe that the way the world is now is reality, but as women begin to notice, label, and conceptualize, they can begin also to learn and to grow and nourish those subjective, intuitive resources within the self. "Sometimes," Schaef adds, "it is difficult to remember what one is not supposed to know" (Schaef, 1981, p. 73).

Schaef's point is carried further by Dumont, who believes that gaining voice can be a difficult task because "silence has made words unavailable or difficult to use in a way that sounds true to one's experience—in addition, gaining voice depends on someone being willing to listen" (Dumont, 1986, p. 15).

Gilligan, in articulating the need for voice, says that "within the framework of relationships, the central metaphor for identifying motivation formation becomes the metaphor of dialogue rather than that of mirroring." She believes that the "subjectively known self" enters into relationships through speaking, being heard, and listening (Gilligan, 1984). If, as Gilligan believes, the "critical interpretive perspective" of the care focus points to deficiencies in the educational system, then higher education must be concerned with how this perspective can be better developed and sustained. It also must develop an awareness of and concern for developing new curricula, teaching and counseling methodologies, administrative structures, books, materials, and so forth—whatever is needed to make higher education more responsive to the needs of women. Women have been successful—at least they have made high grades—in higher education perhaps because "nice girls" fulfill other people's expectations, especially authority figures, such as teachers and parents. Energy that could perhaps be spent on learning is often transformed into efforts to please others. Even when they do make good grades, however, female students often experience a loss of personal and career confidence during their college years. Evidently, achievement in our educational system neither guarantees self-esteem nor generates self-confidence in women.

In a recent study by Clinchy, Belenky, Goldberger, and Tarule, the authors have listened, as Gilligan does, to the voices of women. A majority of these women were "simply students" in institutions of higher education, and their various voices give some beginning insights into what is needed to better educate women. Clinchy et al. refer to a kind of education they call "connected" education. "In connected classes," the authors report, "teachers and students construct knowledge together, and they nurture each other's ideas." It is important in these kinds of classes that teachers present themselves as genuine and that they trust students' experiences. Uncertainty is seen as a positive part of tentative, evolving thought, and authority is not equated with certainty (Clinchy et al., 1985).

From their research, Clincy and her co-authors believe that "most women want and need an education where connection is emphasized over separation, understanding and acceptance over judgement and assessment, and collaboration over debate." The authors believe that a curriculum that respects and includes firsthand experience, as well as a system that helps women to define their own questions, are critical for the education of women and certainly can embellish the education of men. They believe also that the "adversarial" model of learning that has dominated higher education in which teachers "put forth opposing notions, encourage debate, and challenge students to defend their ideas, does not facilitate women's learning" (Clinchy et al., 1985). Analysis and dualistic "either-or" thinking appear to be less natural to women's learning styles than are synthesis and bridging. Also, in women's learning style, the concept of "bringing together" is often more comfortable than the concept of "tearing apart."

Gilligan's concept of "different voice" suggests some needed expansions of the learning environment in higher education. Gender and racial differences need not be viewed as inferior but as adding to, or enlarging, the range of human possibilities. This concept brings added creativity and new ways of constructing and using knowledge that will improve, rather than hinder, the human condition. New learning environments should, as Gilligan has suggested, "not teach answers but rather raise questions that initiate the search for knowledge" (Gilligan, 1985). Perhaps men can benefit from this method as well as women. If the motivators and the rewards in the educational system have been concerned with issues of competition and of following the rules, perhaps they can be altered to include caring and helping each other to learn. This happens in women's reentry centers in the community colleges, where women share baby-sitting, children's clothes, and transportation, as well as help each other study and prepare papers. They would rather help each other and all get passing grades and, moreover, really learn than compete for As. Could this be a model for what higher education could become? Women's studies programs and women's centers, in both colleges and universities, provide a safe place for women to come together and gain support while developing this different voice and seeking answers for their different questions. Women sharing equitably in positions of formal leadership in higher education is also a must for enhancing the collegiate atmosphere for women and for men. These women provide role models for both women and men students and bring needed perspectives for creating a more complete educational system.

More cooperative approaches to learning need to be initiated in which there is more equality than in the present traditional hierarchy of teacher-as-authority figure, and student-as-learner. Emphasis on talking, sharing, and completing projects together in a more equal way are hallmarks of these cooperative approaches (Clinchy et al., 1985). There is a vulnerability for students taking a class, but there is also some vulnerability in teaching, and in being an administrator.

Perhaps in sharing these vulnerabilities or lack of "all the answers" with each other, we can come to develop a better and more humane system of learning.

To be viable today, educational institutions must respond to women's needs to consider issues of intimacy as well as career issues. The question here, according to Gilligan, is, "can women be responsive to themselves without losing connections to others and can they respond to others without abandoning themselves?" (Gilligan, 1984, p. 28). Classes or centers should be provided for dialogues on these and other issues, and men need to be a part of some of these dialogues as well. Equality of opportunity for women cannot be achieved by merely providing encouragement to move into nontraditional career areas and by eliminating barriers to various professions. Equality requires changes in educational preparation, changes in the ways in which work places are structured, and changes in relationships between men and women.

The task for women is to realize that knowledge is *not* sexually neutral and that to bring change to higher education, women's knowledge, the more obscure language, must be discovered, developed, and institutionalized. Classes and textbooks need to be developed that help women (minority/majority) and minority men to both understand and feel pride in their uniqueness and in their special contributions, as well as to legitimize their voices.

Women need to better understand what they need to know and how best to learn it. They must realize that their identity did not spring, like Athena, fully defined from the heads of men, but instead must be created by women themselves. It is important for women to understand that being female and caring does not imply an image of self-sacrificing femininity that invites inequality but rather a feminine image of strength. It is important to know that women can achieve in all areas of male achievement, but that the approach and manner of acting may be different. Women must understand, also, that the harder knowledge, caring and connection, creates the self but can also preserve the planet. Women's voices are another tongue speaking out of the life within this life, giving an additional dimension, an additional knowledge. They must be listened to, however, to bring reality. Like the unheard tree falling in the forest, women's unique moral voice appeared not to exist until Gilligan, and others, heard it.

Gilligan does not believe that it is possible to measure women's moral and human development with the present standards. "The task for women," she stresses, "is to realize that they have a perspective and that the way they see things is valued and that there is truth in what they know" (Gilligan, 1985). The task for men is to hear and honor that voice, in women and in themselves.

REFERENCES

CHODROW, NANCY. *The Reproduction of Mothering, Psychoanalysis and the Sociology of Gender.* Berkeley: University of California Press, 1978.

CLINCHY, B. M., BELENKY, M. F., GOLDBERGER, N., and TARULE, J. "Connected Education for Women." *Journal of Education,* 167(3), 1985, 28–45.

DESJARDINS, CAROLYN. Self-Perceptions of Women Across the Adult Life Span (ages 21–59). Unpublished doctoral dissertation. Arizona State University, 1978.

DUMONT, MICHELE. Carol Gilligan: The Two Moral Voices. Unpublished manuscript. Mt. St. Mary's College, Los Angeles, 1986.

GILLIGAN, CAROL. Adolescent Development Reconsidered. Paper. Health Futures of Adolescents Conference, Daytona Beach, Florida, 1986.

GILLIGAN, CAROL. Untitled speech given at a coding workshop, Harvard University, June 1985.

GILLIGAN, CAROL. Remapping Development: The Power of Divergent Data. Unpublished mongraph. Harvard University, 1984.

GILLIGAN, CAROL. *In a Different Voice.* Cambridge, Mass.: Harvard University Press, 1982.

HEILBRUN, CAROLYN G. *Reinventing Womanhood.* New York. W. W. Norton, 1979.

JOHNSON, KAY. Two Moral Orientations—Two Problem Solving Strategies: Adolescents' Solutions to Dilemmas in Fables. Unpublished doctoral dissertation. Harvard University, 1985.

KOHLBERG, L. "Stage and Sequence: The Cognitive Development Approach to Socialization." In D. A. Goslin (ed.), *Handbook of Socialization Theory and Research.* Chicago: Rand McNally, 1969, pp. 347–380.

LYONS, NONA P. "Two Perspectives: On Self, Relationships and Morality." *Harvard Educational Review* 1983, p. 53.

SCHAEF, ANNE WILSON. *Women's Reality.* Minneapolis: Winston Press, 1981.

SCHEMAN, NAOMI. "Individualism and the Objects of Psychology." In Harding, S., and Hintikka, M., (eds.), *Discovering Reality.* Dordrecht, Holland: D. Reidel, 1983.

SHAKESHAFT, CHAROL. "A Gender at Risk." *Phi Delta Kappan,* March 1986, pp. 499–503.

STERNHILL, CAROL. "Life in the mainstream." *Ms,* July 1986.

VAN GELDER, L., "Carol Gilligan: Leader for a Different Kind of Future." *Ms,* January 1984.

PART TWO

Learning Environments Shaped by Women

In asking what are the educational needs of women, we are not asking a new question. In fact, all educational enviroments designed for, and often shaped by, women have addressed it. The answers of different institutions and projects—from women's colleges, to women's studies programs, to women's centers, special programs, and women's athletics—are the subject of this section of *Educating the Majority*. These approaches and programs began as a response to exclusion or discrimination and, once in place, reflected an evolving understanding of the educational process. Together these colleges and programs designed for women offer a rich legacy that can be of great practical use to institutions and individuals committed to providing quality education to women today and in the future.

Higher education designed for women began in America with women's colleges. Certainly by contemporary standards their initial focus was hardly progressive. In Barbara Miller Solomon's words (*In the Company of Educated Women*, 1985), "women's colleges—like Vassar, Wellesley, Smith, and Bryn Mawr—were initially designed to produce Christian women better prepared to assume their duties in the domestic sphere, as wives, mothers, and only if need be, as school teachers" (p. 48). Yet to provide an education for women equivalent to that available to men, whatever the rationale, was a major step forward for women. And, while addressing the "special needs of women" then may have meant preparing women for domesticity and perhaps even compensating for women's presumed weakness of mind and body, increasingly over the years, it has come to mean equipping women to compete equally with men, both intellectually and professionally. And the record of women's colleges described in this section by Elizabeth Tidball and by Abigail McCarthy is impressive. Women's colleges are remarkably effective in educating women for success and leadership, for to them women are important and valued.

Coeducational schools have until recently assumed that it was enough simply to open their doors to women. Indeed, to too many, providing anything special for women had an old-fashioned ring to it, reminiscent of arguments for "a women's place." With the advent of the contemporary women's movement, however, came new questions and issues. Women began to demand equal access to athletic opportunities, to nontraditional careers, and to high-prestige employment. They demanded services that recognized the realities of their lives—like day care, evening classes, conditions for safety (adequate lighting of campus parking lots and other areas), and sexual harassment policies. They requested—or took things in their own hands and formed—women's centers, women's studies programs, and other strategies to learn about themselves, to understand and remediate gender inequality, and to take charge of their own destinies by helping one another. "Sisterhood," women said, "is powerful."

Women became sophisticated about articulating their need for separate places to learn to hear and honor their own voices and points of view and about defining and recognizing sexism in its many guises. Virtually every aspect of major institutions were critiqued as to their patriarchal elements, and women's commissions began studies documenting the scarcity of women in the faculty and administration, and the discrepancy between male and female salaries. Traditional styles of teaching in which the teacher is invested with all the authority and knowledge, while the student is seen as the passive recipient of knowledge to then to judged by the authority, were challenged. In women's studies classrooms, and in the governing committees of many women's organizations, alternative, more participatory and equalitarian structures were explored. In the latter, leadership was often rotated in order to empower everyone and to develop everyone's leadership ability. Many women's groups then and now experimented with consensual decision-making rather than majority rule.

The development of feminist scholarship, women soon discovered, required the same kind of fundamental questioning. It was not enough simply to add a new content area to the curriculum. Doing so required recognizing and challenging the unwritten rules of the academy about what is legitimate to study, what kinds of questions can be asked, and what kinds of methods are legitimate to use in answering them. The more work that was done, the more apparent were the omissions. Women's studies programs, populated primarily by white women, tended not to recognize or address the issues particular to Black women, so Black women began Black women's studies courses and programs with the important results outlined by Guy-Sheftall and Bell-Scott in this section. So, too, many women concerned with the hesitancy of women's studies programs to identify and address their heterosexual bias, began lesbian women's studies courses and programs, and more recently Asian, Hispanic, and American Indians have begun to add their voices to the new knowledge on women.

Yet, women rethinking everything—about teaching, governance, scholarship, about their relationships with one another and with men, and about their relation to the institution in which they worked and studies—found themselves compelled to enter a frustrating and complex situation. On the one hand, they were asking—even demanding—full participation in cultural institutions. On the other hand, they were critiquing those institutions and saying they were inherently inequitable—sexist, racist, and classist. Women wanted their scholarship, programs, and concerns legitimated by the very institutions they were critiquing. Gaining approval and support required translating into the hierarchical language of academe. Alternative approaches needed to articulate with traditional organizational modes and structures to survive as part of the institutions.

Different women dealt with this complexity in different ways. Some focused on developing alternative ways of doing things and translated as best they could to the institution as a whole. Others simply segmented the critique and operated by the institution's assumptions. Still others, believing that working and learning in a sexist institution was inherently too compromising, set up alternative institutions. While such experiments are beyond the province of this book, many are extremely interesting and innovative. Such experiments (for example, Sagaris, a feminist institution, and California, a freestanding feminist educational collective named after a legendary Black Amazon goddess), are the subject of an interesting and noteworthy study by Charlotte Bunch and Sandra Pollack, (*Learning Our Way: Essays in Feminist Education*, 1983). Most, however, found ways to reconcile feminist and institutional goals. Indeed, the majority of women emphasized their commonalities with institutional commitments (quality education, the full development of each student, fair and equitable processes) and the existence of a common enemy—sexism. Sexism was identified in two primary ways: (a) institutional, or structural, sexism evidenced itself in exclusionary or unequal policies, and (b) internalized sexism was reflected in the form of limiting attitudes and ideas—especially unconscious biases. The conscious-raising groups so prevalent in the 1970s on campus and off were a means to help both men and women recognize the ways they have internalized limiting gender assumptions so that as individuals they could be more whole, authentic, and liberated.

The combined success of all this effort has had a cumulative effect which, while not eradicating sexism, has significantly changed many learning environments. Publications such as *The Classroom Climate: A Chilly One for Women?* (Hall and Sandler, 1982), which clearly identifies sexist behaviors and makes recommendations on how to remediate them, are now widely used by colleges and universities. Professional associations in most disciplines have women's studies sections, and it is becoming less academically respectable to undertake studies of human behavior that ignore or devalue women.

In addition to campus-based programs and disciplinary associations, several national educational associations developed innovative approaches and programs to call attention to women's issues and to foster women's participation and influence in the academy. The Association of American Colleges established its Project on the Status and Education of Women in 1972. The project is best known for its newsletter, *On Campus with Women*, which for more than a decade and a half has called attention to the kinds of overt and covert discrimination women face on campus and made valuable recommendations for change. The American Council on Education's Office of Women in Higher Education, reestablished in 1973, also addresses a wide range of issues affecting the status of women in academe. In 1977 this office launched its National Identification Program (ACE/NIP), a national, state-based network of women and men in administration who are committed to the full and equitable participation of women in the academy. ACE/NIP women are powerful role models in the institutions in which they serve, and additionally many translate women's perspectives for the academic community. The National Women's Studies Association (NWSA), created in 1977, promotes women's studies concepts, programs, and projects and is a valuable network of feminist educators who are committed to these goals. The National Association of Women Deans, Administrators, and Counselors, in existence since 1918, experienced a renewal and intensification of their continuing support of women educators and students and thereby provides another organization in which professional academic women can celebrate women's culture and values. Many other organizations, networks, and programs also emerged to give increased attention to women's needs and aspirations and recognize the commonalities in the impact of the sexist climate in which women students, faculty, and staff all function. (Many of these are listed in the Resources section of this book).

Changes in the learning environment have included changes in campus programs and services. Partly because of the competition for the new market of returning women, and partly because of feminist demands, many campuses now provide day care and special counseling services for women. Most have sexual harassment policies and many discourage the use of noninclusive language, such as "chairman" and the generic "he." Because of federal law, campuses routinely have affirmative action offices and Title IX officers, and many routinely monitor faculty salary equity studies. Over five hundred colleges and universities have women's studies programs, and a small but growing number have projects to integrate feminist scholarship into the curriculum. Women students have greater access to athletics than in previous generations, and expect their intellectual and career ambitions to be taken seriously.

With every success has come some problems. Feminists worry that as women's perspectives on the issues gain more widespread acceptance, they tend to get watered down. Two authors in this section, Marilyn Boxer and Jane Gould, show concern that women's studies programs and women's centers are losing their original radical impulse. As women faculty, staff, and students become more accepted, they have more to lose by rocking the boat, and consequently may be less willing to risk, either in the pursuit of knowledge or in demanding fundamental reforms in the way institutions are run. Sometimes conservative trends are the result of necessary political trade-offs. As Leotus Morrison explains, women coaches have argued that women's athletics should be different from men's athletics. Title IX provided important access to athletics for women, but at the same time, it virtually ensured that women's athletics would develop entirely on a male model.

Very likely time will cure these ills, as more and more feminist ideas gain the widespread acceptance that access to education for women did in the late nineteenth century and equal pay for equal work did in the 1970s. However, at present, programs for women on some campuses still suffer from marginality. Women's programs tend to be seen as outside of the mainstream of the real work of the institution. Still, a growing number of imaginative and farsighted administrators are recognizing that women are a major force in the present and the future, and therefore the future will and should be increasingly egalitarian. Such administrators are making gender issues front and center in their institutions. At the same time, many campuses are only now starting women's centers and women's studies programs, and raising initial questions about salary and employment equity for women. All such current activities can build on the efforts of programming designed for and often by women.

The seven articles that follow were selected because they illustrate institutional characteristics, approaches, or programs designed specifically to address the concerns and needs of women students. Each essay reports on actual programming that is based upon a holistic and pluralistic view of the woman student, a strong sense of her interconnectedness with others, and a recognition that the concerns of men and women are sometimes congruent and sometimes not. Integration of mind, body, and spirit is a common theme. Surely these programs, designed with women in mind, have valuable lessons for all of us.

The first two articles outline the impressive contribution of women's colleges. M. Elizabeth Tidball, in "Woman's Colleges: Exceptional Conditions, Not Exceptional Talent, Produce High Achievers," argues that "Women's colleges are a valuable national resource as institutional models for the education and employment of women." Women's colleges, she notes, "have an unparalleled record of graduating women who attain a variety of measurable post-college attainments" because such colleges have the education of women as their first priority and because they typically provide students with faculty and peer role models of strong women who take women and their achievements seriously.

Abigail McCarthy, in "A Luminous Minority," outlines the impressive contributions of Catholic women's colleges. "Catholic women's colleges," she explains, "have led the way in offering innovative new programs for women to meet new needs . . . such as weekend colleges and external degree programs," and their graduates are "strongly oriented toward service," so they tend to make contributions to their communities and work. Finally, says McCarthy, Catholic women's colleges fostered "international exchange and a global outlook," values currently reflected in the Neylan conference vision for the "establishment of a collaborative international effort to serve women's educational needs around the world."

The next two articles explore the growing discipline of women's studies. Marilyn J. Boxer, in "Women's Studies, Feminist Goals, and the Science of Women," traces the development of women's studies from its origin as the "academic arm of a political movement" to the vehicle for a "fundamental critique of the dominance in the humanities and social sciences of methods of research and interpretation that tend to distort understanding of both sexes while disadvantaging women . . . "Women's studies," Boxer continues, "aims to restore full humanity to women by revisioning the very basis of intellectual endeavor." To understand the full import of women's studies, it is necessary to recognize that it is not simply a matter of "women's rights," but "it is essential to the fulfillment of the university's commitment to the search for truth."

In discussing the development of women's studies, Boxer traces major themes and problems, noting that women's studies programs have not always met the needs of all women. Indeed, just as the rest of the university has often not noticed the exclusion of the concerns of women, women's studies programs have too often focused on the concerns of white, middle-class women. In doing so, they have inadvertently excluded the concerns and perspectives of other women, thus depriving themselves of the richness of a more pluralistic approach and intellectually impoverishing women who were rendered invisible by virtue of class, race, religious preference, sexual orientation, or disability.

The result has been the creation of a variety of programs such as Black women's studies, Hispanic women's studies, lesbian women's studies, and so forth as doubly excluded groups formed their own programs to explore their own issues and heritage. Beverly Guy-Sheftall and Patricia Bell-Scott in "Black Women's Studies: A View from the Margin," outline the substantial achievement of Black women's studies. They conclude that "Black women's studies scholars are in a unique position because of their ability to explore the intersection of race, sex, and class as experienced by Black women in ways that are impossible for other segments of the population. The study of Black women also renders invalid many of the generalizations that abound in the historiography of American women and are considered 'universal.' The ultimate challenge is for women's studies scholars to recognize that Black women's studies is in fact women's studies . . . Educators everywhere should commit themselves to building institutions and providing experiences that promote the self-empowerment of women of color."

The next two articles focus on programs that are designed as catalysts to change institutions or individuals. Jane S. Gould's "Women's Centers as Agents of Change" describes the growth and development of women's centers, which were "created to raise and examine new questions about women's lives, roles, and expectations; to help women develop a feminist consciousness; to combat feelings of isolation; and to establish a sense of community among women." Although the focus of women's centers differ, they tend to make strong community connections and to play a networking role on campus as well as provide direct services to women and to the institution. The need for such centers and "for a feminist presence on campus remains paramount."

Mary M. Leonard's and Brenda Alpert Sigall's "Empowering Women Student Leaders: A Leadership Development Model" describes a project that recognizes women students' diversity of attitudes and experience and offers strategies to develop their leadership abilities. The model responds to the needs of four kinds of women: (a) women who have not tried to develop any leadership role; (b) women who are leaders but are male-identified; (c) women who identify with women's issues yet are unable to act; and (d) women who are leaders and identify women's agendas as part of their commitment. The model describes ways to develop appropriate skills and awarenesses for each type of woman. "As women students become increasingly aware of feminist issues and attain the skills to lead," say Leonard and Sigall, "more of the seats of power in our colleges and universities and in the greater society will be occupied by women who will use their voices to influence policy and practice."

The last article in this section explores the complicated phenomenon of women's athletics. L. Leotus Morrison, in "From the Playing Fields and Courts," traces the development of women's athletics with special attention to the tension between the desire to develop a uniquely female approach to sport and the desire to gain the resources, status, and advantages of male athletics. Morrison argues that "the rapid growth and demise of a new model for athletics administration, the Association for Intercollegiate Athletics for Women, represents an unfortunate consequence of the pull toward the status quo. The need for a new model still exists. Additionally, our society, as well as our individual citizens, could truly benefit from a concept of sport that values cooperation, the joy of participating, and the love of physical activity as well as winning."

In one way or another, almost every author, writing independently from one another, has identified the difficulty of meeting women's needs fully within the philosophical and structural confines of institutions designed with men in mind. Each found that although the programs described had admirable and impressive accomplishments, those accomplishments were limited by the pressure to conform to institutional or cultural patterns that either ignore or devalue women or that continue to act as if men's activities and ideas set the standard. The next two sections, therefore, go further to raise even more fundamental questions, the answers to which require much more fundamental change than providing separate programming for women. Instead, they suggest the need to transform the larger philosophical and institutional context in which women's education occurs.

REFERENCES

BUNCH, CHARLOTTE, and POLLACK, SANDRA. *Learning Our Way: Essays in Feminist Education.* Trumansburg, N.Y.: The Crossing Press, 1983.

HALL, ROBERTA, and SANDLER, BERNICE. *The Classroom Climate: A Chilly One for Women?* Project on the Status and Education of Women. Washington, D.C.: Association of American Colleges, 1982.

SOLOMON, BARBARA MILLER. *In the Company of Educated Women: A History of Women in Higher Education.* New Haven: Yale University Press, 1985, p. 48.

12

Women's Colleges:
Exceptional Conditions, Not Exceptional Talent, Produce High Achievers

M. ELIZABETH TIDBALL

In 1985, Dr. Benjamin Bloom and his colleagues at the University of Chicago published the results of their five-year study of exceptionally talented young people. Among their findings they note that the potential for talent is more common than most people have assumed, and that such potential is brought to fruition by sustained encouragement from the home, teachers, schools, and society. They also point out that these same influences can be responsible for "great wastage of human potential" (Bloom, 1985). Similarly, human resource studies have regularly demonstrated that even outstanding talent requires training, direction, provision for a sphere of action, and rewards to reach fruition (Committee on the Education and Employment of Women in Science and Engineering, 1983).

Women's colleges have an unparalleled record of graduating women who attain a variety of measurable post-college accomplishments. Accordingly, they represent a strong force for the advancement of women. For the women's college story is one of nurture,

157

caring, discipline, high expectations, and appropriate rewards, all brought together in an environment that embraces the wholeness inherent in the academic, cocurricular, and extracurricular facets of the collegiate experience.

Two basic questions may be asked about women's colleges in acknowledging their unequaled record of producing high achievers: What do they do, and how do they do it?

What they do is quite simple, but unique: women's colleges have, as their first priority, the education of women. They are the only institution in all of higher education that do (Dunkle, 1974). How they do it depends upon each institution's governance, location, financial resources, size, and particular history.

About two-thirds of women's colleges are still closely associated with a religious denomination, primarily the Roman Catholoc church. One-fourth of women's colleges are located in Southern states, typically a conservative region. Only about one-fourth of women's colleges are neither church related nor Southern. The current number of four-year women's colleges is less than half of the all-time high of 214 in 1960 (Tidball, 1977). Mergers and the opening of admissions to men have been the most frequent ways they have ceased being women's colleges (National Council of Independent Colleges and Universities, 1984), although some have found it necessary to close entirely.

DIFFERENCES AND LIKENESSES AMONG WOMEN'S COLLEGES

Among the currently existing women's colleges, some distinctive features emerge by which subgroups can be characterized. The Roman Catholic colleges form one such group, comprising about half of all women's colleges. They have the highest proportion of women presidents of any group of colleges or universities in the country (Office of Women in Higher Education, 1984). Both in terms of opportunities for professional women and in terms of role models for women students, this is an asset of considerable value. Roman Catholic women's colleges have pioneered a variety of educational delivery systems—the weekend college, summers-only programs, competency-based education, credit for noncollege experience, contract learning—many of which have been especially beneficial to women with meager financial resources and minimal previous contact with higher education. In these ways the Roman Catholic colleges have adapted their dedication to service to the modern era and, in particular, to serving women who would otherwise remain underserved. Yet it is precisely because this ministry is unusual, performed on a local scale, and delivered primarily to women (often poor), that the colleges involved are not always viewed in the so-called "mainstream" of American higher education. These colleges fail to fit a standard mold or stereotype of what a college "is" or "should be." Often they find themselves in a constant struggle for financial survival, even though the many educational reforms that they pioneered are all slowly finding their way into a broader spectrum of higher education institutions.

Another identifiable subgroup of women's colleges is that composed of institutions located in the South. Although a number are church-related, they are not Roman Catholic. Two thirds of these colleges still have men presidents, the largest proportion of women's colleges to continue to do so. Often there has been a tradition of having as president a minister of the religious denomination with which the college is affiliated, and such practices have effectively excluded women from consideration as presidents. Yet even as this old tradition is fading, the ministers have been supplanted by other men. As if to circumvent this impediment to women's opportunities, there is an array of strong, active women deans. In very recent years, however, a number of these colleges have appointed women presidents for the first time. It is quite apparent that these women are providing their colleges with vision, energy, and life. Many Southern colleges for women appear vigorous and determined, growing within but not irrevocably attached to a southern culture they are helping to shape. Like the Roman Catholic colleges, the Southern women's colleges draw their students primarily from their own immediate geographical region, though the Roman Catholic colleges do so more frequently from urban areas than the Southern colleges.

If the Roman Catholic colleges are imbued with a kind of ecclesiastical authoritarianism, and the Southern colleges shadowed by a kind of benign paternalism, the independent women's colleges walk a path in between. Mostly in the Northeast, though there are some notable exceptions, these colleges stand on their own, with three quarters of them under the presidential leadership of women. They are probably the colleges best known to those outside the education community. They are, as a group, the least regional. The five of the Seven Sisters that are still women's colleges—Barnard, Bryn Mawr, Mount Holyoke, Smith, and Wellesley—are members of this subset and contribute to the group's recognizability. Some of the less well-known colleges, such as Hood, Chatham, and Mills, have also assumed leadership roles in higher education of women and have been very effective in promoting women's colleges.

The only legitimate commonality, therefore, and the only bona fide identifier for all women's colleges is the fact that their primary purpose is the education of women. No other colleges or universities can make this claim. Many institutions state publicly that their mission is the higher education of men and women, but there is not even one that purports to educate women and men. Such is the responsibility taken up by the women's colleges, even as they have been and continue to be the pioneers in learning what this means and proceeding to put it into action. Documenting these assertions is a body of research carried out since the late 1960s which shows that graduates of women's colleges are more likely to become achievers than are the women graduates of coeducational institutions.

THE BACCALAUREATE ORIGINS OF WOMEN ACHIEVERS

During the period 1910–1979, more than 9 million women graduated from four-year colleges and universities in the United States. These women, and the institutions from which they graduated, have been the subject of a series of research studies assessing institutional productivity (Tidball: 1970, 1973a, 1974b, 1975a, 1980a, 1985, 1986; Tidball and Kistiakowsky, 1976). The findings from these studies show that, using nationally accumulated and published databases and registries, 343 out of every 10,000 graduates of women's colleges and 116 out of every 10,000 women graduates of coeducational institutions have attained a measurable and documented intellectual or career accomplishment during the seven decades. A summary of several such studies is presented in Figure 12.1.[1]

The criteria for being categorized as a selected or other institution varies for the different studies, but in all cases the criteria were comparable for both women's and coeducational institutions. By studying outcomes only of women who had actually graduated from college, including all women graduates for the particular years encompassed by a given study, and studying several different outcomes for differing time periods, the likelihood of biasing the research results by some consistently present factor operating always in the same direction is negligible. It is clear that the environment of women's colleges is more enabling of women than is that of co-

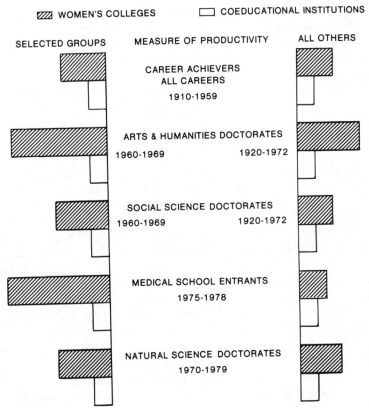

WOMEN'S COLLEGES   COEDUCATIONAL INSTITUTIONS

SELECTED GROUPS   MEASURE OF PRODUCTIVITY   ALL OTHERS

CAREER ACHIEVERS
ALL CAREERS
1910-1959

ARTS & HUMANITIES DOCTORATES
1960-1969   1920-1972

SOCIAL SCIENCE DOCTORATES
1960-1969   1920-1972

MEDICAL SCHOOL ENTRANTS
1975-1978

NATURAL SCIENCE DOCTORATES
1970-1979

FIGURE 12.1. Relative institutional productivities of women achievers, 1910–1979

educational institutions. The differences are quite dramatic. There is no way to dismiss the productivity of women's colleges, nor to imagine that somehow the vast majority of bright women and potential achievers have for decades only chosen to attend women's colleges, most of which are highly regional, small in size, and not especially selective in admissions. To make such an assertion would be to assign to women who chose coeducational institutions low levels of motivation, intelligence, talent, and enlightenment. Clearly this is not the case. Rather, the appropriate concern on behalf of women students attending coeducational institutions should be the tremendous loss of their talent to the wider society (Tidball, 1973a), or, in Bloom's terms, "the great wastage of human potential" (Bloom, 1985).

It should be noted that the focus of these studies has been on identifying the baccalaureate origins of women achievers. It is an *institutional* achievement of the greatest magnitude that, over the past seventy years, women's colleges have consistently emerged and reemerged as the type of higher education institution most likely to graduate women who subsequently are noted for their societal accomplishments. Men have no such institutional counterpart.

THE COLLEGIATE WOMAN

It is appropriate, of course, to acknowledge that students bring with them to college their accumulated academic record, their aspirations, and their personal histories. And what they bring with them does have something to do with how they perform in college. But clearly this is not the whole story. The whole story is much more elusive.

Young women of college age differ in a number of ways from young men. Psychologically, young women go about their identity formation by pursuing intimacy as a means of learning who they are (Douvan and Adelson, 1966; Tidball, 1973a, 1973b) rather than proceeding in the sequence of identity-intimacy suggested by Erikson from his studies of young males (Erikson, 1963). Additionally, young women of college age are more likely than young men to believe that their achievements are due to forces outside themselves rather than to their own skills and hard work (Maccoby and Jacklin, 1974). Achievement motivation and self-concept for the college-age woman therefore require more attention and nurturance if her talent is to emerge and flourish.

A. Astin reported in his major work, *Four Critical Years* (1978), on a number of institutional variables and the importance of their effects on students. He found that students in women's colleges had greater involvement in academic areas, in interaction with faculty, and in verbal aggressiveness. Additionally, there was a positive effect on intellectual self-esteem and a greater degree of satisfaction with virtually all aspects of college life as compared with women students in coeducational colleges. Finally, Astin found that women's college students were more likely than their coeducational counterparts "to attain positions in leadership, to become involved in student government, to develop high aspirations, and to persist to graduation." His study provided a description of behaviors for students attending various college types, although he did not indicate the characteristics that linked any given type to the likelihood of subsequent accomplishments of students.

Pascarella (1984) related the degree to which various student characteristics as well as institutional, environmental, and structural variables affected students' aspirations. He framed theoretical models for women and for men at both more and less selective institutions and reported a number of environmental situations that affected women and men differently. One of his conclusions states that the nurture and reinforcement of women's aspirations would be most likely to occur in an environment such as that of "small, financially well-endowed, women's institutions with low student-faculty ratios." He also noted that collegiate-type activities, such as social functions, intercollegiate athletics and conformist student behaviors, inhibited women's aspiration level. His model, however, did not attempt to match student aspirations with eventual outcomes.

Other research has focused more directly on the relationship of certain structural variables to actual student outcomes (Tidball, 1973a, 1974b, 1980a). Greater selectivity in admissions, higher faculty salaries, and a particular institutional size were all found to be associated with greater institutional productivity of women achievers for both women's and coeducational colleges. Nonetheless, graduates of women's colleges were regularly at least twice as likely to become career achievers as were women graduates of coeducational institutions when the variable under study was analyzed for comparable institutions. For example, less-selective women's colleges were more productive than less selective coeducational colleges, a finding of considerable import according to Block (1980), and the one that provided the clue for expanding an appreciation of the importance of the *totality* of the collegiate environment.

Academic Women in Context

Summarizing much of his work on the family, Bronfenbrenner (1982) makes clear that, in order to understand what is going on and why, it is necessary to examine not only the individual family members but also the complex web of interactions between and among them. So, too, with the learning environment. Studying the situation only for women students (their aspirations, opinions, even outcomes) or only for women faculty (their salaries, rate of promotion, levels of self-esteem) does not provide an assessment of the dynamic interactions between and among various campus constituencies. Yet these interactions and resonances are undoubtedly a major factor contributing to outcomes for women students and to self-esteem and productivity for women academic professionals.

An appreciation of the importance of such interactions is gained by assessing the relationship between the number of women faculty and the number of women students who go on to their own post-college accomplishments. The importance of adult women to younger women in the higher education setting can thereby be defined numerically and statistically. For both women's colleges and coeducational institutions, the number of women achievers per one thousand women faculty was found to be the same; but the women's colleges had almost twice as many women faculty per one thousand women students as did the coeducational institutions. The number of women faculty and the number of women achievers for all types of institutions are dependent variables with a statistically significant, positive correlation coefficient (Tidball, 1973a). That is, the dependence of the two variables is not a matter of chance. A pictorialization of this relationship between women faculty and women career achievers has been published previously (Tidball, 1980a), as has a similar one for the relationship between women faculty and women graduates between 1970 and 1979 who subsequently earned a research doctorate in one of the natural sciences (Tidball, 1986). Figure 12.2 depicts data from forty institutions (Tidball, 1985) demonstrating a comparable relationship between women faculty and women graduates, in this case for women who entered medical school from 1975 through 1978. Briefly summarized, the development of young women of talent into achieving adults is directly proportional to the number of same-sex role models to whom they have access. The implications of these findings may surely be extended to include other women associated with the institution, including peers, administrators, trustees, honorees, and guest speakers, all of whom are of major importance to women students vis-à-vis the actualization of their talents and capabilities during and after college (Macoby and Jacklin, 1974; Tidball: 1973a, 1973b, 1974a, 1975b, 1976a, 1980).

Other research indicates that, regardless of the type of institutions in which they are employed, women faculty are more concerned about women-related issues than are men faculty (Tidball, 1976c). However, the number and proportion of women faculty on most campuses is so small that their voices, at best, are difficult to hear and, at worst, easy to ignore. Some critical mass of women faculty is therefore necessary for women's concerns to emerge and be addressed. The size of this critical mass seems to depend upon the collection of characteristics at any given institution (Tidball, 1976d, 1983).

Studies have also demonstrated a statistically significant and neg-

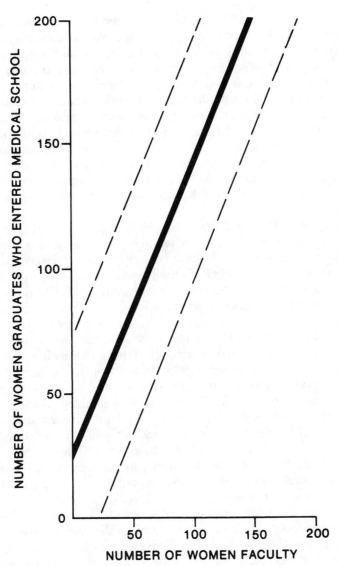

FIGURE 12.2. Relationship between women faculty and women medical school entrants

ative correlation between the number of women achievers and the proportion of men students on campus. There is no statistically significant relationship between women achievers and the number of faculty who are men (Tidball, 1973a). The quality of the men faculty seems to be important to women students: the men who teach in women's colleges are the most concerned about women-related issues among men faculty at all types of educational institutions (Tidball, 1976c). Women's colleges therefore offer women students faculties (of both women and men) that are the most supportive of women of any faculties in any learning environments. The combination of nonstereotypic career competent women and nurturant men makes an important contribution to the exceptional conditions conducive to the development of women achievers. Women's colleges have also had administrators and trustees, as well as faculty, evenly divided between women and men for the past three decades, making them the only truly "coeducational" institutions in all of higher education.

Pascarella (1984) and Ware, Steckler, and Leserman (1985) suggest that encouragement from women peers as well as teachers is important to women students' development of interest in academic achievement. Earlier, Tidball and Kistiakowsky (1976) had concluded, from their extensive demographic studies of doctoral recipients, that a favorable climate for intellectually capable and motivated women students is one which, among other characteristics, enrolls a large number of women students; and Bloom has recently reported that talent development occurs more readily if achievement is valued in the environment (1985). In the women's college environment, the value assigned to various tasks and accomplishments is not only influenced by women but is also established in a context devoid of counterproductive stereotypes. Thus, women students are free to excell in their academic work without fearing a concomitant loss of femininity as judged by their peers (Gilligan, 1979; Miller, 1976; Tidball, 1973a, 1976a). Similarly, in their extracurricular pursuits, these students have unlimited opportunities to participate on the follower-leader axis at whatever level they desire. In mixed-sex groups it has been demonstrated that both females and males overwhelmingly choose males as leaders unless the task is a traditionally "feminine" one (Lockheed, 1977). Thus, women in coeducational settings are far less likely to have tested either their interest or their skills in leadership roles.

As if there were not already a multiplicity of advantages for women participants in women's colleges, considerable attention is also accorded to their alumnae. The interaction of the women's colleges alumnae with the colleges is an important symbolic relationship. There are many ongoing events, both on campus and in innumerable communities across the country, planned for and by alumnae. Alumnae are regularly and extensively involved in promoting career networks, student recruitment, fund-raising, and other activities (Tidball, 1979). Thus, the contact, assistance, and relationships continue in both time and space. Ties with the people who made the college years significant are maintained and nurtured, contributing to kinship relationships that are known to be highly significant in the continuing process of human development (Rubin, 1985). The attachments both the the institution and to the people who were or are the institution regularly reinforce this sense of affiliation so characteristic of women's preferred mode of being in the world (Gilligan, 1977; Miller, 1976; Tidball, 1976a). These are exceptional conditions, indeed, in the service of women's achievement.

The Invisible Majority

It might be imagined, then, that everyone—women and educators especially—would be major supporters if not champions of women's colleges. Not so! Repeatedly, from their earliest beginnings, the serious education of women has been a target for disparagement, neglect, and harassment. For Emma Willard's Troy Female Seminary, the New York legislature approved its charter but refused to vote funds (Goodsell, 1931). Some one hundred-fifty years later, surveyors regularly fail to note institutions' contributions of women and men achievers separately (Fuller, 1985; Hall, 1984), thereby submerging institutions' records for women as well as the records of the women's colleges. In a thoughtful article on the education of women, Jean Walton (1986) acknowledges some of the developmental differences between women and men and points out ways in which most colleges are organized to address men's needs but not women's. But she does not take the next logical step and discuss women's colleges as institutional models exemplifying many of the practices deemed appropriate and helpful to women (Tidball, 1973a, 1976a, 1976c, 1980c).

One important consequence of the poor or neglected public treatment of women's colleges has been their inordinate struggle for survival. No other identifiable segment of higher education has responded so variably and creatively as have the women's colleges. Some, however, have ceased being women's colleges in order to exist at all. Since a number of these women's "change colleges"—women's colleges that now recruit and admit men students—have been operating for close to two decades, it is instructive to look at how this change has affected women's achievement and position.

In Anderson's study of change colleges (1977), Anderson concluded that, for women's colleges that began admitting men, "the change to coeducation had serious and undesirable environmental consequences at the hitherto female colleges." Tidball has documented achievement outcomes for women from both women's change and men's change colleges and finds distinctly lower productivities of these institutions with respect to the proportion of women who enter medical school (1985) or earn a doctorate in one of the natural sciences (1986) as compared with women graduates of women's colleges. It should not be surprising to learn also that the proportion of women faculty at these change institutions is smaller than for women's colleges. Analysis of the current faculty composition at a substantial number of small colleges is depicted in Table 12.1.

In addition to the smaller proportion of women faculty at all kinds of coeducational institutions, there are other indicators of the diminished value of women to be found in their lower salaries, promotion and tenure rates, and general deployment (Committee on the Education . . . , 1983; Reagan and Maynard, 1974). These indicators, coupled with a lack of recognition for the value of women's colleges as exemplars of the importance of women to the education and future employment of women, continues to the disadvantage of women and the perpetuation of gender bias. The existence of an intellectual double standard, or double standard that includes a mental dimension, has been noted for many years (Tidball, 1976d). Yet, gender bias remains. An example of these deleterious affects on one system is contained in the recent report of the New York State Task Force of Women and the Courts, in which gender bias was found to be pervasive throughout the state's court system, with adverse affects on all women who interface with the system: women litigants, women attorneys, and women who work as court employees (Mann, 1986). The parallels to other societal institutions, such as higher education, are obvious and abundant.

TABLE 12.1. *Proportion of Women Faculty in Several Types of Colleges*

COLLEGE TYPE	% WOMEN FACULTY
Women's colleges	50
Women's change colleges	36
Coeducational colleges	23
Men's change colleges	16

NEW DIRECTIONS

What, then, can be concluded from studies of women's colleges that has relevance for the education of women wherever they may be found? Throughout history and across all cultures women have been the chief and often sole supporters of other women in whatever tasks are assumed or assigned (Greer, 1984). Clearly there cannot be an appropriate environment for women students in the absence of an appropriate environment for women faculty, administrators, trustees, guests, and alumnae. All learn from each other. Men in coeducational settings could contribute to a more positive environment for women by emulating the men faculty in women's colleges and working cooperatively with women toward common and valued goals in adult-appropriate fashion (Tidball: 1976a, 1976c, 1976d, 1980b). Many years ago, in response to Tidball's work, the Carnegie Commission stated: "These accomplishments of the graduates of women's colleges are worthy of emphasis . . . significantly in terms of potential influence as they suggest how changes in policies and faculty attitudes in coeducational institutions could affect the accomplishment of their women students" (1973). The point is well taken and still relevant.

Women's colleges are a valuable national resource as institutional models for the education and employment of women. They have demonstrated their specialness over and over again as they have encouraged, trained, directed, empowered, and rewarded women. In their splendid variety of size, location, tradition, and particular specialization they are the very essence of the diversity that reflects all women. Women's colleges personify women in all their wonderful strengths and foibles and certainties and confusions. Thus, to deprecate or ignore women's colleges is, in effect, to deprecate or ignore women. It is in this sense that the continued health of women's colleges is important to *all* women who participate in higher education, whether or not they choose to teach or study in the environment of a women's college. Celebrating and supporting women's colleges for their contributions to women and to higher education must therefore occur regularly and often by all who profess concern for and would participate in the development of an equitable and humane society.

NOTE

1. Achievements able to be documented and enumerated were having been cited for career accomplishments in *Who's Who of American Women*

(Tidball, 1973a); having received a research doctorate in the arts and humanities, social sciences, or natural sciences according to the Doctorate Records File of the National Academy of Sciences (Tidball and Kistiakowsky, 1976; Tidball, 1980a, 1986); and having entered an American medical school according to records of the Association of American Medical Colleges (Tidball, 1985). Institutional productivities were calculated by dividing the number of women achievers by the total number of women baccalaureate recipients for each appropriate year and institutional type. Databases used to identify women achievers had to (a) be available to individual researchers or be subject to design and commission; (b) be national in scope and precisely defined; (c) list women separately; (d) designate baccalaureate institution of origin; (e) include year of baccalaureate degree; and (f) record some generally accepted and recognizable intellectual or career accomplishment.

REFERENCES

ANDERSON, RICHARD E. *Strategic Policy Changes at Private Colleges.* New York: Teachers College Press, 1977.

ASTIN, ALEXANDER W. *Four Critical Years.* San Francisco: Jossey-Bass, 1978.

BLOCK, JEANNE H. Personal communication. October 1980.

BLOOM, BENJAMIN S., ed. *Developing Talent in Young People.* New York: Ballantine, 1985.

BRONFENBRENNER, URIE. "Child Development: The Hidden Revolution." In *Issues and Studies.* Washington, D.C.: National Academy Press, 1982, pp. 40–55.

CARNEGIE COMMISSION ON HIGHER EDUCATION. *Opportunities for Women in Higher Education.* New York: McGraw-Hill, 1973.

COMMITTEE ON THE EDUCATION AND EMPLOYMENT OF WOMEN IN SCIENCE AND ENGINEERING. *Career Outcomes in a Matched Sample of Men and Women Ph.D's.* Washington, D.C.: National Academy Press, 1981.

COMMITTEE ON THE EDUCATION AND EMPLOYMENT OF WOMEN IN SCIENCE AND ENGINEERING. *Climbing the Ladder.* Washington, D.C.: National Academy Press, 1983.

DOUVAN, ELIZABETH, and ADELSON, JOSEPH. *The Adolescent Experience.* New York: John Wiley, 1966.

DUNKLE, MARGARET. "Commentary: Higher Education, A Chilly Climate for Women." In L. Hall and associates, *New Colleges for New Students.* San Francisco: Jossey-Bass, 1974.

ERIKSON, ERIK H. *Childhood and Society.* New York: W. W. Norton, 1963.

FULLER, CAROL H. *An Analysis of Leading Undergraduate Sources of Ph.D.'s Adjusted for Institutional Size.* Ann Arbor: Great Lakes College Association, 1985.

GILLIGAN, CAROL. "In a Different Voice: Women's Conception of the Self and Morality." *Harvard Education Revue* 47(1977):481–517.

GILLIGAN, CAROL. "Women's Place in Man's Life Cycle." *Harvard Education Review* 49(1979):431–446.

GOODSELL, WILLYSTINE, ed. *Pioneers of Women's Education in the United States.* New York: McGraw-Hill, 1931.

GREER, GERMAINE. *Sex and Destiny.* New York: Harper and Row, 1984.

HALL, ALFRED E. "Baccalaureate Origins of Doctorate Recipients in Chemistry." *Change* 16(1984):47–49.

LOCKHEED, MARLAINE E. "Cognitive Style Effects on Sex Status in Student Work Groups." *Journal of Educational Psychology* 69(1977):158–165.

MACCOBY, ELEANORE EMMONS and JACKLIN, CAROL NAGY. *The Psychology of Sex Differences.* Stanford: Stanford University Press, 1974.

MANN, JUDY. "Sex Bias in the Courts." *The Washington Post*, April 25, 1986, p. C3.

MILLER, JEAN BAKER. *Toward a New Psychology of Women.* Boston: Beacon Press, 1976.

NATIONAL COUNCIL OF INDEPENDENT COLLEGES AND UNIVERSITIES. "A Report." Washington, D.C.: June 1984.

OFFICE OF WOMEN IN HIGHER EDUCATION, AMERICAN COUNCIL ON EDUCATION. "Women Chief Executive Officers in U.S. Colleges and Universities." Table X, December 1984.

PASCARELLA, ERNEST T. "College Environmental Influences on Students' Educational Aspirations." *Journal of Higher Education* 55(1984):751–771.

REAGAN, BARBARA B., and MAYNARD, BETTY J. "Sex Discrimination in Universities Through Internal Labor Market Analysis." *AAUP Bulletin* 60(1974):13–21.

RUBIN, LILLIAN B. *Just Friends.* New York: Harper and Row, 1985.

TIDBALL, ELIZABETH PETERS. "Women's Colleges vs. Coeducation: A Question of Creative Involvement?" *Mount Holyoke Alumnae Quarterly*, 54(1970):176–178.

TIDBALL, M. ELIZABETH. "Perspective on Academic Women and Affirmative Action." *Education Record* 54(1973a):130–135.

TIDBALL, M. ELIZABETH. "Teaching: Two Sides of the Coin." *Mary Baldwin* 21(1973b):8–13.

TIDBALL, M. ELIZABETH. "Women Role Models in Higher Education." *Proceedings of American Association of University Women* (1974a):56–59.

TIDBALL, M. ELIZABETH. "A Search for Talented Women." *Change* 6(1974b):51–52, 64.

TIDBALL, M. ELIZABETH. "Wellesley Women in Science." *Wellesley Alumnae Magazine* 59(1975a):1–3.

TIDBALL, M. ELIZABETH. "Women on Campus—and You." *Liberal Education* 61(1975b):285–292.

TIDBALL, M. ELIZABETH. "On Liberation and Competence." *Education Record* 57(1976a):101–110.

TIDBALL, M. ELIZABETH. "Equality and Success." In Dyckman W. Vermilye, ed.: *Individualizing the System.* San Francisco: Jossey-Bass, 1976b, pp. 192–199.

TIDBALL, M. ELIZABETH. "Of Men and Research: The Dominant Themes in American Higher Education Include Neither Teaching nor Women." *Journal of Higher Education* 47(1976c):373–389.

TIDBALL, M. ELIZABETH. "Toward Developing a Common Perspective." *Living at Russell Sage College* 2(1976d):5–6.

TIDBALL, M. ELIZABETH. "Women's Colleges." In Asa S. Knowles, ed.: *The International Encyclopedia of Higher Education.* San Francisco: Jossey-Bass, 1977, pp. 4389–4398.

TIDBALL, M. ELIZABETH. "Encore." Speech delivered on the occasion of the 100th anniversary of the Wilson College Alumnae Association. June 1979.

TIDBALL, M. ELIZABETH. "Women's Colleges and Women Achievers Revisited." *Signs: Journal of Women in Culture and Society* 5(1980a):504–517.

TIDBALL, M. ELIZABETH. "To Use All Their Talents." *Vital Speeches* 46(1980b):380–384.

TIDBALL, M. ELIZABETH. "Educating the New Majority: Women and Achievement." *Scan* 56(1980c):12–15.

TIDBALL, M. ELIZABETH. "The Ideal Gas, A Critical Mass and Homeostasis: Three Lessons from the Sciences." *Women's Studies Quarterly* 11(1983): 5–7.

TIDBALL, M. ELIZABETH. "Baccalaureate Origins of Entrants into American Medical Schools." *Journal of Higher Education* 56(1985):385–402.

TIDBALL, M. ELIZABETH. "Baccalaureate Origins of Recent Natural Science Doctorates." *Journal of Higher Education* 57(1986):606–620.

TIDBALL, M. ELIZABETH, and KISTIAKOWSKY, VERA. "Baccalaureate Origins of American Scientists and Scholars." *Science* 193(1976):646–652.

WALTON, JEAN. "Can You Really Be Both?" *AAHE Bulletin* 38(1986):11–15.

WARE, NORMA C., STECKLER, NICOLE A., and LESERMAN, JANE. "Undergraduate Women: Who Chooses a Science Major?" *Journal of Higher Education* 56(1985):73–84.

13

A Luminous Minority*:
The Contributions of
Catholic Women's Colleges

ABIGAIL MCCARTHY

The story of women religious in higher education in the United States is a story of high achievement despite enormous difficulty. It is also an untold story—and because it is untold, the nation and the Church may lose a precious resource.

Take only one example. In June of 1984 television and newsprint were alive with the prospect that a woman, for the first time, might be nominated for the vice presidency of the United States. In a rare demonstration of cooperation, three of those mentioned—Congresswomen Barbara Kennelly, Barbara Mikulski and Mary Rose Oakar—united to endorse another woman representative, Geraldine Ferraro. All four of these women who had come close to the second highest office in the land were educated—not in the nation's great universities, not in the famed Seven Sisters of the Ivy League—no, they were educated in small Catholic women's colleges. Trinity, Mt. St. Agnes, Ursuline, Marymount Manhattan—the names of their colleges are a mini-litany.

'First used by Patricia Roberts Harris, former Secretary of the Department of Health, Education, and Welfare, to describe women's colleges.

How and why did these women advance into the highest ranks of leadership in the country? There are various reasons, of course—reasons having to do with personality, family, opportunity—but surely one of the reasons has to do with their preparation in institutions with special characteristics. These characteristics have only begun to emerge in recent research.

For most of their history the institutions founded by women religious have been institutions for the education of women. Their colleges share with other women's colleges the strengths discovered in research over the last ten years: (a) their graduates achieve success at a higher ratio than women graduates of coeducational institutions; (b) they have been twice as likely to enter professional schools and to pursue doctorate degrees and two to three times more apt to choose fields like mathematics, chemistry and biology; (c) they are also more apt to complete their degrees and pursue career plans; (d) according to Alexander Astin and others, they were more likely to be self-confident and entertain high aspirations.

Although the religious women sponsoring colleges, their cooperating lay faculties, and alumnae have been proud of individual colleges, it is not until recently that they have become aware of the uniqueness of their collective contribution to higher education. As a speaker at a recent conference put it, they "found little time to reflect on the quality of their achievements or the effect of their actions in higher education." Yet in the 1960s, famed Harvard sociologist David Riesman was able to say that "some of the most adventurous educational leaders have been sisters" and that of their colleges "the best are very good indeed;" and Notre Dame sociologist Robert Hassenger was able to point out that their students were in general more intellectual and more socially concerned than were men in Catholic colleges.

Most of the Catholic women's colleges educated a different population from that of other colleges and, as David Riesman pointed out, they were phenomenally successful in lifting the freshman who came to them from one educational plane to another. Thus they contributed to their students' social mobility. Moreover, they differed in emphasizing occupational and professional preparation as well as an education in the liberal arts. They dealt with students who might well need to earn a living.

Many of these colleges pioneered in raising traditional women's occupations to a professional level. The first bachelor of science in nursing degree was offered at a Catholic college, and the first bachelor in secretarial studies at another. Professional librarians, medical technologists, physical education and health teachers, home economists raised to dieticians—all these emerged from such colleges. The relationship of this fact to the economic well-being of women has yet to be measured.

From the beginning, the stronger Catholic women's colleges differed significantly from the men's colleges. They were deeply influenced as to curriculum by the already established Seven Sisters. They shared with them an underlying assumption that to educate women was to improve society—that women were the bearers of culture.

Perhaps because many of the founding generation of religious were determined that their institutions would equal other institutions for women, or perhaps because sisters preparing for the faculties found secular universities more open to them than were Catholic institutions, their colleges led the way in breaking out of cultural isolation. They led the way in seeking accreditation by state, regional, and national agencies. They themselves joined, or were represented by, lay faculty in national education associations and in professional associations. They saw to it that their students were made eligible for the most prestigious and influential of national and specialized honor societies. It was the College of St. Catherine which was the first Catholic institution *of any kind* to be awarded a Phi Beta Kappa chapter.

Another cause for the strengthening of standards in the women's colleges lay in their need to raise funds. Sisters had to rely heavily on their own contributions, on tuition, and on the support of friends. As a result some of the colleges of women religious were among the first to seek and win help from public sources and private foundations like the General Education Fund of New York, the Carnegie Corporation of New York, and the Rockefeller Foundation. Qualifying for such grants meant that they opened themselves freely to comparison with nonsectarian colleges and state institutions and was yet another way in which they led the Catholic community in breaking out of its cultural isolation.

There were other things which distinguished Catholic women's institutions. From the beginning they differed, in degree at least, from both other women's colleges and men's colleges in the way in which they fostered international exchange and a world outlook. This was in part because of the strong ties which bound the international communities of women religious, in part because of the missionary orientation of others, in part because of the strong departments of music, art, and modern languages—all with a European emphasis—in others.

It was at a women's institution, i.e., St. Mary's College at Notre Dame, that complete courses and majors in theology and philosophy were first made available not only to women but to lay persons. The liturgy as a means of formation was made available to Catholic women in the Benedictine colleges and at the Pius X School of Liturgical Music at Manhattanville. Who can doubt that in these beginnings were sown the seeds of the current struggle of women for fuller participation in the life of the Church?

In fact, until very recently at least, the graduates of these institutions were marked by special qualifications to serve the Church and the world well. First, they were strong in a sense of shared values. The singleness of purpose which originated in the commonality of the sponsoring religious community held students and faculty together and drew alumnae back year after year to renew their sense of community. As Alice Gallin, O.S.U., wrote in an article on the history of the College of New Rochelle, "Without using the word community the nuns really built one and immersed us in it."

Secondly, the majority of these graduates were strongly oriented toward service. Only a few years ago the Higher Education Research Association estimated that there was a 30 percent difference in this orientation between their graduates and those of other institutions. Congresswoman Mary Rose Oakar of Ohio puts it this way: "It was borne in on us that caring for the human family was a logical extension of what education had prepared women for in the past. Social issues, seeing and serving the needs of others, came naturally to us." In sum, the sponsoring bodies could well claim that the ministry of higher education was indeed a ministry. The potential for personal and social change inherent in forming and influencing the development of so many is the very potential of the gospel and of creation continued.

THE STRENGTH OF HISTORY

One of the special characteristics of the Catholic women's colleges lies in their history. From the beginning, the institutions founded by women religious were a testimony to the worth of woman in herself; their existence meant that she had worth apart from her biological function and apart from her ability to give pleasure to, and to sustain men. In post-revolutionary America, according to Emily Taft Douglas, author of *Remember the Ladies*, the story of the women who helped shape America, girls who sought more than an elementary education, "sought it in certain sectarian institutions such as those of the Ursuline Nuns in New Orleans." That Ursuline convent was founded in 1727. Behind that convent lay a two-hundred-year struggle of women religious with church and state authorities for the right to teach girls and women. The Ursulines (as well as other women religious) held, according to one of their historians, that "woman has a *right* (italics mine), as a man has, to the full development of the gifts she has received from God."

It was the convent-educated women who elicited the admiration of John Adams, Benjamin Franklin, and Thomas Jefferson, who came to the French court from an America where women were, at best, semi-literate.

The ancestors of today's women religious poured out of the towns and villages of France, Italy, and Germany in the seventeenth, eighteenth, and early nineteenth centuries, intent on educating girls and women, intent on the mission of the church. They came to America and what they accomplished was prodigious. Only recently an article in a major news magazine summed up their accomplishment: they built the most far-flung and accessible system of higher education for women the world has ever known.

In America they took the daughters of frontiersmen and immigrants and lifted them from one level to another and, in so doing, transformed families and communities. Convent education in either the French or German model was important in the "civilizing" of frontier after frontier and was sought by leading settlers for their daughters whether they were Catholic or not. Convent education helped shape the country and from many of these convents sprang the strong colleges later founded by women religious.

In the early nineteenth century "higher education" for women meant academy education, although the courses offered and the ages of matriculation were often the same as those in men's institutions already called colleges, even universities like Georgetown and Harvard. Private Catholic girls' schools—as distinguished from the parochial schools which developed later to provide education for tide after tide of immigrants—were among the best of these. By the last quarter of the nineteenth century, such Catholic academies were spread from Maine to California and from Minnesota to Texas.

Long before 1880, some of these schools offered college-level courses and extra years of study. Some few had degree-granting charters awarded in approximately the same time frame as those of the earliest women's colleges. Elmira was chartered in 1855 and Vassar in 1865. St. Mary of the Woods had a similar charter in

1848 and St. Mary's at Notre Dame by 1862. It was undoubtedly only religious restraints that deterred their foundresses from calling them colleges. This long history in liberal education was one of the strengths of the women religious who were to found the later colleges or to develop them from existing academies.

Parallel to that history was an equally long history in the training of teachers. Many religious orders brought developed methods of education and courses of study with them from Europe. American-founded groups of sisters instituted training courses of their own—Mother Seton's nuns at Emmitsburg, Maryland, for example, were given professional training for their work in 1810, and in the 1820s the convents in Kentucky had such courses taught by professors from nearby Mt. St. Mary's College.

Over the years this emphasis on the education of religious for their work in teaching and other professions created a community of educated women. In 1983, Sister Lucille McKillop, R.S.M., president of Salve Regina: The Newport College, could say—with no fear of contradiction—that American religious are the most highly educated group of women in the world!

When the degree-granting Catholic women's colleges finally emerged at the turn of the century they had "a living endowment" of supporting sisterhoods with experience in administering institutions, with professional training, and a history of relating to and meeting the needs of the wider community. Between 1896 and 1910 nine such colleges were founded and double that number in the decade following. Not only did their foundresses see higher education as "the need of the times" but they were soon making it clear that the times demanded not only education for mothers, teachers, and nurses but for such highly trained women as industrial and scientific specialists, physicians and lawyers. They emphasized the need for proper accrediting and rating by national agencies. Graduate preparation of faculty became a priority. In the 1920s, American nun educators were being prepared in universities like Oxford, Munich, and the Sorbonne as well as the best universities in this country. By 1955, there were 116 Catholic baccalaureate colleges for women, plus 24 two-year colleges.

THE PICTURE TODAY

What of the institutions of women religious today? The ranks of nun educators diminish; the prospective student pool is declining; the women's colleges feel the pressure of competition from newly coeducational colleges. Some colleges have been closed. Others have lost their identities in mergers. Nevertheless, the strengths of the institutions sponsored by women religious are there to be built upon in new ways and under new circumstances. Sisters in the ministry of higher education are drawing together to discern the promise in the future. And what do they see?

They see that not only are they the most highly educated group of women in the world but, more important, they are a group with the longest history and brightest record as *educators.*

Forty percent of the women's colleges in the United States today are sponsored by women religious. They also sponsor eighty or more small coeducational colleges. The distinguishing mark Riesman found so important endures—the difference these colleges have made in the lives of their students.

A Profile of Women's College Presidents, issued by the Women's College Coalition, reports that "both women and men presidents of historically Catholic colleges are overwhelmingly first-generation college graduates themselves. These presidents thus confirm, by personal experience, the often-stated special role of the historically Catholic college in opening higher education and higher education leadership to new populations."

In a later report the Women's College Coalition makes it clear that Catholic women's colleges have led the way in offering innovative new programs for women to meet new needs. In citing colleges which have pioneered in nontraditional programs for women and which have later been adapted to and adopted by coeducational institutions (such as weekend colleges and external degree programs), they name four Catholic colleges to one secular one.

The study unearthed other facts which suggest that religious educators remain true to the spirit of mission. Women faculty are more likely to be tenured in their institutions than in other women's colleges, which may indicate a heightened sensitivity to justice. They also show an increasing commitment to the enrollment of minority students.

To see women in leadership positions—to have strong role models—is the normal experience for women in these institutions. Today, most of the presidents of the colleges founded by women religious are women, as are almost all of the presidents of the Catholic women's colleges. These women presidents, moreover, are widely involved in leadership positions beyond their own schools. They serve on nonprofit and corporate boards, thus making highly competent and effective women visible in the community at large. Over half of the faculty are women and the proportion is even higher in disciplines thought nontraditional for women—that is, the natural and mathematical sciences.

The importance to women of such role models has been strongly stated by M. Elizabeth Tidball: "The development of young women of talent into career successful adults is directly proportional to the number of role models to whom they have access." This is especially important to women in the Church because more and more Catholic women are going to college—many from Catholic groups in which there was once a certain hostility to education for women. In 1978–79, women were 54 percent of the total enrollment in Catholic colleges and universities. In 1981 they were 57 percent. In other independent colleges they were only 48 percent. This means that the emerging generation of educated Catholics will be comprised of more women than men. How these women see themselves, how they view their service to the Church and the world, is of utmost importance.

The promise lies, finally, in the attachment lay women demonstrate for the institutions of women religious. Most reentry women seek out their campuses and say that they feel more comfortable, and find the help they need, there. Women's colleges have the best records of alumnae-alumni giving in all higher education and that giving has risen significantly in recent years. Recently the rise has been higher in alumnae giving to the Catholic women's colleges than in other sectors. The loyalty of so many women to these institutions suggests a bright future for networking and the possibility of forming strong alliances among Catholic educated women.

Sisters looking to the future can also see in their institutions promise for men. Men have for too long carried the burden of life and decisions in our society, and they have not known or been able to see how they could share this burden and use the gifts of the other half of the human race. The institutions of women religious in higher education provide them with a unique place of learning.

As faculty members they share on a more equitable basis with women than they would in other institutions where women are apt to comprise only 25 percent or less of the faculty. Their department heads are apt to be women. They work with women deans and presidents. Their interaction with women students, studies have shown, is also on a more equitable basis than it would be in male-dominated institutions where women may well be brighter students but tend to defer to males. Studies also give us every reason to believe that the above factors have a discernible effect on these men's attitude toward women and way of thinking about them.

They tend to think about them as persons, as colleagues and friends rather than as "the other." Their opinion of women's ability is higher than that of men without like experience. They tend to acknowledge discrimination against women and the exclusion of women from the networking process in academia and the work place and believe in working to eliminate these. They believe in equal pay for equal work and approve equal pay for work of equal value. They believe in maternity leave and benefits; they approve of "flextime." One could go on.

It is too soon to know what the effect has been on men students of their experience in the institutions sponsored by women religious; one can only assume that it is similar. More and more male students are attending women's colleges as part-time students in special courses, as exchange students in consortia, or as graduate students. In addition to seeing women in administration and faculty leadership positions, they see women students as campus leaders and experience the more healthy give and take in classes where women are on an equal basis with men.

Postscript:

AND THE VISION CONTINUES*

"A Luminous Minority," which concentrates on the traditional mission and concern of Catholic colleges, founded by sisters, for the education of women, particularly Catholic women, was written for the Neylan Commission for presentation at the first Neylan Conference held in 1983. The 127 Neylan Colleges are those U.S. colleges founded by and still related to orders of women religious. They are both women's and coeducational colleges whose collective mission is to create an effective voice for their common heritage and sense of values. The 1983 conference marked the first time that women religious gathered to discuss the higher education mission of their orders, past, present, and future. Approximately 325 attended.

The Neylan Commission, which sponsored the conference, is part of the Association of Catholic Colleges and Universities, named for Edith and Genevieve Neylan, two sisters who provided the support for its creation. Through triennial conferences and other meetings and projects, the commission provides a forum for the discussion,

*Prepared by Brigid Driscoll, R.S.H.M., President, Marymount College, Tarrytown, N.Y., and current chair for the Neylan Commission; and Alice Gallin, O.S.U., Executive Director, Association of Catholic Colleges and Universities.

clarification, and preservation of the philosophies and values that undergird member colleges.

The first Neylan conference, "A Call to New Leadership: Women Religious in the Ministry of Higher Education," was designed to bring a new cooperative focus to the collective efforts of the colleges to educate their students who are primarily women. The energy was electric and the discussion powerful. All went away with a renewed sense of purpose and support.

Three years later came the next step in the quest for a vision for the future, "A Call to New Leadership II: Definitions and Directions for the Higher Education Apostolate." This conference indeed produced a new vision—establishment of a collaborative effort to serve women's educational needs around the world. A critical link was made between the education of women and the potential to solve the overwhelming, worldwide problems of famine, disease, and conflict.

Is it possible to make even a small dent in these massive and complex international problems? The women who attended this conference believe it is. In most developing countries the primary producers of food and, most certainly, the caretakers of children are women. Providing such women with education will have a direct and lasting impact on them, their families and their countries. According to Joel Read, S.S.S.F., President of Alverno College and Chair of this second conference, "over 500 million women in these primarily agricultural societies are illiterate. It is presently not possible for them to make the changes that can bring a positive difference to their societies."

Collectively, these colleges have the resources to make a significant impact in these areas if they can build a collaborative program drawing on their considerable strengths—175,000 current students, 600,000 alumnae, assets of nearly 1.5 billion, linkages with one another and collaboration with other ministries of their religious communities in eighty-two other countries. A resource we cannot overlook is the many lifetimes of dedicated service by women religious to humankind.

The practicalities of the collaboration that would need to be put in place have not yet been developed, but using all the sophisticated technologies and programs that are currently available and maintaining the will to make such an effort work, their vision can and should be translated into practical programs. Prospective women students (as well as men) from around the globe could be linked together in very meaningful ways through the new technologies of teleconferencing and educated according to their needs. They could prepare for study in one-another's countries, they could share problems and possible solutions to recurring and emerging problems, they could provide a forum for the open discussion of differing values, and possibly develop new methods for understanding, appreciating, and allowing for cultural differences to flourish rather than to be the focal point of conflict. Tall orders? Indeed, but so initially was the creation of a system for educating American women in the early twentieth century, and they met and are meeting that challenge every day.

14

Women's Studies, Feminist Goals, and the Science of Women

MARILYN J. BOXER

Following commencement ceremonies at a large urban university recently, a student graduating with a major in women's studies was asked what she intended "to do" with her degree. "I'm going to think," she replied, leaving her computer-specialist interrogator momentarily speechless. If her answer might have dismayed some of her more activist feminist foremothers, it also provides insight into the potential, as well as the problems and paradoxes, of women's studies that are the subject of this essay.

The founders of women's studies, activists in the women's liberation movement during the late 1960s, intended by recovering a lost heritage of women's experiences and perceptions to foster feminist consciousness.[1] As "consciousness-raising" through small-group discussions was intended to move participants to action that would achieve the social, economic, and political equality of the sexes, so "female studies" would provide an intellectual foundation for the almost forgotten but recently renewed struggle for women's rights. Though a few of the earliest courses were offered in nonacademic settings, or in community-based "free schools," the locus of the women's studies movement, reflecting the preponderant role of university students, faculty, and in some cases staff, was the world of higher education. With the support of faculty and administrators (often sensitized to the validity of feminist claims through recent experiences with Afro-American or Mexican-American studies), women-oriented courses, largely in the humanities and social sciences, were developed, and women's studies programs were established.

During the decade of the 1970s, with a momentum and magnitude that defied an overall retrenchment of higher education, women's studies grew to include thousands of courses on hundreds of campuses across the nation, more than three hundred of which established integrated women's studies programs (including a few departments). Innovative in structure as well as content, they appeared first in the Northeast, Northwest, North Central, and Far West, by 1973 also in the Midwest, Southeast, and Southwest regions of the United States; at public and private institutions, including two-year and four-year colleges, church-affiliated as well as independent, research universities and technical institutions. The expansion of women's studies throughout the 1970s and into the mid-1980s, from two programs in 1970 (at San Diego State and Cornell) to 150 in 1975 to 300 in 1980 and 450 by 1985, testifies to the continued vitality of the feminist impulse in the grass roots of America, despite periodic pronouncements of the decline of the women's movement and the advent of "post-feminism." It also reflects an extraordinary expansion of scholarship about women.[2]

SCHOLARLY APPROACHES AND ACHIEVEMENTS

Beginning with preparation for the first courses on women in history and women in literature, women's studies scholars undertook a microscopic search for forgotten feminists, literary figures, and women unorthodox enough to have made a mark on a civilization, where a women's virtue was said to reside in her submission and her treasure to consist of her children. Measured by the traditional values of androcentric knowledge, it often appeared as if women were universal victims. But the painstaking resurrection of neglected sources (published as well as unpublished) soon revealed that some women indeed had risen to positions of influence and that most, though submerged and anonymous, had contributed vitally to the development of social and economic as well as family life.[3]

These discoveries led to a second stage in the production of women's studies scholarship. As they examined what traditional scholars had to say about women, the new researchers found purportedly "scientific" studies about women riddled with value judgments. Darwin's inference that "if men are capable of a decided preeminence over women in many subjects, the average of mental power in man must be above that of woman," Freud's pronouncement of the "inferiority of the clitoris," Erikson's characterization of a female's identity as "already defined in her kind of attractiveness" to men, Moynihan's diagnosis of matrifocality among American blacks as "pathological," anthropologists' identification of woman with nature and man with culture, sociologists' assimilation of women's status to men's, economists' exclusion of women's nonwaged work from definitions of labor activity, all illustrate biases present in allegedly neutral social science. Furthermore, feminist scholars universally recognized the denigration of women implicit in conventions of language, the "he/man" speech, that turned them into a "marked" and "muted" variation on the (male) model of human being.[4]

Like the practitioners of the "new social history" who sought to rewrite the human record "from the bottom up," researchers in women's studies focused their lenses on women's lives in women's own terms: woman as subject not object, women as producer of goods and reproducer of families, woman as constructor of culture. This scholarship was heavily influenced by a number of essays that were quickly labeled "classic," in recognition of their impact on all the disciplines that constitute women's studies. So many key scholars contributed to this flurry of scholarly activity that it is impossible to recognize them all here. However, the alacrity with which the insights of such scholars as historians Gerda Lerner, Joan Kelly-Gadol, and Carroll Smith-Rosenberg, anthropologists Gayle Rubin, Sherry Ortner, and Michelle Rosaldo, psychologists Sandra and Daryl Bem, Phyllis Chesler, Matina Horner, and Naomi Weisstein, sociologist Pauline Bart, political scientist Jo Freeman, literary critics Barbara Smith, Annette Kolodny, Kate Millett, and Elaine Showalter, linguist Robin Lakoff, poets Adrienne Rich and Alice Walker, and other early contributors infused work across disciplinary lines may be explained partially by the great thirst of the first generation of female scholars who understood the epistemological implications of male-centered bodies of knowledge. Like "Copernicus shattering our geo-centricity, Darwin shattering our species-centricity," they used their training in research methods and critical analysis to expose the fallacies of androcentricity. Conventional assumptions about "femininity" and socially constructed definitions of women's "nature" were reexamined with a new "double vision" that allowed female perspectives to emerge.[5]

From the work of Gerda Lerner and Joan Kelly came the recognition that commonly accepted interpretations of "watershed" events or periods in history ignored or distorted their impact on women; they maintained that the European Renaissance and the Jacksonian era in the United States, respectively, enhanced opportunities open to men but ushered in eras of relative decline in the status of women. Smith-Rosenberg countered prevailing assumptions about the psychological and social significance of "homosocial" relationships by demonstrating the common and casual acceptance of lifelong emotional ties among women in eighteenth- and nineteenth-century America, which she linked to the rigid gender-role differentiation of Victorian marriage.

Rosaldo and Rubin used cross-cultural studies to argue, respectively, that the source of asymmetry in the cultural evaluation of women and men lies in the dichotomization of human activities into public and domestic spheres and in the creation of a "sex/gender role system" through which societies translate human biology into culturally prescribed notions of femininity and masculinity. Ortner also drew on anthropological research to trace societal evaluation of the sexes to the identification of femaleness with nature and maleness with culture, where the latter signified the superiority of human consciousness and control over bodily functions and infantile modes of relationship.

The pioneering contributions of the Bems, Horner, and Weisstein all raised new questions about research on sex differences. They showed the influence of preconceived definitions of femininity and masculinity and of social structures on researchers, teachers, and experimental subjects in the building of psychological theories. For example, Weisstein showed how both clinical psychologists and experimental psychologists erected "Kinder, Kuche, Kirche" into "scientific law," limiting women's world to children, cooking, and church, by failing to put their own reflections and observations to the test of evidence.

Horner, in a controversial study of achievement motivation, attributed women's allegedly low achievement drive to an internalized "fear of success." Her successors pointed to external factors that made repression or denial of achievement needs a means some women adopted to avoid social penalties for "unfeminine behavior." The Bems showed how social assumptions about sex roles trained children from the earliest ages to value females less than males, creating a "nonconscious ideology" that belied the allegedly free choice of career offered to adult women. Sandra Bem went on to develop a new "androgyny" scale that permitted subjects to score highly on sets of traits labeled both masculine and feminine. Thus, an androgynous person could be "sympathetic," a supposedly feminine characteristic, as well as "athletic," a stereotypically masculine characteristic. Later research analyzed the personality differences between persons of both sexes who show high and low levels of androgyny.

Sociologist Pauline Bart, who today teaches in a psychiatry department, stimulated the reappraisal of diagnoses of female mental illness, especially "Portnoy's Mother's Complaint." Her study of clinically depressed middle-aged women demonstrated that it was typically "feminine" women, who under social pressure eschewed self-fulfillment for service to family, that suffered most.

Jo Freeman parlayed her experience as a graduate student in one of the first community groups active in the 1960s "rebirth of feminism" into a prize-winning book on the politics of women's liberation. She traced the origins of the new movement to both an "older," highly structured and nationally-active group of women with close links to government and an informal network of "younger," grass-roots groups that grew out of the New Left, student and civil rights movement of the 1960s.

In literature and linguistic studies, influential early work demonstrated anew—the historian Mary Beard was insistent on this in the 1930s—the power of language to affect human consciousness, attitude, and behavior. Lakoff showed how exclusionary terminology (the "generic man"), and Kolodny, masculinist imagery ("rape of the land," "the virgin soil") helped narrow "woman's place." Smith and Walker pointed out that even white feminist scholars often ignored Black women's lives and contributions; they not only stimulated salutary self-criticism of racism within women's studies programs but also provided important new ideas, images and inspiration. After recovering such writers as Zora Neale Hurston, Margaret Walker, and Alice Walker herself—as well as heroic historical figures like Harriet Tubman, Sojourner Truth, and Mary McLeod Bethune—white feminists could no longer claim the name "woman" for themselves alone.

For Showalter, revision pointed toward a new "feminist criticism." She claimed that women's experience might offer an authentically different aesthetic and consciousness from that of men, which was labeled, in the accepted literary canon, "universal." Adrienne Rich envisioned a new world, "when we [women] dead awaken." Writers or readers, we would cease to live primarily in men's eyes. Seeing anew, we would rename ourselves—and through that audacity, change the world.

Exhilarated by the new work, women's studies pioneers freely shared their research and teaching experiences. Led by Florence Howe and Sheila Tobias, who compiled and published the earliest *Female Studies*, they mimeographed and photocopied scholarly articles and course outlines and passed them from coast to coast. They presented papers at academic conferences, published articles in established disciplinary journals, and in 1972 created three of their own, the cross-disciplinary *Women's Studies, Feminist Studies*, and *Women's Studies Newsletter*. By 1975, supported by such sterling institutions as the University of Chicago Press, Barnard College, and the Ford Foundation, *SIGNS: Journal of Women in Culture and Society* joined a list of scholarly periodicals that today, expanded with more specialized journals, includes at least two dozen. Similarly, academic women founded their own caucuses and committees in the major professional associations of most disciplines. In 1977, university faculty joined with practitioners at all levels, community as well as campus, to form the National Women's Studies Association.

By the decade's end, some women's studies scholars had moved beyond the restoration of women and women's perspectives to accepted canons and the critique of androcentric interpretation and methodology to suggest that women's studies constituted more than a multidisciplinary accumulation of new content on neglected topics. Examining the histories of traditional disciplines, philosophical definitions of the concepts of disciplinarity and interdisciplinarity, and debates about the structure of knowledge, Sandra Coyner used the work of Thomas Kuhn on scientific revolutions to argue that women's studies had become an emergent discipline. The common core of premises shared by the women's studies professional community appeared to constitute, at least in embryonic form, the paradigmatic basis upon which a new science of women would be built.

Coyner herself decided to discard her professional identity as a historian, and to define herself as a "woman's studiest." Elsewhere, scholars in women's studies adopted the label "feminology." Used as early as 1900 to describe studies of women, this term would lend itself to the more graceful occupational title of "feminologist." It might facilitate acceptance of women's studies as a new science of women. However, it would also deemphasize the radical, pro-woman mission of the new scholarship which, ironically, its very success served to obscure.[6] "Women's studies," most felt, must remain undeniably feminist studies.

During the 1970s, however, its emphasis moved beyond criticizing the omission and distortion of women in traditional bodies of knowledge, past the political stance that blamed male conspiracy for the oppression of women, toward a critical analysis of the epistemological foundations of male-biased curricula and androcentric cultures. The goal remained the same: to dismantle error, to rebuild knowledge, to transform teaching, and to educate women and men of all classes and races equally for social roles of their choice.

Women's studies became less the "academic arm" of a political movement than the vehicle of fundamental critique of the dominance in the humanities and social sciences of methods of research and interpretation that tend to distort understanding of both sexes while disadvantaging women. Since the ancient Greeks, who took "man as the measure of all things," woman has been defined by Western philosophy and science as a "partial man, or a negative image of man, or the convenient object of man's needs." Women's studies aims to restore full humanity to women by revisioning the very basis of intellectual endeavor. It challenges male hegemony over not only culture and society, but also over the structure of educational institutions and the content of knowledge itself. Thus, it marks a new departure in the history of higher education as well as the history of women. Learned women today seek to widen not only their own orbit but also to expand the "circumference of truth."[7]

THE HISTORICAL CONTEXT

In the nineteenth century, when universal public education began to offer new opportunities to men, it tendered to women little that would broaden their view beyond the family circle. Rousseau's famous prescription for Julie (Emile's ideal wife) "to be pleasing in [man's] sight, to win his respect and love, to train him in childhood, to tend him in manhood, to counsel and to console, to make his life pleasant and happy," became the basis for female education. Girls were taught to conform their aspirations to domestic and nurturing roles. When, after centuries of playing a central role in providing for their family's subsistence, "women of the people" were marginalized by the reorganization of production, they were, in the new era of industrial revolution and "careers open to talent," enjoined to remain "eternally feminine" and to deny individual aspiration. For the good of society, women were to become Victorian ladies, pious, pure, submissive, and above all, domestic, to cater to their families' emotional needs and to safeguard social virtue.[8]

When the establishment of public school systems created a demand for numerous low-paid teachers, women were recruited to work but denied equal opportunities for advancement. Often sharing prevailing assumptions about femininity, female educators sometimes utilized notions of maternal instinct to argue that women made superior teachers and deserved greater power in their profession. The "bonds of womanhood" that limited their grasp might, they hoped, also produce collective strength. But the earliest higher education for women rested firmly on assumptions of psychosexual differences. Female students were to be trained to serve in feminine ways. As "Republican mothers" educating sons for citizenship in the new American nation, or as "Daughters of the Nation" raised to be "worthy wives for the Great Men" of the new French republic, they needed to develop their moral sensibility, not their mental acuity. If unmarried, however, they might also fulfill "woman's sacred office" as teacher.[9]

In the latter nineteenth century, leaders of the developing women's rights movements in European countries as well as the United States postulated new motives for women's education. They stressed access to higher education, and the opening of the liberal professions, as demands central to women's "emancipation." Not content with "special education," a ladies' curriculum that often excluded classical languages, modern history, and laboratory sciences, they set out to disprove prevailing "scientific" notions of female intellectual inferiority. Proving they could master the "men's curriculum," some women won degrees at prestigious universities (especially in Europe) and founded women's colleges modeled on men's, which were designed to be as rigorous as the institutions that educated society's elite. Educators such as Henry Durant, who founded Wellesley College in 1857, and M. Carey Thomas, who became first dean of Bryn Mawr College in 1885, said "Women can do it" and made no concession to sex differences. Often the first generation of college graduates eschewed "femininity" and female roles altogether. Carey Thomas said, "Our failures only marry." Women, it seemed, had to choose between family and career.[10]

But most of the girls and women who won the privileges of higher education became "coeds." Reflecting a conventional sexual division of labor, some of the first coeducational institutions required different assignments of women and men (health reformers suggested women students make beds or wash clothes as physical education). In 1911, 60 percent of women faculty in coeducational universities taught home economics—even though their doctoral degree might be in American history! For decades the percentage of degrees granted to women lagged far behind their proportionate enrollment as undergraduates. By the mid-twentieth century, however, when the numbers of women attaining degrees at U.S. colleges and universities began to approach that of men, few exceptional requirements remained, and it was widely assumed that coeducation offered equal opportunities to both sexes. The most significant contribution of the new feminism of the 1960s and 1970s to the education of women lay in its perception that sexism in the curriculum—in textbooks ("the pioneer and his wife moved west"), course outlines (only male writers included in "Twentieth-century American Fiction"), and bodies of knowledge (generalizations about human experience based exclusively on male subjects)—made "coeducation" a myth. Or, more precisely, another social experience that reinforced the secondary, companionate status of women (the *female* as coed). The "men's curriculum" was just that: largely about, by, and for men. To collegiate women, coeducation meant fitting into a model that alienated aspects of themselves that transcended conventional, ascribed social roles.[11]

In criticizing the content, method, and purposes of scholarship about women, much contemporary feminist analysis faults the positivism that permeates the social sciences. As it developed in the late nineteenth century, the "science of society" incorporated, along with faith in "objectivity" and empiricism, the Comtean concept of a functionally necessary sex division of life and labor. Based on his belief in the "perpetual infancy" and "natural subordination" of women, Comte declared that "sociology will prove that the equality of the sexes . . . is incompatible with all social existence, by showing that each sex has special and permanent functions that it must fulfill in the natural economy of the human family." Attributing to women greater moral and spiritual sensitivity than to men, Comte denied them intellectual power, considering the feminine qualities "hostile to scientific abstraction and concentration." Furthermore, he asserted with the authority of nineteenth-century science, that the "indubitable organic inferiority of feminine genius has been confirmed by decisive experiment." While Comte gained repute as the "father of modern sociology," the impetus toward gender equality that had flourished among his own precursors, the Saint-Simonians, faded. Comte's "positive philosophy" offered women "veneration" rather than emancipation. It employed new, allegedly neutral scientific terminology to support old prejudices.

EPISTEMOLOGY, STRUCTURES, AND VALUES

Women's studies scholars, often accused of bias for their women-oriented stance ("where are the men's studies?"), tend to reject even the possibility of objectivity. Indeed, they deny that value-free knowledge is possible. They criticize the dichotomies conventionally used to define masculinity and femininity—rational/irrational, logical/emotional, active/passive, field-independent/field-dependent— as not only ahistorical, class- and culture-bound, but more importantly as derivatives of a philosophical dualism and acceptance of a subject-object split that cannot survive the scrutiny of a Heidegger or Derrida. Social scientists of the nineteenth and twentieth centuries, who assumed with Comte a stance of scientific objectivity, developed a definition of female nature that reinforced the biases of ancient philosophers. Women's studies has mounted a broad and sustained attack on all forms of knowledge that consider women as objects and "lesser men," that ignore female subjectivity or that abstract women from their social position. Drawing on the science of hermeneutics, feminist scholars insist that knowledge is never "objective," for the knower is always grounded in a specific historical and cultural context. Phenomenologists and deconstructionists agree.[12]

This critique of epistemology is paralleled in women's studies by criticism of the fragmentation of knowledge into discrete disciplines, of the separation of modes of learning into affective and cognitive, and of the compartmentalization of individual lives into professional and personal pursuits. The impulse toward wholeness reflects not only the "interdisciplinary" nature of women's studies, but also the salience for academic feminists of resolving the conflict between scholarship and politics.

From its origins in the liberation movements of the 1960s, women's studies has been linked with women's liberation. Absent the women's liberation movement of the 1960s, women's studies might not exist on U.S. campuses; but students in the 1980s frequently do not know or understand this. Instructors today must teach their students the heritage of that period as well as of others more remote. To survivors of that rebirth of feminism and pioneers of women's studies, the danger of the mid-1980s seems less that "consciousness-raising" and community action—strategies occasionally confounded with higher education in the founding years—might corrupt the academic enterprise, than that "cooptation" will, as predicted by some early skeptics, lead to loss of feminist identity. As scholars in women's studies become more accepted in academe, they have more to lose by appearing radical. The pressure to forego the early thrust toward structural change is strong; many women's studies faculty facing the dangers of marginality and witness to the object lessons of well-publicized tenure battles in the late 1970s and early 1980s, focus more on research than on reorganization of the classroom, the university or the social world. Still, in the pursuit of knowledge they strengthen not only their own case for tenure, promotion, and professional distinction, but also the presence of women and women's studies in an environment still overwhelmingly male. Women—feminist women—with power to influence the decisions of faculty committees (and university administrators) are essential to a continued attack on sexist scholarship, teaching, and behavior.

Feminists sensitive to social process have linked the fight against women's oppression to struggles against bias based on age, class, race, religion and sexual preference. Women's studies teachers similarly understand the necessity of pluralism in their own work, and they incorporate materials and perspectives relevant to all women whenever possible. Yet, while the study of women and women-oriented perspectives continues to expand across the traditional curriculum, women's studies itself must acknowledge internal gaps. All too often the norm in women's studies courses has been the white, middle-class woman. Only in the past few years has significant research begun to appear dealing with women of color; except for a few programs or departments where they reside together, women's studies and ethnic studies intersect more in theory than in practice. Women of lesbian identity likewise appear infrequently in course materials and topic outlines; heterosexuality tends to be assumed in discussions of family relationships, sex role socialization, healthy sexual behavior, and political perspective. There is concern within women's studies to create both a body of knowledge and an environment that fosters growth and development of all women and men. A continuing distrust of hierarchical and institutional power, still largely in male hands and organized to women's disadvantage (the "clockwork of male careers" impeding the advancement of women), tempers the increasing integration of women's studies and its advocates into "mainstream" academia.[13]

PROGRAM MODELS

After almost two decades of subjecting higher education to feminist analysis, and producing both highly sophisticated critiques of the disciplines (critiques that unfortunately are more often unheard and unread than answered by traditional scholars) and prodigious quantities of new research on women, women's studies practitioners today may point to a formidable array of institutions dedicated to pursuit and transmission of the new knowledge. In four to five hundred colleges and universities, women's studies programs draw faculty and financial resources from established departments to offer not only thousands of courses but hundreds of degrees. According to a 1984 listing, 24 institutions offer the A.A., 195 the bachelor's, 50 the master's, and 18 the Ph.D., while 205 award undergraduate and ten graduate minors and 54 give certificates. Many of these programs depend for administration and development on a crossdisciplinary committee coordinated by a faculty member assigned either to a traditional department or jointly to women's studies and to a department.

While this structure may facilitate the spread of women's studies across campus, it also tends to limit possibilities for development of a carefully articulated and stable program. At worst, the committee must depend entirely on volunteers; not even release time is provided by the university. Even with some institutional support the coordinating committee has little, if any, authority and its need may be ignored when personnel decisions, class schedules, and budget allocations are made. Faculty dedicated to women's studies sometimes find themselves unable to teach preferred courses or even penalized for devoting time to nontraditional scholarship and service. More autonomous programs, with faculty lines in women's studies, are able to create a stronger focus for women's studies in the university, to stimulate new research and develop new courses, to provide the ground for optimal testing of the potential of women-oriented scholarship and teaching.

The most common model today is one that combines a small number of full-time tenured women's studies faculty who teach "core" (often interdisciplinary) courses with part-time or adjunct instructors who teach specialized courses linked to specific disciplines and housed in traditional departments. Examples of the former might include the core courses taught at San Francisco State University, "Feminism: The Basic Questions," "Translating Women's Experience," "Comparative Models of Women's Experience," "Women in

Groups," and "Women as Creative Agents." Typical of the latter would be courses such as "Women in American History," "Psychology of Women," "Black Women Writers," or "Women and Economic Development."

Whatever the structure of women's studies programs, they depend for success on the commitment of dedicated faculty and supportive administrators willing to place resources in women's studies. Women's studies is most successful where it is integrated into academic structures fully enough to command a goodly share of instructional and research funds, the respect of faculty, and the attention of students. To that extent, it must become a "discipline" like any other.

LIBERAL EDUCATION AND RESEARCH ON WOMEN

Buttressing the women's studies programs are more than forty major centers for research on women, a few recently established with million-dollar endowments. Collectively they secure and enhance the productivity of thousands of scholar-teachers and provide stability and continuity for the new professional community. These centers participate in the National Council for Research on Women, a consortium that fosters collaborative work among some two thousand men and women scholars engaged in feminist research, policy analysis and educational programs in the United States and abroad. It also functions to coordinate the storage and retrieval of information about research by women.

Founded in 1981, the National Council for Research on Women has been supported by grants from the Ford Foundation (which has contributed over $5 million over the past decade to research on women sponsored by participating centers) and from the Carnegie Corporation of New York. The major purpose of the council is to foster research on women and provide for the dissemination of that research to society at large with particular emphasis on adding to the knowledge base and informing public policy development.

To help fulfill the ultimate goal of women's studies of transforming the traditional curriculum, several dozen funded projects, and many others, are now devoted to incorporating the new scholarship into basic instruction across the spectrum of courses designated to fulfill "general education" requirements. The reinstitution of breadth requirements on many campuses, and the concurrent "back-to-basics" trend, in some cases pose a danger that newer curricular offerings such as women's studies may be eliminated from degree programs or dismissed as frills by students intent on quick fulfillment of graduation requirements and attainment of professional goals. Therefore, projects for transforming the liberal arts curriculum through the incorporation of the new scholarship on women have devised means to broaden the outreach of women's studies. They run faculty development workshops and conferences, plan strategies for curriculum revision, prepare sample course outlines and materials, provide consultants, and emphasize the value of "gender-balancing." Some focus on issues of race and class as well as gender. These projects, which depend on women's studies scholarship and leadership, although they may be institutionally independent, help to assure that women's studies reaches an ever-growing audience.[14]

Moving to correct notions, sometimes held by persons unfamiliar with the new scholarship, that women's studies is simply feminist politics, leaders in the field have pointed out that, on the contrary, it is quintessentially a part of the liberal arts and belongs in the core as well as throughout the curriculum. Historian Carolyn Lougee, in a forum on the "rebuilding" of general education through reinstitution of required humanities courses, has called attention to the "necessity of keeping the corpse [of traditional western civilization course] from being resurrected intact." For the absence of women in the vast panorama, she notes, reflects a narrow purpose.

Celebrating the superiority of the European cultural heritage that it largely retold, the traditional humanities curriculum assumed a community of values among the peoples and nations of Western Europe and North America; it also conveyed a "homogenizing and normative" judgment about what in human experience was important. Lougee shows that its implicit ideals and aesthetics, linked to civic and political participation or embodied in specific disciplines or genres, served to eliminate the contributions of women and other nondominant groups, whose roles and responsibilities limited them to personal lives and "useful arts." Therefore, requisite to a new and broader definition of humanities is "the need to understand community life as more than public, as a continuum of private and public, and to define the audience as adults rather than merely citizens, as men and women rather than merely men. . . . The challenge is seeking a dialectic of commonality in and through difference rather than denying it in the name of a unitary image to which all should aspire or conform."[15]

While Lougee thus argues eloquently for transforming the traditional curriculum through inclusion of women, Florence Howe, a founder of the women's studies movement and editor of the *Women's Studies Quarterly*, shows that women's studies serves the goals of liberal education in five fundamental ways: by its interdisciplinary, synthesizing approach, its emphasis on critical analysis, its problem-solving stance, its elucidation of the role of value judgment in the creation of knowledge, and its promotion of socially-beneficial goals (advocacy through scholarship being shared historically with such other "disciplines" as anthropology and sociology, which were established with goals of promoting, respectively, cross-cultural understanding and social harmony).

Many other educational leaders, today engaged in ardent self-criticism, have also suggested an appropriate role for women's studies. Recognizing that the ideal shape of liberal learning requires study of traditional academic disciplines in depth, so that students may gain insight into the complexity and coherent nature of academic inquiry, they point to the value of interdisciplinary studies as a balance for the narrow compass of some individual disciplines. Because they require comprehension and integration of several approaches to knowledge, they may also serve to link liberal and professional studies. As the recent report of the Association of American Colleges ("Integrity in the College Curriculum") pointed out,

> Where interdisciplinary studies are focused on major world problems . . . they offer an attractive bridge between intellectual discipline and career preparation. Real life, we need to remember, is interdisciplinary.

For professional as well as liberal arts students, the report noted, the skills in critical analysis and generalization learned from women's studies and similar fields, are essential. It also recommends experience in "self-conscious examination of the claims and mode of the discipline," including "theory, history, ethics, and style" in professional as well as liberal fields.[16]

If women's studies thus is easily justified as integral to the liberal arts curriculum—as compensation for omission, as catalyst for criticism—it offers more directly to individual students (and especially to women) a key to the goal, once explicit among young people entering college and always implicit, of developing a personal and intellectual identity. To form what used to be called a "philosophy of life," or a "personal world-view," students must recover their heritage and discover new horizons. Many students today have peered far beyond the kitchen window, which was the framework of many women's views in the generation of Charlotte Perkins Gilman.

A turn-of-the-century writer and lecturer, Gilman saw the limits on women's development as harmful to the advancement of the human species. As long as the world was man's home, but the home was woman's world, evolutionary progress would be impeded.[17]

Some women today still find themselves caught without a broad vision in a changing world, where gender roles, the permissible and the mandatory, are uncertain. They need liberal education, for it aims toward the development, by women and men, of the knowledge of self and society requisite to the building of a coherent world view. For such students of both sexes, women's studies offers compensation for the omission of women from books and elsewhere, a catalyst for criticism of received knowledge, and a reevaluation of women's worth. Demonstrating by its very existence that women are important, it challenges all aspects of society that suggest otherwise. Above all, it challenges women—and feminist men—to use the power of knowledge to change themselves and their world. Education, after all, means "to lead out."

CONCLUSION

Women's studies began as politics. It became a passion for the creation and teaching of new knowledge. As the science of women, it is essential to the curriculum, to the education of all students, and to the academy itself. The transformation of the curriculum to include women is more than a question of women's rights. It is essential to fulfillment of the university's commitment to the search for truth. To serve this goal, faculty and administrators must be alert to the continuing neglect of women-oriented perspectives and materials in most parts of the curriculum. They must watch for opportunities both to remove bias wherever it appears and to transform fundamental approaches toward understanding human experience. They need to support scholarship and teaching devoted to the new knowledge by hiring more faculty with appropriate interests and training—a task facilitated by conceptualizing departmental needs and describing job openings specifically to include women's studies. They must use their influence to allocate a greater share of research support and released time to projects concerning women. They must promote faculty development programs to broaden the circle of informed scholars. They must seek to build the most outstanding women's studies program they can and then to create an atmosphere in which its academic strength is recognized and valued.

Only then will women's studies, which began life in the 1960s, cease to be academia's foundling and enjoy the equal status in the community of scholars essential to fulfillment of its potential and its mission. Then women will be taken as seriously as men, and women students as well as men students will be free to claim an education, in classics or computer science or women's studies, that prepares them "to think" as well as "to do." This will happen where educators possess the courage as well as the power to change.

NOTES

This essay is in a profound sense the work of many contributors whose work I have assimilated in fifteen years of teaching women's studies. I am heavily indebted for inspiration as well as ideas to Gloria Bowles, Sandra Coyner, Florence Howe, Gerda Lerner, Catharine Stimpson, my colleagues in women's studies at San Diego State University, and many others. I thank Bonnie Zimmerman for her helpful comments on a first draft.

1. For a history of the development of women's studies in the United States and analysis of debates over goals, conflicts, theories, and structures, see Marilyn J. Boxer, "For and About Women: The Theory and Practice of Women's Studies in the United States," *Signs: Journal of Women in Culture and Society* 7, no. 3 (Spring 1982), pp. 661–695. Issues of contemporary concern are discussed in a special issue of *Women's Studies International Forum* 7, no. 3 (1984), ed. Gloria Bowles. For discussion of the impact of women's studies on specific disciplines, see Ellen Carol DuBois et al., *Feminist Scholarship: Kindling in the Groves of Academe* (Urbana: University of Illinois Press, 1985), especially Ch. 5, "Ten Years of Feminist Scholarship: The Response of the Disciplines;" also *Soundings*, special issue on "A Feminist Perspective in the Academy: The Difference It Makes," Elizabeth Langland and Walter Gove, eds., LXIV, no. 4 (Winter 1981), and *Men's Studies Modified: The Impact of Feminism on the Academic Disciplines*, ed. Dale Spender (Oxford: Pergamon Press, 1981).

2. Regional patterns of women's studies development are analyzed from the perspective of innovation research by Donna J. Wood, "The Adoption of Academic Women's Studies Programs," *Knowledge: Creation, Diffusion, Utilization* 5, No. 4 (June 1984), pp. 509–536.

3. An early advocate of the latter position, herself neglected by historians until recently, was Mary R. Beard; see her *Woman as Force in History* (New York: Macmillan, 1946) and Ann J. Lane, ed., *Mary Ritter Beard: A Source Book* (New York: Schocken, 1977).

4. On Charles Darwin, see Ruth Hubbard, "The Emperor Doesn't Wear any Clothes: The Impact of Feminism on Biology," *Men's Studies Modified*, pp. 213–235, especially p. 225. On Freud, "Some Psychical Consequences of the Anatomical Distinction between the Sexes," in Sigmund Freud, *Col-*

lected Papers, ed. Ernest Jones, vol. 5, Ch. XVII (New York: Basic Books, 1959), pp. 186–197. On Erik Erikson, "Inner and Outer Space: Reflections on Womanhood," *Daedalus: Journal of the American Academy of Arts and Sciences* 93 (Spring 1964), pp. 582–606. On Daniel Moynihan, *The Negro Family: The Case for National Action* (Washington, D.C.: Government Printing Office, 1965). For "he/man" speech, Wendy Martyna, "Beyond the 'He/Man' Approach: The Case for Nonsexist Language," in *Signs: Journal of Women in Culture and Society* V, no. 3 (Spring 1980), pp. 482–493; for muted groups, Shirley Ardener, ed., *Perceiving Women* (New York: John Wiley, 1975), pp. xxii–xvii and 21–25.

5. For early, influential essays, see Gerda Lerner, "The Lady and the Mill Girl: Changes in the Status of Women in the Age of Jackson," *American Studies* 10, no. 1 (Spring 1969), and "Women's Rights and American Feminism," *The American Scholar* 40, no. 2 (Spring 1971) and "Placing Women in History: Definitions and Challenges," *Feminist Studies* III, nos. 1–2 (Fall 1975); Joan Kelly-Gadol, "The Social Relations of the Sexes: A New Methodology for Women's History," *Signs: Journal of Women in Culture and Society* I, no. 4 (Summer 1976), pp. 809–823, and "Did Women Have a Renaissance?" in *Becoming Visible: Women in European History*, ed. Renate Beidenthal and Claudia Koonz (Boston: Houghton Mifflin, 1977), pp. 137–164; Carroll Smith-Rosenberg, "The Female World of Love and Ritual: Relations Between Women in Nineteenth-century America," *Signs: Journal of Women in Culture and Society* I, no. 1 (Autumn 1975), pp. 1–29, and, with Charles Rosenberg, "The Female Animal: Medieval and Biological Views of Women in 19th-Century America," *Journal of American History* 59 (1973), pp. 331–356; Gayle Rubin, "The Traffic in Women: Notes on the 'Political Economy' of Sex," in *Toward an Anthropology of Women*, ed. Rayna R. Reiter (New York: Monthly Review Press, 1975), pp. 157–210. Sherry Ortner, "Is Female to Male as Nature Is to Culture?", *Woman, Culture and Society*, ed. Michelle Zimbalist Rosaldo and Louise Lamphere (Stanford, Calif.: Stanford University Press, 1974), pp. 67–87; Michelle Zimbalist Rosaldo, "Woman, Culture and Society: A Theoretical Overview," in *Woman, Culture and Society*, pp. 17–42; Naomi Weisstein, "Psychology Constructs the Female, or the Fantasy Life of the Male Psychologist," in *Roles Women Play: Readings Toward Women's Liberation*, ed. Michele Hoffnung Garskof (Belmont, Calif.: Brooks/Cole, 1971), pp. 68–83; Matina S. Horner, "Femininity and Successful Achievement: A Basic Inconsistency," in *Roles Women Play*, pp. 97–122; Sandra L. Bem and Daryl J. Bem, "Training the Woman to Know Her Place" in *Roles Women Play*, pp. 84–96; Pauline B. Bart, "Depression in Middle-aged Women," in *Woman in Sexist Society*, ed. Vivian Gornick and Barbara K. Moran (New York: Basic Books, 1971), pp. 163–186; Jo Freeman, *The Politics of Women's Liberation* (New York: David McKay, 1975); Barbara Smith, "Toward a Black Feminist Criticism," *Conditions: Two*, no. 2 (Autumn 1979); Annette Kolodny, "The Land-as-Woman: Literary Convention and Latent Psychological Content," *Women's Studies* I, no. 2 (1973),

pp. 167–182, and "Some Notes in Defining a 'Feminist Literary Criticism,'" *Critical Inquiry* 2, 1 (Autumn 1975), pp. 75–92; Elaine Showalter, "Introduction," in *Women's Liberation and Literature*, ed. Elaine Showalter (New York: Harcourt Brace Jovanovich, 1971), pp. 1–5; Robin Lakoff, *Language and Woman's Place* (New York: Harper and Row, 1975); Adrienne Rich, "When We Dead Awaken: Writing as Re-Vision," *College English* 34, 1 (October 1972), pp. 18–25; Alice Walker, "In Search of Our Mothers' Gardens," *Ms.* 2 (May 1974), pp. 64–70. On Copernicus and Darwin, Elizabeth Kamarck Minnich, "Friends and Critics: The Feminist Academy," in *Toward a Feminist Transformation of the Academy: Proceedings of the Fifth Annual Great Lakes Colleges Association Women's Studies Conference* (Ann Arbor, Mich.: Great Lakes Colleges Association Women's Studies Program, 1979).

6. In the early fall of 1970, Sheila Tobias compiled and the feminist press Know, Inc., published *Female Studies I*, the first in a ten-volume series of syllabi, reading lists, and discussions on the practice of teaching women's studies. *Female Studies II*, edited by Florence Howe and also published by Know, Inc., appeared in December 1970. *Female Studies VI: Closer to the Ground—Women's Classes, Criticism, Programs 1972* and three of the later volumes were published by the Feminist Press, which Howe, with Paul Lauter, founded in Baltimore in 1970 and moved to the State University of New York, College at Old Westbury, in 1972. On Kuhnian revolution and women's studies as a discipline, Sandra Coyner, "Women's Studies as an Academic Discipline: Why and How to Do It," *Theories of Women's Studies*, ed. Gloria Bowles and Renate Duelli-Klein (London: Routledge and Kegan Paul, 1983), pp. 46–71; on naming, Marilyn J. Boxer, "For and About," pp. 664–665, no. 11, and Marilyn J. Boxer, " 'A Course in Feminology': Women's Studies in France Circa 1902," *Women's Studies Quarterly*, International Supplement no. 1 (January 1982), pp. 24–27.

7. On woman as partial man, Marcia Westkott, "Feminist Criticism of the Social Sciences," *Harvard Educational Review* 49, no. 4 (November 1979), pp. 422–430, especially p. 423; on learned women and the circumference of truth, Natalie Zemon Davis, "Gender and Genre: Women as Historical Writers, 1400–1820," in Patricia H. Labalme, ed., *Beyond Their Sex: Learned Women of the European Past* (New York: New York University Press, 1984), pp. 153–182, especially pp. 157 and 174–175.

8. J. J. Rousseau, *Émile*, trans. Barbara Foxley (New York: Dutton, 1911; reprint ed., 1955), p. 328. On Victorian ideals of womanhood, see J. A. and Olive Banks, *Feminism and Family Planning in Victorian England* (New York: Schocken, 1964), especially Ch. 5, "The Perfect Wife," pp. 58–70; Linda L. Clark, *Schooling the Daughters of Marianne* (Albany: State University of New York Press, 1984), especially Ch. 2, "Prescribing Values and Behavior: Feminine Images in Textbooks, 1880–1914," pp. 26–59; Carol Gold, "Prescription for Girls: Education in Early 19th Century Denmark," paper presented to Western Association of Women

Historians, Mills College, May 11, 1985; and Barbara Welter, "The Cult of True Womanhood, 1820–1860," *American Quarterly* XVIII (Summer 1966), pp. 151–174.

9. The dual significance of the "bonds of womanhood" is analyzed by Nancy F. Cott in *The Bonds of Womanhood: 'Woman's Sphere' in New England, 1780–1835* (New Haven: York University Press, 1978; for "Republican Mothers," see Linda K. Kerber, "Daughters of Columbia: Educating Women for the Republic, 1787–1805," in Stanley Elkins and Eric McKitrick, eds., *The Hofstadter Aegis: A Memorial* (New York: Knopf, 1974, pp. 36–59; and "The Republican Mother: Women and the Enlightenment—An American Perspective," *American Quarterly* 28, no. 2 (Summer 1976), pp. 187–205; for daughters of the French nation, Nicolas Baudeau, "De l'Education nationale," *Ephemerides du Citoyen, ou Chronique de l'esprit national* 4, no. 4 (May 12, 1766), trans. Karen M. Offen, in Susan Groag Bell and Karen M. Offen, eds., *Women, the Family, and Freedom: The Debate in Documents*, Vol. I, 1750–1880 (Stanford: Stanford University Press, 1983) pp. 73–76. Teaching as "woman's sacred office" is discussed in Nancy Hoffman, *Woman's "True" Profession: Voices from the History of Teaching* (Old Westbury, N.Y.: Feminist Press, 1981).

10. On Durant, Thomas, and mastering the "men's curriculum," see Florence Howe, "Myths of Coeducation," lecture given at Wooster College, November 2, 1978, and elsewhere, also in Howe, *Myths of Education: Selected Essays, 1964–1983* (Bloomington: Indiana University Press, 1984), pp. 206–220. For the early experience of American women in higher education, see Barbara Miller Solomon, *In the Company of Educated Women* (New Haven: Yale University Press, 1985), especially Ch. 6, "Women and the Modernizing of Liberal Education, 1860–1920," and Ch. 7, "Dimensions of the Collegiate Experience."

11. For statistics on women's education, 1870–1980, see Nancy Woloch, *Women and the American Experience* (New York: Knopf, 1984), p. 543. On Florence Robinson, who endowed a chair in history at the University of Wisconsin because, despite her Ph.D. in American history, she had found employment only in teaching home economics, see Solomon, *Educated Women*, pp. 86–87.

12. For Comte on the nature of women and the social relations of the sexes, see Bell and Offen, I, pp. 219–226. For feminist criticism of scientific objectivity, see Gloria Bowles, "The Uses of Hermeneutics for Feminist Scholarship," *Women's Studies International Forum* 7, no. 3, pp. 185–188, and Westkott, "Feminist Criticism," especially p. 152.

13. On the burdens imposed on women by the structure of academic institutions, see Arlie Russell Hochschild, "Inside the Clockwork of Male Careers," in Florence Howe, ed., *Women and the Power to Change* (New York: McGraw-Hill, 1975), pp. 47–80. For recent and in some cases radical feminist perspectives on academic feminism, see Charlotte Bunch and

Sandra Pollack, eds., *Learning Our Way: Essays in Feminist Education* (Trumansburg: N.Y.: Crossing Press, 1983). On Black women's studies, see Gloria T. Hull, Patricia Bell-Scott, and Barbara Smith, eds., *But Some of Us Are Brave* (Old Westbury, N.Y.: Feminist Press, 1982).

14. The best source for recent information on women's studies programs, research centers, and projects for transformation of the curriculum is *Women's Studies Quarterly*, especially Vol. X, no. 1 (Spring 1982), Vol. XI, no. 2 (Summer 1983), Vol. XII, no. 1 (Spring 1984), and Vol. XII, no. 3 (Fall 1984).

15. See Gilbert Allardyce, "The Rise and Fall of the Western Civilization Course," and comments by Carolyn Lougee and others, *American Historical Review* 87, no. 3 (June 1982), pp. 695–743; also Lougee, "Women, History, and the Humanities: An Argument in Favor of the General Studies Curriculum," *Women's Studies Quarterly* 9:1 (Spring 1981), pp. 4–7.

16. For Florence Howe, "Toward Women's Studies in the Eighties: Pt. 1," *Women's Studies Newsletter* 8, no. 4 (Fall 1979); for Association of American Colleges report, *Chronicle of Higher Education* (February 13, 1985), pp. 12–30.

17. See, especially, Charlotte Perkins Gilman, *Women and Economics: The Economic Factor Between Men and Women as a Factor in Social Evolution* (New York: Harper and Row, 1966 [orig. 1898]).

15

Black Women's Studies:

A View from the Margin

BEVERLY GUY-SHEFTALL
AND PATRICIA BELL-SCOTT

Two of the most important improvements in postsecondary education over the past two decades have been curriculum reform and
faculty development in Black studies and women's studies. Less
well known but equally as significant has been the development
within the past several years of a new field of study—Black women's
studies—which emerged in part because of the failure of Black and
women's studies to adequately deal with the experiences of Black
women in America and throughout the world. Black women's studies
is the scholarly investigation of the history, cultures, and experiences
of Black women. This new field confronts the problem of gender
bias in Black studies and racial bias in women's studies and analyzes
the ways in which gender/race form an "otherness" both in relationship to Black men and in relationship to non-Black women. All three
of these movements call into question the philosophical frameworks
and values of the American college curriculum.

The most noteworthy developments in Black women's studies
have come from a small but growing group of women scholars
who have been teaching and doing research on Black women for
the past twenty-five years. The pioneering work of educator Anna

J. Cooper, who wrote *A Voice from the South by a Black Woman of the South* (1892), has the distinction of being the first scholarly publication in the area of Black women's studies, though the concept had certainly not emerged during this period. Eighty years later, the publication of Professor Gerda Lerner's documentary history, *Black Women in White America* (1972) underscored the importance of treating the experiences of American Black women as distinct from those of white women and Black men. More recently, the publication of the first interdisciplinary anthology in Black women's studies, *All the Women Are White, All the Blacks Are Men, But Some of Us Are Brave* (Hull, Smith, and Bell-Scott, 1982), which includes essays, bibliographies, and course syllabi, provided concrete evidence of the wealth of material available to the teacher and researcher in Black women's studies. The founding of *SAGE: A Scholarly Journal on Black Women* in 1984 was a milestone in promoting research on Black women and an obvious manifestation of the "coming of age" of Black women's studies.

Proponents of the Black studies and women's studies movements have argued convincingly that the typical college curriculum is based upon a world-view that does not reflect the fact that more than half the world's population is female and nonwhite. Women and minorities have come to represent a significant segment of the college student population and have increased their demands for balance and pluralism in the curriculum. Responses to the demand for nonsexist and nonracist college curricula have taken many forms, among which are:

1. the development of separate departments and programs, in Black studies, women's studies, or ethnic studies;
2. the integration or "mainstreaming" of content on women and Blacks into selected, disciplinary curricula;
3. the creation of extracurricular, administrative units (e.g., women's centers, Black research or cultural centers, university-wide committees for women's and Black concerns) that enrich the formal curriculum;
4. the proliferation of new scholarly journals (e.g., *The Black Scholar, SIGNS, Women's Studies Quarterly, Callaloo*);
5. the establishment of a few university chairs for senior scholars with expertise in Black or Women's studies (e.g., the Robinson-Edwards Chair in History at the University of Wisconsin at Madison, held by Gerda Lerner);

6. the creation of several national professional associations (e.g., The National Council for Black Studies and The National Women's Studies Association) committed to the study and education of Blacks and women.

In addition, several disciplinary, professional associations of scholars have emerged. The Association of Black Women Historians, the Association of Black Women in Higher Education, the Committee on Black Women's Concerns of the American Psychological Association, the Association of Black Women Sociologists, and the Minority Women's Caucus of the Modern Language Association are representative of the burgeoning number of academic groups committed to scholarship in Black Women's Studies.

Also important is the publication of several major works on Black women suitable for classroom use. They include Harley and Terborg-Pann, *The Afro-American Woman: Struggles and Images* (1978); Bell, Parker, and Guy-Sheftall, *Sturdy Black Bridges: Visions of Black Women in Literature* (1979); Christian, *Black Women Novelists: The Development of a Tradition, 1892–1976* (1980); Hooks, *Ain't I A Woman: Black Women and Feminism* (1981); *The Black Woman* (1980); Giddings, *When and Where I Enter . . . The Impact of Black Women on Race and Sex in America* (1984); Sterling, *We Are Your Sisters, Black Women in the Nineteenth Century* (1985); Wade-Gayles, *No Crystal Stair: Visions of Race and Sex in Black Women's Fiction* (1984); Jones, *Labor of Love, Labor of Sorrow: Black Women, Work, and the Family from Slavery to the Present* (1985); Davis, *Women, Race and Class* (1981); and White, *Ar'n't I A Woman? Female Slaves in the Plantation South* (1985).

Despite recent efforts to improve women's studies curricula on many college campuses and despite the proliferation of publications on Black women, several problems remain. First, it is still the case that too many women's studies courses include only token, if any, treatment of women of African descent. When material on women of color is included, it tends to ignore these who live outside the United States. Relatively few courses exist in women's studies or Black studies that focus entirely on Black women, and these deal primarily with American Black women. The majority of undergraduate women's studies degree programs are located at predominantly white institutions, and the majority of women's studies programs are in large, northern institutions. Only a few of these programs have specific international or comparative emphases. Very few historically Black colleges or universities have women's studies programs, and many of these offer no women's studies courses. Apart from the Africana Women's Studies Program at Atlanta University, no degree program in women's studies focuses on women of African descent.

Attempts over the past several years to bring Black women into the college curriculum follow a pattern similar to the development of Black studies and women's studies. Though no separate department or academic program in Black women's studies has been established at the undergraduate level, separate courses within Black studies, women's studies, American studies, and English and history programs and departments have emerged. The largest number of courses that focus on Black women are about Black women writers. This phenomenon can be attributed to the wealth of primary and secondary works by and about Black women writers. Black women's history and interdisciplinary, social science courses have begun to increase in significant numbers also.

Unlike the core curriculum, Black studies and women's studies programs have been impacted by the slow but steady growth of courses and resources on Black women. The results of this impact are best exemplified by the following projects:

1. The Southern Black Women's Culture Project of the University of Alabama at Tuscaloosa, which was designed to promote the development of a model course on southern Black women's culture. The resulting publication was *The Culture of Southern Black Women: Approaches and Materials,* which was edited by Nancy Conklin and Brenda McCallum and published by the University of Alabama Press in 1983.
2. The National Black Women's Archives of the Mary McCleod Bethune Historical Project, which was established by the National Council of Negro Women and was designed to promote the collection of primary source materials and to support research on Black women. The archives, located in Washington, D.C., serves as the repository for several major collections on Black women.
3. The Great Lakes College Association Summer Institute in Women's Studies incorporates content on Black women.
4. The University of Massachusetts at Amherst, and Smith College faculty seminar/workshop series addressed issues of race and gender in Black studies and women's studies.
5. The Feminist Press–initiated project to promote the incorporation of content on women and minorities into college-level

American literature survey courses. An intended outcome was the promotion of networking and resource-sharing among scholars in women's studies, minority studies, and American literature.

6. The Minority Women's Program Area of the Wellesley College Center for Research on Women initiated a FIPSE-funded project to do faculty and curriculum development in Black women's studies for faculty in historically Black colleges and two-year colleges.

7. The Organization of American Historians and the Association of Black Women Historians cosponsored a project to incorporate content on Black women into survey American history courses.

8. The Institute of the Black World Black Studies Curriculum Development Project focused upon the absence of content on women in many Black studies programs.

9. The establishment of three women's research centers in the South whose focus is minority women—the Women's Research and Resource Center at Spelman College (1981); the Center for Research on Women at Memphis State University (1982); and the Africana Women's Center at Atlanta University (1983).

The aforementioned projects represent some of the most outstanding efforts to incorporate content on minority women into a single discipline; develop and collect resources on Black women that might be used by researchers and experienced teachers; and encourage dialogue, networking, and resource sharing among experienced women's studies scholars, Black studies scholars, and scholars from traditional disciplines with a focus on race and gender—but not necessarily Black women.

ENDURING ISSUES

Three questions have been central to the historical development of formal, higher educational opportunities for Black women: (a) Should the higher education of Black women be separate or coeducational? (b) Should the educational curriculum for Black women be different from or similar to the curriculum in institutions which are predominantly male and/or white? (c) Do Black women have special psychosocial needs that must be considered by educational planners?

Though these are not the only questions that have emerged in the higher education of Black women in the United States, they represent some of the most debated and enduring ones. As early as 1944, for example, Spelman College, the oldest college for the education of Black women in this country, hosted a conference on the "Current Problems and Programs in the Higher Education of Negro Women." The purpose of this historic gathering was to explore those psychological and socioeconomic factors related to the academic success and failure of Black women.

The question of whether the educational curriculum for Black women can and should be different from or similar to the curriculum in institutions that are predominantly white and/or male is an old one and is closely related to those purposes attributed to women's education generally. Historically, preparation for marriage and family living, the enhancement of moral and Christian character, and the preparation of intellectual and social leaders have been the basic objectives of curricula for women. Through the establishment of home economics, religious education, and liberal arts curricula, educators in institutions of higher learning have sought to meet the aforementioned objectives.

The curriculum at Spelman College has historically had a strong orientation in the liberal arts and religious education. Early circulars of the college reflect the classical and religious flavor of the curriculum, which included courses in Latin, geometry, moral philosophy, astronomy, and Bible studies. The early curriculum of Spelman has been likened to the curricula at Mount Holyoke and the Oread Collegiate Institute—schools from which Spelman's founders graduated—as well as the curricula of institutions such as Oberlin College.

After its transition to a women's college in 1927, Bennett College (established initially as a coeducational institution in 1873 for newly emancipated slaves) began a heavy emphasis upon preparation for marriage and family living in the educational curriculum. In a 1938 article about Bennett College, Constance Marteena asserted that "when you educate a woman you educate a family . . . the entire curriculum is geared to provide the students the type of education that not only will make them intelligent, alert, and progressive, but will go a long way towards helping them establish homes and happy families as well" (Marteena, 1938). At the time Marteena's article was written, all students at Bennett, regardless of their major, were required to take a course in "The Art of Living," which was strongly oriented toward the development of homemaking skills.

The trends and developments in the curricula at predominantly male and/or white institutions of higher learning have had some impact upon the design of curricula at Spelman and Bennett, as well as Black coeducational colleges. From the early 1880s to the 1930s, a trend toward industrial and vocational education swept the country. The impact of this movement upon Black higher education is best reflected by the emergence of Booker T. Washington as a political leader, as well as the phenomenal growth of the school he nurtured—Tuskegee Institute. Washington's desire to encourage the development of educational programs to provide Blacks with marketable skills such as tailoring, brick-masonry, carpentry, and scientific agriculture gave impetus to the formalization of home economics for women and industrial arts for men as professional fields of study.

Just as the curricula at Bennett and Spelman have been influenced historically by trends in the curricula at other institutions, so do they continue to be influenced. Because of the need to train Black women for potential leadership roles, both Spelman and Bennett have placed considerable emphasis upon the participation of students in community life and civic affairs. This kind of participation was institutionalized in the extracurricular acitivities of the colleges via the development of the YWCA on campus, women's choral societies, and service-oriented clubs. Bennett's Women for Leadership Roles in International Service is just one of the newly established programs at the college that illustrates its continuous efforts to provide for the special needs of women.

Similarly, the newly established Women's Research and Resource Center at Spelman (the first of its kind on a Black college campus) is the most recent example of the college's commitment to the educational development of Black women. The center conducts research on Black women, sponsors outreach activities to women in the community, and develops courses in women's studies, especially Black women's studies. Bennett's interdisciplinary program in women's studies (which began in 1975–1976) was the first women's studies program on a Black college campus. Both colleges have also seen a need for collecting books and other material on Black women; the development of the Afro-American Women's Collection at Bennett was initiated during the early 1940s, and the Margaret Nabrit Curry Collection on Women opened as part of the Quarles Library at Spelman in 1970. Since the decade of the 1960s, when there was tremendous growth in professional education, Spelman and Bennett have entered into cooperative arrangements with neighboring coeducational and predominantly male institutions in an effort to make engineering, law, and medicine courses available to their students.

CASE STUDIES

Despite their progressive stances in other areas of curriculum reform, most notably Black studies, Black colleges have lagged behind the rest of the academy in the evolution of women's studies (with a few notable exceptions), in spite of the fact that their student populations are heavily female. Spelman's historic mission to provide for the unique educational needs of Black female students enabled the college to engage in pioneering work in women's studies in the context of minority women's experience. "Women's courses" began to emerge as electives in the Spelman curriculum in 1969 when Psychology of the Sexes was offered for the first time. A chronology of the development of additional women's studies courses over the next decade follows: Psychology of Women (1970–1971); Women in Africa (taught in 1972–1973 by a guest professor and discontinued after one year); Images of Women in Literature (1973–1974); Human Sexuality (1974–1975); Images of Women in the Media (1976–1977); Women, Values, and the Law (1978–1979); Women of the Bible, Sociology of Women, Woman As Writer, Women in Drama, Women, Literature and Identity, and Women in Management of Organizations (since 1979).

Though these courses remained tangential, for the most part, to the curriculum, they helped to create an environment, at the very least, that was receptive to the idea of women's studies at Spelman. The absence of hostility to women's studies on the campus made it less difficult to carry out a Ford Foundation–funded project that would incorporate Black women's studies into the core curriculum. This curriculum development project, which began in 1983, was the first "mainstreaming" or "curriculum integration" project in women's studies to take place on a Black college campus.[1] Since many women's studies courses as they were presently being taught focused on white, middle-class northern women, Spelman's curriculum revision project, carried out under the auspices of its Women's Center, was designed to reconceptualize women's studies in such a way that material on women of color would be incorporated into required core courses.

A thorough examination of the Spelman curriculum revealed that despite the presence of women's studies courses (which far exceed such offerings in other Atlanta colleges and in most Black colleges), the curriculum was still not "gender-balanced" or sufficiently sensitive to Black women's studies. Furthermore, most of these courses were electives in the major or minor. Relegating attention to women, and Black women specifically, to a set of elective offerings at the margin of the curriculum had not provided our students with a comprehensive understanding of the diverse experiences and contributions of women generally or an appreciation of the roles of Black women in society and as subjects of scholarly inquiry.

While a cross-disciplinary team of faculty had discussed the possibility of expanding the women's studies minor, this group concluded that a more comprehensive approach was required. This approach has been characterized by women's studies scholars in the following manner:

> The major thrust of the second decade will be toward directing the movement outward, towa∶d "mainstreaming." Despite a decade of new scholarship, Women's Studies has so far made little progress toward its "ultimate strategy" of transforming the established male biased curriculum." (Howe, 1982)

Specifically, the objective was to invigorate our liberal arts curriculum by redesigning courses so that they would reflect the new scholarship on women. The process of bringing about a gender-balanced curriculum represented an attempt to de-ghettoize women's studies and to keep it from being separated from the rest of the academic enterprise. In order to bring this about, a carefully articulated program of faculty development, course refinement and modification, and course development was initiated. Course modification and refinement to include increased emphasis on women, especially women of color, was targeted to appropriate courses throughout the curriculum and more explicitly to those courses that comprised the general education core curriculum and those that were basic, required introductory courses to the disciplines and majors. An interdisciplinary faculty team of twenty, which included the academic dean and division chairs, was involved in this curriculum development project. Four colleges in the Atlanta area were also involved—Agnes Scott (predominantly white, all female); Clark (historically Black, coed); Kennesaw (predominantly white, community, coed); and Morehouse (historically Black, all male).

At Spelman ten courses in the core curriculum were redesigned, which included Freshman English, World Civilization, World Literature, Introduction to Sociology, Introduction to Psychology, Survey of Fine Art, World Religion, Afro-American History, Introduction to Philosophy, and Science and Society. Much of the "pioneering" work involved the English Department, which compiled a new race- and gender-balanced reader that is international in focus and includes short stories, poems, essays, and excerpts from the personal narratives and autobiographies of major thinkers and writers. Many of the selections had never been anthologized and others, while known to scholars, are not accessible to students in freshman courses. The extent to which Black women's studies was incorporated into this core requirement is also apparent in the English Department's decision to use Maya Angelou's *I Know Why the Caged Bird Sings* as the one complete text that all first-year students would read in English 101-102. The English Department also designed a new world literature course that represents a radical and refreshing departure from conventional world literature courses in most colleges and universities in the United States, which focus unduly on the West. The new course is truly a *world* literature course and is cross-cultural in its approach.

As a result of the Ford-funded Curriculum Development Project in Black Women's Studies at Selected Southern Colleges, Spelman now has the distinction of being the only historically Black college with a viable women's studies program (which includes a minor) *and* a mainstreaming project in women's studies. Spelman's project is also unique because of its special attention to minority women and its cross-cultural dimension. Its pioneering effort at developing a world literature course that would in fact include the literature of the world *and* be at the same time race- and gender-balanced is truly a remarkable accomplishment. This course can indeed serve as a model for other colleges seriously committed to transforming their curricula.

By concentrating on the humanities and the social sciences during the project, Spelman avoided some of the more difficult challenges facing those who would incorporate women's studies in all of the disciplines. The rationale for this approach was simple. The desire was to reach the largest number of students at the beginning of their college careers. For this reason, Freshman English, World Literature, and World Civilization—all required courses—were important courses on which to focus. Despite considerable progress, the work of curriculum reform at Spelman is not complete. It will be necessary to continue monitoring course offerings with respect to their sensitivity to the new scholarship on women, particularly women of color, especially at the core level. More effective strategies to include more men of color in mainstreaming efforts need to be devised. Efforts at curriculum revision in Black women's studies at predominantly white colleges, especially in the South, need to be intensified.

During the same time period (1983–1985) another major project in Black women's studies was being conducted on another campus in the Atlanta University Center—Atlanta University, the graduate institution that has the distinction of having the only degree program in women's studies in the United States that focuses on women of African descent. Though plans had been underway for several years, the program was actualized in 1983 with the establishment of the Africana Women's Center. The center's primary aim was to address the obvious need for comparative research and teaching about women of African descent. A conscious decision was made to emphasize research and teaching that focused on the conditions, activities, and concerns of Africana women in Africa, the Caribbean, and the southern region of the United States. The major objectives of the program were:

1. to provide opportunities for students to systematically analyze gender bias in the history of knowledge and to examine its consequences for women;
2. to encourage and support examinations of the intersection of race, class, and sex bias and its consequences for Africana women;
3. to promote the comparative examination of the contributions, strategies, perspectives, and ideologies of Africana women;
4. to provide a forum for dialogue and exchange of international and comparative research on women, especially women of African descent;
5. to build a resource base for research on Africana women;
6. to develop interest in and expertise in teaching about Africana women;
7. to promote theoretical and comparative research in feminist theory;
8. to encourage and support the comparative study of poor and rural women;
9. to promote research, projects, and activities leading to improvements in the lives of Africana women;
10. to contribute to a reduction in global oppression based on class, race, and sex. (Lewis and Hoytt, 1985)

A grant from the Fund for Improvement of Post Secondary Education (FIPSE) made it possible in 1983 for ten faculty members from Atlanta University and twenty faculty members from four undergraduate colleges and universities (Hampton University, Atlanta Junior College, Southern University and Jackson State University) to participate in the program. The program consisted of intensive training institutes, research projects (individual and collaborative), and developmental activities such as the development of course outlines and bibliographies, course piloting, and the integration of courses in existing academic programs.

Thirty courses (eleven graduate level and nineteen undergraduate), which can be used as models by teachers of Black and women's studies in a variety of disciplines, were developed. They include Women in Contemporary African Fiction; The Way We Love: Intimacy and the African-American Woman; Health Issues of Africana Women; Southern Rural Black Women; Third World Women and Development; Personality Development of the Black Woman; Black Women in American Politics; Images of Black Women in the Trinidadian Calypson and in the Afro-American Blues, 1920–1950; Africana Women in Politics: A Comparative Examination; Africana Women in Criminal Justice; Resources in Black Women's Studies; and Women in History.[2] This impressive and pioneering series, though not definitive, is offered as a guide to scholars, programs, and institutions interested in transforming the traditional curriculum and integrating information about Africana women into existing Black and women's studies courses.

CONCLUSION

Black women's studies scholars are in a unique position because of their ability to explore the intersection of race, sex, and class as experienced by Black women in ways that are impossible for other segments of the population. The study of Black women also renders invalid many of the generalizations that abound in the historiography of American women and are considered "universal." The ultimate challenge is for women's studies scholars to recognize that Black women's studies is in fact women's studies, and that "the Black female experience, by the very nature of its extremity, illuminates the subjugation of all women" (Aptheker, 1982). Such a perspective would render Black women's studies unnecessary over the long run or at the very least redundant.

And finally, it is still the case that women of color are being educated away from themselves despite the blossoming of Black studies and women's studies. Unfortunately, few introductory courses in these areas really reflect the experiences of women as a group. The steady increase of curriculum materials on women of color makes the argument that there is no scholarship or literature in Black women's studies an empty one. Since women and people of color should be prepared to run the societies on this planet in the future, it is imperative that we design educational curricula that reinforce who we are and teach us how to be more human. Educators everywhere should commit themselves to building institutions and providing experiences that promote the self-empowerment of women of color. For the strength of women of color is crucial to us all.

NOTES

1. The most recent issue of *Women's Studies Quarterly* 13 (Summer 1985) contains articles on curriculum integration projects and scholarship throughout the country. See Margot C. Finn, "Incorporating Perspectives on Women into the Undergraduate Curriculum: A Ford Foundation Workshop," for further discussion of Spelman's involvement in the curriculum integration movement, and Dorothy O. Helly, "Recent Books on Curriculum Integration," for a comprehensive listing of publications in the area.
2. A complete listing of all course syllabi developed during this FIPSE-funded program can be found in *Africana Women's Studies Series, Course Syllabi*, Volume 1, which is available from the Africana Women's Center, Atlanta University, Atlanta, Georgia. Bibliographical material developed in connection with course offerings are available in *Africana Women's Studies Series: Course Bibliographies*, Volume 2. These two volumes contain the largest amount of material on the development of Black Women's Studies at an American university. Volume III in the series is a Cross-Cultural Bibliography of Africana Women, and Volume IV is the proceedings from the first National Conference of Africana Women's Studies in the United States.

REFERENCES

Africana Women's Studies Series, Vol. 1–4. Atlanta University: Africana Women's Center, 1985.

ANGELOU, MAYA. *I Know Why the Caged Bird Sings*. New York: Random House, 1969.

APTHEKER, BETTINA. *Woman's Legacy: Essays on Race, Sex and Class*. Amherst: University of Massachusetts Press, 1982.

BELL, ROSEANN, PARKER, BETTYE J., and GUY-SHEFTALL, BEVERLY. *Sturdy Black Bridges: Visions of Black Women in Literature*. New York: Anchor/Doubleday, 1979.

The Black Woman: An Anthology. New York: New American Library, 1970.

CHRISTIAN, BARBARA. *Black Women Novelists: The Development of a Tradition, 1892–1976.* Westport, Conn.: Greenwood Press, 1980.

CONKLIN, NANCY, and MCCALLUM, BRENDA. *The Culture of Southern Black Women.* Tuscaloosa: University of Alabama Press, 1983.

COOPER, ANNA J. *A Voice from the South by a Black Woman of the South.* Xenia, Ohio: Aldine Printing House, 1892.

DAVIS, ANGELA. *Women, Race and Class.* New York: Random House, 1981.

GIDDINGS, PAULA. *When and Where I Enter . . . The Impact of Black Women on Race and Sex in America.* New York: William Morrow, 1984.

HARLEY, SHARON, and TERBORG-PANN, ROSALYN, eds. *The Afro-American Woman: Struggles and Images.* Port Washington, N.Y.: Kennikat Press, 1978.

HOOKS, BELL. *Ain't I A Woman: Black Women and Feminism.* Boston: South End Press, 1981.

HOWE, FLORENCE. "Feminist Scholarship, The Extent of the Revolution." *Change* 14 (April 1982), 12–14.

HULL, GLORIA, SMITH, BARBARA, and BELL-SCOTT, PATRICIA, eds. *All the Women Are White, All the Blacks Are Men, But Some of Us Are Brave, Black Women's Studies.* Old Westbury, N.Y.: The Feminist Press, 1982.

JONES, JACQUELINE. *Labor of Love, Labor of Sorrow.* New York: W. W. Norton, 1984.

LERNER, GERDA. *Black Women in White America: A Documentary History.* New York: Pantheon, 1972.

LEWIS, SHELBY, and HOYTT, ELEANOR. *Africana Women's Studies Series: Course Syllabi,* Vol. 1. Atlanta: Africana Women's Center, Atlanta University, 1985, pp. 3–4.

MARTEENA, CONSTANCE. "A College for Girls." *Opportunity* 16 (1938), 306–307.

STERLING, DOROTHY. *We Are Your Sisters, Black Women in the Nineteenth Century.* New York: W. W. Norton, 1985.

WADE-GAYLESS, GLORIA. *No Crystal Stair: Visions of Race and Sex in Black Women's Fiction.* New York: Pilgram Press, 1984.

WHITE, DEBORAH GRAY. *Ar'n't I a Woman? Female Slaves in the Plantation South.* New York: W. W. Norton, 1985.

Women's Studies Quarterly, Volume XIII, Number 2, Summer 1985.

16

Women's Centers as Agents of Change

JANE S. GOULD

The creation of women's centers on college campuses was a natural response to the growing awareness in the late sixties and early seventies of the unmet needs of women. Acknowledging the extent and the depth of discrimination against all women, campus women's centers were created to raise and examine new questions about women's lives, roles, and expectations; to help women develop a feminist consciousness; to combat feelings of isolation; and to establish a sense of community among women. The goal was to provide or to help institutions to provide programs and services which would enable women to achieve equity in all aspects of their education, work and life.

These new women's centers were many things to many people, and the character of each center was shaped by those who came together to create it as well as by the institutional response. Hence, center programs were diverse. Some focused on general services for women students; some concentrated on emerging women's studies; some tried bringing together women active in the community with women on campus; some were the focal point for early studies of dis-

*The research for this piece was supported by the Russell Sage Foundation. Similar information will appear in a forthcoming book, Marian K. Chamberlain, ed., *Women in Academe: Progress and Prospects* (New York: Russell Sage Foundation, 1988).

crimination in such areas as salary equity and women's safety; some provided a place for women to be together to raise questions, address issues, and "be themselves"; some were mainly concerned with helping women develop their careers and deal with the concomitant issues of family and life-style; some were dedicated to giving women control over their bodies by providing health information and helping them to be more assertive with the health establishment; and some tried to play many different roles. Indeed, many succeeded admirably in these diverse and multiservice capacities by becoming comprehensive women's resource centers.

THE EARLY YEARS

Campus activism of the middle and late 1960s both gave impetus to women's activities on campus and galvanized women to focus on their own needs and take more control of their own lives. By 1970, as new legislation, executive orders and regulations were slowly being developed and put into place to address discrimination against women in higher education, there was a buildup of explosive energy among women on campuses. Women were frustrated and angry at the rigidity of their institutions, eager to see some immediate changes, and at the same time aware that an important first step to effect change was raising women's own awareness of their status. With few exceptions, new structures had to be created for this work. In most cases institutions did not know how or whether to respond and some were not immediately receptive, although a handful of continuing education programs for women did respond to this new climate by broadening their focus.

On most campuses in the early 1970s the only special office for women was a Dean of Women's Office, which in rare cases became or continued to be a focal point for responding to these changes. There was no affirmative action office, rarely a women's studies program, only a sprinkling of women's studies courses and continuing education programs for women; there were few women faculty and even fewer women in top administrative positions. Even (and sometimes especially) at women's colleges, there was a reluctance to address any of the special issues for women, in part because of a general agreement that providing a "superior" education for women in a supportive atmosphere—that is, the same education available to men—was quite enough.

In this climate, the emergence of the early women's centers followed a fairly general pattern, varying slightly from institution to institution. Small groups of women (including some combination of students, faculty, staff, adminstrators, alumnae, and on occasion women from the larger community) met, established themselves as a committee or task force, and devoted months and even years to preparing the necessary groundwork to convince their adminstration of the need for a women's center. Sometimes a rape incident on campus or a pending lawsuit by a woman faculty member hastened the process. In a few instances the impetus came from a chancellor or president, who, aware of new federal quidelines on affirmative action or enlightened by women administrators or faculty, would appoint a task force to assess women's needs on campus. It cannot be underestimated how important outside pressures for and against women's programs have been—and will continue to be. Campus issues have never, in fact, been isolated from the larger community.

On some campuses administrators were willing to make a temporary commitment and provide minimal budget and space, often in a location far from the center of campus. Occasionally, student governments responded with initial funding and support. If not, women learned to use some of the strategies and tactics that had worked in the late 1960s to move intransigent administrations. Taking over a building or taking down the walls between offices to create "space" when they were told there was no space, holding an all-campus rally with an outside speaker, and sitting in the president's office were all effective ploys resorted to when an administration was unreceptive and when women felt they had exhausted normal channels.

Although there has always been great diversity among women's centers, their institutions, and the historical circumstances surrounding their origins, they have shared common goals and values. All of them tried to speak to a broad range of women's issues, going far beyond immediate undergraduate needs. Most opened their doors to all women, both on and off campus, partly in recognition that many women had been excluded from higher education and the means to develop skills and hence independence. They also acknowledged an important feminist truth that their programs and services would be enriched by including the full diversity of women's experience. A few centers limited their services only to women within their institutions, and some even to young undergraduates. Among these, many services were student-initiated, student-run, and funded by undergraduate associations. Although from the start they played an important role in providing a "new space" for women's concerns, they were simply one of many student activist groups.

CENTERS AS AGENTS OF CHANGE

No matter what the focus of the center was, it almost inevitably had an impact on the campus. Of course, there were some success stories and some failures. But for the most part the centers played crucial, catalytic roles on many campuses. Individually and collectively, women's centers raised the general level of consciousness and concern about issues of women's equity while providing a safe haven for women to clarify their own ideas and positions. By providing this place, they enabled women to discover the power they had collectively to make change within the institution as well as in the larger society.

Clearly, any group trying to create change must have the space and time to develop its vision. Many times the women's centers on campuses contributed to the articulation of what a campus environment might be like if it were to be fully reflective of and committed to women.

These early centers were often viewed as marginal operations, as part of a fad that could be expected to last for a few years and then fade away. Yet, amazingly, these centers flourished and functioned with an incredibly high energy level, filling important unmet needs on their campuses. Directors managed with few resources, often functioning within an experiential nonhierarchical structure, sometimes working collectively even to the point of sharing the one salary. To enhance the work of small, fragmented staffs, centers depended on dedicated paid student workers and volunteers as well as on developing internships and practicums for both undergraduate and graduate students. This same innovative spirit was used to transform dreary, limited space into comfortable attractive quarters and, sometimes, even to acquire more space.

The range of programs and services offered by these women's centers was remarkably broad, including lectures, workshops, seminars, conferences, films, poetry readings, and art exhibitions; issuing a community calendar of women's events; serving as a reentry center for returning women students and as a drop-in center with information and referrals on such subjects as health, housing, child care, divorce, abortions, legal rights, and employment; offering peer counseling and, at a few centers, professional personal counseling; having a library of books, articles, periodicals, clippings, and other printed material on women's issues; organizing consciousness-raising and support groups; giving noncredit courses on the new scholarship on women as well as on many areas of women's rights and on such topics as self-defense and assertiveness training. Other activities included publishing a newsletter, bibliography, and publications of presentations from center programs. Some of the centers got involved in issues and concerns related to campus safety for women, child care, and improved health services for women, but most of these issues came later. In the beginning the emphasis was on personal empowerment and on identifying some of the emerging issues for women that were not addressed anywhere else on campus.

All these activities generated a sense of excitement and pride in breaking new ground in both process and content, and in making connections between women who had heretofore been isolated from each other. In addition to presenting perspectives that were directly related to the new thinking about women, most centers went to great lengths to include the participation and the particular experience of women of all ages, of different race and class backgrounds and sexual preference. Recognizing the commonalities as well as the differences among women and understanding that all women could benefit from this enrichment were new concepts and led to bringing to campuses provocative programs and strong women, often from a wider variety of backgrounds than academia usually admits.

By reaching out and including community women and their concerns in center programs, women's centers developed strong ties between the institution and the larger community. To everyone's surprise, this bridging proved to be an unexpected, inexpensive, and important public relations asset for institutions. At institutions where there was no continuing education center for women, it was not unusual for women's centers to play a role in the recruitment and retention of reentry women. The mix that community women provided to center programs was an unexpected dividend that contributed to the vitality of women's centers, and through them, to the whole institution—a vitality not always welcome.

Tensions between the institution and women's centers were inherent from the start, despite the benefits centers brought. Although these tensions put centers on the defensive and demanded an excessive amount of time and energy, they also forced women's centers to think through each issue carefully. The result was often the development of articulated, shared convictions perhaps earlier than otherwise would have happened, and often ahead of such consciousness elsewhere on campus.

This was particularly true of the issue of lesbianism, an issue that most women's centers handled with a forthright decision to work with all women who supported their basic goals. Many lesbian women were in the forefront of the women's movement and saw women's centers as an important advocacy agency and a vehicle for expressing their views and concerns. It was crucial that centers take a strong position and not succumb to the homophobia that pervaded higher education, the larger society, and even the women's movement at that time, and most did so.

In a broad sense, most women's centers linked feminism with social change. Hence, wherever possible, programs reflected this commitment and solidarity, an approach which strengthened all programs and led some centers into addressing other inequities, such as examining how war, oppression, racism, and unemployment affected women both at home and abroad.

FURTHER INTO THE 1970S

On this strong base the mid-1970s saw the expansion of women's centers, the establishment of new ones, and the proliferation of women's groups on campuses. Women's centers were positioned and ready to serve as the coordinating links between women's groups and as the liaison between the institution and various groups within the larger women's community. Many of these groups turned to campus based women's centers for advice, support, and cosponsorship of programs. Occasionally, these groups challenged the centers to consider new ideas and issues and to expand programming to meet new needs. The positive links were particularly true of beginning women's studies programs and of student groups as women students were beginning to seek their identity as women and wanted programs reflecting this concern.

During these years many centers were able to acquire more space and higher budgets, which represented an acknowledgment on the part of administrations that the centers were serving a useful function on campus and had a powerful constituency. It became clear that women's centers were often speaking for large numbers of women whose needs had been ignored at a time when moral indignation about the status of women was exploding. It was the recognition of this power and understanding how to use it that enabled now-seasoned women's centers members to be effective in helping their institutions make needed changes for women.

Gradually by the late 1970s, across the country, the emphasis of the centers changed from personal support and direct services to advocacy and institutional change. While continuing to offer programs and services for self-development, consciousness-raising, and the dissemination of new knowledge about women, women's centers began to play a much more important role in identifying women's issues affecting women within the institution and providing leadership in setting up machinery to find solutions. A handful of women's centers went one step further and stated publicly that they would serve as an advocate, not only for women on their campus, but would take an activist position on feminist legislation and social policy in the larger community.

Women's centers became concerned about such issues as rape, child care, health services, sexual harassment, and athletics. They learned to play a dual role. On the one hand, they worked behind the scenes, cooperating with appropriate offices or departments on campus on a problem, often getting an office, department, or top administration to take action. They also served as whistle-blowers when problems affecting women on campus needed action or when incidents occurred, by publicizing the incident, getting speakers, holding public forums, and organizing the campus community around the incident and the larger issue.

Specifically, this role meant some centers started or helped to start programs or services that subsequently became institutionalized, as in the case of child care centers, rape crisis centers, or drop-in counseling centers for women. Center directors and staff learned to exert pressure on administrations, an approach that resulted in achievements such as gaining a half-time appointment of someone whose job would focus on the status of women as part of faculty affirmative action or the addition of free Pap smears and pregnancy tests to the campus health service.

The 1970s was also a period of dramatic increase in research on women. Recognizing that the core of higher education is academic and centers around the curriculum, women's centers responded with an expansion of programs. Fostering the new scholarship on women that continuously challenged the basic underpinnings of traditional scholarship was a high priority for some of the centers. They also tried to support and encourage women faculty whose research and teaching reflected the new scholarship. These were important steps in opening up the campus to necessary institutional changes in the academic arena.

In addition to offering programs and services that were on the cutting edge of the new scholarship on women, many centers developed extensive resource collections of books, articles, bibliographies, directories, pamphlets, and special issues of journals and carried subscriptions to large numbers of newsletters and periodicals. Emphasis was always placed on significant material rarely found in traditional library collections—for example, classic feminist writings published by small out-the-way presses or publications that tended to go out of print quickly.

By the late 1970s a number of women's centers began to focus on research: some of the new centers included a research component in their functions or at least as one of their goals, while a few of the older established ones added research to their many services. Adding a research component required a major increase in budget. Necessary funding for research usually came from outside sources, and centers found that donors, both individuals and funding agencies, were sometimes wary of the more provocative, activist programs. Hence for some centers, there was a gradual shift in priorities and a move away from the founding, sustaining activism.

Since the early 1970s we have witnessed a number of changes characterized by increases in the numbers of women's studies programs and/or courses, projects concerned with women faculty and administrators, research centers on women, and transformation of the curriculum projects. In the 1980s these changes have occurred in a conservative political climate. Although it is significant that most of the several hundred multiservice and resource campus-based women's centers have survived, only a few new centers were established in the 1980s.

REACHING OUT: PRIORITIES AND ISSUES FOR WOMEN'S CENTERS

Has the need for an active feminist presence on campuses disappeared? Have woman achieved equity in their education, work, and lives? Has the fact that some centers have become more firmly institutionalized necessarily made them less controversial and less effective? And are they in danger of being graciously phased out or folded into the institutional structure?

Indeed, women still face many persistent, if somewhat more subtle, barriers to full and equitable participation in the academy. And it is already evident that when those with authority to make institutional change do so without fully comprehending the message and magnitude of the changes being sought, the changes are likely to be superficial and lost within institutional structures. The answers to these questions lead us to the conclusion that women's centers or women's spaces are still very important to the welfare of women on campus, and therefore to meeting the campus problems of the 1980s and beyond. The problems centers still face are those of marginality, insecure funding, competition between programs, homophobia, the scarcity of women at the policymaking level, across-the-board budget cuts, and conservatism in students and administrators.

Whatever the problems, however, it is abundantly clear that we have an imposing task if we are to create a truly supportive atmosphere for women in higher education. The bright future we saw when we started in the early 1970s has become a different and more difficult reality in the mid-1980s, and many strapped institutions feeling the pressure to keep the institution functioning do not view women as a priority.

We still need women's centers or some construct like them to lead us into the next decade and to keep women's issues in the forefront as a major part of the future higher education agenda. We must help institutions to see that correcting the problems identified on behalf of the new majority of their students help not only those students but the entire institution as well.

Center leadership can help all women's groups grow stronger by building support networks among them. Cooperating on programs, sitting on each other's advisory commitees, sharing resources and information on plans and problems, all serve to cut down on divisive competition, unify the women's community, and make possible the strength in numbers that can make women's needs rate higher on the institutional agenda. Developing and keeping strong working ties with women's groups off campus is also important, especially since the power and impact of the centers has rested partially on their ability to reach beyond the academic community for service and for support.

It is essential to extend cooperation and support within the academy to all academic departments, programs, and administrative offices, either by taking the initiative or responding to a suggestion from a department or program to work together on an issue or a special event of interest to the department. Since many campus units fear collaboration with women's centers because they may seem "political," it is important for women's center staff to exercise skill, patience, and persistence without watering down the basic philosophy of the center.

Reaching out to make new friends can be an important means of finding new support. Alumnae have responded with expressions of pleasure in learning that their institution has a women's center and have come forth with support, often contributing much-needed funds. Asking important alumnae, sometimes trustees, to serve on executive or advisory committees can prove invaluable. If they accept, the probability is that within a short time they will become among the center's strongest supporters and serve as a wonderful liaison between the center, the administration, the board of trustees, and/or the alumnae association.

Finding and cultivating supportive administrators—both women and men—at the policymaking level can also make a difference in the kind of institutional support a center is given. Often people who are asked for advice eventually give their support.

Centers need to continue being a voice for women on campus. Part of monitoring the well-being of women on campus is keeping tabs on statistics on gender relationships affecting faculty, student, staff, and administration, as well as information on incidents and their resolution. This is usually difficult to do and sometimes requires prodding appropriate offices and faculty and administrative committees to obtain figures or at least to point to the need for more research. In addition, many centers have taken on the more active role of seeing that an unpleasant incident or grievance gets proper attention and does not get lost in a maze of bureaucracy, by lobbying, holding special meetings, and publicizing the grievance.

CONCLUSION

Although impressive progress has been made in institutionalizing the new scholarship on women and in beginning to transform the curriculum, there is still a tendency to play down women's issues and to avoid activism at many institutions in an attempt to seem more acceptable and mainstream. It is crucial, I believe, for women's centers to continue to stay on the cutting edge and to bring activists into as much of programming as possible. We must hear the experiences of women from different backgrounds who can give us firsthand knowledge of issues such as poverty, peace, reproductive rights, single parenting, jobs, health, and hazards in the workplace. Centers would do well to continue to encourage the involvement of community women so that the academic community of women can come to understand the commonalities that bind all women. Wherever possible, activist issues should be integrated into academic programs. An excellent example is the Barnard Women's Center Scholar and Feminist conferences, which have been held annually since 1974.

Each conference examines an aspect of the impact of feminism on traditional scholarship, underscoring the inextricable relationship between theory and practice, and always includes activist experiences on the same platform as feminist research and theory. It is noteworthy that these conferences attract a rare mix of several hundred scholars, artists, administrators, and activists of all ages.

The need for a feminist presence on campus remains paramount. In those few institutions where there is a serious commitment to women at the top level, the results are stunning. Programs flourish, and money comes in for special programs such as institutes, lecture series, grants for women scholars, and faculty development. Elsewhere, in the absence of such support and of community revitalization, women must continue to struggle to build the power bases they need to achieve equity both on and off campus.

REFERENCES

GIRAUD, KAREN L., SORCE, PATRICIA A., and SWEENEY, JOAN L. "Increasing the Effectiveness of Women's Programs on College Campuses: A Summary of the Activities and Accomplishments of the National Women's Training Project." National Women's Centers Training Project, Everywoman's Center, University of Massachsetts/Amherst and U.S. Department of Health, Education and Welfare. Unpublished, no date. Chapter 4. Women's Centers and Higher Education Conference, pp. 41–55.

MINNICH, ELIZABETH KAMARCK. *Special Progress for Women in Higher Education.* A report from the Barnard College Conference, March 14–16, 1979. Written in cooperation with the Barnard Women's Center. New York: The Women's Center, Bernard College, 1979.

17

Empowering Women Student Leaders:

A Leadership Development Model

MARY M. LEONARD AND
BRENDA ALPERT SIGALL

Where are the women student leaders on college and university campuses today? Why do we see so few? Has feminism affected only women over the age of twenty five? This article attempts to address these questions through an examination of the phenomenon of women student leadership on coeducational campuses and the presentation of a model for identifying the variables crucial to its development. This model, ideally, will give educators, counselors, and student affairs staffs a framework within which to understand undergraduate women's dilemmas and to intervene more effectively to encourage women's leadership potential. The model was developed out of eight years of reading, thinking, and creating leadership groups for undergraduate women.

If women are going to be equal partners with men in running our cities, schools, factories, state legislatures, religious and professional organizations, hospitals, unions, and federal government, they need to begin taking their place beside their male peers in school, having a say in how things are run. Although undergraduate women are involved in some leadership activities that would have been unheard of twenty years ago—take-back-the-night marches, lobbying state legislators, women's awareness weeks, rape crisis hot lines, abortion referral centers, escort services, picketing against pornography, lobbying for women's studies courses, and supporting feminist scholars—the more startling reality is what has not changed for undergraduate women. For the most part, they remain unwilling or unable to take their places next to their male peers in running college campuses (Weidman, 1979).

CAMPUS CLIMATE

One explanation for the difficulty women have in becoming leaders can be found in the context in which undergraduate women live. The campus environment is filled with contradictions. On the progressive side there is the increased attention to sexual harassment and date rape. Title IX of the Education Amendments Act of 1972 protects women from discrimination in admissions, curriculum, financial aid, and athletic participation. Women's studies courses are flourishing around the country, and the new scholarship has been introduced into many disciplines. On the regressive side, 40 percent of undergraduate women all over the country report experiencing sexual harassment from male students, faculty, and staff. Graduate and undergraduate women alike are affected, and few know what steps to take to protect themselves (Bogart and Truax, 1983). One large coeducational university reported that 80 percent of the reported rapes were "acquaintance rapes" (Atwald, 1984). The Supreme Court, in *Grove City vs Bell* (February 1984), severely limited the scope and impact of Title IX. Further, women continue to report sexist jokes, less eye contact, fewer follow-up questions, and other covert dismissal behavior by professors plus critical omission of materials on and by women in the classrooms (Hall and Sandler, 1981; Bogart, 1982).

The overall impact of the campus environment may be related to some negative outcomes for college women. Women's grades from freshman to senior year in college decrease notably, reversing women's performance in high school. In addition, women's career aspirations fall and self-esteem decreases during the four years of college, while men's grades, career aspirations, and self-esteem improve from freshman to senior year (Hall and Sandler, 1981; El-Khawas, 1980). The incidence of eating disorders is increasing, and 95 percent of the reported cases are women. Current statistics suggest as many as 15 percent of undergraduate women have some kind of eating disorder (Halmi, Falk, and Schwartz, 1981).

In examining the campuses nationwide, one finds that only 27 percent of faculty, 20 percent of administrators, and 10 percent of presidents of colleges and universities are women (Ottinger, 1987, tables 119, 130; Office of Women, 1984). Most student organizations are now coeducational, and males tend to hold the leadership positions. So the context in which undergraduate women exist is one which does not provide an experience in which women are leading and succeeding in proportion to their numbers. Given these realities, it is difficult for women to flourish in college. It has been observed that women who have early positive leadership experiences are more likely to be successful in their careers, with attendance at all women's colleges increasing the likelihood of this outcome. Graduates from these colleges achieve greater career advancement and community involvement than women graduates of coeducational schools (Tidball, 1973).

UNDERGRADUATE WOMEN

In working with students who are struggling to become leaders and become more powerful within themselves, we have found they face a number of problems. They are encountering biased treatment, including not being taken seriously and having to work harder to be better than men to be respected or get ahead. Feeling intimidated by male competitiveness is another common experience, along with the fear of loss of approval if and when they do assert themselves. When, for example, they speak up forcefully, they are frequently labeled as "too smart" or "pushy." Such women report receiving anger and rejection from male and female colleagues when they appear to be powerful. Weighing the benefits of affiliation versus being in charge, they often feel that the price of leadership may be loss of acceptance or social isolation. Role conflict, combining family responsibilities with those of work or school, seems to be a problem for women whether young, old, single, or married.

Many young women in the 1980s are dealing with these realities primarily through denial. While they say discrimination is a phenomenon of the past, they act as if they had no real opportunity for leadership. Or they implicitly equate leadership with masculinity and emulate male ways of doing things. This male identification results in a rejection of those human qualities, traditionally associated with women, that are positive and healthy: nurturance, caring, gentleness, and warmth. They may express little empathy for women or even become contemptuous of some women's problems. While women in the latter group are sometimes successful in breaking into leadership roles, they do so at a heavy psychological price—an internal disjuncture between their sense of self-esteem and the realities of their gender identity.

Having been born into the accomplishments of the second wave of the women's movement, they were shielded from the earlier struggles. Unlike earlier generations of women, they have missed many blatant experiences of discrimination and have not been aided in recognizing its more subtle forms. They have not yet had what Gloria Steinem calls the radicalizing experience of getting older. They sometimes see the leaders of the leadership workshop or vocal women leaders in general as overly reactive, polemic, or stuck in the past. When they do experience discrimination they do not know how to deal with it, for they lack conceptual understanding, response skills, and a network of support for coping with it.

Yet, even with all these problems, leadership skills for women rarely are discussed directly in psychological literature. What research is found comes under the categories of achievement motivation, fear of success, women and management, and, in small group research, sex differences in leadership. Little of this work touches directly on why women are less likely to assume leadership positions in college or explains the exceptional successes of the few. Some of the literature that does address this topic suggests that developing a sense of identity is related to political attitudes (Stein and Weston, 1982), conflicting expectations of achievement (Dickerson and Hinkle, 1978) and participation levels in activities (Weston and Stein, 1977). Most of the material that focuses on developing women leaders has come out of homegrown programs which often started as seminars on leadership, Women's Week presentations on women and power, assertiveness training, developing personal potential weekends, values clarification exercises, etc. Some of this work has just begun to be presented at the larger professional conventions (Frampton and Clark, 1984; Leonard et al., 1984).

THE LEADERSHIP MODEL

The Women's Leadership Matrix (see Figure 17.1) has been developed out of concern for finding a conceptual framework that can inform effective interventions to increase women's leadership participation. The model was developed out of the recognition that women are not a monolithic group on campus. There cannot be one intervention or one approach that would help all women to become better leaders. Their diverse needs and backgrounds require different responses.

The initial premise of the model is that leadership has a broad definition and application. Leadership defined strictly as holding elected or appointed offices is too narrow and rules out many of the opportunities women have to express or test their capacities. The definition needs to be expanded to include all those activities in which the person takes a stand, gathers support, pushes for something, and is recognized as a participant in the struggle. This view opens the door to nonhierarchical relationships, brief campaigns, and small as well as large projects.

DEGREE OF LEADERSHIP SKILL

	Low	High

	TYPE I
	
	Who: Women who have not yet developed any leadership role (includes majority of women students)
	
	Challenge: Connect
	    Awaken
	    Inform
	    Develop
		TYPE II
		
		Who: Women who are leaders but are male-identified (includes many elected leaders in student government, dorms, sororities)
		
		Challenge: Connect
		    Awaken
		    Inform
		    Involve

	TYPE III
	
	Who: Women who identify with women's issues but are unable to take on leadership roles (includes some returning women, some women's studies students, some others)
	
	Challenge: Develop
	    Instill hope
	    Empower
		TYPE IV
		
		Who: Women who are leaders and identify women's agendas as part of their commitment (includes some elected leaders, directors of women's centers, rape crisis hot lines, etc., some women's studies students, others)
		
		Challenge: Nurture
		    Network
		    Avoid burnout
		    Model

CONCERN FOR WOMEN'S ISSUES — Low / High

FIGURE 17.1. THE LEONARD/SIGALL WOMEN'S LEADERSHIP MATRIX

The second premise of the model, which resonates to Gilligan's (1982) concept of voice, is the notion that a woman needs more than just the traditional leadership skills to be a leader. She needs to be able to speak for herself as a person, for herself as a woman, and for her constituency of women. She needs to be able to identify and address causes that impact women directly and differentially. Understanding what these issues are and acknowledging their importance are necessary if one is to put them on the agenda despite lack of support from those who may trivialize these concerns or give them very little priority.

The two key variables in the Women's Leadership Matrix are degree of leadership skill and concern for women's issues. The matrix helps explain four types of women: (a) women who do not try to develop any leadership role; (b) women who are leaders but are male-identified; (c) women who identify with women's issues yet are unable to act; and (d) women who are leaders and identify a woman's agenda as part of their commitment.

Some examples of the two variables are in order. A woman high in leadership skill would be one who could write a good, clear letter, speak her mind, hold her own in group discussions, and talk to an administrator. She could organize a meeting, plan a demonstration or charity drive or a dance, run a campaign, a lobby, a hot line, a sorority, or a woman's awareness week. Women who are unskilled are more likely to be unassertive and fearful, with low self-esteem, and would have difficulty with most of the above actions.

Awareness of women's issues involves the recognition of women's needs and problems as discussed earlier. A woman with low awareness ignores historical economic or cultural influences, viewing people as individuals who are pushed and pulled only by inner forces. She does not identify politically as a woman or with women as a group. In their development of an extensive leadership program for students at a women's college, Frampton and Clark (1984) made consciousness-raising one of the four components of the program, seeing this as a crucial part of the work.

Minority women's identification with women's issues presents a complex picture. For the most part, what is said throughout this article applies to all women, majority and minority. But there are some special aspects relating to minority women in the context of this article that require additional comment. For example, minority women generally seem aware of race discrimination, and identify with their racial or ethnic group. They may be skilled leaders but may not be concerned with women's agendas. Sometimes they are pressured to show allegiance to their racial/ethnic roots, placing low priority on women's issues that may appear to be white women's issues, thus detracting from minority concerns. The minority woman, then, has the difficult task of resisting such pressure and being able to be effectively responsive to women's as well as ethnic/racial concerns.

The Quadrants

The Women's Leadership Matrix shown in Figure 17.1 includes four categories of women—described in each of the following quadrants—according to strength and weakness on two variables: leadership skills and awareness of women's issues.

Quadrant I holds women who are low in leadership skills and low in awareness of women's issues. They appear to represent the majority of our sample of women students. The challenge here is to connect with, awaken, inform, and develop these women. *Quadrant II* represents those women who are high on leadership skills and low on concern for women's issues. The women here include many elected leaders in student government, dorms, sororities, and other campus groups. They represent a very small percentage of women. The challenge here is to awaken them politically and help them to become identified with women's issues. *Quadrant III* holds women who are low on leadership skills and high on concern for women's issues. They represent a substantial minority of women observed. They include graduate students, returning women, women's studies students, and a small number of undergraduate women. The challenge here is to develop and empower them. *Quadrant IV* holds women high in leadership skills and high in concern for women's issues. They, like Quadrant II leaders, account for a very small percentage of women. They are typically the heads of women's centers, hot lines, rape crisis and abortion-referral networks. Some elected leaders and women's studies students are also often in this quadrant. The objective here is to give them support, to teach them self-nurturance, networking skills, and ways of avoiding burnout, and to engage them as teachers and models for Quadrant I, II, and III women.

It is clear how diverse these women are and that their needs for leadership development vary. What seems consistent among all the traditional-aged undergraduate women is the reality of the world in which they live and the similarity of the developmental tasks they face. As Jessie Bernard (1981) observed,

We all live in the single sex world and most of what we know from history, the humanities, the behavioral sciences deals with the male world. What we do know about the women's world from the male researchers is how it impinges on the male world. (p. 1)

Further, Bernard feels that women between the ages of eighteen and twenty-five are in their prime time of attractiveness and popularity. The culture is telling them they should get married. Relationships with men are put ahead of friendships with women, and academic success is often not their major concern.

RESEARCH FINDINGS

Whether a woman is in Quadrant I or IV, she still has to contend with society's messages and expectations. Farmer (1976) documents that reduced academic self-confidence first appears in college and speculates it might be related to a marriage-career conflict. Bardwick (1971) concurs and feels the ambivalence between achievement and affiliation with the opposite sex leaves the woman fearful that one will rule out the other. Leonard et al. (1984) found that men felt a romantic relationship would enhance their grades, while women felt if they had a romantic relationship, their grades would fall.

A number of researchers (Alper, 1974; Weidman, 1979; Gilligan, 1982; Pearson and Pope, 1981) identify the unique problems experienced by traditional-aged undergraduate women: achievement verses affiliation, attachment versus separation, and a personal versus a diffuse identity. These women have to face a dilemma that their male colleagues never have to consider: will becoming powerful lessen their chances for marriage? Becoming powerful includes developing leadership skills, initiating relationships with men and women, holding positions of influence, being committed to their education, and basing their personal and career decisions on their goals and abilities and not on their fears and concerns. How or if a woman reconciles these problems will depend on a number of factors. What educators need to keep in mind is that these are central concerns which cannot be ignored.

What is the picture of the traditional-aged college woman? They are young women concerned with love, acceptance, and marriage who have an ethic of caring and responsibility to others. They are at once women who are beginning their personal and career development, often embarking on unchartered waters.

INTERVENTIONS

What general approach do these insights suggest? First, women's concerns with relationships and marriage should be affirmed. They need to talk about how important relationships and family are to them. Second, the value of caring for one's self needs to be emphasized. Women can be encouraged to examine their often reflex selflessness and to consider the positive aspects of self-centeredness and personal development. This can be done through a variety of vehicles: nonsexist therapy, feminist reading, consciousness-raising groups, support groups, Outward Bound programs, and physical exercise, to name a few.

A discussion of recommended interventions follows, beginning with general campus actions and going on to specific exercises developed for use in small group settings.

Quadrant I Women

With Quadrant I women, who are low in leadership skills and low in consciousness of women's issues, connecting with or reaching them may be the most difficult task. Offering a leadership seminar will usually yield few takers, and those who do sign up are typically not Quadrant I women. They may be reached, however, through personal development workshop offerings such as those on values clarification, self-esteem, and assertiveness training. These can be run through the student union, counseling center, women's center, sororities, or dorms. In addition, traditional undergraduate women are usually quite receptive to either classroom experience or assignments for participation in some kind of self-development workshop. One approach that has been successful at the University of Maryland is a program of workshops run in conjunction with a class. To protect students and observe ethical guidelines, this kind of classroom involvement is freely chosen and not graded.

Once the Quadrant I women have chosen to participate, the next two challenges are to awaken them to themselves and to help them develop leadership skills. In terms of the awakening process, the overall approach needs to be to help them become aware of women's issues, their feelings about them, and identification with them, and to heighten their sense of unity with other women.

There are a wide range of options available for this process. Some possibilities are: reading, interning in women-oriented organizations, writing papers on women's issues for courses, attending women's events, watching television news for bias in coverage, interviewing women who have been discriminated against, investigating the school's process for handling sexual harassment charges, and participating in the group exercises later described.

Once the Quadrant I women have begun identifying with women's issues, they need to develop their leadership skills and quickly get plugged into some project that interests them. They can develop the skills most efficiently and thoroughly by enrolling in a leadership training class.

Quadrant II Women

Quadrant II women, those who are high in leadership skills and low in concern for women's issues, are probably the most difficult women to reach. They don't need skills training and they don't identify with women's issues. They are unlikely to be in any self-development group or women's studies class. They might enroll in a class on leadership or be involved in a retreat for school leaders. After contact is made, there are a number of suggestions for working with them. First, acknowledge their position and power. Often they feel that their work has not been appreciated and will welcome the recognition. Frame women's issues in the broader terms that they can understand and respond to: for example, rape is a safety issue; child care is a productivity issue; women studies funding represents the needs of 52 percent of their constituency.

It is important to help these women gain perspective on their experiences as women leaders on campus. Some questions that will be useful to raise with them include: How would you compare the recognition and acclaim you get for your leadership on campus versus that of your male peers? Have there been times when you felt dismissed or ignored by male peers in leadership positions?

Women students may initially need help in identifying such experiences. For example, one women student government officer on a major commuter campus did all the research on the need for lighting on campus, and three of the men who did none of the library work took the prize of testifying before the state legislators. The observation that she worked hard and deserved the recognition was very supportive to her. With that kind of validation, she was able to confront her colleagues. As a result of this experience this leader, who previously had little interest in women's issues, began to identify with women and eventually became a strong supporter of women's concerns.

Another recommendation is to try to build women's coalitions. For example, one could get the key women leaders from various campus groups together, have them form working teams, and respond to common concerns—for example, campus safety, female faculty tenure, classroom climate.

It is important for Quadrant II women to be exposed to leaders who are concerned with women's issues. By facilitating their working together, suspicion can recede and mutual respect grow. Once Quadrant II women have been contacted and express some interest in women's issues, many of the exercises suggested below for Quadrant I women apply.

Quadrant III Women

Quadrant III women, those who are low in leadership skills and high in concern for women's issues, require leadership skill, development, hope, and empowerment. The self-development and awakening interventions used for Quadrant I women are applicable here. Giving these women an historical perspective with which to identify is helpful. Since so little of women's history is taught in elementary and secondary schools, reading about famous and accomplished women and examining their struggles can be a very validating and powerful experience at the college level. Examining historical successes can be followed by looking at current successes in one's own and other's lives. Finally, data can be presented that show how far women have come, and just how much social, legal, and economic change has occurred.

A few approaches to empowering women include having them: (a) list their strengths, or ask their closest friend to list their strengths; (b) set goals for themselves and develop plans for reaching them; (c) break attractiveness rules—for example, walk around one day in sloppy clothes, no makeup or obligatory smiling; (d) get a critical mass of women at a meeting to sway the group; (e) observe verbal dominance in interpersonal situations (noting how often they are interrupted, cut off, asked their thoughts, or praised); (f) participate in an assertiveness-training class; (g) write letters to newspapers, congress people, and others on matters of concern; (h) interview successful women who identify with women; and (i) keep a journal of their thoughts and experiences during the group or workshop to document change and growth.

The goals of all the empowering exercises are to encourage the woman to get in touch with her own wishes, to act on them, and to develop a heightened awareness of sex-role stereotyping and how it controls and/or affects her.

Quadrant IV Women

Quadrant IV women need to be nurtured, connected with other supportive people in the community, and provided with positive experiences through role models. These leaders, high on both leadership skills and concern for women's issues, are often overcommitted, overlooked, and undersupported by their constituency or the administration. If they are leaders in traditional student organizations, they may have the additional burden of promoting concerns their colleagues do not share. All these women, whether they run the women's centers or sororities, need to find and receive support and learn to give to themselves. They often need help in setting limits, saying "no," and taking time for themselves, their relationships, their studies, and their futures.

Since these women are often heads of nontraditional and/or high-stress services, they can become isolated from other undergraduates and often feel lonely and disconcerted. They need to be taught how to create and maintain relationships with other kinds of services, key administrators, other student leaders, and supportive faculty, along with their natural constituency. It would seem helpful for them to reach out to services like their own in the community or on other campuses, as well as to sympathetic state legislators, newspaper columnists, or other influential persons. As they learn to talk with, influence, lobby, jockey for funds, and apply pressure, they are likely to feel more powerful in their jobs, more connected to the resources in the university and the local community, and feel revived.

Quadrant IV women can be used in leadership or self-development classes as role models to talk about themselves, their successes, and their failures. This will help the Quadrant I and III women, especially, and provide more support and appreciation for the Quadrant IV women.

SMALL-GROUP EXERCISES FOR EMPOWERING WOMEN LEADERS

The exercises described on the chart at the end of this article represent the authors' work with small groups and can be adapted to meet the needs of a particular group of women or particular leaders. These exercises are crucial elements of leadership training programs for women for a number of reasons. They help the women get in touch with their *feelings* and thoughts about a number of threatening topics. They help them face their fears and self-doubts. They give the women a safe environment to try out new behaviors, to experiment, and to practice skills and approaches before they have to use them more publicly or in less safe situations.

(1) Adjective Checklist

The first exercise, The Adjective List, is useful for Quadrants I through IV, but is especially effective for Quadrant I and II women. Group members individually list all the adjectives they associate with the words "femininity" and "leader" respectively, then share their lists with the group. Observing that there are rarely any words from the "femininity" column under "leader," the women are then asked to consider a series of questions: (a) What does it mean to you that few words associated with femininity are associated with leader? (b) With which words under femininity and leader do you identify? (c) Which words under leader would you be uncomfortable being called by your boyfriend, father, spouse, or brother? (d) Are there words under leader that sound positive when applied to men but negative when applied to women? Conflicts, contradictions, and overlaps between the lists are examined. The origin of the participant's word associations, personal experiences with the conflicts, and possible effects of the attitudes are considered.

(2) Risks to Being Powerful

A follow-up exercise, Risks to Being Powerful, which has the women consider the consequences of being powerful, is appropriate for Quadrants I through IV. Inevitably the women identify conflicts with boyfriends, husbands, or male colleagues as the major difficulty with being powerful. Fear of rejection, loss of love, loss of the relationship, and fear of hurting the male ego are cited as the major concerns, followed by discomfort with power and a reluctance to see themselves as powerful. The women are then asked to explore their fears by encouraging them to talk to the men from whom they anticipate rejection, and to talk to the group about their difficulty accepting power as a part of their self-image.

(3) Obstacles to Being a Leader or Being Powerful

The next exercise, Obstacles to Being a Leader or Being Powerful, is appropriate for Quadrant I and III, with Quadrant IVs acting as models. Here the women are asked to identify an area in which they would like to be more powerful and to think about what stands in their way. In addition to external—for example, institutional—problems, women repeatedly identify lack of assertiveness skills and inexperience with the world outside of home—for example, work situations—as personal obstacles.

In groups of three, members work on clarifying problems, developing strategies, and coming up with specific plans for action. Each person carries out her plan, feeling free to call other members of the triad for assistance, and everyone reports back to the group in one or two weeks. One of the objectives of this exercise is to encourage women to turn to each other for help, introducing both the idea and the experience of networks of support. Whether or not goals are reached, the women feel validated. They feel less isolated in their viewpoint and can receive valuable feedback. The probability of success is increased, and an understanding of the externally imposed as well as internally generated limitations is enhanced. As an adjunct, a leadership assessment can be done, asking the women to list their leadership strengths. Strengths are underscored, with a focus on how to utilize them. At this point books, self-help groups, women's organizations, and informal support groups are sanctioned and encouraged as legitimate resources. This is a place where Quadrant IV women can be drawn into the process as role models, gaining credit and visibility for themselves.

(4) Guided Sex-Role Fantasy

The Guided Sex-Role Fantasy asks the women to reflect on how their lives would have been different had they been born male. With eyes closed, they are slowly taken back through time to when they were born, beginning with experiencing their reactions to their grandparents joy over "It's a boy"; to their toys; clothes; friends; school experiences; rules; participation in sports (especially team sports); police patrol; altar boy (if Catholic); privileges; jobs around the home; bar mitzvah (if Jewish); first date; first use of the car; sex; curfews; after-school and summer jobs; the emphasis on vocation; college, marriage, children, and career. Examining their mother's lives or projecting into their daughter's futures via fantasy can facilitate confronting cultural limitations for those who have difficulty seeing them in their own experiences.

In another guided imagery, the participants go back in time to when they were ten years old (fifth grade). They think about who their friends were, what their family life was like, what teacher they had, how they felt about school, sports, friends, pets, clothes, and so forth. They are asked to be that ten-year-old girl and introduce herself to the group. Speaking in the first person, she talks about all aspects of her life. The women recall relationships, restrictions, and responsibilities. Often they get in touch with a spunkiness and vitality they had forgotten they had. By asking what happened to the liveliness, the strength, the spunky little girl, many of the women realize that during adolescence their lives were narrowed to stereotyped feminine activities and options. This is possibly the most powerful and usually the saddest exercise to do. It is allowed by an examination of how they were prepared for marriage, encouraged or discouraged from seriously pursuing a career, studying, or developing interests and talents. One frequent experience was having homemaking and child care responsibilities while brothers were free to spend their time playing, studying, or socializing. The older the women, the stronger the sex role stereotyping seems to be. Applicable to all women, these exercises are especially useful for women with low awareness—that is, Quadrants I and II.

(5) The Shoulds

The Shoulds helps the women examine what they were taught by word and example about what they *should* be, do, say, feel, look like, and so forth. They are instructed to list all of these messages and try to remember their respective sources—parents, school, movies, and the like.

Multiple, limiting, and conflicting expectations emerge with passive dependency as common themes. They are encouraged to express their feelings about this and think about how it gets played out in relationships and careers.

(6) Role Conflict

In the Role Conflict exercise, appropriate for Quadrants I and IV, the women get in touch with their potentially conflicting needs for affiliation and achievement. More mature women with families seem to profit most from this exercise. These women are balancing the demands of multiple roles and most often experiencing the resulting guilt and frustration from not being able to be all things to all people at all times. Often the younger or single women are out of touch with the reality of sexism and the different expectations which exist for men and women. They do not anticipate any problems combining family, school, and career. Inevitable conflicts, need for choices and priorities, limits on time and energy, and the cost of trying to be superwoman are dealt with in this discussion.

(7) Attitudes Towards Women Scale

Another exercise asks women to fill out the Attitudes Towards Women Scale, developed by Spence and Helmreich (1972), and then in small groups discuss their responses. Often they are surprised by the sexist beliefs group members, or even they themselves, express.

Discussing the concept of misogyny with historical and cultural examples is a powerful way for the less-experienced, more traditional women to become more educated and sensitized to sexist attitudes. Hearing the more experienced and politically aware women give examples of discrimination in their own lives, the less-experienced women typically begin to remember episodes of biased treatment that they had not recognized as such. They begin to relate experiences in which they were given sexist treatment. It is important for the women to get in touch with their own negative feelings toward women and begin to replace those attitudes and values with positive images of women.

Common examples of unconscious sexism include voting for a woman only if they knew her, versus voting for a man based on his platform; distrust and discomfort with a woman boss; assuming a work group of women will be backbiting while a group of men willl be cooperative; preference for male friends; assuming women friends are more interested in your boyfriend or spouse than you; questioning a woman if she said she knew how to do something, but assuming a man knew if he said he did; assuming men would make a better appearance than a woman speaking for the group; being more comfortable with a man chairing a meeting; thinking it odd if a man made coffee or took notes for a meeting; and so forth. Unevenness in awareness is common. In one arena, women may quickly demonstrate insight into sex-role stereotyping and in the next breath refer to forty-year-old women as "girls" while always referring to forty-year-old men as "Mr." It is important for the women to understand that all people have some stereotypic views of men and women, and that the goal is to identify and replace them.

CONCLUSION

As women students become increasingly aware of feminist issues and attain the skills to lead, more of the seats of power in our colleges and universities and in the greater society will be occupied by women who will use their voices to influence policy and practice. To this end, educators must create environments where women are taken seriously, as students and as potential and actual leaders. This requires acknowledgement and respect for women's knowledge and perspectives. As Adriene Rich (1979), in her last injunction to students at a recent women's student conference, said,

> To think like a woman in a man's world is thinking critically, refusing to accept the givens, making connections between the facts and ideas which men have left unconnected. And to me the most difficult thing of all, listening and watching, in all the descriptions we have been given of the world, are the silences, the absences, the nameless, the unspoken, the uncoded. It is there that we should find the knowledge of women. And in breaking those silences, naming ourselves, uncovering the hidden, making ourselves present, we begin to find the reality that resonates to us, which affirms us, which allows the woman teacher and the woman student alike to take ourselves and each other seriously, meaning to begin taking charge of our lives. (p. 245)

REFERENCES

ALPER, T. G. "Achievement Motivation in College Women: A Now-You-See-It Now-You-Don't Phenomenon." *American Psychologist* 29(1974), 194–203.

ATWALD, C. Sexual Assault: A Chance to Think. Videotape accompanying lecture presented at the Counseling Center Research and Development Session, University of Maryland, College Part, Md., Fall 1984.

BARDWICK, J. *Psychology of Women.* New York: Harper and Row, 1971.

BAR-TAL, D. and FRIEZE, I. H. "Achievement Motivation for Males and Females as a Determinant of Attributions for Success and Failure." *Sex Roles* 3(1977), 301–313.

BERNARD J. *The Female World.* New York: Free Press, 1981.

BOGART, K. *Institutional Self-study Guide on Sex and Equity for Post Secondary Institutions.* Washington, D.C.: Project on the Status and Education of Women, 1982.

BOGART, K., and TRUAX, A. Sexual Harassment in Academe: A New Assessment. Symposium presented to the National Women's Studies Association Conference, Columbus, Ohio, 1983.

DICKERSON, K. G. and HINKLE, D. E. "Expected to Achieve—But Not Too Much: Conflicting Expectations for Entering College Freshmen Women." Monograph. *College Student Journal* 12(1978), Part 2.

EL-KHAWAS, E. H. "Differences in Academic Development During College." *Men and Women Learning Together: A Study of College Students in the Late 70's the Report of the Brown Project.* Office of Provost, Brown University, Providence, R.I., 1980.

ERKUT, S. "Exploring Sex Differences in Expectancy, Attribution, and Academic Achievement." *Sex Roles* 9(1983), 217–231.

ETAUGH, C., and RILEY, S. "Evaluating Competence of Women and Men: Effects of Marital and Parental Status and Occupational Sex-typing." *Sex Roles* 9(1983), 943–952.

FARMER, H. S. "What Inhibits Achievement in Women?" *The Counseling Psychologist* 6(1976), 12–14.

FRAMPTON, M., and CLARK, J. R.I.S.C. Leadership training at Rivera College. Unpublished manuscript, 1984.

GILBERT, L. A., GALLESICH, J. M., and EVANS, S. L. "Sex of Faculty Role-model and Students' Self-perception of Competency." *Sex Roles* 9(1983), 597–607.

GILLIGAN, C. *In a Different Voice.* Cambridge: Harvard University Press, 1982.

GUMP, J. and RIVERS, L. "The Consideration of Race in Efforts to End Sex Bias." In E. Diamond (ed.), *Issues of Sex Bias and Sex Fairness in Career Interest Measurement.* Washington, D.C.: U.S. Government Printing Office, 1975.

HALL, R. M. and SANDLER, B. R. *The Classroom Climate: A Chilly One for Women?* Washington, D.C.: Project on the Status and Education of Women, 1981.

HALMI, K. A., FALK, J. R., and SCHWARTZ, E. "Binge-Eating and Vomiting: A Survey of College Population." *Psychological Medicine* 11(1981), 697–706.

ILLFELDER, J. K. "Fear of Success, Sex-role Attitudes, and Career Salience Anxiety Levels of College Women." *Journal of Vocational Behavior* 16(1980), 7–17.

LARSON, J. H., ALVORD, R. W., and HIGHER, K. "Problems Related to Academic Performance." *College Student Journal* 16(1982), 335–342.

LELAND, C. *Men and Women Learning Together: A Study of College Students in the Late 70's.* Report of the Brown Project. Providence, R.I.: Brown University, 1980.

LENNEY, E., GOLD, J., and BROWNING, C. "Sex Differences in Self-confidence: The Influence of Comparison to Others' Ability Level. *Sex Roles* 9(1983), 925–942.

LEONARD, M., SIGALL, B., PEARSON C., TOUCHTON, J., McMULLAN, Y., and MICHAUD, M. Slaying the Dragons: Leadership Development for Undergraduate Women. Presentation at the American College and Personnel Association Conference, Baltimore, MD, April 1984.

McKEACHIE, W. J., and LIN, Y. G. "Achievement Standards, Debilitating Anxiety, Intelligence, and College Women's Achievement." *The Psychological Record* 19(1969), 457–459.

O'DONNELL, J. A., and ANDERSON, D. G. "Decision Factors Among Women Talented in Math and Science." *College Student Journal* 11(1977), 165–168.

OFFICE OF WOMEN IN HIGHER EDUCATION, AMERICAN COUNCIL ON EDUCATION. Personal conversation with Judy Touchton, data based on Office of Women files. Washington, D.C., Nov. 14, 1984.

OLIVER, B. "Female Teachers, Student Achievement and Attitude in Coed Instruction." *Education* 103(1982), 139–144.

OTTINGER, CECILIA. *1986-1987 Fact Book on Higher Education.* New York: ACE/Macmillan, 1987, tables 119, 130.

PEARSON, C., and POPE, K. *The Female Hero in American and British Literature.* New York: Bowker, 1981.

RANDOUR, M. L., STRASSBURG, G. L., and LIPMEN-BLUMEN, J. "Women in Higher Education: Trends in Enrollments and Degrees Earned." *Harvard Educational Review* 52(1982), 189–202.

RICH, A. *On Lies, Secrets, and Silence.* New York: W. W. Norton, 1979.

ROWE, M. The Saturn's Rings Phenomenon: Microinequities and Unequal Opportunity in the American Economy. In P. Bournes and V. Parness (eds.), *Proceedings of the NSF Conference on Women's Leadership and Authority.* Santa Cruz, Calif.: 1977.

RUHLAND, D., GOLD, M., and FELD, S. "Role Problems and the Relationship of Achievement Motivation to Scholastic Performance." *Journal of Educational Psychology* 70(1978), 950–959.

SIGALL, B. Eating Disorders. Paper presented for staff development. Counseling Center, University of Maryland, College Park, Md, Fall 1984.

SMALL, A. C., and TEAGNO, L. "Identification and Academic Achievement in College Females." *College Student Journal* 14(1980), 54–59.

SPENCE, J. T., and HELMREICH, R. L. *Masculinity and Femininity: Their Psychological Dimensions, Correlates, and Antecedents.* Austin: University of Texas Press, 1978.

STEIN, S. L., and WESTON, L. C. "College Women's Attitudes Towards Women and Identity Achievement." *Adolescence*, Vol. XVIII, No. 68, Winter 1982, pp. 895–899.

STORMS, M. "Sex Role Identity and Its Relationship to Sex Role Attributes and Sex Role Stereotypes." *Journal of Personality and Social Psychology* 10(1979), 1779–1789.

TEGLASIE, A. "Sex-role Orientation, Achievement Motivation, and Causal Attributions of College Females." *Sex Roles* 4(1978), 381–397.

TIDBALL, M. E. "Perspective on Academic Women and Affirmative Action." *Educational Record* 54(1973), 130–135.

VEROFF, J. "Process vs. Impact in Men's and Women's Achievement Motivation." *Psychology of Women Quarterly* 1(1977), 282–293.

WEIDMAN, J. C. "Nonintellectual Undergraduate Socialization in Academic Departments." *Journal of Higher Education*, Vol. 50, No. 1 (1979), 48–62.

WESTON, L. C., and STEIN, S. L. "The Relationship of the Identity Achievement of College Women and Campus Participation." *Journal of College Student Personnel* 18(1977), 21–24.

ZUKERMAN, D. M. "Women's Studies, Self-esteem, and College Women's Plans for the Future." *Sex Roles* 9(1983), 633–642.

18

From the Playing Fields and Courts

L. LEOTUS MORRISON

From 1970 to 1976 participation by girls in high school competition increased approximately 600 percent nationwide (National Federation of State High School Associations, 1978). Between 1966 and 1985 the number of collegiate female competitors increased from approximately 16,000 to over 78,000 (*NCAA News*, 1984). This phenomenal growth exceeded the predictions or hopes of those working to establish sport opportunities for girls and women.

Women's interest in sport, ranging from competitive athletic teams to individual activities such as jogging or aerobic exercise, reflects a fundamental change in societal attitudes toward the role of sport in the lives of girls and women. Currently, 51 percent of the students in higher education institutions are women. They pay 51 percent of the tuition support of higher education and 51 percent of student fees that many campuses use to pay a major portion of athletic costs. As important consumers they are entitled to sports programs that meet their particular interests and needs.

The rapid growth and demise of a new model for athletics administration, the Association for Intercollegiate Athletics for Women, represents an unfortunate consequence of the pull toward the status quo. The need for a new model still exists. Additionally, our society, as well as our individual citizens, could truly benefit from a concept

250

of sport that values cooperation, the joy of participating, and the love of physical activity as well as winning.

THE EARLY DEVELOPMENT OF WOMEN'S SPORTS

Throughout the history of education, girls and women had limited or no opportunity to participate in competitive sports programs in any organized structured fashion. Society's assessment of the position of women, myths regarding the impact of strenuous activity on the female, cultural acceptance of vigorous sport as a "rite of passage" for masculine maturity, and protectionism of women from the "evils of competition" combined to close off sport and athletic options to all but a few females. For those few, options were limited to involvement primarily in activities valued for gracefulness or limited in vigor by modification from boys' games.

Early women leaders in physical education (largely in separate departments and professional organizations) watched the exploitation of some talented female athletes and the corruption of early intercollegiate programs for men. In reaction they placed greater emphasis on instructional programs and advocated "a sport for every girl and every girl in a sport." Intramural programs were stressed; intercollegiate programs were frowned upon. In actuality, women leaders gave priority to programs for the majority and underestimated the needs and interests of the athletically talented.

Women leaders who had chosen physical education as a career were a unique breed. In choosing physical education, the only career option for "female athletes" at that time, they were revolutionists of a sort, and certainly each had to cope with the stereotypical definitions of the gym teacher, ranging from comments on their "masculine walk" to unspoken questions threatening an individual's femininity. These women believed in the published, articulated goals of sport participation. They were committed to providing programs that fulfilled the philosophical goals expressed by educational theorists *through* physical activity. This approach to the educational potential of physical activity and sport experiences emphasized process (participation plus instruction) rather than product (wins/losses).

The large number of women's colleges and the pattern of separate departments and separate facilities in colleges and universities allowed and encouraged a different type of physical education program for women. This separate organizational structure offered growth and advancement opportunities for its leaders and was a natural support network providing female role models, mentoring, and encouragement to move ahead professionally. Success was measured through contributions to a program, to an institution, and to a professional group rather than to moves up the administrative hierarchy or to personal status or financial gain. This service motif to students and profession was "a strong cause" and was passed down from generation to generation.

The history of "female movements" indicates that, as long as those movements do not threaten the status quo or call for change in established "male patriarchal values or patterns of organization," women are allowed a great deal of latitude in running their own show. Certainly this was true with women's physical education, and women leaders asserted strong control. Yet they also were a part of a patriarchal society and were influenced by societal attitudes. Far too often they accepted artificial limitations on the physiological capabilities and skill expectations of female students. In matriarchal governance and for the good of those who played, they protected that play, designed its competitive structure, and controlled the players. Thus, women leaders inadvertently participated in limiting athletic opportunities and in perpetuating myths and patriarchal beliefs.

The civil rights battles, legislative achievements, and the student revolutions of the 1950s and 1960s raised questions regarding equality in the minds of younger women in physical education. A break with the past was not an easy step to take, for overt refutation of the ideals passed to them was a perceived denial of a valued heritage. Almost without articulation and without conscious revolt some voices were raised questioning the neglect of the talented athlete. Professional organizations that had staunchly denied varsity programs began to discuss the potential values of interscholastic and intercollegiate programs for women, albeit with different emphases and controls than those prevalent in men's programs. On individual campuses, especially in those state colleges and teachers colleges with strong physical education programs for women, limited varsity programs were initiated and coached by women physical educators and supported largely out of departmental budgets and out of the pockets of students and student organizations. National conferences were held to discuss the possibility of interscholastic and intercollegiate competition. An increasing number of women recognized they had been denied options for athletic development and a chance to strive for excellence in physical skill and prowess. They wanted additional options for their students, and a new cause was born.

Concurrently, those few women athletes who had competed at

international levels had not achieved to the satisfaction of Olympic leaders and a project was initiated to develop a higher level of expertise in teachers of selected sports. Jointly, the Women's Board of the Olympic Development Committee and the Division for Girls and Women's Sports (a professional organization of women that had been the voice of women in sport since 1899) sponsored five national institutes to train coaches and teachers in more advanced skills. Each of these institutes emphasized one or more sports and selected women leaders from each of the states to attend. Those attending were obligated to return to their state and conduct two or more local workshops to pass on their acquired knowledge. Thus, within a short period of time techniques, skills, and strategies were passed to colleges and high schools, sports new to girls and women were introduced, and competition was initiated or encouraged.

Once competitive groups were in operation, it was natural that these groups would desire a culminating event or tournaments to assess their accomplishments and test their skill. In 1966 the Division of Girls and Women's Sports (DGWS) announced the creation of the Commission on Intercollegiate Athletics (CIAW) to sponsor invitational championships conducted within the published guidelines of DGWS philosophical principles and standards. The first DGWS/CIAW championship was held in 1967. The response was overwhelming, but with it came numerous problems regarding selection of teams, conduct of the championships, support of the program both in financial terms and in time cost to the volunteer leaders, and responsibilities of institutions recognizing or sponsoring the teams. Another organization, the National Association for Physical Education of College Women (NAPECW), with regional substructures had been assessing needs for intercollegiate programs and encouraging the formation of state and local associations to direct and control the direction of women's athletic programs.

In 1971, DGWS called a meeting that included representation from its executive board, the commissioners of CIAW, and representatives from all NAPECW regions and from community and junior colleges to consider the creation of an organization to govern women's intercollegiate athletics. Increased interest in athletics by women and the positive response to DGWS/CIAW championships pointed to a need for an organization with institutional membership and elected representation.

Invitations for membership were sent to community and junior colleges, accredited colleges and universities; 278 institutions became charter members of the Association for Intercollegiate Athletics for

Women (AIAW) in 1971–1972. AIAW took on the responsibilities of CIAW but was an institutional membership organization within the overall associational structure of AAHPER (American Association for Health, Physical Education and Recreation) and its substructure DGWS. The organizations (DGWS, AAHPER, CIAW, NAPECW), which were influential in developing and supporting athletic programs for women, were all professional education organizations.

Thus, a collegiate athletic governance organization was created by women educators interested in additional sport options yet influenced by a philosophical heritage with primary concerns for (a) the personal benefits of participation, (b) the right of athletes as students and the avoidance of exploitation of athletes by coaches and institutions, and (c) the importance of women educators as leaders and role models.

The initial thrust toward increased sports opportunities resulted from "a women's movement" in physical education, though those very women did not and many still do not define themselves as feminists nor as political advocates for change.

A second impetus for the growth of women's sports was increased television coverage of the Olympics, highlighting the accomplishments of women athletes from other countries such as Olga Korbut and the Japanese women's volleyball team and pinpointing an early lack of success by our female athletes as well as the decreasing success of male U.S. athletes. This highly visible injury to national pride led to increased support and funding of year-round programs to identify and develop Olympic level athletes, both male and female.

Probably the most far-reaching influence contributing to the growth of women's sports was the passage of Title IX of the Educational Amendments Act of 1972. High schools and universities, especially those with highly visible male athletic programs and limited or nonexistent programs for women, added women's teams. In many cases these programs were structured in athletic departments rather than in physical education departments, and policy decisions were the responsibility of the male athletic director. In 1971–1972, 15.6 percent of all college athletes were women. By 1980–1981, nine years later, 30 percent of all collegiate athletes were women (*NCAA News*, 1984).

The athletics section of the Title IX regulations generated a great deal of negative attention from the male-dominated athletic establishment, while leaders in the general women's movement came to view it as a critical measure of women's programs. The threat of withdrawal of federal funds, the projected cost of replicating the existing male model of athletic programs, and the ultraconservative views on female participation in athletics held by many in athletic governance led to strong opposition to Title IX. Repeated attempts to modify and weaken the regulations were made by the National Collegiate Athletic Association and by individual colleges and universities involved in large scale athletic programs for men.

Leaders in the women's movement easily identified a gold mine of clear-cut, countable, discriminatory practices and procedures in athletic programs. A number of colleges and universities had no programs for women. Existing women's programs were limited in the number of sports offered, the number of participants and events, the amount of financial support, the number and quality of coaches, uniforms, equipment, facilities, media attention, and institution-wide support services ranging from medical and athletic care to secretarial and administrative services.

Initially, many of the leaders in the general women's movement had little experience with sport. In the limited career options open to them, intellectual and academic achievement was stressed. Yet, as their sensitivity to discrimination was raised, they were exposed to a vision of sport as a training ground for success. They supported the right of women to athletic opportunity, but the only model they could envision was one identical to existing male athletic programs—one that is a rite of passage to success, advancement, power in a patriarchal society. This society defines success in terms of wins and the marketability of those wins and power over others as opposed to the potential of sport participation for self-knowledge. This lack of understanding on the part of educational leaders and feminists alike concerning the need for an alternative approach to athletic governance, added to the difficulty of creating a program that emphasized the potential of women and the athlete as a student.

The growth of women's collegiate athletics during the 1970s was phenomenal and AIAW was successful way beyond the projections of its early leaders. Increased opportunity, improved budgets and support services, provision of equipment and facilities led to greater levels of skill development and higher expectations for and by collegiate players. But perhaps the greatest success was a fundamental change in societal attitudes toward the role of sport in the lives of girls and women. More women (from joggers and aerobic dancers to the Olympic gold medal winners) have had the opportunity to become more confident with their physical selves. Through sport they have had the chance to learn commitment to a cause, to strive toward individual or group goals, to develop self-discipline, and to develop the cooperation necessary for equitable competition.

Despite continuing opposition from women leaders, and some

men who understood the importance of alternative governance in sport, athletic governance organizations which previously had conducted programs only for men began programs for women. In 1981 the NCAA enacted governance and championship plans which ultimately led to the dissolution of AIAW by AIAW Executive Board action. It seemed that neither the colleges and universities nor the male athletic establishment could cope with or tolerate a separately functioning new model of governance for competitive athletics for women—or for men.

Powerful organizations seek additional power and control, especially over groups that threaten existing practices or pose successful competition. By the late 1970s it was evident that women's athletics was not a passing fad and that AIAW would not self-destruct through incompetence and lack of support. In addition, alternatives to existing NCAA regulations, emphasizing allowing the same options to athletes as to other students relative to such areas as scholarship amounts, transfer status, and due process, threatened the control of NCAA over athletes and institutions. Within the ranks of women, success raised expectations for greater success and quicker gratification in terms of financial support and media exposure.

Acknowledgment of women's athletics as a viable program, the failure of attempts to undermine Title IX, the threat of alternative models, the reported simplicity of administering men's and women's programs under the same organization were factors influencing the NCAA initiation of programs for women and the subsequent dissolution of AIAW. The fight of AIAW for increased opportunity was a successful one. The thrust of AIAW for a different model of athletics has suffered severe setbacks. The opportunity for higher education to experience the positive effects of a fresher, potentially more student-centered and less-corrupt model of athletic governance was, at least for the time being, lost.

CURRENT CONCERNS

Our society has supported and developed, during a seventy-five-year period, an athletic system for male athletes that encourages every young boy to learn a sport at an early age. This acceptance of the importance of sport to masculinity and to the average "American male" provides a mammoth pool of potential athletes. Extensive community programs (for example, midget leagues, little leagues, recreation programs) provide early instruction and encouragement to be a member of a team. As a youngster progresses through elementary and secondary school, the more highly skilled from the talent pool are selected. At the collegiate level the selection (recruiting) process becomes even more stringent, and the competition for the "blue chipper" intensifies. With the attraction of potential television and marketing monies and the increased importance placed on athletic success to reflect success of the institution, the athlete has become a marketable item and the athletic program an essential ingredient to the image of institutional prestige and accomplishment. In a large number of institutions there are no "walk-ons" and program decisions are influenced by economic and political factors rather than by the interests of students or by the educational potential of the varsity experience. This is a system that serves primarily the institution—not the student. The athlete is a valuable commodity, and many regulations are designed to protect the investment of the institution.

Women's athletics, though increasingly forced into this model, has not had the same developmental history. Societal attitudes toward the role of sport in the life of a woman have changed, but the broad horizontal entry opportunities of community programs do not exist, nor is there the same importance attached to sport as an essential skill for career success. Young girls usually learn sport skills later than young boys, and there is some question that their motivations for sport participation may be different from their brothers or at least that their concern for interrelationships may influence their type of participation in athletics. Much has been written about the gender gap in politics; some women believe there is also gender distinction in the developmental role of sport. The recent research and writings of such authors as Carol Gilligan pose many questions that have relevance for both athletics and education. Increased options in sports for women only addresses these questions in part. Additionally, women/girls and women's sports need increased numbers of programs at earlier ages stressing participation and instruction rather than concentration on organized league competition.

Following the model of men's athletics, some trends toward classicism and racism are evident in women's athletics. There is continuing attitudinal pressure on women (minority and majority) to enter such sports as gymnastics, swimming, tennis, and golf. Early skill instruction in those sports is costly and primarily limited to those who can afford private clubs and coaches. Minority women and men, too, often are counseled and directed toward certain sports. In fact, part of the "clustering" phenomenon of minorities in a few sports is due to a lack of opportunity for instruction in others. There is also peer pressure to avoid sports dominated by upper-class white men and women and for Black men, for example, to pursue sports such as basketball as a way "up and out" vis-à-vis scholarship opportunities. The lack of professional opportunities in women's sports makes decisions about scholarships, provision of academic support and encouragement to complete degrees especially critical for the minority women athletes and for some majority women, as well.

Society, education, and research tend to assess women's behavior, and physical and psychological capabilities or reactions in sport, as in other aspects of society, in comparison to levels of function. In other words, we measure the male level of function, assume that level as a standard, and compare female data to that "norm." Consequently, we report such physical observations on females (for example, lean body mass or oxygen uptake) as a certain percentage of that of males. The inference here is value-laden, assumes sameness, and automatically designates "first-class" and "second-class" status. In curricular and cocurricular program construction, we impose similar pressures for sameness. We ignore or overlook the implications of observations and research that present the "different voice of women," alternative motives for involvement, or different emphases at various states of chronological and developmental stages. We replicate programs designed for white men, for minority women and white women; then we appoint predominantly upper-middle-class white males to administer these programs. Higher education leaders need to identify, encourage, appreciate, and support value differences and diversity. The question has been asked: "What do women want in athletics?" One answer is a different model of athletics and acceptance of differentness as "equal to" and "as good as." A major loss in the dissolution of AIAW was in the loss of a possible alternative athletic philosophy, structure, and organizational pattern.

The past five years have brought changes to women's athletics. Some changes stem from pressures to fit the structure of existing male-dominated athletic organizations and some from the decreasing interest of governmental agencies to enforce the mandates of civil rights legislation in large part due to the 1985 Supreme Court decision on *Grove City* vs. *Department of Education*. This decision considerably altered the scope and coverage of Title IX.

There has been a drastic decrease in the number of women leaders in athletics and in physical education. This decrease of women leaders is found among coaches, officials, teachers, and athletic administrators. Title IX required opening gender-segregated classes but did not require joint administrative structures. However, many institutions have merged separate physical education departments and separate athletic programs. In almost all cases men have been appointed to the top decision-making posts and women leaders have been relegated to assistant or associate positions. In 1984, 86.5 percent of women's intercollegiate programs were under the supervision of a male athletic director and, even more alarming, 38 percent of the intercollegiate programs for women in the United States have no female involved in athletic administration (Acosta and Carpenter, 1985).

The situation relative to the coaches of women athletes is similar. In the early 1970s, male coaches of women's teams in colleges were a rarity. By 1984, only 53.8 percent of the women's teams were coached by a female head coach and five of the ten most popular NCAA sports for women have more male coaches than female coaches. The preponderance of male coaches reinforces a societal attitude that males are more knowledgeable and capable in the sport arena.

In addition, many institutions have combined men's and women's teams and appointed the same coach, usually a male, to coach both. This pattern not only has decreased the number of female coaches, but also has lead to the conduct of joint competitions that have resulted in decreases in squad size and in the numbers of events within joint competitions (for example, swimming and track meets). Since there are fewer events for women to begin with, a decrease that appears equitable (that is, one for one) disproportionately affects opportunities for women.

The increase of male coaches at the high school and college level imposes male athletic standards, values, and practices on female athletes and teams and contributes to the continuation of questionable practices of the past. In effect, these trends encourage the development of a male athletic program for women, diminish the impact of different ideas, and eliminate strong female mentors and role models.

The decline of women in athletics may be influenced also by a climate in higher education that discourages entry and promotion of women in administration. In 1983, according to the National Research Council, over 40 percent of the doctorates and 72 percent of the master's degrees in education were granted to women, yet we do not see those proportions represented on faculties or in administration. Many highly qualified women are leaving the education profession. In an article examining fundamental fallacies in policy and programs for sex equity, Marshall (1984) questions if the crisis in quality of education is linked to the decline in women educational leaders. Current bureaucratic business models of administration emphasize hierarchical control and decisions from above. The leadership style of most women is more democratic and seeks wider input into the decision-making process. Marshall suggests: "Perhaps intelligent, highly educated women are leaving education because they despair over the unwillingness of education chieftains to listen to their ideas or grant legitimacy to their leadership style" (p. 29).

In addition to changes occurring because of pressures within education for bureaucratic control and homogeneity, the conservative political wave bringing deemphasis or nonenforcement of civil rights legislation has also affected women's athletics. There appears to be both a relaxed concern regarding possible consequences of inequality and inequity and an attitude that the problems of sex discrimination have been solved. Unintentional or unconscious acts or attitudes are the most difficult forms of discrimination to combat. The atmosphere in higher education today is not as sensitive to equity or equality as previously. It is interesting to note that gender equity has not been addressed in most of the critiques of education published in the 1980s. A commitment to a change in social policy and the necessary procedures to support equity is not evidenced in the expressed concerns of education leaders.

Educational policy and education leaders should be focusing on developing human potential—female and male. Athletic programs are used to reflect an image of success, to generate contributions from alumni and corporations, and to earn television revenue through in-season and championship contests. The athletic program increasingly serves the interests of institutional promotion and public relations rather then the interests or needs of students and society. Marketing the university on the basis of its athletic success has increased pressure to win at any cost and undermines the value of sport participation as an educational experience. Young people learn from the actions of their elders more readily than from their verbiage. What we say about athletics and the decisions we make or do not make relative to athletics are creating double standards and value confusion.

In the full realization of human potential, the college experience provides opportunities to develop independence and the ability to make responsible choice decisions. Treatment of athletes, both in the recruitment process and after enrollment, is different from that of other students. They receive special consideration, special protection and direction, special additional support services. This treatment perpetuates dependency by the athlete on a paternal support system

and contributes to the failure of many athletes to become independent and direct their own lives and choices. A large number of athletes
have not achieved academically because they were not expected to
achieve. Many teachers/counselors, beginning in secondary schools,
have subconsciously reinforced a belief that athletes are not capable
of intellectual accomplishment. Once a pattern of lower academic
expectation is set, most athletes rise only to that level of expectation.

THE FUTURE

Women's athletics is beginning to show symptoms of the ills that
men's athletics has developed. The problem is not whether women
and men will cheat, but that the athletic system, as constituted today, corrupts. Treatment of athletes, rules and regulations, the institution's use of athletic success, higher education administrative and
management styles contribute to perpetuation of a system that demands constant success measured in wins and increased revenue
production. Athletic programs have become tools of the university
rather than programs for students. There are few individuals in athletics and higher education who do not genuinely believe in the educational potential of athletic participation, but they are increasingly
caught up in moral dilemmas between decisions that benefit individual students and those that contribute to wins and public acclaim.
The system needs drastic change, and the changes needed will require courageous leadership from college and university trustees and
presidents, athletic administrators, coaches, parents, and the public.
    A first brave step would be to require all issues at the NCAA as-
sembly to be voted on by all institutions. The current trend toward
federation, different rules for different divisions, and competition
based on conferences encourages voting motivated by institutional
or conference self-interests rather than by a desire to create programs that provide educational opportunities for students.
    In a country where scientific advances have dramatically length-
ened the average life span, education should be concerned with the
quality of that life. The potential of physical, psychological, social,
and emotional benefits acquired through sport participation, both as
a student and as a college graduate, suggests two program considerations. Basic curricula for both men and women should include a
commitment to the role of physical activity as a vital ingredient of
the liberally educated person. Second, universities should provide a
continuum of sport competitive experiences for its students. It will

be necessary to change current athletic programs drastically in order to accomplish such aims. A continuum of competitive programs could include: a few selected varsity teams, a broad spectrum of club teams supported in part by the institution, comprehensive intramural and recreational programs, and provision of sport facilities for informal use.

Sport (athletics) can be a unique human experience through which students learn about themselves. Developing a physical skill can be beneficial, but perhaps more important are the possibilities to test one's abilities physically and emotionally, to strive for excellence, to set personal and group goals and evaluate the degrees of success, to discipline oneself, to experience mastery over time, space, and objects, to respond to stress, and to appreciate the joy of skillful movement. Both men and women would gain from programs that allow students to benefit from sport as opposed to involvement in programs that exploit students.

The decrease of women in leadership should be a major concern to higher education and to women. If higher education really intends to educate women rather than merely collect tuition and fees, each institution has the responsibility to create an administrative and educational environment that utilizes and encourages women at all levels. A necessary concomitant emphasis is to encourage alternative administrative/management styles using creativity and innovativeness. Women in leadership can bring a different voice, a unique perspective to athletics and to the entire vision of higher education.

The increase in the number of majority women and minority women and men in higher education plus the projected increase in the number of students of foreign-born parents should forewarn us of an expanded and more diverse undergraduate population in the future. Mere acceptance of students from diverse subcultures and molding students to a white-upper-middle income image will not be sufficient. Higher education needs to change its image, value the uniqueness of our various subcultures, incorporate the new knowledge from Women's Studies, Black Studies, Asian Studies, American Indian Studies, and Ethnic Studies into the mainstream of course content as well as encourage continued research and study in those distinct fields. Perhaps most important, faculty and administrators that appreciate diversity and are representative of anticipated constituencies must be hired.

Only a limited number of women or feminists and even fewer men have understood the distinctions between athletic programs for individual development and programs for institutional purposes.

Those who do understand have been negligent in expressing those ideas in publications read by feminists or by the general public. Most feminists have spoken out for athletic opportunities but have not analyzed the potentials of different models of athletic programs. Women now need to accept the responsibility to understand the influences athletic programs can have on individuals and fight for programs that benefit people.

This effort requires increased instructional opportunities for young girls in community programs and school programs; demands for change in the organization and administration of athletic programs; support for women coaches, administrators, and leaders; and examination of the role of sport in educating young men and women.

There is a value crisis in athletics today. It is a women's issue, but more important it is a societal issue. Reevaluation of the uses we make of athletic programs could benefit higher education and the female *and* male students who should be the reasons for its existence.

REFERENCES

ACOSTA, R. VIVIAN, and CARPENTER, LINDA JEAN. "Women in Athletics—A Status Report." *Journal of Physical Education, Recreation and Dance,* August 1985, 30–34.

BOUTILIER, MARY A., and SANGIOVANNI, LUCINDA. *The Sporting Women.* Champaign, Ill.: Human Kinetics Publishers, 1983.

"82-83 A Year Of Growth In Men's, Women's Sports." *NCAA News,* February 29, 1984, 1 and 20.

GILLIGAN, CAROL. *In a Different Voice: Psychological Theory and Women's Development.* Cambridge, Mass.: Harvard University Press, 1982.

MARSHALL, CATHERINE. "The Crisis in Excellence and Equity." *Educational Horizons,* Fall 1984, 24–30.

NATIONAL FEDERATION OF STATE HIGH SCHOOL ASSOCIATIONS. *1978 Sports Participation Survey.* Elgin, Ill.: 1978.

SLATTON, BONNIE, and BIRRELL, SUSAN, eds. *The Politics of Women's Sports. Arena Review.* Boston: The Institute for Sport and Social Analysis, July 1984, Vol. 8, No. 2.

WEST, CHARLOTTE. "The Female Athlete—Who Will Direct Her Destiny?" In *Rethinking Services for College Athletes.* San Francisco: Jossey-Bass, 1984, pp. 21–30.

PART THREE

Reconceptualizing the Ways We Think and Teach

Inherent in the programs shaped by women in Section II is a tension between the needs of women as understood by women and the values and priorities of the dominant social and institutional environments in which they find themselves. The result more often than not has been compromise programming on a spectrum, with the more established and establishment programming having the benefit of being more accepted by their institutional environment and with programs struggling on the periphery experimenting in more fundamental ways. As ideas are tested and proven effective in the programs on the margin, however, they are often incorporated in more mainstream efforts.

It is not surprising, then, that many such ideas, spawned in programs designed especially for women, required reconceptualizations that have implications way beyond those programs. For example, it was argued originally that women needed to learn about women's history so that they would have adequate and empowering role models. While this argument still has validity, a more compelling argument for women's history today is that history that leaves out half the human race is seriously flawed; thus, women's history is as important for men as for women.

If women are learning the history of males in their "regular" history courses and supplementing that knowledge by taking women's history courses, they still will be more fully educated than a student, male or female, who takes only the traditional courses, believing those on women are for women only.

If women experience programming designed by women for women and at the same time programming designed for men, they often experience dual or multiple realities while most white males experience only one. (Minority women and men similarly experience multiple realities, with minority women experiencing double overlays of race and sex.) As a result, women begin raising questions and having expectations that seem unprecedented: in their "regular" courses—which still tend to exclude information on women—women are not asking, what were the women doing? After learning to link personal experience to theory in women's studies classes, women are less likely, in other classes, to passively accept theories that contradict their own experience. And they are not simply assuming that the male way of doing things is the only way. They are daring to assert their equality with men while also exploring and honoring their differences from them.

Chronologically and historically, women and the culture at large have gone through at least three levels in understanding difference.[1] All the levels coexist in today's world, with some people at one stage and others at another. Briefly, the first level of truth about gender and difference holds that men and women are inherently and innately different and that difference translates into different roles and social expectations. In this view there is no true difference without heirarchy, so that men are seen as superior and women inferior, with men holding greater political and economic power.

The second level of truth emphasizes equality for women and in doing so deemphasizes difference, maintaining that men and women are essentially the same (with perhaps a few minor, but relatively insignificant differences). This was a radical notion in its time and has been responsible for the concept of equal pay for equal work and the offering of nontraditional employment to women, even positions of relatively great power. In educational terms, this meant offering women, for the first time, access to the same education available to men. This great breakthrough required, however, that women demonstrate and earn their equality by proving that they were as good as—meaning the same as—men. Elizabeth Kamarck Minnich, in "From the Circle of the Elite to the World of the Whole: Education, Equality, and Excellence," explores the implications of this view for higher education. While women have been highly successful in demonstrating that they can be successful when judged by male standards, the result has been the loss to many women, and hence to the society at large, of the distinctly female perspectives emerging out of uniquely female experiences.

The third level recognizes difference in a context of equality. Adopting this stance for many people requires a major cognitive leap equivalent to the paradigm shift. As Thomas Kuhn describes in *The Structure of Scientific Revolutions* (1962), a paradigm shift occurs after too many unexplained "facts" accumulate that cannot be accounted for by the old theory. A new theory is required that will do so. When the experiences of women and minority males are ignored, the old paradigms seem to work. However, the more previously invisible information comes to the fore, the more inadequate the old ways of seeing the world become. At first people simply tamper with the old paradigm, such as adding a unit on women (minority and majority) here, on the minority experience there; but the more you know, the more inadequate the old paradigm appears. The result is a major paradigm shift in which new information is not simply added on, but the entire way of organizing and arranging knowledge is rethought and reconfigured.

At level three, therefore, it is possible to conceive of men and women as being both similar and different and to see differences as a form of human richness. In a context of equality it is possible to recognize that differences of experiences and perspectives exist without translating that awareness into limitation for any group. Instead of relegating groups to particular roles on the basis of their particular abilities, we can learn from one another and benefit in all areas of life from diversity.

This new paradigm comes easiest to majority women and minority women and men because their cognitive dissonance is greater, and therefore belief in the old paradigm is harder to maintain. However, majority males on the forefront of knowledge and theory are experiencing a similar paradigm shift, sometimes as the direct result of feminist challenge, but also because of more synchronous change. As Judith Harris et al. note in "Educating Women in Science," the revolutions in thinking in modern physics and biology are movements from more traditionally male ways of seeing the world—as a separate discrete object acted upon by a value-free scientist—to a more female way of envisioning the world which emphasizes interconnectedness: the scientist is viewed as in relationship with the phenomena being studied.

It is interesting to trace the ways that insights and points of view characteristic of women in general converge with the cutting edge theories in many fields. Is this because women have less to lose in moving past the old paradigm and hence resist change less than most men? Is it because the culture is, as Carl Jung predicted, reintegrating the feminine? Or is it simply that women have had to be more cognitively complex because they have had to understand at least two systems—and minority women three or four—while majority men have had to learn only one and thus have not had the experience of cognitive challenge that motivates growth?

William Perry's scheme of cognitive complexity (*Forms of Intellectual and Ethical Development in the College Years*, 1968) is useful here. Level-one thinking about sex roles parallels his stage two (out of nine stages of cognitive complexity). It is characterized by a belief in absolute truth, absolute standards, dualism, and a reliance on the judgment of authorities. Unfortunately, many academics, ordinarily quite cognitive complex, retreat to a stage-two arguments when faced with the feminist challenge, fearing that integrating material on women, minority and majority, or minority men will lower standards—as if those standards were absolute. In Perry's scheme, stages three and four are various responses to multiplicity and to the relativity of knowledge. At stages three and four, we either uphold a "new truth" absolutely or we explore ways of developing standards adequate for dealing with a relativistic, multiplistic universe. At stage five, we become relatively comfortable with making contextual, not absolute, judgments.

The feminist challenge requires a reconceptualization of the way we think and teach that requires cognitive complexity. If the standards of white males are not absolute—and the job of majority women and minority women and men is *not* to learn to act and think as much like majority males as possible—then how are we to establish standards? What are the new standards for teaching and for scholarship?

Academics have assumed that it is their responsibility to guard academic freedom, and have occasionally responded to those who wish to integrate scholarship on women—minority and majority—

and minority men into their classrooms as if feminists were threatening it. The irony here is that the real threat to academic freedom occurs on the curriculum committees and the hiring committees that, consciously, or unconsciously, systematically censor the insights of people other than majority males by declaring them to be lowering standards.

In the past fifteen years, there has been a veritable explosion of research and theory on rethinking the ways we think and teach. Challenges to the content and methodologies of most disciplines are now widely available as are now a number of books about the process of transforming the curriculum of institutions. These include JoAnn M. Fritsche's *Toward Excellence and Equity: The Scholarship on Women as a Catalyst for Change in the University* (1984), and Betty Schmitz's *Integrating Women's Studies Into the Curriculum* (1985). Works bringing together diverse research on gender related to questions of pedagogy are not yet so readily available. Taken together, research on learning styles, decision-making, cognitive development, and leadership suggest a compelling need to rethink not only what we teach but how we teach it. Recent research on personality and learning styles, moreover, suggests that traditional ways of teaching may be geared more to men's preferences in ways of knowing than women's. For example, according to David Kolb (*Experiential Learning*, 1984), 59 percent of men prefer to learn by abstracting knowledge from its context. Fifty-nine percent of women, however, prefer to grasp information in context. This may explain why traditional male college environments prize objectivity and abstraction so highly. It may also explain why women's colleges and women's studies programs have taken the lead in developing internship programs and other experiential approaches to learning.

Research on decision-making suggests a similar difference in approach preferred by the majority of each sex. According to the Myers-Briggs Typology Index, discussed by Gabelnick and Pearson in Part One, 60 percent of men prefer to make decisions with an analytical, objective, "thinking" process, while 60 percent of women prefer a more contextual and narrative decision-making process, which the index describes as a "feeling" mode of cognition (Myers and Myers, *Gifts Differing*, 1980).

It is important to remember that the difference in preference noted by both Kolb's and Myers-Briggs' research are not absolute. Although 60–61 percent of each sex prefer to learn and make decisions like the majority of their own sex, the other 40–41 percent prefer to learn and to make decisions like the majority of the other sex. The slight difference in preference noted on both instruments, however, may explain research that suggests significant differences in group behavior in all male, all female, or mixed sex groups, since groups tend to function like the majority of their members (Bernard, *The Female World*, 1981).

Carol Gilligan's research on moral decision-making (*In a Different Voice*, 1982) identifies similar gender differences. A female "voice" predominates in women and a male "voice" in men, but both men and women are capable of moral reasoning in either voice. The male voice sees moral dilemmas in terms of conflicting moral values, which are decided hierarchically by determining which value is more important. The female "voice," however, tends to see the world in terms of interrelationships. Moral problems occur when relationships break down. Problems are resolved through communication, which responds with a sense of community and caring. The male voice strives to remove the "self" from the situation so as to be objective and to find a solution which is fair in an abstract sense. The female voice seeks to be honestly subjective—to acknowledge fully her own biases—and to seek a solution that is good for all the people involved.

Gilligan's research suggests that, for men, moral development entails an escape from their own subjective self-interest. For women, the problem is a belief that morality requires complete selflessness, and therefore the issue for women is not so much escaping from egotism but learning to factor in their own needs and to care for themselves as effectively as they care for others.

A study by Mary Belenky, Blythe Clincy, Nancy Goldberger, and Jill Tarule (*Women's Ways of Knowing*, 1986) built upon Gilligan's approach to look at women's cognitive development. Conducting interviews with women from several different colleges as well as community service projects, this team of researchers identified five different types of learners: (a) silent women, who do not perceive themselves as capable of learning; (b) receivers, who learn by listening, unquestioningly, to authority; (c) subjectivists, who learn by listening to their inner voices; (d) procedural knowers, who have learned to form their own opinions by reflecting on information and theories of others; and (e) constructed knowers, who know there are no absolutes, yet comfortably create models for understanding the world.

Overall, Belenky et al. found that women differ from men in two major ways: (a) women have less confidence in their own abilities and approaches than men (in general) do; and (b) more women prefer "connected" rather than "separate" learning. Briefly, "separate" learning is isolated and emphasizes doubt and competition. Separate learners work on their own, raise doubts about everything before learning it (may even judge whether the subject is worth learning), and defend their position against others. The reward for proving their worth as a scholar is eventual admission to the community of scholars and being recognized as peers with their instructors.

Conversely, "connected" knowledge is an interactive experience in which bonding precedes learning, and learning precedes judgment. Learning occurs in a community that establishes bonds of caring and in which people are assumed to bring important abilities and knowledge to the learning experience. The mode of understanding is empathic and believing: the connected approach requires the learner to attempt to understand fully a theory (or a person) before judging it. Class discussions are collaborative; classmates build upon each other's perceptions to construct together a more adequate understanding of the truth.

This learning team also noted that although many women were very good at abstracting, women almost always named "out-of-school experiences," experiential learning, as "their most powerful learning experiences" (p. 200). Belenky et al. conclude from these findings that colleges and universities should provide learning environments for women that are reinforcing, collaborative, interactive, and integrative (of theory, experience, and application), and in which connection and bonding support learning.

Literature on women's leadership styles cites similar gender patterns to those noted by learning theorists. Marilyn Loden, in *Feminine Leadership, or How to Succeed in Business Without Being One of the Boys* (1985), delineates models of masculine and feminine leadership. Briefly, the "masculine" leader is competitive, hierarchical, and rational and strives to maintain control and to win. The "feminine" leader is cooperative and team-spirited, and combines intuition with rationality, striving for collaboration and "quality output."

While Loden argues that women's leadership styles should be valued and appreciated, Alice Sargent (*The Androgynous Manager*, 1981) goes further to argue that both male and female leadership abilities should be encouraged in both men and women.

Together, current research in the areas of curriculum, learning styles, decision-making, cognitive and moral development, and management and leadership styles suggests the need for a radical rethinking of the ways we think and teach in the classroom and in our leadership and career development programs. They also indicate a need to be mindful of the hidden and unexamined assumptions and biases that precede the subliminal curriculum taught by our institutions. We communicate basic assumptions about the nature of reality and of learning by dividing knowledge into subject areas, by quantitative student credit hours, by grades, and even, as Elizabeth Dodson Gray's article in this book, "The Culture of Separated Desks," points out, by the physical layout of a typical lecture hall. This subliminal content—generally unexamined by either faculty or students—reinforces a traditional "male" perspective on reality.

Carol Gilligan found in her research that men tended to envision the world in terms of ladders, while women were more likely to emphasize nets or webs of human connectedness. Men aspire to making it to the top of the ladder; women fear the isolation at the top. Women aim to encourage communication and connectedness between people, while men fear becoming entrapped in these very webs of interconnection (Gilligan, 1982). Administrative organizational charts reflect this "male" perspective by graphically showing us who is on top (and conversely who is at the bottom), thus concentrating on who has power over whom. Our competitive and pyramidal grading systems do the same thing, in a somewhat different way, by showing who rates high and who is low, who has proved their superiority, and who has failed. In universities and colleges, the tenure and promotion system concentrates on whether a faculty member has proved he or she is good enough to join the hierarchy of the tenured professors.

How might women who (according to Gilligan) prefer nets and webs to ladders do things? If the emphasis is on interconnection and communications, organizational charts might focus on questions of communication flow: Who needs to know what from whom? What does each person contribute to the good of the organization? Instead of people fitting into their job descriptions, job descriptions could be written to utilize the full talents of the individual involved and describe the ways and places those talents could be used. The job of a teacher would not so much be judging or grading an individual, but helping him or her to understand his or her actual or potential contribution to the class and eventually, to the world at large. In short, the job of the teacher would be to identify, name, and nurture the individual gifts of every student.

Tenure decisions would not be based upon an abstract determination of whether this person "measures up," but on the more personal arena of relationships: will the continuing relationship between the institution and the individual be positive for both?[2] To answer this question, both the institution and the individual would have to take the time to know themselves well and to communicate their needs and desires to one another.

Although we do not fully know what would be required to design institutions that recognized diverse human contributions and
achievements, we do have the experience of experiments of the contemporary women's movement to show us how women, left to themselves, might structure organizations. Women in the contemporary
feminist movement put together organizations very differently from
established male-dominated models. Sometimes they formed collec-
tives and other nonhierarchical groups and, other times, simply networks. In these networks, emphasis was not on who, "up" there, had
power, but on the identification of a core, responsible for supervising
and facilitating information exchange. In both, concern was not so
much on determining who was worthy of leadership as on empowering everyone. This "female" organizational voice has at its basis of
belief that quality in institutions is a result of tapping everyone's full
potential, rather than simply identifying and turning over power to a
seemingly, superior few. A gender-equitable institution could profit
by incorporating some aspects of both "male" and "female" organizational approaches.

The essays that follow were selected because they make arguments that we found to be particularly provocative of the new thinking as it relates to higher education.

The first two essays stress the need for completely rethinking the
curriculum—first in the arts, humanities, and social sciences, and
second in the sciences. Elizabeth Kamarck Minnich, in her groundbreaking article "From the Circle of the Elite to the World of the
Whole: Education, Equality, and Excellence," exposes the logical in-
consistencies and distortions underlying the curricula of most of today's colleges and universities and calls for a curriculum which reflects the perspectives and experiences of people. She calls upon us
to "imagine a culture, predicated on equality, in which no kinds of
people, no kinds of art, no kinds of public participation, no kinds of
music, no kinds of religion are judged a priori insignificant, of poor
quality, uninteresting. Imagine, finally, a citizenry educated to think
and make judgments about what is significant, interesting, good, and
useful that do not replicate the old false judgments made and built
into our very modes of thinking when only the few were considered
really human, let alone important."

Judith Harris et al., in "Educating Women in Science," explores
ways in which recognizing a female perspective can and is improving science, arguing that "Many of the women pioneers in
science have made major contributions *because* they saw science
as underlain by the principles of selves-in-connection, rather than
selves-in-separation." Furthermore, "by educating women in a peda-

gogical milieu suited to" their tastes, "more women can be enamored of science and be encouraged to bring their own special world view to that science."

The second group of articles delineate ways we can rethink pedagogy, leadership development, and career development, respectively. Barrie Thorne, in "Rethinking the Ways We Teach," gives practical advice about how to teach in a pluralistic classroom, one in which multiple perspectives are encouraged and valued. Urging professors to use their power to ensure equal and full participation of all their students, she notes that this "process involves taking all people seriously and urging them to take themselves seriously. This may be especially important for women whose oppression often takes the form of being trivialized, laughed at, sexualized, called 'girl,' defined by their appearance instead of their minds, told they have no serious future other than being a wife or mother. This kind of treatment—amply documented in the settings of higher education—mutes the spirit, diminishes self-esteem, and drains aspirations. I believe one of the greatest gifts a teacher can give is to help others find a sense of agency in their lives."

Carolyn M. Shrewsbury explores the contributions of women's studies programs to developing and reconceptualizing leadership and ways that women's strategies and goals coalesce with the best, most forward-looking theories about the kinds of leadership required for the twenty-first century. Noting that "major theorists about leadership have emphasized the very qualities we find in women leaders as the kind of leadership most needed in the contemporary world," Shrewsbury shows how "feminist pedagogy itself develops leadership skills by making the class itself a leadership lab" where responsibility is shared.

Elizabeth Dodson Gray, in "The Culture of Separated Desks," first examines the culture of separation, looking at what the ideal of autonomy, self-sufficiency, and independence have done to our classrooms and to our students. She further addresses what separation as a mindset has meant to our thinking. "To live by cosmic theories of separation when we are actually within an interconnected reality system," says Gray, "is dangerous to the health and well-being of human society on this endangered planet." Raising alternatives that would reflect a more female perspective, Gray suggests that an emphasis on learning that is profoundly relational and contextual provides a model for recognizing both diversity and uniqueness. By extension, this valuing of relationship in context allows us to recognize not only diversity of gender but all forms of difference. The issue is no longer for individuals and groups to prove themselves to show they have something worthy to share. The issue is for all of us to hear from and learn from diversity, so that we will have the collective wisdom necessary to solve the great problems of our time.

Finally, Carole W. Minor, in "Toward a New Concept of Career Development," traces ways that career development programs can promote the full development of women students. "Facilitating the career development of women students, traditional-aged, returning, of differing ethnic backgrounds, or life-style preferences, should be part of every institution of higher education." Doing so requires a reconceptualization of the function of the career development office and of career development, so that education for satisfying and productive work is a cooperative effort between and among all relevant parts of the institution from the classroom to the counseling center and internship office. Minor's essay leads us into Part IV in its emphasis on the attitudinal and systemic changes needed at the institutional level to promote the full development of women students.

The changes suggested in these reconceptualizations are sweeping and would require massive transformations in our institutions of higher learning. The final section, then, explores the change process, identifying factors necessary for such positive transformation to take place.

NOTES

1. The concept of "levels of truth" as used here comes from Anne Wilson Schaef's *Women's Reality: An Emerging Female System in a White Male Society* (Minneapolis, Minn.: Winston-Seabury Press, 1981). The application to levels of truth about difference is original with the editors.
2. Such a "tenure system" has been used successfully at the Pendle Hill Community in Pennsylvania, according to Dean Parker Palmer of Pendle Hill.

REFERENCES

BELENKY, MARY FIELD, CLINCY, BLYTHE MCVICKER, GOLDBERGER, NANCY RULE, and TARULE, JILL MATTUCK. *Women's Ways of Knowing: The Development of Self, Voice, and Mind.* New York: Basic Books, 1986.

BERNARD, JESSIE. *The Female World.* New York: Free Press, 1981, pp. 489–99.

FRITSCHE, JOANN M. *Toward Excellence and Equity: Scholarship on Women as a Catalyst for Change in the University.* Orono: University of Maine, 1984.

GILLIGAN, CAROL. *In a Different Voice.* Cambridge, Mass.: Harvard University Press, 1982.

KOLB, DAVID. *Experiential Learning.* Englewood Cliffs: Prentice-Hall, 1984.

KUHN, THOMAS. *The Structure of Scientific Revolutions.* Chicago: University of Chicago Press, 1962.

LODEN, MARILYN. *Feminine Leadership, or How to Suceed in Business Without Being One of the Boys.* New York: Times Books, 1985.

MYERS, ISABELLE BRIGGS, and MYERS, PETER BRIGGS. *Gifts Differing.* Palo Alto, Calif.: Consulting Psychologists Press, 1980.

PERRY, WILLIAM. *Forms of Intellectual and Ethical Development in the College Years.* New York: Holt, Rinehart and Winston, 1968.

SERGENT, ALICE G. *The Androgynous Manager.* New York: AMACOM, 1981.

SCHAEF, ANNE WILSON. *Women's Reality: An Emerging Female System in a White Male Society:* Minneapolis, Minn.: Winston-Seabury Press, 1981.

SCHMITZ, BETTY. *Integrating Women's Studies into the Curriculum: A Guide and Bibliography.* Old Westbury, N.Y.: Feminist Press, 1985.

SMITH, DONA M., and KOLB, DAVID. *Users Guide for the Learning Style Inventory: A Manual for Teachers and Trainers.* Boston: McBer and Co., 1986.

19

From the Circle of the Elite to the World of the Whole:
Education, Equality, and Excellence

ELIZABETH KAMARCK MINNICH

BREAKING THE CIRCLE: THE PARTIALITY
OF CIRCULAR REASONING

If a faculty member, intrigued by the new scholarship in women, takes a syllabus for a new course to her colleagues on the curriculum committee, she is still likely to hear variations on this theme: Should you teach a course that is only about women? Isn't it peculiar to talk about the (history, literature, psychology . . .) of women without mentioning men (the assumption being that to talk about women is to exclude men, an assumption that reverses the usual, that to talk about men is to include women). Did you choose these works because they are good or because they are by women? If another faculty member brings in a syllabus in which not a single women author is represented, and not a single book that deals with women is included, no such questions are asked. A list of white male authors writing about themselves is still not seen as exclusive. Quite the contrary. Such a list is fully acceptable for a literature course, for example, in a way that a list of black female authors is not. The latter is questioned:

Is there room for it in a crowded curriculum? Is it too specialized? Is it too political? And through all the discussion runs the concern that women's literature can be included only at the price of lowering standards.

Several things are happening in the curriculum committee's responses to these two lists. First, the committee is simply replicating the dominant culture's notion that the white male Euro-American heterosexual privileged male is the generic human. He alone need not have prefixes. His history is "history." His psyche, along with the behavior of white male rats, is written up as "psychology." His writings are "literature." As we move down the hierarchy central to the tradition, the number of prefixes, or "markers," increases. There are "women writers," "Black women writers," "Black Third World women writers." The first conceptual problem we have when we confront the curriculum committee is, as we will see, basically the same as the problem of confusing sameness and equality: only the few who have been educated and educators and subjects of education over the centuries are seen as "real" humans. The classic Broverman study (Broverman et al., 1970) gives us a vivid example of this bizarre conceptual error. The Brovermans asked one hundred clinical psychologists, psychiatrists, and psychiatric social workers to describe a "normal" human, a "normal" man, and a "normal" woman. They found that the descriptions of the "normal" human and the "normal" man coincide, leaving a woman with the option of being a "normal" woman and therefore an "abnormal" human, or a "normal" human and therefore an "abnormal" woman. The real thing is the male (white, heterosexual, usually Euro-American). The rest of us are deviants from the norm, are kinds of humans to their assumed central humanity, and are, therefore, at best subtopics of knowledge. When the part defines itself as the whole, the rest of us become "minorities," which, in fact, we are not, and we are put in the absurd position of having to fight to be seen as the same as the minority that is in the defining center in order to be considered "real."

Needless to say, the conceptual confusion here is rampant, and is equaled by the existential. And then both our ability to think clearly and our ability to live truly are compromised again by a curious circularity of thinking that characterizes the dominant meaning system as we still find it in our curricula. The real and the best become conflated as well. To "be a man" is not just to be a male. It is to achieve something worthy. The supposedly inclusive term "man" serves as a normative term as well, even an ideal. Women are not just women: we are not-men, and hence are lesser humans. Throughout American history, men have stood up and said, "You can't treat me that way . . . I'm a man!" The same phrase, uttered by a woman, has an entirely different meaning. At most, "I'm a woman" in this context seems to be laying claim to special care and courtesy and protection: "You can't ask me to help build the barn. I'm a woman." "I'm a woman" in the dominant meaning system calls forth no existential claim to human worth that transcends any particular culture or state or law. Only "man" is used both as mere description and as a claim to prior, unargued, worth.

In the curriculum this peculiar closed circularity is revealed neatly when we bring our syllabus back to the curriculum committee, this time with some works on women's art added to the History of Art listing. Insofar as the works by women we have added are virtually the same as those by men, we will be greeted only by the now-familiar concern that we are lowering the quality of what our students will be studying. But if we are claiming equality, are bringing forth the different art works that women have done not in imitation of men but on our own from within our own lives, we are charged with destroying the category of "art." "Art," that is, is already defined in a way that excludes what women have done. We are greeted in the same way when we propose studying what women have done in politics: it is interesting, but not really politics! "Perhaps it belongs in sociology?" What women have done as women was defined out of the categories that now inform the curriculum from the beginning, and then these same categories are used to prove that we *ought* to stay out. That is circular reasoning.

When art history was developing as a field, certain sorts of works were already considered "art." Canvas art was held in great esteem, and certain sorts of subjects and certain painters were already established as "the best." The growing field of art history took these works, and some sculpture and some architecture, as its subject matter, the "art" of which it was a history. Definitions of art grew from that subject matter, and standards for "good" and "great" art developed along with careful demarcations of works into genres. Obviously, kinds of works that were not already included in art when the field developed did not appear in the examples of good and great art, in the genres, or in the acceptable exemplars of the various definitions of art.

When the founders of political science studied only the workings of governmental institutions, the workings of nongovernmental institutions come to be, by definition only, less important than the "truly political." When the founders of literary scholarship studied only the already acceptable forms of writing, all other forms came to be called "non-" or "sub-" literary. When the founders of philosophy as an academic discipline taught only certain texts already published and accepted by the few educated men, all other texts became "non-philosophical," no matter how close they were to the supposed center of philosophizing, the quest for wisdom.

In all fields, the definition of the "real" subject matter and the standards subsequently deduced from and used within the field have developed in such tight relation to each other. There is nothing shocking about this realization: all human knowledge starts with some particular subject and/or question at some particular time in history in some particular culture and therefore simultaneously excludes other subject matters and develops standards that justify that exclusion. Every field we teach has been expanded, redefined, reordered as other subject matters and methods and questions have been struggled with. Few retain nothing but the definitions and standards with which they began, although many give centrality and prime worthiness to their originating subjects (consider the primacy of Italian Renaissance printings).

Almost all, however, reveal their core circularity—their inability to see different subject matter as different within an inclusive kind rather than lesser—when challenged by feminist scholarship, especially that which is more than an effort to retrieve the women who did the same things as men. To analyze what women were doing, making, thinking, being in any field is precisely to work outside the boundaries of that field as presently defined because *women* were defined outside the boundaries. Until feminist political science came along, it seemed evident to political scientists that what women did was private, not political, and that what was done *to* women was also private, not political, since "political" means what men did in very particular arenas from which women were actively excluded (which act of exclusion was not itself analyzed as a political phenomenon). Until feminist anthropology came along, it seemed evident to anthropologists that the best informants were men because what men did was taken to be culture-defining, which led to male informants becoming culture-defining (whatever the male role really was in the culture itself).

And in all fields, until recently, sex/gender was ignored as an analytic category, as a subject matter, as the defining universal human construct it is. Had it been otherwise, no fields could have claimed the sort of generality they have claimed. All subsequent theorizing and research prior to that which takes account of sex/gender, race, class, ethnicity in their intricate intertwinings must then be seen as partial and therefore fallacious insofar as it claims generality (let alone universality). And that means that all standards of judgment that claim generality are equally suspect.

Knowledge is a human construct and carries within it on the deepest levels the assumptions its authors make that they do not even know are assumptions. The ensuing edifices of knowledge tend, therefore, not only to perpetuate but to validate those assumptions. They become, those assumptions, available for us to think about only when they are apprehended as assumptions, and that usually happens when they are challenged. Feminist scholarship constitutes a challenge precisely to the excluding definitions and standards of judgment of that which has been central to the curriculum, because women have been excluded and judged lacking in the culture that produced that scholarship.

That sort of reasoning traps us in old mistakes, old false generalizations that went too far on the basis of too few. It is not excellence we put in jeopardy when we question circular reasoning. Quite the contrary. Applying definitions of what is "real" and/or central to any field, and applying the standards of judgment derived from that category to categories for which they were never designed, leads to sloppy—and cruel—thinking, not to preservation of excellence. Standards of greatness derived from the dominant Western tradition of art do not apply to the dominant Eastern traditions. Should Western standards appear to force us to judge Eastern art lacking, it is the standards of judgment used, not Eastern art, that are revealed to be inadequate. Similarly, definitions and standards derived from the study of men that, applied to the study of women, show women to be less "real" and less worthy than men are simply inadequate definitions and standards.

Excellence demands that we use our conceptual tools more carefully, and that we support feminist scholarship to keep us from replicating the same old errors.

EQUALITY AND SAMENESS

In America, right along with a heritage of struggles for equality, we have maintained an undercutting confusion about the relation of equality and sameness. Without realizing it, we have continued to believe that these two near-opposites are interchangeable terms. Feminists still hear that we are "trying to be *like* men," to be the same as men, when we work for equality. Teachers still say proudly that they serve equality in their classrooms by treating all students *the same* regardless of their sex, or race, or ethnicity. And, at the same time, those who advocate equality are still often taken aside to hear, "But you know perfectly well that the problem is that we really are not all the same—we start with different abilities of all sorts," as if equality were made impossible, rather than essential, by the fact of human difference. Affirmative action, in recognizing difference, serves equality as insistence on an unobtainable and undesirable sameness with the dominant few cannot.

This confusion between sameness and equality is entrenched in the dominant meaning system on several different levels. It tends to begin with the old worry that de Tocqueville articulated so well, the belief that working for equality means leveling. That is, it is assumed that equality requires sameness, and if the sameness must include everybody, then we must level all down to the lowest common denominator. There is another assumption here, of course, and that is that "the lowest" cannot be raised to the level of "the highest," so we have no option but to level. And behind those assumptions there is yet another, and that is that hierarchy is not only real and natural but essentially value-related: we would not have to level to achieve equality if we humans were not already ranked, supposedly by Nature, in ways that make some of us better, some worse. So long as that assumption is with us, it implies that giving serious attention to "lower" humans means lowering values. De Tocqueville and many far less favorably disposed gentlemen of the Old World worried that raising "the common man" to a position of full citizenship meant raising commonness—that is, vulgarity, crudeness, and rudeness—to become acceptable citizenly qualities. Opponents of suffrage for women worried that raising the female to a position of full citizenship meant emasculating the role of citizen, and that meant to them lowering it—letting in weakness, frivolity, overemotionalism.

The hierarchy we find here reveals itself to be based on notions about "Nature" and "Nature's God." From the position that humans are naturally arranged in ranks by kinds, feminists and suffragists advocating equality for women must be seen as advocating that women be the same as men, which, it is deeply believed by many still today, violates Nature and Nature's God . . . and His hierarchy. And this belief is not a quaint outdated one, or held only by fundamentalists. Faculty members who consider including works by and about women in their courses but worry that they are lowering standards—letting in the second-rate, probably oversentimental and/or overly political posturing of lesser thinkers, writers, artists—are within the American tradition of assuming that established elites are based only on merit. They are less likely than antifeminists or antisuffrage people to invoke Nature and Nature's God as the source of the hierarchy of worth they wish to defend, but they are no less likely to spring to the defense of the hierarchy that has made the curriculum a white male sanctum through the generations. Not wanting to think that America has a class and sex/gender and racially stratified system that is effective "even" in the Academy, such faculty members cannot see the principles of inclusion and exclusion in the curriculum as anything other than rational principles of judgment of merit, significance, interest. Precisely the same situation holds with those who see affirmative action as "reverse discrimination."

That working for a feminist transformation of the Academy should uncover these assumptions is not surprising at all. We follow in the footsteps of thinker/activists such as W. E. B. Du Bois (1969), who wrote of the quest for freedom of his people that it focused first on manumission; then, freedom from slavery having failed to deliver freedom, turned to suffrage. Suffrage having failed, education became the dream and the hoped-for road. It is, of course, equality that he spoke of: freedom for those who have been exploited and oppressed requires equality. The problem has been that there is no real possibility of equality in systems predicated on hierarchy—by race, by class, by sex, by religion. It is precisely the centrality of such hierarchy that is revealed by confusions of equality and sameness, and the related concern lest equality threaten excellence.

De Tocqueville's formulation is a classic:

> When I survey this countless multitude of beings, shaped in each other's likeness, amid whom nothing rises and nothing falls, the sight of such universal uniformity saddens and chills me, and I am tempted to regret that state of society that has ceased to be. When the world was full of men of great importance and extreme insignificance, of great wealth and extreme poverty, of great learning and extreme ignorance, I turned aside from the latter to fix my observation on the former alone, who gratified my sympathies. (de Tocqueville, 1945)

It is the lack of rising and falling, the threat of "universal uniformity" (there being here no notion whatsoever that differences can be of interest and value unless they are ranked, vertical, invidious differences), that saddens this particularly honest and sensitive thinker. He needn't have worried, of course. The rise of white property-owning men to citizenship in America did not remove slavery, nor poverty, nor sex hierarchy, nor any other of a number of related rankings of groups that added up to the vast majority. As John Adams wrote to

Abigail Adams in 1776, in response to her plea that the promised liberty and equality of the new revolutionary government be applied not just to males:

> As to your extraordinary code of laws, I cannot but laugh. We have been told that our struggle has loosened the bonds of government everywhere; that children and apprentices were disobedient; that schools and colleges were grown turbulent; that Indians slighted their guardians, and Negroes grew insolent to their masters. But your letter was the first intimation that another tribe, more numerous and powerful than all the rest, were grown discontented. (Schneir, 1972)

Except for his laughter, Adams was right: Women were the majority, and with all the others the white men never meant to include in their new equality, constituted the majority of Americans who did take for themselves the dream they were not supposed to share. There was no loss of peaks and valleys under contemplation in this radical new venture in the American colonies. There was also no restriction on dreaming.

There was a principle of equality that has transcended the intentions of most, if not all, of its original promulgators. It was and is a dream that we too have shared and called on, one given force by its original translation into political principles set above even the political institutions created to serve it through the instrumentality of a written constitution. Those principles have served the struggles of the groups originally excluded as they served their authors—not as grounds for unambiguously recognized claims but as rallying grounds for movements that have fought for rights never yet given, but on occasion won. Women were not "given" the vote. Women won the vote. But remembering our history of struggle does not mean we have saved our understanding of equality from the pull toward sameness. By the history most of us were taught, those who have fought for their share of the American dream have been after a piece of the pie . . . a chance to live and be the same as those who were already in. Those who have understood that getting into the boys' clubhouse means becoming one of the boys, and that that is hardly an unambiguous good, have certainly been around and fighting through our history, but their reasoning has largely not been preserved for us. How many even among feminists know of the radical positions taken in opposition to Stanton and Anthony by Matilda Joslyn Gage (1980), for example?

The content, structure, and population of educational institutions provide one of the clearest grounds on which we can see the struggle for equality, and its confusions, continue. Black women and men, and white women, fought for the right to education and are continuing to do so. Moving from separate schools that were finally seen as inherently unequal because *not the same* as those designed and run by and for white males, we have continued struggling to receive *the same* education. The earlier waves of feminism, and the fight for education for Blacks and all other minority groups, aimed at access to the dominant schools and the dominant curriculum—the same schools and curriculum that had justified and perpetuated the excluding. Some women's schools and some Black schools still pride themselves on offering the same curriculum as white men's schools. It wasn't until women's colleges found themselves threatened with extinction by attrition that they became aware of the need to emphasize the differences in what they offered—to return, in some cases, to the liberationist rhetoric of their founders. Still, many women's colleges feel the need to prove their legitimacy by *not* having women's studies programs. They fear the brand of "feminist," and still more the equation of "feminist" with "lesbian," thereby contributing to the power of those terms to serve as threats.

When the white men's schools opened their doors to women, it was largely because they too feared falling enrollments. They opened to women with trepidation, heightened at times by their lively sense that they could be, if they weren't careful, swamped by females. Quotas were common, at least as transitional devices—and it is worth noting that *those* quotas aroused none of the ire that affirmative action goals have.

And still women flocked to the male bastions. The hierarchy remained intact: institutions founded of, by, and for privileged white males continued to be seen as the best. Efforts to increase the mix in the student body were, and are, greeted by expressions of concern over loss of excellence. Quotas designed to protect white male undergraduate institutions from too many females all at once seemed fine, just as discriminations practiced in admissions through the years continued to seem fine. Athletes, sons of graduates, flute players when needed, representatives from underrepresented parts of the country or world—all continued to receive special attention at those schools that had given it to them before, while quotas designed to guarantee a sex and racial mix were called the very epitomy of injustice.

That is, where conscious efforts of any kind were and are made to include those who have been purposefully excluded as a category (a race, a sex, an ethnic or religious group), "equality" provides both the rationale for so doing (Americans like to sound as if they are for equality) AND a set-up for the objection: "Equality may be well and good, but not if it interferes with excellence," which it is still seen as doing. Educational institutions are dedicated to excellence, and hence not to equality, in this view. And so we have seen Black people admitted to institutions that continue to offer the same curriculum they offered when Black people were excluded . . . an overwhelmingly if not exclusively all-white curriculum. This, it is assumed, is the right thing to do because it "maintains quality." Women gain access to all-male curricula, and that is assumed the right thing for us, a step moving us closer to equality because it reflects the fact that women are to be treated the same as men.

The full absurdity of assuming that a Black woman, studying a curriculum that is by and about white men, is having the same experience, learning the same things, as a white man studying alongside her is still not fully evident to some educators. A woman of any group is supposed to assume she is simply being educated when she learns nothing at all about women and all kinds of things about all sorts of men. The variety of white Euro-American men in the curriculum is somehow supposed to stand in for the variety of humankind. In fact, it simply furthers the notion that variety belongs to this group while all others, the majority of humankind, can be covered by a course or two, a mere mention or two, a token female administrator here and there.

The irony increases in the treatment of women and minorities after college, where they are allowed to succeed in businesses and the professions to the degree that they act almost the same as majority males, thus depriving the world of the particular contributions that their differences of experience and perspective could provide.

If we would think and act well together and have the benefit of the contributions of diverse groups, we cannot continue to conflate sameness and equality. Equality, allowed into the Academy and beyond, helps us, forces us out of old errors of exclusivity and clears the space to allow us to think better. There is no threat to excellence here but, instead, a challenge to unexamined notions of "excellence" that carry old exclusivities unexamined within them. Excellence and prejudiced elitism are not the same.

THE IMPORTANCE OF A FEMINIST CRITIQUE

A feminist critique futhers the cause of excellence by requiring us to rethink the formulation most of us take for granted. When we plan courses, programs, curricula, and all institutional policies including hiring, promotion, and tenure with regard for equality no longer misunderstood as sameness within the old excluding tradition, we are freed—even forced—to be creative both about what we should continue to teach and how, and about new ways of thinking and learning. When we are no longer trapped within the circular self-justifications of the old definitions and standards, we are able to think much more effectively about what ought to be covered in a field called "art history" and what ought to be considered significant enough to include in a course called "psychology." That is, we find ourselves asking questions as basic, and difficult, as "What *is* the subject matter of philosophy? What *does* make an act of historical significance? What qualities *should* a good administrator or faculty member have—and promote in others?" And those questions take us back to the originating vision and passion of the quest for new knowledge and forward to visions of fields of knowledge that not only allow us to think about humankind but that require that we do so.

To critique is not just to react, it is to go behind, to find out what makes something be what and as it is: it is to see it *as* it is, which is, in and of itself, to become free of it. Critique is learning to see ourselves seeing, to think about our thinking, and that is empowering in and of itself. Critique reminds us that we have always with us not just our individual consciousness within and playing on our shared social consciousness, but the very ground of human intellectual freedom, our consciousness of consciousness itself.

We can, then, adopt a radical doubt, assert our freedom from patriarchal consciousness, and approach the dominant tradition afresh, having suspended belief in its centrality, its adequacy, its accuracy with regard to anything or anybody or any investigation beyond itself. In doing so, we shrink the boundaries of the dominant tradition so that it becomes visibly what it has always been: the tradition of a particular group within a particular culture and a particular history.

When what has been taken to be central and defining is seen as one among others, difference moves into the place previously held by sameness: we now have room for diversity to be significant not as deviation but as the essential thread of a highly articulated and multiform changing real world. For example, when we recognize that it is not necessary to see classical Greece as the origin of "Civilization," we can see it as a fascinating moment in a story that began well before the dates we used to hold almost sacred and as a culture that drew on others well beyond its own boundaries. We can see, for example, the effects of India and Africa on Greece as well as Greece's effects on Rome in ways that help us understand all four profoundly influential cultures, and in a spirit that emphasizes the complex interrelatedness of histories too often taught in isolation from each other.

First, then, in our effort to break the circularity of sameness, we can add the prefixes, or markers, to all the terms within our curricula and educational institutions that lack them, on the grounds that accurate scholarship, truth-telling itself, demands that we name our sample. If a course covers only white people, and/or is taught from the analytic perspectives developed within an exclusively white tradition, it should be so labeled and the perspective claimed as such.

The possibilities for improved thinking and enlivened classrooms that emerge when we demystify the unprefixed minority are intriguing. We all live as endangered creatures, working to become women and men as our society defines those highly complex and not at all natural roles. We all live as embodied beings whose experience of ourselves in the world is necessarily mediated through a socialized consiousness. To insert into the historic quest for self-knowledge a full recognition of sex/gender in its cultural, political, economic contexts is to raise questions, complexities, abiding human concerns rarely before raised in the classroom. Courses titled "Man and His World" can still be taught, but now as courses in which gender analysis is central, not weirdly absent.

Still, courses on "Woman and Her World" are at this moment in history much more important to teach than courses on "Man and His World." Immersion in a different world than that which has variously contained us helps us see the boundaries of the old better, perhaps, than anything else. To leave America—even to leave your neighborhood—for a while is the best way to come to know it, and yourself. We cannot now send students abroad for immersion in a nonpatriarchal culture, but we can give them as much as possible of what we do indeed have from and about women all over the world.

A TRANSFORMED CURRICULUM

We are, therefore, working together designing curricula in response to the demanding challenge of equality. Right now, there are women's studies courses and programs being taught that combine critique of the dominant tradition with immersion in the rich world and works of women, with a growing knowledge of the necessarily related critique and subject matter of other "special" programs.

And, in addition to these courses and programs, there are available models of many "curriculum transformation projects" designed to help faculty members change their courses to take account of the critique, the new scholarship on women, and the multicultural content and approaches of the other "special" studies areas. Almost any approach one can think of has been and is being used to change the curriculum, to both correct and enrich it. There are now, on our campuses:

- projects that make women's studies the activating center for change across the curriculum;
- projects that use faculty development in the new scholarship on women not only to change courses but to build support for women's studies programming;
- projects that come from the initiative of administrators who take seriously their task of holding the faculty to high standards of scholarship and teaching and so recognize the inadequacy of perpetuating old errors in the curriculum;
- projects that come from student initiative, usually such that a course or two is offered and then expanded into a program as more and more faculty become involved;
- projects that make use of a range of techniques, including consultants and faculty workshops; all-college addresses giving a critique of the liberal arts tradition, and of the disciplines within it; sending key faculty members to special conferences and institutes on the new scholarship; running regular faculty discussion groups that explore both transdisciplinary theory and intradisciplinary research developments; sessions on pedagogy that prepare faculty members to work with their classes in ways that do not perpetuate male/female power hierarchies; sessions with faculty and administrators and students that explore the intrinsic relations between sexism, racism, classism, ethnocentricity, homophobia in an effort to ensure that new courses and teaching methods go as far as possible toward eliminating the old crippling divisions and exclusions.

These projects have taught us four general rules: (a) Change-directed projects need to start from and build on strength, rather than being aimed at areas of weakness. It is helpful to have women's studies expertise on campus to begin with if possible, and/or to support those who will be carrying the burden of work rather than those who raise all the objections. Experience has shown us that it is, indeed, often wisest to ignore the most vocal opposition lest it deflect needed energy. (b) Given the variety of faculty members and the tenacity of established institutions, it is important to use, eventually, as many different techniques and approaches as possible because we all hear some kinds of arguments better than others. (c) Follow-up is very important—we cannot change the heritage of millennia, nor the institutions that carry it implicitly within their structures, overnight. (d) Since persistence is critical, as is the use of a variety of approaches, it is both important and possible that each of us, from our different positions and with our differing commitments and temperaments and abilities, work in ways that are for each of us energizing and compatible. There is no one right way for institutions to go about changing.

Although we can envision a curriculum in which every student in a highly diverse student body would feel equally recognized and validated and extended and challenged beyond her or his limits, and in which no one tradition dominated but many intertwined throughout, such a curriculum does not exist yet. Even those who understand the need for it do not know enough. Neither the essential critique nor the production of new knowledge can have done their jobs so quickly. What has taken millennia to establish can hardly be transformed in twenty years.

And it is doubtful in any case if returning to conversation about gender-free "humans" is a desirable goal. Certainly it is not desirable to *return* to talk about "humans" as if gender analysis were something to get past as quickly as possible. Let us for now consider dwelling with difference for a while longer. It is essential to any accurate notions of "humankind" that we do so, with great care and respect, and that we follow the lead of "special" programs we do have on our campuses, those in women's studies along with those in Afro-American and Jewish, and Asian-American and Hispanic and Native American studies. These programs have, in many cases, already broken out of the molds that constrain so much of education today. They engage students with new and passionate questions; they introduce voices that push the limits of understanding of some students and deeply validate the unnamed experiences of others; they return to the curriculum the context of that which has ruled for so long as if it were all there is, thereby correcting old errors; they encourage student research on issues of deep personal concern; they bring to campus "experts" whose knowledge comes from lives of activism as well as research; they not only allow but call for personal reactions to subject matter; they uncover the political and economic bases of culture; they look for what is significant and interesting and revealing where it can be found and not where, and in whom, the dominate culture has judged it to be; and they all provide a perspective on the world without which our understanding continues to be partial, and so both intellectually and ethically flawed. Because of these programs, we have available to us the work of experienced educators from a wonderful array of traditions.

A curriculum built from their wisdom would take not the old, narrow view of excellence but, rather, a new understanding of equality to be the ground and the goal for a "sound" education. It would not be built on the assumption that what students need is to be "exposed to" greatness and predetermined by cultural elites; but would, rather, take it to be critical for students to learn to find their own meaning in conversation with many others, both like and radically unlike them.

EQUITY AND TRUTH

Equality is, in fact, the precondition for, not the opposite of, a dedication to excellence. It is the precondition, that is, so long as we do not confuse excellence, the expression of the universal human ability to transcend, with exclusivity. Old notions of excellence celebrate hierarchy; the democratic notion celebrates the opportunity for self-expression, for diversity, for growth.

The task we have before us is an exciting one, on the order of the Copernican and the Darwinian revolutions: we too are reordering the whole. We are changing androcentricity. And that means, as did those earlier basic shifts in how knowledge was henceforth to be ordered, that all must be rethought. To some, the blow to old ego constructs will be great, and the magnitude of the task too daunting. But for many of us, the freedom to think freshly about everything, to find new research opportunities everywhere, to teach students as enlivened as those in women's studies classrooms always are, to cross disciplines so that our own is enriched and challenged, to team teach with friends and colleagues as we relearn our fields together, to bring our personal and political commitments to equality together with our intellectual and professional commitments to truth and excellence, is deeply moving and life-giving.

Imagine the pleasure of a curriculum that emerges as a complex weave of many stories, many voices, in which the effort and the horror and the glory of what it means to be human opens up to and challenges as many of our students as possible. Imagine white male students learning the stories, the passions, the gifts, the intense personal and the telling political lives of all those people who are, now, still unknown to them—learning about others as all others now learn about them in our schools. Imagine a Mexican-American woman coming to college and learning her history, an appreciation and understanding of her cultural heritage, an ability to think critically and creatively from her own centered and validated experience. Imagine women students of all sorts learning about what women have been and done so that they, and the real world, emerge from the shadows cast by the distorted abstractions that an all-male curriculum casts.

Imagine a culture, predicated on equality, in which no kinds of people, no kinds of art, no kinds of public participation, no kinds of music, no kinds of religion are judged a priori insignificant, of poor quality, uninteresting. Imagine, finally, a citizenry educated to think and make judgments about what is significant, interesting, good, and useful that do not replicate the old false judgments made and built into our very modes of thinking when only the few were considered really human, let alone important.

We may not know enough yet to teach "Humans and Their World," but we do know enough to join our students in thinking about what such a level of understanding might spring from, to join them in reading works by and about women across time and cultures that challenge and enrich our human, and our self, understanding. It is time now, I believe, to concentrate on "Woman and Her World" so that, this time, we do not lose over half the human race when we rush to generalizations about us all. Truth itself demands that we finally pay some heed to a democratic understanding of equality as a condition for any adequate comprehension of what it means to be human, let alone for an inspirational vision of excellence worthy of us—of all of us.

ACKNOWLEDGMENTS

There is a lot in this essay that is uncredited, and I am deeply sorry about that. I have thought with and learned from many wonderful people while trying to understand what we do in our educational systems, and I cannot begin to cite—or adequately thank—them all. Still, let me mention that in this piece I am aware of drawing on Patricia Palmieri's research on the history of education. I have also drawn on my own years of work with and for women's colleges (sometimes working with the Women's College Coalition)—for example, for the comments on quotas in formerly male colleges and other observations on equity for women in education. Marcia Sharpe of the Coalition is very helpful in such areas, as are Donna Shavlik and Judith Touchton of the ACE Office of Women, and Bernice

Sandler of the Project on the Status of Women of the AAC. Then there are the years I have worked on "curriculum transformation projects" with some fifty colleges and universities and a large number of special projects (perhaps the most fruitful of which was the Great Lakes Colleges Association's Summer Institute on Feminist Scholarship). Recently I have also worked with Peggy McIntosh of the Wellesley Center for Research on Women on feminism and curricular change (specifically, under a Ford Foundation grant to write a book on the implications of feminist scholarship for the humanities). I have learned a great deal from literally hundreds of faculty members who have participated in course-change workshops as in the research for the book with Peggy, and I thank them for their openness, their questions, their challenges. For years I have also learned from the work of thinker-activists such as Barbara Smith, Cheryl Townsend Gilkes, Patricia Bell-Scott, Gloria Hull, Elizabeth Higginbotham, Beverly Guy-Sheftall, Bonnie Thornton Dill, Gloria Joseph, Paula Giddings, Angela Davis, and other women who have not only worked within and on feminist scholarship but have created Black women's studies to go deeper, and beyond. Their writings and the talks I have been privileged to hear are essential. The thoughts in this piece are now my own, but no thoughts come without the support and challenge of conversation and reading.

REFERENCES

BROVERMAN, INGE K., et al. "Sex-Role Stereotypes and Clinical Judgments of Mental Health." *Journal of Consulting and Clinical Psychology* 34 (1970), 1–7.

DE TOCQUEVILLE, ALEXIS. *Democracy in America,* Vol. II, Henry Reeve text, revised by Francis Bowen, edited by Phillips Bradley. New York: Vintage Books/Random House, 1945, p. 350.

DuBois, W. E. *The Souls of Black Folk.* London: Signet Classic/New American Library, 1969. (See especially "Of Our Spiritual Strivings," pp. 43–53.)

SCHNEIR, MIRIAM, ed. *Feminism: The Essential Historical Writings.* New York: Vintage Books/Random House, 1972, p. 4.

GAGE, MATILDA JOSLYN. *Woman, Church and State.* Watertown, Mass: Persephone Press, 1980. (See the Introduction by Sally Roesch Wagner.)

20

Educating Women in Science

JUDITH HARRIS, JOANN SILVERSTEIN, AND DIANNE ANDREWS

That the true business of civilization has been in the hands of men is the lesson absorbed by every student of the traditional sources. How this came to be, and the process that kept it so, may well be the most important question for the self-understanding and survival of the human species. (Rich, 1979, p. 135)

For the past two decades there has been public concern about the dearth of women in science. This has resulted in numerous studies (Briscoe and Pfafflin, 1979; National Research Council, 1979, 1983; Cole, 1981; Humphreys, 1982; Bruer, 1983; Vetter and Babco, 1986, National Science Foundation, 1986) and several National Science Foundation programs. A number of culprits have been accused. In K–12 education math and science anxiety in girls, lack of proper science background for girls, and lack of serious attention for girls in science classes have been suggested (Mallow, 1981; Bybee and Kahle, 1982; Kahle, 1982; Kahle and Lakes, 1983; Knox, 1983). In addition, it has been pointed out that science is characterized as masculine (Keller, 1978) and that there is a cultural belief that women are less scientifically competent than men (Zuckerman and Cole, 1975), thus inhibiting women from entering science. Covert and overt discrimination are also rife within the sciences (Briscoe and Pfafflin, 1979). Beyond these causes, however, are more fundamental ones: (a) the historic exclusion of women from universities, and thus from science; and (b) the overmasculinization of scientific theory, practice, and pedagogy. Until we remedy the underlying male bias in science and scientific pedagogy, we shall continue to see only the small fluctuations in the percentage of women in science that have been present since the 1920s (Humphreys, 1982).

In order to achieve a permanent change in the numbers and influence of women in science, we must feminize science and its pedagogy, transforming it to include values and methodologies associated with the female gender, such as are discussed below. Without such a radical philosophical transformation, the existing sexism will remain and any changes will be purely cosmetic.

THERE ARE SO FEW WOMEN SCIENTISTS

Of the 1477 living members of the National Academy of Sciences, only 51 are women. Of these, 6 were elected in 1975 and 26 since 1975. (Personal communication, National Academy of Sciences, October 1986)

From the beginnings of scientific endeavor in the United States, women's place in science has been peripheral (cf. Mozans, 1913; Rossiter, 1982; see also references in Aldrich, 1978). Women were effectively prohibited from exploring science from its inception because they were excluded from university education. This prohibition of women from training and working in science has continued well into the twentieth century, and at a more subtle level still remains a problem.

Until the twentieth century women in the United States remained predominantly uneducated and, often, illiterate; there was no requirement that they, as noncitizens, attend secondary school. Well into the 1900s those women who were educated were confined to women's colleges, both for education and for employment. Women frequently conducted their research alone, as they had little access to the best research laboratories and were considered by the male scientific establishment to be incapable of good research. Many women had no research opportunities at all and were restricted to teaching. Women were also denied membership in most scientific societies and other professional organizations (Rossiter, 1982). In this manner, they were essentially segregated from the white, male domain of "real science," being denied the interaction and facilities necessary for scientific activities. Those few who were able to work in research laboratories were confined to support staff, the equivalent of "women's work" within the professions (Gornick, 1983). This remains a problem today, as can be observed in almost any working laboratory. In addition, many of the elite universities excluded women until a few years ago, effectively eliminating us[1] from the elite of science, participation in policy-making, and from access to the forefronts of research (Rossiter, 1982).

Today women are redefining and enlarging our place within the world of science, but many of us still meet barriers which prevent us from reaching the degree of participation equal to our aspirations and qualifications. Women have been entering undergraduate and graduate programs and the scientific labor force in record numbers: we earned almost 40 percent of the bachelor's degrees and nearly one quarter of higher degrees in science in 1980, but in 1984 we constituted only 12 percent of the scientific and engineering labor force (National Science Foundation, 1986). Vetter and Babco (1986), however, show that the tide has turned and there are actually fewer women now entering science. Most of the gains have been in the social and biological sciences, although in the physical sciences women made up about 11 percent of the work force in 1984 (ibid.), in contrast with 1980, when we made up 1–5 per cent (Vetter, 1981 and 1982). In all fields, and at all degree levels, female graduates of science programs are less likely to find employment in our fields and are more likely to be without work than comparable men. Nearly three quarters of a million women who earned at least one degree in science and engineering over the last twenty-five years are not currently employed as scientists and engineers (Vetter, 1981 and 1982). Thus, we see that in spite of the touted gains, "science and technology, by and large, have survived into the 1980s as a white, male club" (Knox, 1983). This may partially explain the recent downturn of women entering science reported by Vetter and Babco (1986). However, in order to understand the exclusion of women from science and university education more fully we must explore the patriarchal bias of science.

PATRIARCHY AND SCIENCE

The widespread assumption that a study of gender and science could only be a study of women still amazes me: if women are made rather than born, then surely the same is true of men. It is also true of science ... both gender and science are socially constructed categories. (Keller, 1985, p. 3)

Patriarchal Bias in Science

The world view of patriarchal Western civilization underlies not only science but also our culture and our educational system (Keller, 1978; Hubbard et al., 1979; Ferguson, 1980; Wallsgrove, 1980; Capra, 1982; Bleier, 1984). In the West this world view became the natural world (Capra, 1982), a "reality" so old and so much a part of our background that it is invisible, as water is to fish.

Chodorow (1978) has characterized men as "selves-in-separation" and women as "selves-in-connection." She has shown that the female-dominated parenting, or mothering, common in our society is pivotal to the way in which males and females develop. This concept is also important to the way in which people see and relate to the natural world. She defines males as selves-in-separation who seek to deny dependence and intimacy in their attempt to identify with their fathers rather than their mothers. They turn instead to independence, solitary endeavor, and competition. In this frame of mind, one sees the universe as dichotomized and without relationship. Females, on the other hand, are selves-in-connection, remaining identified with their mothers and developing a complex interdependence with others. This sets up a conflict living in the male or patriarchal world of selves-in-separation, especially for the woman in science. This dichotomy also makes it very difficult for men to see anything but selves-in-separation, thereby dismissing selves-in-connection through lack of recognition.

The patriarchal world is a universe built by selves-in-separation where the individual form, rather than the community of relationships, is of utmost importance. Here every cause has one physical effect, and every effect one physical cause, rather than being complexly interconnected; change occurs linearly and progressively, not cyclically and recurrently. It is a universe that is hierarchically ordered, information going from "top" to "bottom" as orders or instructions, not a web in which all is interwoven. In this universe the main interactions are competition and domination, rather than exchange and mutual empowerment. It is within this hierarchical system with its interactions of competition and domination that science and male/female relationships operate.

This patriarchal world view has existed for millennia, at least in Western Europe, and it has traditionally associated women with nature, and men with mind and spirit. Accordingly, the relative status of women in partriarchy is interrelated with the culture's attitudes toward nature at any particular time. Some scholars believe that it was not until the sixteenth and seventeenth centuries that the old matriarchal world view really began to lose its respect and power. Merchant (1980) documents this change historically. She demonstrates that earlier the earth was viewed as female, giving birth in her womb to all living and nonliving things. Paracelsus, for example, "compared the earth to a female whose womb nurtured all life" (ibid. pp. 26–27). During this time period infringing upon the womb of the mother was not socially acceptable and thus mining was frowned upon. As the feminine lost value, the plight of women worsened and concepts of the world shifted. The connection of women to earth as positive and spiritual broke down, and woman became less the "earth mother" and more the whore to be raped, the slave to be bound. Bacon, the father of the scientific method, was foremost in the use of domination and rape metaphors. He speaks of nature being "bound into service" and made a "slave" and that "neither ought man to make scruple of entering and penetrating into these [nature's] holes and corners" (Merchant, 1980, pp. 168–169).

This degraded view of nature and the feminine developed hand-in-hand with science. Connection as an organizing principle in science was greatly diminished. The increased emphasis on our separation as individuals from each other and from our source, whether this be our human mother, our mother the Earth, or our mothers the Universe, emphasized dualities—dichotomized pairs that are irreconcilably split: mind/body; rational/feeling; good/evil; man/woman (Watts, 1963). In this intellectual milieu nature is an object or a machine. Women, while accustomed to this general world view, are, as selves-in-connection, uncomfortable with this way of perceiving the world, as they are uncomfortable with the dualistic equation of women with nature and men with mind and spirit. This view denies women the possibility of being fully and completely human.

We can piece together the old gynocentric world view in which the earth was seen as our source and mother from the world view of the female subculture today. It was one in which women were highly honored and where connection and community were of utmost importance. Here cause and effect was a complicated matter, with many interconnections, some of which were not physical; time was not linear but cyclical; there the focus was not on progress but on continuation and recurrence. The universe was structured with interconnected levels. There were polarities—one extreme irrevocably connected to the other—rather than dualities. Nature was alive and part of us, not an object or a machine.

The split between these two points of view, which has become genderized into "male" and "female," has allowed a stituation to develop in which there is a "public sphere" dominated by "male" values of individualism, separation, and justice and a less-prestigious "private sphere" to which "female" values of cooperation, interaction, and caring have been relegated (Gilligan, 1982). The separation of the world into different spheres, with different world views and values has dichotomized culture with resultant dire consequences. The public sphere has developed in a way which is out of balance with nature and in danger of collapse, because we have neglected our interrelationships and the ethic of caring (Capra, 1982; Gilligan, 1982) and the private sphere has become undervalued, along with the degradation and trivialization of women. Our science, which is part of this public sphere, is also underdeveloped in the area of interrelationships and is unable to explain complex interactive phenomena or to foresee many of the results of technology (Daly, 1978; Griffin, 1978; Ferguson, 1980; Koen and Swaim, 1980; Capra, 1982). With the integration into science of ideas of interconnection and cooperation, relegated to the private, female sphere, these problems could be better understood and perhaps even solved.

The patriarchal bias in science is reflected in science education. We will explore how this bias affects women and how it has operated to keep women out of science.

Patriarchal Bias in Scientific Education

Women students in today's educational system must attempt to fit into the male scientific subculture as well as learn about the nature of the physical universe. This subculture manifests in patriarchal modes of thought; pervasive male bias; and hierarchical, teacher-centered pedagogy. The lack of a feminine perspective, such as one can find in the humanities, the almost complete lack of women professors and teaching assistants, and the low numbers of other women students leave these women stranded in a foreign, and often hostile, culture.

MALE MODES OF THOUGHT. Male modes of thought are part of the unseen background on which science is painted. These modes of thought are part and parcel of being raised as "selves-in-separation" (see footnote 1). Objectivity, for example, is one of the cornerstones of the scientific method. It has been perhaps the most important single philosophical idea in the development of science, and has enabled scientists to pursue, unchallenged, a description and manipulation of the natural world that is unequaled. However, on its negative side, the pursuit of objectivity has led to the objectification of nature and ourselves. The attempt to separate the "observer" from others and from nature, the subject which is being studied, leads to alienation (Keller, 1985). Rationality is one of our most important abilities as humans and is, of course, absolutely necessary in science, as it is in life. Unfortunately, in science it has been dichotomized with feeling, empathy, and intuition, which have been excluded as rationality has been sanctified.

The concepts of competition and domination have also been important in science and technology. They lie beneath most technological development. These ideas stem from the assumption that power and resources are limited and that the universe is hierarchically structured. For women especially (Chodorow, 1978) it can be difficult to maintain an integrated self in a milieu where objectification, rationality, competition, and domination are unduly important while feeling, intuition, and cooperation are denied or undervalued.

ANDROCENTRISM.   There is male bias both in the choice and definition of scientific problems and in the design and interpretation of scientific work. Male bias is most obvious in the social and biological sciences, although it is also present in the underlying paradigms of the physical sciences. In psychology, for example, most "normal" developmental patterns and psychological states have been defined on the basis of studies of male subjects (Gilligan, 1982). Male bias in anthropology has given us "Man the Hunter" as a major paradigm (Linton, 1971; Tanner and Zihlman, 1976; Bleier, 1984). Biological and anthropological studies "proving" the inferiority of women and the "natural" place of women in society have existed since the beginning of these sciences (Darwin, 1874; Wilson, 1975), and are present today in the field of sociobiology. Darwin, for example, states in *Descent of Man* (Chapter 19, as excerpted in Agonito, 1977) that "The chief distinction in the intellectual powers of the sexes is shewn [sic] by man's attaining to a higher eminence, in whatever he takes up, than can woman—whether requiring deep thought, reason, or imagination, or merely the use of senses and hands." He attributes this difference to sexual selection. This type of thinking has continued until the present day with articles appearing continually in respected journals such as *Science* and *Journal of Human Evolution* on the lack of mathematical ability and smaller intellectual capacity of girls and women (cf. Benbow and Stanley, 1980, 1983; Kolata, 1983; Bleier, 1986; Velle, 1984). This work does not, of course, deal with the intellect alone. Barash (1979, as quoted in Bleier, 1984) "demonstrates" how rape is "natural" and also that the current conservative social structure is "natural": "Because men maximize their fitness differently from women, it is perfectly good biology that business and profession taste sweeter to them, while home and child care taste sweeter to women" (Barash, 1979, p. 114, in Bleier, 1984, p. 36).

Male bias also occurs at deeper philosophical levels, as emphasis on *competition* in the biological sciences, on *independence* as necessary for psychological maturation (Bettelheim, 1977), and on the importance of matter (that which is tangible and separate) over energy (that which is intangible and inseparable) that has persisted in most sciences.

In order to study science in such a milieu we must, as women, deny our female selves and accept the first level of male bias—the tacit elimination of women from fields of study, or the denigration of women by science—the equivalent to laughing at sexist jokes. The second level of bias, the philosophical, permeates our scientific tradition and is alien to people in our society who are raised to be selves-in-connection rather than selves-in-separation. Thus, the discipline of science itself as currently conceptualized feels foreign to us. Until we are advanced enough in our studies and confident enough in our abilities, we do not realize why there may be a certain dis/ease with our methodologies and lack of wholeheartedness in our pursuit of our work

TRADITIONAL, TEACHER-CENTERED PEDAGOGY.   Too often science classes are taught in an authoritative, outline-form lecture style. Freire (1970), in his critique of traditional education, discusses this type of educational authoritarianism brilliantly and at length. Rogers (1983) has since referred to this as the "jug-and-mug" theory of education. In these classes the student is the receptacle, or mug into which the teacher pours his [sic] font, or jug, of knowledge.

Although this method of teaching has been critiqued as classist (Freire, 1970) it has not often been recognized as a patriarchal mode.

The definition of the teacher as actor and the student as passive receptacle parallels many scientists' attitudes about nature as well as patriarchal attitudes about sex roles, where men are defined as active and women as receptive.

These attitudes deny the abilities and experiences of the student;

there is no respect for the knowledge of the student and her/his ability to teach; no acknowledgment of the validity of his/her personal experience; no possibility of dialogue; no critical evaluation of the subject matter; no reference to feeling or intution; and no understanding of science and learning as a process in which we all participate. In order to educate more women in science we must break out of this traditional mold and engage in a more integrated kind of teaching/learning.

FEMINISM AND SCIENCE

Having defined the problem as nothing less than an enveloping patriarchal consciousness and a more than 4000-year-old patriarchal civilization that has ordered social behaviors, forms of social organization, and systems of thought, including science, how can we view the possibilities and directions for change? Over the past decade and a half, feminist activists and scholars have begun a revolutionary movement in thought and behavior so profound and so rooted in a transformed consciousness that it will not stop until all Western consciousness and civilizations are transformed. (Bleier, 1984, p. 199).

Feminist Pedagogy in Science

Radical changes in the attitudes of the scientific community and university teachers are necessary to make science and scientific pedagogy more human endeavors that engage the whole person, man and woman, and work for humane goals in society.

Although hierarchy, competition and domination are deeply rooted, an *immediate* shift from these ideas can occur in a classroom by a shift to nonhierarchical egalitarianism on the part of the professor. This can have immediate and profound effect on the students, transforming them into alert, interested, contributing members of the classroom who think independently.

In addition to attitudinal changes, many methodological changes are necessary to retain women in the sciences. Both radical and feminist pedagogies stress experience as a basic part of learning. In this milieu knowledge is a process rather than a product; we are all teachers and students; and teaching/learning[2] is the other hand of action.

Feminist pedagogy stresses the importance of respecting one's experience and feelings. This idea is an outgrowth of consciousness-raising[3] and advocates developing an atmosphere of mutual respect, trust, support, and nurturance in the classroom. In essence, it is the joining of the heart with the mind. We will explore these pedagogical concepts below.

INTERACTION, COOPERATION AND TRUST. Interactive classrooms are necessary to foster learning by the whole being, to foster cooperation and support, and to value one's own thoughts. Interaction can be encouraged by setting aside significant amounts of time for discussion, even in large lectures; by encouraging single students or groups of students to give lectures, to lead and/or take part in discussions, labs, and field classes, and to have brown-bag lunch discussions in which they present their own work or ideas; by breaking classes into small groups; and by allowing many kinds of media for "papers" and other projects.

CONNECTED, HOLISTIC THOUGHT. In science classes the hard data lecture in linear outline is the most common teaching technique. For example, in a geology class the professor might come in, put an outline on the board, and proceed to tell the class about the different kinds of sedimentary rocks and in what situations each is deposited.

The advantage of linear outlines is that they break down information into manageable chunks and organize them in a way that facilitates memorization. There are also serious disadvantages. One serious drawback is that the medium is the message. Whether we look to modern quantum mechanics or ecology, it is clear that nature is, instead, profoundly relational and process-oriented. The process of our teaching tends to inculcate in students a philosophical paradigm that is outdated, yet since it is not recognized or challenged explicitly, can be left unquestioned, perhaps throughout a student's career.

In nature things are profoundly interconnected. The emphasis on linear thought in science has constricted our understanding of the world as an integrated web and hampered our ability to develop a methodology with which to study such a world (the attempts of systems theory notwithstanding). To supplement or supplant the lecture/outline method, more imaginative exercises can be developed to help students understand the processes and interdependence characteristic of natural processes. For example, a geology student could be asked to imagine herself to be piece of sand in a river, and then to imagine what would happen to her as that piece of sand under different conditions, thereby really understanding the hydrological and sedimentary processes.

INTUITION AND INSIGHT. As scientists we actually use all methods of thought—rational, intuition, empathy, and insight—and we need to consciously employ and teach, not *deny*, all of these modes of thought. Too often stereotypically male qualities like rationality and objectivity are overemphasized to the exclusion of more stereotypically female qualities like intuition, empathy, and caring. Although we may think of intuition as innate or instinctive knowledge, it comes from experience. We are merely unaware that we are gathering the information that gives it to us. It is really the synthesis of many sensory data that we have unconsciously "observed." We learn to be intuitive about people, for example, by attending to people, and about rivers by attending to rivers. This type of fixing of attention occurs in the university in laboratory and field courses—which accounts in part for the great value that science instructors attribute to these kinds of courses. We should provide as many of these kinds of experiences as possible for students and, in addition, we should discuss with them the quality of intuition and its origins.

Closely related to intuition is empathy—the capacity to know something from the inside out, to put yourself in its place and imagine what the world is like from its vantage point. Good science requires us to develop that "feeling for the organism" that Barbara McClintock, the 1983 Nobel laureate in medicine, talks about (Keller, 1983), or "become the tumor" in order to understand why it is growing, as the anonymous woman scientist in Goodfield's (1981) book suggests. If we can empathize with our material to that degree, we can notice things that cannot be observed when we are separated or alienated from our material. It is empathy that allowed McClintock to see the tiny chromosomes in *Neurospora*, the bread mold, well enough to follow their reproductive splitting (meiosis). In addition, her total attention to the daily details of growth in every corn plant that she grew, similar to the attention one must give a growing child, allowed her to accurately predict the genetic background of each and every change she witnessed. We must encourage students to practice this subtle and empathic art of observation. This does not mean that we project our feelings onto the material but that we keep ourselves open enough to "feel," and thus understand, the material.

Insight is somewhat different; it is the "answer" to a problem that just "pops up." It is the stuff that radical new theories are made of, such as the "jumping gene" model of McClintock (Keller, 1983). Gould (1984) describes this kind of thought as the "simultaneous integration of many pieces into single structures." It has a more magical quality to it than intuition, but it too can be developed—mainly through calming the mind and feeling and respecting our unconscious mind.

JOINING FEELING AND THINKING. Traditional scientific thought and pedagogy have discouraged us from exploring the possibility of an appropriate and necessary interaction between feeling and our work. First we need to approach our work with passion—to care for it passionately in order for it to be good. We must also use our feeling in our attitudes toward the implications and use of our work and the work of others in the marketplace, the military and other potential areas of abuse. Denying feeling has led us to a place of psychic numbing in which anything, even including nuclear holocaust, can either be rationalized or ignored (Caldicott, 1984).

Students often react with strong feelings to what they are learning in class, indicating that they are integrating new information and ideas. Such expressions of emotion are usually unacknowledged and even discouraged, although they are necessary for learning and development. Keeping a journal or a notebook in which to write ideas, insights, observations, and feelings about what they are learning can serve to focus the students' attention on whether their life experiences, their understanding of the world, and their feelings correspond with what they are learning. If they do not, this needs to be discussed. If the students are encouraged to thus actively participate in what they are learning, checking to see whether it makes sense and feels right, they will be more likely to really understand the science, to make important contributions, to critically evaluate their world, and to make ethical and moral judgments about the direction of their scientific research.

SOCIAL RESPONSIBILITY. Although today there are restrictions on the use of both human and animal subjects in the laboratory, there are no such restrictions on dealing with nature when it is not in the laboratory. Every science student needs to explore her/his own personal feelings about to what degree we should continue to impinge on nature. If science students had been encouraged in the 1950s to examine their feelings, values, and ethics (and to investigate the *connections* between actions and their likely outcomes) about putting toxic and radioactive waste into the environment or developing nuclear weaponry, we would probably live in a less-polluted and dangerous world today. Classroom and community projects are an excellent way to foster a socially responsible attitude. For example, a class could study the effect of the local dump on groundwater supply and pollution in order to learn about groundwater flow and properties.

Feminist Science

> We live in a scientific age, yet we assume that knowledge of science is the perogative of only a small number of human beings, isolated and priestlike in their laboratories. This is not true . . . Science is part of the reality of living . . . (Carson, 1961)

People familiar with the best in contemporary scientific research and teaching, by men and by women, may react to our generalizations by saying that what we describe as *male* science and teaching is simply *bad* science and teaching. In part, they are right. Both males and females in the forefront of knowledge are advocating or practicing what we have described here as a female mode. This is happening as part of a major paradigm shift in the culture from a patriarchal to a more balanced, androgynous way of seeing and being in the world. This recognition does not change the fact, however, that most science teaching and theory (and most scientists) are still locked into patriarchal ways of seeing the world. Not surprisingly, most of the scientists consciously or unconsciously acting on different, nonpatriarchal premises are women.

We predict that the entrance of larger numbers of women into science will ultimately help change science into a more whole, human endeavor in which the hierarchy will give way to the web, in which we develop complicated methodology able to deal with this web that is nature (cf. Bleier, 1986). This is, however, a classic chicken-and-egg situation. The more the field changes, the more women will enter it, and the faster they enter, the more it will change. We cannot afford to study the universe from any single perspective; we must have the entire human perspective, and we must recognize that we each are *a part* of this universe rather than *apart* from it.

Many of the women pioneers in science have made major contributions *because* they saw science as underlain by the principles of selves-in-connection, rather than selves-in-separation. Ellen Swallow and Rachel Carson in ecology, the first seeing nature as home, the second seeing how we are fouling that home; Lynn Margulis in cellular biology showing us the incredible possibilities of cooperation in nature—the symbiosis between the bare cell and other organisms known to us now as mitochondria and chloroplasts, which gave rise to the modern eukaryotic cell; Jane Robinson, Rosalind Franklin, and

Barbara McClintock, who so closely empathized with what they were studying that they were able to learn its secrets; Jane Robinson in knowing how the ancient seagoing reptiles, the plesiosaurs, swam by becoming a plesiosaur (personal communication); Rosalind Franklin, who detailed the molecular structure of DNA; and Barbara McClintock, who decades before anyone else understood that genes move from place to place within the chromosomes because she had the ability to "get inside" those chromosomes.

These women are among the few who have managed to let their selves-in-connection survive and create in the scientific milieu. We feel that, by educating women in a pedagogical milieu more suited to our tastes, more women will be enamored of science and be encouraged to bring their own special world view to that science. When *both* a male and a female perspective are valued and nurtured in science, science will be more consistently a force *for* humanity and the planet rather than a force *against* it.

NOTES

1. The pronoun "we" is used to refer to women, that is to refer to ourselves, in order to avoid the distancing and objectification that can occur when the third person is used.
2. Danish has a single verb, *at lore*, to teach/to learn (Elizabeth Van Couvering, personal communication).
3. Consciousness-raising is the unconditional sharing and hearing of feelings and experience in order to validate them and know their cultural extent. It arose among small groups of women in the 1960s as a grass-roots part of the women's movement.

REFERENCES

AGONITO, ROSEMARY. *History of Ideas on Woman: A Sourcebook.* New York: Perigee Books, G. P. Putnam's Sons, 1977.

ALDRICH, MICHELLE. "Review Essay: Women in Science." *Signs* 4:126–135, 1978.

ARDITTI, RITA. "Feminism and Science." In Arditti, Rita, et al., eds., *Science and Liberation.* Boston: South End Press, 1980, pp. 351–368.

BARASH, D. *The Whisperings Within.* New York: Harper and Row, 1979.

BENBOW, C. and STANLEY, J. "Sex Differences in Mathematical Ability: Fact or Artifact?" *Science* 210(1980):1262–1264.

———. "Sex Differences in Mathematical Reasoning Ability: More Facts." *Science* 222(1983):1029–1031.

BETTELHEIM, BRUNO. *The Uses of Enchantment.* New York: Vintage, 1977.

BLEIER, RUTH. *Science and Gender: A Critique of Biology and Its Theories on Women.* New York: Pergamon Press, 1984.

————, ed. *Feminist Approaches to Science.* New York: Pergamon Press, 1986.

BRISCOE, ANNE, and PFAFFLIN, SARA. *Expanding the Role of Women in the Sciences.* New York: Academy of Science, 323(1979):1–344.

BRUER, JOSIAH. "Women in Science: Lack of Full Participation." *Science* 221(1983):1339.

BYBEE, RODGER, and KAHLE, JANE. "Biology Education: Beyond the Status Quo." In Hickman, Faith, and Kahle, Jane, eds., *New Direction in Biology Teaching: Perspectives for the 1980s.* Reston, Va.: National Association of Biology Teachers, pp. 141–165, 1982.

CALDICOTT, HELEN. Speech delivered in Boulder, Colorado, Nov. 1984.

CAPRA, FRITJOF. *The Turning Point.* New York: Simon and Schuster, 1982.

CARSON, RACHEL. *Silent Spring.* Boston: Houghton Mifflin, 1961.

CHODOROW, NANCY. *The Reproduction of Mothering: Psychoanalysis and the Sociology of Gender.* Berkeley: University of California Press, 1978.

COLE, JOHNATHAN. "Women in Science." *American Scientist.* 69(1981):385–391.

DALY, MARY. *Gyn/Ecology.* Boston: Beacon Press, 1978.

DARWIN, CHARLES. *The Descent of Man,* 2nd ed. rev. London: John Murry, 1874.

FERGUSON, MARILYN. *The Aquarian Conspiracy.* Los Angeles: J. P. Tarcher, 1980.

FRANKLIN, R., in a personal conversation with the author, Boulder, Colorado, Oct. 1976.

FREIRE, PAOLO. *Pedagogy of the Oppressed.* Trans. by Myra Ramos, 1970. New York: Seabury Press, 1970.

GILLIGAN, CAROL. *In a Different Voice.* Cambridge: Harvard University Press, 1982.

GOODFIELD, JUNE. *An Imagined World.* New York: Penguin Books, 1981.

GORNICK, VIVIAN. *Women in Science.* New York: Simon and Schuster, 1983.

GOULD, STEPHEN. "Triumph of a Naturalist." Review of *A Feeling for the Organism: The Life and Work of Barbara McClintock* by Evelyn Fox Keller, 1983. New York Review of Books 31(1984):3–6.

GRIFFIN, SUSAN. *Woman and Nature: The Roaring Inside Her.* New York: Harper and Row, 1978.

HARDY, SARA. *The Woman That Never Evolved.* Cambridge: Harvard University Press, 1981.

HUBBARD, RUTH; HENIFIN, MARY SUE; and FRIED, BARBARA, eds. *Women Look at Biology Looking at Women.* Cambridge, Mass.: Schenkman, 1979.

HUMPHREYS, SHEILA, ed. *Women and Minorities in Science.* Washington, D.C.: American Association for the Advancement of Science, Selected Symposium 66, 1982.

KAHLE, JANE. "The Disadvantaged Majority: Biology Education for Women and Minorities." *The American Biology Teacher* 44(1982):351–356.

————, and LAKES, M. "The Myth of Equality in Science Classrooms." *Journal Research Science Teaching* 20(1983):131–140.

KELLER, EVELYN. "Gender and science." *Psychoanalysis and Contemporary Thought* 1(1978):409–433.

―――. *A Feeling for the Organism: The Life And Work of Barbara McClintock.* New York: W. H. Freeman, 1983.

―――. *Reflections on Gender and Science.* New Haven: Yale University Press, 1985.

KNOX, HOLLY. "Math, Science Improvements Must Involve Female and Minority Students." *Education Week,* May 11, 1983, p. 24.

KOEN, SUSAN, and SWAIM, NINA. *Handbook for Women on the Nuclear Mentality.* Norwich, Vt.: WAND, 1980.

KOLATA, GINA. "Math Genius May Have Hormonal Basis." *Science* 222(1983):1312.

KUHN, THOMAS. *The Structure of Scientific Revolutions,* 2nd ed. Chicago: University of Chicago Press, 1970.

LINTON, SALLY. "Woman the Gatherer: Male Bias in Anthropology." In Jacobs, Sue-Ellen, ed., *Women in Perspective: A Guide for Cross-Cultural Studies.* Urbana: University of Illinois Press, 1971.

MALLOW, JEFFRY. *Science Anxiety: Fear of Science and How to Overcome It.* New York: Van Nostrand Reinhold, 1981.

MERCHANT, CAROLYN. *The Death of Nature: Women, Ecology and the Scientific Revolution.* San Francisco: Harper and Row, 1980.

MOZANS, H. *Women in Science.* 1913. Reprint, Cambridge, Mass.: MIT Press, 1974.

NATIONAL RESEARCH COUNCIL. *Climbing the Academic Ladder: Doctoral Women in Academe.* Washington, D.C.: National Academy Press, 1979.

―――. *Climbing the Ladder: An Update on the Status of Doctoral Women Scientists And Engineers.* Washington, D.C.: Academy of Science Press, 1983.

NATIONAL SCIENCE FOUNDATION. *Women and Minorities in Science and Engineering.* National Science Foundation, Washington, D.C.: 1986, 86–301.

RICH, ADRIENNE. *Of Woman Born.* New York: W. W. Norton, 1976.

―――. "Toward a Women-centered University (1973–1974)." In *Lies, Secrets and Silence.* New York: W. W. Norton, 1979.

ROGERS, CARL. *Freedom to Learn for the 1980s.* Columbus: Charles E. Merrill, 1983.

ROSSITER, MARGARET. *Women Scientists in America.* Baltimore: Johns Hopkins University Press, 1982.

SMALL, M., ed. *Female Primates: Studies by Women Primatologists.* New York: Alan Liss, 1984.

STONE, MERLIN. *When God Was a Woman.* New York: Dial Press, 1976.

TANNER, NANCY, and ZIHLMAN, ADRIENNE. "Women in Evolution. Part I: Innovation and Selection in Human Origins." *Signs* 1(1976):585–608.

VELLE, W. "Sex Differences in Intelligence: Implications for Educational Policy," *Journal of Human Evolution* 13(1984):109–113.

VETTER, BETTY. "Women Scientists and Engineers: Trends in Participation." *Science* 214(1981):1313–1321.

―――. "Labor Force Participation of Women Baccalaureates in Science."

In Humphreys, Sheila, ed., *Women and Minorities in Science*, American Association Adv. Science, Sel. Symp., 66, 1982.

————, and BABCO, ELEANOR. *Professional Women and Minorities—A Manpower Data Resource Service*. Washington, D.C.: Commission on Professionals in Science and Technology, 1986.

WALLSGROVE, RUTH. "The Masculine Face of Science." In Brighton Women and Science Group, eds., *Alice Through The Looking Glass*. London: Virago, 1980.

WATTS, ALAN. *The Two Hands of God*. New York: Collier Books, 1963.

WILSON, E. O. *Sociobiology: The New Synthesis*. Cambridge, Mass.: Harvard University Press, 1975.

ZUCKERMAN, HARRIET, and COLE, JOHNATHAN. "Women in American Science. *Minerva* 13(1975):82–102.

21

Rethinking the Ways We Teach

BARRIE THORNE

What are the meanings of silence in the classroom? What can silences teach us about knowledge, about processes of teaching and learning, about the nature of social and political life?[1]

In the last decade educators have become increasingly aware of the tacit centering of knowledge around the lives and experiences of the privileged. Women of all social classes, ethnicities, and sexualities, and minority, working class, and gay men are relatively absent from traditional bodies of knowledge. These distortions and gaps in the content of what we teach raise questions about the experiences of students and teachers. What are the effects on those whose lives and histories have been, and in many ways still are, enveloped in silence or distortion? And what are the effects on the privileged—the Euro-American, the heterosexual, the class-privileged, the men and boys—whose specific experiences have been inflated as universal knowledge?

One can explore these questions by examining the effects of masculine "generics" (the use of male terms like "he" and "man" in contexts where gender is not specified, as in "the evolution of man" or "every student should pick up his assignment"). I have asked women students how they experience themselves when they hear or read the masculine "generic." One woman said, "I blank out; I hear or read the

311

words, but my mind is blank." Another said, "I feel schizophrenic; I try to force myself into the 'he,' but I'm straddling the whole time, partly in and partly out."

Cumulative research evidence shows that discomfort with, and alienation from, masculine "generics" is widespread. The singular "they" has been used for centuries,[2] and people sometimes use "she" in generic contexts—for example, to refer to elementary school teachers or secretaries, some of whom are male. Why would these usages persist if "he" were a fully workable generic? Recent research by psycholinguists provides further evidence that "he/man" are false generics. In separate experiments Wendy Martyna and Donald MacKay both found that when male and female subjects hear or read the masculine "generic," they mentally picture men and boys.[3] Martyna found that 40 percent of men had mental imagery (of males) when they read "he" or "his" in generic contexts, but only 10 percent of the women had any imagery at all; like my student, the women "blanked out."[4]

A classroom experiment undertaken by Cathryn Adamsky suggests that the experience of "blanking out" can be turned around, with a release of psychic energy.[5] While teaching an undergraduate course in child psychology, Adamsky consistently used "she/her" generic contexts (the abstracted individual lurks at the center of psychology, providing many occasions for using a singular generic). Examining students' written work, Adamsky found that over the course of the term both men and women reduced their use of "he" as the generic singular (as a control, she looked at writing from an earlier term, when she used the masculine "generic"; there was no such shift). Adamsky asked students to reflect on their experiences of her use of the "generic she." Women students felt included by the use of "she"; one wrote that the "generic she" gave me a sense of equality—power even"; another wrote, "I felt surprisingly proud when I used it."[6] Interestingly, the majority of the men said they did not feel excluded by the usage; the "she" was educative. Both women and men felt that "she" is not the final answer and that our language needs a fully inclusive pronoun.

The other side of "blanking out" is the inflated sense of presence and self-importance that accompanies privilege. Robert Coles uses the term "entitlement" to refer to the emotional expression of "familiar, class-bound prerogatives of money and power."[7] The essence of entitlement is to take one's privilege for granted, to not notice, and hence to perpetuate, patterns of inequality and control. The masculine "generics" (including a whole array of terms, like "mankind" and "chairman") encourage boys and men to take masculine presence for granted at the core of language. This detail of entitlement may be small, but it is recurring; MacKay estimates that in the course of a lifetime a highly educated American is exposed to generically used "he" a million times.[8]

Heterosexual, white, and middle-class, as well as male, assumptions permeate knowledge; all of these forms of entitlement are perpetuated by being taken-for-granted. For example, "couple" is assumed to mean "heterosexual couple"; prefixes ("*lesbian* couple") designate marginality and subordination. The choices of example and bits of humor that sprinkle classroom talk usually assume that everyone is caught up in heterosexual dating and intends to marry. As Marilyn Frye observes, even women's studies courses take heterosexuality for granted: "the searching out of careers and 'feminist men,' the development of 'egalitarian marriages' and the management of heterosexual sex and the family."[9] At best, many women's studies courses include lesbian and gay male experiences as a bounded "topic." How do heterosexual assumptions affect the felt presence of lesbians and gay men within classrooms? Is it a service to heterosexuals to reinforce their taken-for-granted privilege?

Invisibility and silence are characteristic experiences of subordinated groups, especially in settings created and controlled by those with structural power. Of course, all groups have lively, talking occasions. But in dominant settings like universities, where white, class-privileged men and their subcultures prevail, those not of the entitled categories may experience a particular kind of silence, infused with feelings of not being quite at home, of anxiety, of self doubt. Adrienne Rich provides a compelling description of this kind of silence:

> Look at a classroom: look at the many kinds of women's faces, postures, expressions. Listen to the women's voices. Listen to the silences, the unasked questions, the blanks. Listen to the small, soft voices, often courageously trying to speak up, voices of women taught early that tones of confidence, challenge, anger, or assertiveness, are strident and unfeminine. Listen to the voices of the women and the voices of the men; observe the space men allow themselves, physically and verbally, the male assumption that people will listen, even when the majority of the group is female. Look at the faces of the silent, and of those who speak. Listen to a woman groping for language in which to express what is on her mind, sensing that the terms of academic discourse are not her language, trying to cut down her thought to the dimensions of a discourse not intended for her (*for it is not fitting that a woman speak in public*); or

reading her paper aloud at breakneck speed, throwing her words away, deprecating her own work by a reflex prejudgment: *I do not deserve to take up time and space.*[10]

Empirical social science studies of classroom interaction underscore Rich's insight. Systematic observations of elementary school classrooms have found that boys tend to make more contributions than girls to classroom discussions and to receive more teacher attention, both positive (praise) and negative (criticism).[11] The problem of "disruptive boys," possibly related to self-fulfilling cycles of teacher expectation, has long been acknowledged. But another recurring situation, which Constantina Safilios-Rothschild calls the "semi-ignored status" of girls in the classroom, has only recently been seen as a problem.[12] As a participant-observer in elementary schools, I have often seen girls who obey the teacher, who work quietly and neatly, who don't take up much space or whisper or talk in class, and who, because of these qualities, are virtually ignored in the give-and-take of the classroom. The spirit of these girls seems muted; some may even be depressed. Teachers usually appreciate the fact that these girls don't make trouble, but rarely query their silence or passivity. They may even use quiet girls as acoustical buffers, seating them next to noisy or distractable children.

There are fewer empirical studies of college than of elementary school classrooms. At all levels of schooling, researchers find significant variation from classroom to classroom. Not all women students are silent, nor do all men students feel free to speak; some studies have found no sex differences in amount of student talk. However, when a statistically significant sex difference has been found, it has thus far always been that in mixed-sex college classes, men students talk more than women.[13] The patterns are complex, and vary from study to study. For example, in an observational study of ten college classrooms, David Karp and William Yoels found that in classes taught by men, male students talked three times more than women.[14] In classes taught by women, the rate of female participation increased, but men students still talked 57 percent, and women students 42 percent of the time. In a study of graduate classes in social work, Virginia Brooks found no sex differences in amount of student talk in classes taught by men, but in classes taught by women, men students spoke significantly more often and longer than women students.[15] In a study of sixty classes, Sarah Sternglanz and Shirley Lyberger-Ficek found no sex differences in student participation in classes taught by women; in classes taught by men, male students more often initiated interaction with the teacher.[16]

These studies were all conducted in four-year colleges and universities, and they take middle-class culture for granted. In *Critical Teaching and Everyday Life*, a wonderfully provocative book about his experiences as a radical teacher in a community college, Ira Shor observes that among working-class people, especially men, to talk a lot and with enthusiasm in front of superiors is to be a "brown-nose" or "ass-kisser," "guilty of collaborating with the enemy."[17] On the other hand, rebellious talk might lead the teacher to consider you a troublemaker. A power struggle surrounds the use of words in work and school institutions, and "there are tense rules and high prices to pay for talking."[18] Shor observes that in his classes, women talk with more ease than men:

> In general, women students find it easier to take public risks by engaging in critical debate. The men are cloaked in a formidable silence, fearing to be proved wrong in their opinions or feelings. Their linguistic style is abrupt and terminal; they are more likely to voice strong conclusions instead of partaking in an evolving dialogue. This kind of reaction is not uniform or universal, but there is a strong male defensiveness against the humiliation of being wrong. Some men have rationalized their withdrawal by saying that *women* talk and argue all the time. To talk too much is to be silly like a woman. Going public with your thoughts and feelings is a threat to macho dignity. Talking a lot in class means commitment to the process; commitment suggests feeling that the discussion matters to you; admitting publicly that something matters to you is a surrender of male coolness, a giving up of the disguised toughness where you tell the world you can make it on your own. Talking openly and seriously in a group is a statement that you need the others, and the men are reluctant to let on that they need anything from anybody. Their aloofness develops over the years, from hearing how worthless they are, from feeling inadequate in meeting the demands of others.[19]

The meanings of masculinity and femininity, and of speech and silence, may vary along lines of class and race. Vicky Spelman has probed the silence of Black women in predominantly white women's studies classes.[20] Black women felt marginalized when white women's experiences were taken as the paradigm, and the experiences of women of color as a source of divergence; they felt marginalized when they were heard and seen as a bloc, with minimal attention to variations among them; and they felt marginalized when their opinions were not challenged and they were treated soley as victims rather than as "members of lively communities with rich cultural identities and traditions."[21] Within the classroom, the silence of Black women, like the silence of the working-class men Shor describes, may be a form of resistance, a way to avoid becoming even more vulnerable. White women, on the other hand, may refuse to engage in talk that would make their privilege more visible, talk which might, for example, reveal their lack of knowledge of Black cultures. As Vicky Spelman, Audre Lorde, and Helen Washington have each observed, the history and presence of racism are loaded with suppressed anger and mistrust, emotions which may infuse some kinds of classroom silence.[22]

In general, silence may be related to fear of saying the wrong thing or of showing emotions. Students may fear the judgment not only of the teacher, but also of other students, who may seem "frighteningly anonymous or frighteningly well qualified," as a student said in a discussion at Oberlin College. In classrooms generally, silence may be a way to avoid taking risks, to avoid getting involved. In most classrooms a few talkers emerge early in the term, setting up a tacit division of labor. When the teacher asks a question, the teacher and the nontalkers may even turn and look at the talkers, expecting and perhaps cueing them to respond.

Feminist pedagogy, like the radical pedagogy Paolo Freire developed for teaching literacy to peasants in Latin America, seeks to break through silence and passivity and to empower subordinated groups.[23] This approach to teaching values dialogue, with the kind of engaged learning that comes from all participants feeling present and respected in the classroom, and ready to speak. How can one empower students, especially those whose silence may be the accumulation of years of feeling invisible, marginalized, afraid, unable or unwilling to become involved? How can one enhance their sense of presence and of freedom to participate in the classroom? And, turning to the more privileged, how can one reveal and challenge assumptions of entitlement? To discover that one's experience is *not* the measure of all things, to come to *see* white, middle-class, male, and heterosexual assumptions as limited and not the universal, and to explore the experiences of other groups are precious forms of learning.

There are no magic classroom solutions to problems of inequality deeply anchored in social and political institutions. But in the process of teaching we can work for equality and the goal of empowerment. Here are an array of specific suggestions drawn from many different sources and people:

TALK ABOUT SILENCE AND EMOTIONS

One can raise, as a specific topic, the question of silence and classroom content and process. Last term I opened an undergraduate course on the sociology of sex and gender with a section on feminist recentering of knowledge. I asked students to think about their past educations, and I explained, with specific examples, varied ways in which subordination and entitlement may infuse knowledge and classroom interaction. We discussed Adrienne Rich's essay "Taking Women Students Seriously," and Mary Helen Washington's evocative article on racial dynamics in a women's studies classroom.[24] Many of the students had already pondered their own biographies of classroom speech and silence. For example, one woman said in a reticent tone, "I talked a lot in high school, but when I talked in one of my first college classes, the professor and the other students just blew it away, so I haven't talked much since." Another said her classroom silence had come to feel like a "shroud," from which she was determined to break free.

We also read Audre Lorde's essay "The Uses of Anger," and talked about connections between thinking and passion, especially feelings of anger.[25] When I taught an interdisciplinary course called "Women's Situations," we went around the room and each student explained why she or he was taking the course. Many of them talked about anger: "I feel angry about my experiences as a woman, and I want to know why"; "I'm a biology major, and I'm in a continual state of rage at the way I'm treated"; "I want to learn about women's studies, but I don't want to feel angry"; "feminists' anger makes me feel defensive as a man." We discussed sources of anger, the risks of getting angry, ways anger can be misdirected but also provide information, spirit, and energy, relationships between anger and social change, anger and hate, and anger as both paralyzing and leading to action. The course was enhanced by making emotions explicit.

NOTICE EVERYDAY DETAILS OF INTERACTION

One can cultivate the habit of noticing the details of interaction in the classroom. (Two good sources for sharpening one's eyes and ears are *The Classroom Climate: A Chilly One for Women?* by Roberta Hall and *Body Politics: Power, Sex and Nonverbal Communication* by Nancy Henley.[26])

Notice the language of space, of high and low, of fixed seats versus a rectangular or round table, of where different students sit. Structures of power and participation can be altered by stepping away from a podium and moving closer to the class, by moving chairs from rows and into a circle, by the teacher's sitting on the side rather than at the end of a rectangular table. Patterns of seating affect patterns of talking. Large classes pose enormous barriers to comfortable discussions, but there are ways to enhance participation. Watch your angle of vision in a large classroom. Students at the front and up the center have been found to be more visible and more likely to talk. You can share this observation with students and ask them to rotate where they sit, to feel what it's like in different parts of the classroom. When you reach an evocative point in a lecture, pause and ask students to discuss the issues with a neighbor for ten minutes. Then draw the class back together and ask them to brainstorm the results. (I always explain that brainstorming is an associative process to get ideas out, with minimal accountability for what one says.)

Notice the language of eye contact, which helps regulate talk. A teacher in a liberal arts college told me that a class discussion of Freire opened the topic of participation patterns in their own classroom; several students observed that men talked more than women. One student suggested that this was partly due to the teacher's habit of looking at men students when she asked a question. Eye contact can invite, and eye aversion can discourage, participation in talk.

Another detail to notice: the construction of turn-taking and the organization of the floor of talk. Lee Jenkins interviewed 77 Latina/o, Black, Asian-American, and Native American students about their experiences in classrooms at San Francisco State University.[27] They told her they were reluctant to participate in classroom discussions when faculty didn't really listen, ignored the speaker's content, interrupted or cut them off, treated them patronizingly or with contempt, or acted surprised when they did well. On the other hand, they were encouraged to participate when teachers called on them by name, offered encouragement in facial expressions and nonverbal gestures, and gave them time to respond. They were also more likely to participate when the course included materials from their cultures, although they didn't like to be singled out as spokespersons for their ethnic groups.

Native American, Latina, and Asian-American students, especially women, mentioned cultural prescriptions against speaking up which carried over to the classroom. But they also felt that faculty, perhaps because of stereotypes of the quiet Asian or the silent Indian, did not expect them to participate, so they did not.

Familiar classroom rituals of talk—the tacit rules that one person speaks at a time, that turns should be requested by a raised hand, that there should be minimal response as a person speaks—fit more closely with white, middle-class, Protestant males than with other speaking cultures. In *Black and White Styles in Conflict*, Thomas Kochman notes that Black students may feel more comfortable speaking out in class rather than raising their hands and waiting for a turn to speak.[28] In Afro-American culture talk is often organized in quick exchanges rather than sequences where people hold forth, at length, one at a time. As Jenkins points out, by ignoring students who "speak out of turn," we may extinguish participation without realizing it.[29]

Rules for talk in college classrooms are anchored in male, as well as white and upper-middle-class, subcultures. Talk among women (to generalize in a way which wrongly suspends class and ethnic variation) tends to be more collaborative and participatory than talk among men. For example, compared with men, women do more "interaction work" (head nods, saying "mmhmm," asking questions to draw out the speaker).[30] Women are also more likely to build upon than to contest one another's comments, to share personal experiences, and, in general, to regard conversation as "a cooperative enterprise, as a mutually constructed product for common interest."[31] As a result, as Paula Treichler and Cheris Kramarae have insightfully argued, the competitive verbal jousting, the continual marking of hierarchies, the efforts to wield control, the declarations of fact and opinion that one finds more often in all-male groups—and in college classrooms—may be especially alienating to women.[32]

By virtue of their role, teachers have enormous power to shape and control the conversational structure of the classroom, to open up or monopolize the floor, to throw it to one person rather than another, to interrupt and take the floor back, to restructure the very nature of the floor. You can give up some of that power, inviting students to shape the rules of talk; you may also use that power to enhance participation. Invite students to help figure out the tacit rules of classroom talk and to devise ways to encourage more participation. For example, after alerting students to notice the silent and to share responsibility for helping everyone feel at ease, open the floor and let people speak without being called upon, or implement a rule that the last person who speaks gets to choose the next speaker. You can talk privately to students who are always silent and ask if there are ways you can help bring them to speech. I made a pact with one student that I would try to be especially sensitive to cues that she had something to say (facial expressions, a clearing of throat, a shift in body posture), and that I would try to call on her, to help her readiness break through her hesitation.

The constructive silence of listening takes work and attention. You can encourage students to draw one another out, to invite and refer back to one another's comments, to ask questions as well as making statements, to generally be aware of the effect they have on one another—for example, through nonverbal expressions of support or impatience. Help students prepare for an upcoming discussion by providing questions for them to think about or by asking them to prepare discussion questions or summaries of readings.[33]

Notice your pattern of calling on students. On whom do you call, and in what sequence? Do you change your tone of voice when you speak to different students, and if so, how and why? Do you call some students by name, and just point to others? Which names do you know? A few years ago when I was teaching a lecture class of one hundred students, I discovered, to my horror, that I knew all of the men's names and fewer of the names of women students (part of my horror was that this was a women's studies class). There were fewer men, so they were more visible. But I also discovered a pattern: I hadn't learned the names of those I clustered into a stereotype of the nice, smiling, silent woman student. I discovered my stereotype when one of the nameless women came to my office hours and said she hoped to go to medical school. I was surprised, and then asked myself why I was surprised and why I had never learned her name.

I try to encourage students to feel visible and acknowledged from the beginning of the term, creating a context where people have names and distinctive identities.[34] Everyone can wear a name tag or place a United Nations–type of name sign in front of them during class. Beginnings are important; if one doesn't talk at the start of the term, chances are slim one will talk later. Creative forms of self-introduction allow everyone to be heard at the start. In a course on women and work we opened with a round of introductions; each student described her own history of work (part, full-time, and summer jobs, including baby-sitting and housework), and then her mother's and her grandmother's work histories. The introductions brought concrete examples of historic changes and social class and ethnic variations in women's work; it also made student diversity more visible. We returned to these examples throughout the term. In my class on the sociology of childhood we each described ourselves in second grade: where we lived, the nature of our households and friendships, memories of what happened in schools and neighborhoods.

Noticing opens the path to action. And our actions, I believe, should be geared to the goal of empowering those who have been socially subordinated, and ending relations of inequality in as well as outside of the classroom. Nancy Hartsock makes an important distinction between power as domination and a feminist definition of power as energy, effective interaction, working together, and empowerment.[35] The feminist challenge is to develop forms based on this alternative vision as a way of transforming institutions based on domination.

This vision can be realized in the classroom, as illustrated by Mischa Adams' description of the transformation of a graduate seminar.[36] During the first few sessions women were relatively silent; they had difficulty entering the rapid freeway of talk between the professor and most of the men students. The talkers controlled the floor through mutual eye contact, throwing the floor only to one another, and a rapid pace of mutual challenging and interruption. The silent students (all of the women, and a few of the men) gathered outside of class, analyzed the patterns, and set out to change them, not by adopting the dominant discourse (barging onto a freeway with interruptions and challenging) but by empowering one another and changing the course of talk. They arrived early and sat in a way that diffused eye contact around the group. They built on one another's comments in the discussion, giving the mutual gift of interaction work (head nods and other signals that one is listening; questions to draw out the speaker); they invited the silent to speak. Rather than overvaluing and imitating the dominant style (monopoly of turn space, interruptions, topic control), they used collaborative patterns to draw in and empower more participants. The teacher, by the way, soon noticed that something had changed; the shift in classroom climate, and the students' explanation of what had happened, led him to rethink his mode of teaching.

We are involved in a long process of rethinking and revising the curriculum and the ways we teach. Above all, the process involves taking all people seriously and urging them to take themselves seriously. This may be especially important for women, whose oppression often takes the form of being trivialized, laughed at, sexualized, called "girl," defined by their appearance instead of their minds, told they have no serious future other than being a wife or mother. This kind of treatment—amply documented in the settings of higher education—mutes the spirit, diminishes self-esteem, and drains aspirations. I believe one of the greatest gifts a teacher can give is to help others find a sense of agency in their lives.

NOTES

This paper began as a talk given in various incarnations at the Claremont Colleges Conference on Women's Studies and a Balanced Curriculum (February

1983), at the Great Lakes Colleges Association Women's Studies Conference (November 1983), and at Carleton College, Oberlin College, and Northeastern Illinois University in January and February 1984. Discussions on all of these occasions greatly enriched what I finally wrote. I would also like to thank Cheris Kramarae, Nancy Henley, Lee Jenkins, Roberta Hall, Beverly Purrington, Mischa Adams, Kay Trimberger, and Bettina Aptheker for their contributions and inspiration.

1. For some provocative thoughts on silence and on language, see Adrienne Rich, *On Lies, Secrets and Silence* (New York: W.W. Norton, 1979) and *Dream of a Common Language* (New York: W.W. Norton, 1978).
2. Ann Bodine, "Androcentrism in Prescriptive Grammar," *Language in Society* 4 (1975):129–146.
3. Wendy Martyna, "What Does 'He' Mean? Use of Generic Masculine," *Journal of Communication*, 28 (1978):131–138; Donald G. MacKay, "Prescriptive Grammar and the Pronoun Problem," in Barrie Thorne, Cheris Kramarae, and Nancy Henley, eds., *Language, Gender and Society* (Rowley, Mass.: Newbury House, 1983), pp. 38–53. Additional studies of the uses and effects of masculine "generics" are annotated in Cheris Kramarae, Barrie Thorne, and Nancy Henley, "Sex Differences in Language, Speech and Nonverbal Communication: An Annotated Bibliography," in Thorne, Kramarae, and Henley, pp. 174–182.
4. Martyna, ibid.
5. Cathryn Adamsky, "Changes in Pronominal Usage in a Classroom Situation," *Psychology of Women Quarterly* 5 (1981):773–779.
6. Ibid. pp. 777–778.
7. Robert Coles, *Privileged Ones* (Boston: Little, Brown, 1977).
8. Donald MacKay, "On the Goals, Principles, and Procedures for Prescriptive Grammar: Singular *They*," *Language in Society* 9 (1980):349–367.
9. Marilyn Frye, "Assignment: NWSA-Bloomington-1980, Speech on 'Lesbian Perspectives on Women's Studies,' " *Sinister Wisdom* No. 14 (1980), p. 5. Frye's article is reprinted in Margaret Cruikshank, ed., *Lesbian Studies* (Old Westbury, N.Y.: The Feminist Press, 1982).
10. Adrienne Rich, "On Taking Women Students Seriously," in *On Lies, Secrets and Silence* (New York: W. W. Norton, 1979), pp. 243–244.
11. See reviews of research in Jere E. Brophy and Thomas L. Good, *Teacher-Student Relationships: Causes and Consequences* (New York: Holt, Rinehart and Winston, 1974); Constantina Safilios-Rothschild, *Sex Role Socialization and Sex Discrimination: A Synthesis and Critique of the Literature* (Washington, D.C.: National Institute of Education, 1979); and Susan S. Klein, ed., *Handbook for Achieving Sex Equity Through Education* (Baltimore, Md.: Johns Hopkins University Press, 1985).
12. Safilios-Rothschild, ibid.

13. A comprehensive, annotated bibliography of studies of gender and inter-action in college classrooms can be found in Sec. V-F-2, "Classrooms," in Kramarae, Thorne, Henley, op. cit. (footnote 3).

     There is another recurring finding: college classes taught by women tend to have more overall student participation than classes taught by men. This may be partly due to women's more collaborative cultures of talk. While this pattern may be put to good pedagogical use by women teachers who want to create participatory classrooms, it may also en-tail a double bind. Anne Macke, Laurel Richardson, and Judith Cooke, *Sex-typed Teaching Styles of University Professors and Student Reactions* (Columbus: The Ohio State University Research Foundation, 1980) found that students judged women professors to be more likable *and* less com-petent, the more they generated student participation in class. Evalua-tions of most men professors were not affected by the amount of student participation in their classes. Radical pedagogies assume that the teacher enters with initial authority that needs to be demystified. If a teacher enters the classroom with minimal authority or credibility (which may be especially true of younger women teachers), the challenge becomes more complex. Feminists have begun to rethink the complicated rela-tionships between teaching and authority; for example, see Amy Bridges and Heidi Hartman, "Pedagogy by the Oppressed," *Review of Radical Political Economics* 6 (1975):75–79; Berenice M. Fisher, "Professing Fem-inism: Feminist Academics and the Women's Movement," *Psychology of Women Quarterly* 7 (1982):55–69; and Susan Friedman, "Authority in a Feminist Classroom: A Contradiction in Terms?" in *Feminist Pedagogy* (Madison: University of Wisconsin Women's Studies Research Center, 1981), pp. 1-9.

14. David A. Karp and William C. Yoels, "The College Classroom: Some Observations on the Meanings of Student Participation," *Sociology and Social Research* 60 (1976):421–439.

15. Virginia R. Brooks, "Sex Differences in Student Dominance Behavior in Female and Male Professor's Classrooms," *Sex Roles* 8 (1982):683–690.

16. Sarah Hall Sternglanz and Shirley Lyberger-Ficek, "Sex Differences in Student-Teacher Interactions in the College Classroom," *Sex Roles* 3 (1977):345–352.

17. Ira Shor, *Critical Teaching and Everyday Life* (Boston: South End Press, 1980), p. 72.

18. Ibid.

19. Ibid., pp. 72–73.

20. Vicky Spelman, "Combatting the Marginalization of Black Women in the Classroom," *Women's Studies Quarterly* 10 (no. 2, Summer 1982):15–16.

21. Ibid., p. 16.

22. Spelman, ibid.; Audre Lorde, "The Uses of Anger," *Women's Studies*

Quarterly (No. 3, Fall 1981):7–10; Mary Helen Washington, "How Racial Differences Helped Us Discover Our Sameness," *Ms.*, September 1981, pp. 60–63.

23. Paolo Freire, *Pedagogy of the Oppressed* (New York: Herder and Herder, 1972).

24. Rich, op. cit. (footnote 10); Washington, op. cit. (footnote 22).

25. Lorde, op. cit. (footnote 22).

26. Roberta Hall, *The Classroom Climate: A Chilly One for Women?* Available for $3 from the Project on the Status and Education of Women, Association of American Colleges, 1918 R St., NW, Washington, D.C. 20009; Nancy Henley, *Body Politics* (Englewood Cliffs, N.J.: Prentice-Hall Spectrum, 1977). Another useful source: Mercilee M. Jenkins, *Removing Bias: Guidelines for Student-Faculty Communication*, part of Judith M. Gappa and Janice Pearce, *Sex and Gender in the Social Sciences*, available for $7.50 from the Speech Communication Association, 5105 Backlick Road, Suite E, Annandale, Va. 22003.

27. Mercilee M. Jenkins, "Guidelines for Cross-cultural Communication Between Students and Faculty," Speech Communication Department, San Francisco State University, 1983.

28. Thomas Kochman, *Black and White Styles in Conflict* (Chicago: University of Chicago Press, 1981).

29. Jenkins, op. cit.

30. Pamela Fishman coined the term "interaction work" in "Interaction: The Work Women Do," in Thorne, Kramarae, and Henley, *op. cit.* (footnote 3), pp. 89–102.

31. Sally McConnell-Ginet, The Origins of Sexist Language in Discourse, unpublished paper, Department of Linguistics, Cornell University, 1982, p. 10. For a review of research on talk among women see Barrie Thorne, Cheris Kramarae, and Nancy Henley, "Language, Gender and Society: Opening a Second Decade of Research," in Thorne, Kramarae, and Henley, op. cit. (footnote 3) pp. 7–24.

32. Paula A. Treichler and Cheris Kramarae, "Women's Talk in the Ivory Tower," *Communication Quarterly* 31 (1983):118–132.

33. Useful suggestions for teaching students the skills of discussion can be found in Nancy Schniedewind, "Feminist Values: Guidelines for a Teaching Methodology in Women's Studies," *The Radical Teacher* 18 (1982):25–28, reprinted in Charlotte Bunch and Sandra Pollack, eds., *Learning Our Way: Essays in Feminist Education* (Trumansburg, N.Y.: The Crossing Press, 1983), pp. 261–271; and in William Fawcett Hill, *Learning thru Discussion* (Beverly Hills, Calif.: Sage, 1977).

34. Schniedewind, *ibid.*, provides many excellent suggestions for working toward this goal.

35. Nancy Hartsock, "Political Change: Two Perspectives on Power," in Quest Staff and Book Committee, eds., *Building Feminist Theory* (New York: Longman, 1981), pp. 3–19.

36. Mischa B. Adams, *Communication and Gender Stereotype*, unpublished Ph.D. dissertation, University of California at Santa Cruz, 1980.

22

Leadership in the University Curriculum

CAROLYN M. SHREWSBURY

Whether we talk about it as the "third wave" (Toffler, 1980) or the "acquarian conspiracy" (Ferguson, 1980), or an information society (Naisbitt, 1982), our future will demand and reward different skills than did the recent past. Already, as analysts discuss the "excellent companies" (Peters and Waterman, 1982) or new management styles (Agor, 1984), the need for most workers to be skilled participants in the decision-making and problem-solving processes of their jobs is clear. Recognition of such needs has paralleled discussions about new visions of leadership. The old image of leaders as the commanders of men is being replaced by a vision of a leader as

> someone who knows how to control her life, and who has a vision of possibilities for other lives apart from her own, for her community, for other women, for example, and who works to make that *vision* visible to others, to share it, without trampling on the other persons, but engaging them, enabling them to work for that vision as well. (Howe, 1983, p. 10).

Such images of leadership have important implications for both the ways in which we participate in and manage our universities, and for the content and process of our curriculum. It is the latter that is the focus of this paper.

Women in general and women's studies courses in particular have much to teach us about the possibilities as well as the practicalities of this new vision of leadership. Women have always been leaders. Although the history books have ignored us, those in formal positions of authority have oppressed us, and even we have undervalued our accomplishments.

As leaders, we have been different from men. If there is any single phrase that might characterize women's leadership, it is the establishment of community. Our history books are full of the names and activities of the founders of business and industry or the politicians and generals. But the social fabric is a woven tapestry of interconnections between all elements of the society. It is this act of connecting that was so typical of women. Women on the frontier, for example, kept up the flow of letters that connected them with family members who stayed in the east or who pushed on further west, or the women's church circle planned and prepared dinners and helped the sick. It was women's groups that furnished schoolrooms, that started libraries, that pushed for sanitation laws. In Minneapolis and St. Paul, for example, it was women's groups that formed aid societies for the thousands of women pouring into the city from the rural farms, while the male legislature focused on laws to aid the cattle shipped in for slaughter.

But besides recognizing the contributions of these women who worked so hard to form community, we must note that it would be hard to cite a few names of "great women leaders," for leadership was often shared by many different women in the group. Women's leadership reflects a world view that recognizes the interconnections between self and others and between autonomy and community.

As we think about the university's role in developing leadership in others, we will be more effective if we include the advantages of women's as well as men's historic leadership styles. Elizabeth Janeway notes:

> the masculine ideal of leadership in the use of power, of *mastery*, calls for individual might, heroic stature, lone suffering that can win, perhaps, a solution born of the mind of a single genius who has achieved a new vision. . . . But of course it is not the only way to solve problems, and it may be particularly inappropriate at a time of multiple, rapid change. Then the shared experience of a purposeful group might afford more insight. . . . And the members who provide diversity must be taken seriously in their differences: it is these differences that matter, that permit marginal, flexible, and original ideas to be put forward out of a hitherto prohibited realm of thought. (1980. p. 254).

The metaphors we use to refer to leadership are telling and they are grounded in the very real experience of men and women. If our metaphors for leadership, which are based on the male experience, have been the military (the general) or sports (the quarterback), women's experience of leadership might well be imagined as parental. Good parents do not master children, they work with them to help them grow and learn, to gain the capacity to take responsibility for shaping their own lives.

The military metaphor emphasizes uniformity. When all goes well, the leader commands and everyone will march in lockstep, not only wearing the same uniform (slightly differentiated by place in the military hierarchy) but even wearing the same expression. Conversely, a successful family encourages children to develop their unique gifts.

Differences are crucial to any emerging vision of feminist leadership. Women leaders emphasize the ways life experiences of women differ from one another as well as the ones we hold in common: the needs of the Black differ from those of the Chicana as both differ from the white; the needs of the poor differ from those who have good careers in industry; the needs of women and men in Nigeria differ from those in France. Differences, moreover, are more than different needs. The lesbian sees society from a different perspective than the heterosexually married women, who sees a different perspective than the celibate woman. And these and other differences are not things to fear but things to spark the creative leadership that recognition of the richness of such diversity can bring about.

Increasingly, major theorists about leadership have emphasized the very qualities we find in women leaders as the kind of leadership most needed in the contemporary world. James McGregor Burns (1978) makes a distinction between two kinds of leadership, transactional and transformational, that highlights the importance of difference. Transactional leadership "occurs when one person takes the initiative in making contact with others for the purpose of the exchange of valued things" (p. 19). It is a kind of bargaining leadership. The relationship is essentially temporary or limited. The conflict in the situation arises because of the attempt to achieve desired things in a circumstance in which resources are limited.

Transforming leadership, on the other hand, "occurs when one or more persons *engage* with others, in such a way that leaders and followers raise one another to higher levels of motivation and morality" (p. 20). Transforming leadership necessitates a much more intensive interaction, but one which results in greater empowerment. Conflict is pervasive, in part because, in Burns' words, leaders need to "see through the posture and defense of public attitudes to the real needs and values behind the protective facade" (p. 40). The tyrant plays on our fears and often uses such conflict to isolate people in parochial groups. The transforming leader helps us understand the needs behind our fears and helps us sense the joy of satisfying these needs rather than placating them.

When we view leadership as a relationship between two or more people rather than a property of one person, we see that there is a reciprocity between leaders and followers, and that the relationship is in process. The actual role of leader or follower may shift. Indeed, a feminist view of leadership is exactly that: leadership may be rotated formally; it may shift informally from task to task; it may be divided with different people performing different leadership roles, or it may literally be shared. In any of these cases, although the roles of leader and follower shift, what remains constant is an ethic of responsibility and a shared sense of purpose.

THE CLASSROOM

Some Women's Studies Programs have consciously developed women students' leadership activities. This task has necessitated a feminist analysis of leadership that includes recovering and making visible the historic dimensions of women's leadership, conceptualizing a morality whereby empowerment is not just "doing your own thing" but finding the connection between autonomy and community, and teaching students to lead and to follow in ways that are neither racist nor sexist nor classist. Feminist teachers emphasize cooperative learning strategies and the development of internal reward structures and critical thinking rather than competitive learning and external reward structures and the acquisition of "facts." A constant interaction between theory and action, experience and theory, self and community is a central part of the learning environment. Students learn to take responsibility for their education and to empower themselves as teachers/learners.

This kind of learning process directly contributes to the development of leadership skills in ways that traditional pedagogies do not. For example, students who take part in developing goals and objectives for a course learn planning and negotiating skills. They also learn how to develop an understanding of, and an ability to articulate, their needs. They learn how to find connections between their needs and the needs of others. They learn about groups and about the different leadership tasks in groups and take different leadership roles throughout the course period. As students struggle with evaluation methods, they learn how to evaluate actions and the connection between objectives and achievement. When things are not working in the classroom, they learn how to analyze the problem and how to find alternatives.

In the feminist classroom, the role of the instructor is more complex than in the traditional classroom. Letting go of some control is very difficult for most instructors. It not only requires a considerable amount of faith and trust in students, but also in oneself and in the process. In this sense, the feminist teacher is above all a role model of a leader. She/he has helped members of the class develop a community, a sense of shared purpose, a set of skills for accomplishing that purpose, and the leadership skills so that teacher and students may jointly proceed on those tasks. Feedback is an important part of any learning process. Learning leadership is no exception. Students need to know when they have been effective at leadership tasks, whether they be roles they play in class discussions or in developing evaluation techniques. And community, so necessary for effective leadership, is enhanced by celebration—as small as a good word or pat on the back, or more formal as in a rite or ceremony.

There is a dynamic between leadership and followership and effective leaders under the more modern sense of leadership are also effective followers. Between the two is a morality based upon shared responsibility. Individuals are responsible for their acts within the context in which they have freedom to act. When the students as well as the teacher have decision-making roles in the classroom, students learn to act consciously and responsibly. As we have seen, feminist pedagogy itself develops leadership skills by making the class itself a leadership lab. In addition, specific classroom activities can augment and complement the general approach of shared leadership within the classroom. For instance, in an introductory women's studies course community speakers are frequently used, both because of the subject matter they discuss and because of their value as models of women leaders in the community.

A similar activity is the use of oral interviews by students as a part of a class. A discovery of the extraordinary strengths of relatives, community residents, neighbors, again models from those we have been taught to ignore or overlook. As we regain our heritage, we not only discover a lost past but also possibilities for the future.

In some introductory classes students are asked to participate in or observe activities—for example, attend a local NOW meeting, volunteer time at a battered women's shelter, participate in a hearing on public housing, or help organize a local conference.

In more advanced courses, students take on more specific leadership roles in the community. In integrating these activities into our courses, we might remember that they are best when integrated, not just add-ons. Students need the same help in such experiential learning as they do with other substantive class material. The connections most important to make are not always obvious. The instructor's role may be to make explicit those connections or otherwise help students identify them. We also need to remember how hard it is to take that first step into any new activity. We as instructors need to be aware of those fears, and to prepare students for them and provide alternative strategies for those who need them (two students working together, going first as a class group, having a council member speak to the class and meet the students and know when they are coming—a friendly hello from the council member will ease the entrance, and so forth).

More typical college experiences also develop leadership potential. Research activities, especially those done in teams or in close working relationship with client groups, can also develop leadership abilities, as can internships. A successful internship requires special attention to sites, ensuring that the site indeed is one where that can happen. But most important is the support of the faculty supervisor in suggesting connections between the student's internship work and previous class work and in debriefing in ways that help the student identify leadership opportunities seized and missed.

CLASSROOM PROBLEMS

The classroom as a site, inter alia, for leadership development is not without its problems. Here, we can only examine a few of the most relevant ones. It is, however, particularly important for administrators to understand the difficulties that faculty face whenever they implement new teaching methods. In addition, variations of these problems occur when administrators change their leadership approach. Recognition of some of the stumbling blocks is most helpful during those transition periods.

Student resistance is one critical barrier. Students resist changes in traditional class structure for a variety of reasons, not the least of which is fear of the unknown. The feminist classroom strives to make students full participants in the classroom. It is difficult for students to believe in that intention. Much of their experience lends credence to that cynicism. Only open, sincere, and continued actions as well as statements by the instructors can make believers out of cynics.

Indeed, much of traditional education has been geared to keep people from making connections between their own lives and the material studied. Students often, when first exposed to information about how women have suffered from discrimination, see how that was true in the past or for other women, but have difficulty making connections between the class material and their own lives. They define themselves as "different." The feminist classroom allows students to break down those barriers between the text and people's everyday lives. When women students begin to discover ways in which they too have been discriminated against, they may respond with rage, anger, and often hopelessness. This may turn to despair, denial, flight, or a random striking out until or unless the student continues her studies and begins to see ways to exercise agency in the system, to understand work for social change. Cheri Register (1979) has suggested that it is particularly important for instructors to be aware of this process and to name it, discuss it with students, empower them by recognizing their right to understand what they are undergoing. Again, the inclusion of a focus on leadership helps this process, not just to intellectualize what is happening but to internalize it and connect it to how people work together to achieve social change.

There is a special joy to being part of a community and feeling empowered within that community (see, for example, Breines, 1982). The classroom can be such a community, modeling a possible set of relations for the larger world and developing the skills for living in that world. Careful attention to leadership is central to that task.

Time is another crucial barrier in several senses of the term. Students resist additional demands made on their time. Classes are short enough. How can we add leadership development to them without either overburdening already overworked students or cutting important substantive material out of the curriculum.

Full discussion of this issue requires a separate paper, but here it is important to note that we need to rephrase this question. We can do things differently. We can even do them more efficiently. Cooperative learning strategies allow a good deal more material to be covered than do individualistic learning strategies. We, however, have a kind of vicious circle. Without cooperative learning strategies, there is no time to give explicit attention to leadership development. But without leadership skills, students are unable to employ cooperative learning strategies. The way to break this cycle is to begin with leadership skills. As students develop their skills in more and more classes, the ability to depend more and more on cooperative learning strategies in the classroom will increase and the tension of time, although always there, is no longer so dominant. Women's studies programs have clearly demonstrated the growth potential of students and teachers and the increase in coverage of materials that this skill development includes.

CONCLUSION

William James has said, "I will act as if what I do makes a difference." If we are to encourage our students to believe their lives can make a difference, we must introduce them to ordinary people whose lives have clearly mattered and provide them with experiences which encourage them to experience a sense of agency and power. For women and other groups whose heroism has not been recognized and explored, their collective accomplishments and the styles of their achievements, must be named and validated.

Administrators can increase leadership opportunities for students through encouraging faculty to incorporate feminist pedagogical techniques into courses, especially if their own leadership practice is in accord with the principles of the new images of leadership. Beyond that, administrators can certainly encourage and support the activities of those on campus who are introducing such principles into their courses. Such support is, of course, not a panacea, but the legitimacy of feminist pedagogy that such demonstrates is crucial for the continued development of feminist pedagogical techniques. Those techniques are crucial to the development of the skills of women as well as for men students that will advantage them in postindustrial society.

REFERENCES

AGOR, WESTON H. *Intuitive Management Integrating Left and Right Brain Management Skills.* Englewood Cliffs, N.J.: Prentice-Hall, 1984.

BREINES, WINI. *Community & Organization in the New Left, 1962–1968: The Great Refusal.* New York: Praeger, 1982.

BURNS, JAMES McGREGOR, *Leadership.* New York: Harper and Row, 1978.

FERGUSON, MARILYN. *The Aquarian Conspiracy.* New York: St. Martin's, 1980.

HOWE, FLORENCE. "New Teaching Strategies for a New Generation of Students," *Women's Studies Quarterly* XI:2(1983), 7–11.

JANEWAY, ELIZABETH. *Powers of the Weak.* New York: Knopf, 1980.

NAISBITT, JOHN. *Megatrends.* New York: Warner, 1982.

PETERS, THOMAS J., and WATERMAN, ROBERT H., Jr. *In Search of Excellence: Lessons from America's Best-run Companies.* New York: Harper and Row, 1982.

REGISTER, CHERI. "Brief, Amazing Movements: Dealing with Despair in the Women's Studies Classroom." *Women's Studies Newsletter* 7:4 (1979), 7–10.

TOFFLER, ALVIN. *The Third Wave.* New York: Bantam, 1980.

23

The Culture of
Separated Desks

ELIZABETH DODSON GRAY

Picture a typical classroom in our educational system. There are row upon row of separated desks, lined up in order and facing an open space filled with one desk or one speaker's podium. What are the unspoken assumptions that lie behind this arrangement of furniture for the learning process?

In answering this question, I am reminded of a cartoon from *The New Yorker* magazine. It shows a vast open business office with vast expanses of glass windows and row upon row of separated desks and office cubicles—five or more wide and fifteen or so rows deep. At the front of the room one man is standing talking to another, and one asks the other, "Who sets the tone here?"

What was crystal clear from the cartoon was that *no one person* set the tone among those rows upon rows of separated desks. The tone had been set by the setting, the layout of the room. The same is true in education. The layout of the room speaks eloquently about the school's assumption about education—and about the expected relationship of student to teacher (or professor) and student to student. Lecterns at the front tell us the teacher is expected to be a dispenser of knowledge. Separated, identical desks imply that education is expected to be an individual experience.

But the question still remains: What are the unspoken assumptions behind and beneath such settings? Why, in education as well as in business, do we fill up our space with separated desks? Clearly, it is because we conceptualize an education as a solitary and autonomous experience. To sit down as a first-grader at a separated desk in one of our school systems is as solitary an experience as for a runner in a track event to put his or her feet in the blocks and take their mark. We are to start running our own course, start learning our letters and math by ourselves, start competing with others for grades, start racing all the others to gain prizes and scholarships and, ultimately, better jobs in the real world that come after the educational world, the real world of adulthood.

Within this conceptualization of education, each of us not only runs our own race and competes with others, but "cheating" is defined as helping each other. There is, almost by definition, little or no cooperative work possible in running this course. Academic courses, and the educational curriculum as a whole, are highly individualistic, each student is to be alone and autonomous, and all are to be competitive from the time we sit down at that first separated desk.

MALE PSYCHOLOGY: THE LONELINESS OF THE LONG-DISTANCE RUNNER

Now I ask you: Where does all that need to separate and compete come from? And why are we so resistant to critiquing it or even to noticing it as an underlying educational issue? To answer this question we must first do a gender analysis of our culture. We must first notice that we are living in a culture that has been constructed from the point of view of *male* life-experience.

Our widespread use of male generic language—"man and the future," "mankind," "he"—is a helpful clue for us that indeed we do dwell within an interpretive bubble, what sociologists Peter Berger and Thomas Luckmann have called "a social construction of reality," (1966), in which men have been the chief actors as well as the chief interpreters of the public life we call "culture." Men have conceptualized all of life and thought from their standing point, the standing point of male life experience and male imagination.[1]

But what is there in life experiences of males that makes life feel like a lonely footrace? Where does this feeling come from, of being a racer, always running alone toward some distant prize?

It is interesting to note that we are not dealing here with simply a phenomenon of modern culture. Several millennia ago in the quite different world of Late Antiquity this footrace image arises again and again to the mind of St. Paul as he writes his letters to the earliest Christian churches. "Do you not know," he wrote, "that in a race all of the runners compete but only one receives the prize. So run that you may attain it. Every athlete exercises self control in all things. They do it to receive a perishable wreath, but we are imperishable" (1 Corinthians 9:24–27).

That same image of the runner comes to his mind again when writing to the Philippians. "One thing I do, forgetting what lies behind and straining forward to what lies ahead, I press on toward the goal for the prize of the upward call of God in Christ Jesus" (Philippians 3:13). Another writer in the Letter to the Hebrews in the New Testament uses this same running image: "Let us also lay aside every weight and sin which clings so closely, and let us run with perseverance the race that is set before us" (Hebrews 12:1).

The 1981 film *Chariots of Fire* was a compelling portrayal of this separation and this drive toward triumph played out in an Olympic competition in the second decade of this century. What is the psychic seedbed of this syndrome of the long-distance runner? Is the basis and motivation for a perennial "Chariots of Fire" embedded in the male of our species? And if so, then why?

At this point we need to look at the psychodynamics of male childhood. Almost without exception boys (and girls) are raised by women. But those women, those mothers, are experienced by little boys differently than little girls experience them. As infancy turns into early childhood and little girls become aware of themselves, they realize they are *like* their mothers, they learn their bodies match their mothers, and they realize they can continue their earlier close relationship and identification with their very important female nurturing figure. Little girls "grow up female" by continuing early identifications and remaining close to and modeling themselves on their mothers or their female mothering-figures.

But being raised by women raises a characteristic problem for boys. They too are close to their mothers in infancy, and are rocked and cuddled, often breast-fed. Boys in infancy also develop a deep and primal relationship with this most important nurturing figure, mother. The psychological rub comes as little boys emerge out of infancy and become aware of themselves as boys, as different than girls and mothers, as boys in male bodies and destined to grow up and become men—and not women. They are very close to their mothers (as little girls are), but their bodies, their lives, their destinies cannot be modeled on the one they have been so close to and identified with until now.

Nancy Chodorow, in her book *The Reproduction of Mothering*,[2] suggests that in very early childhood little boys resolve this psychological dilemma by pulling away from their close relationship with their mother, by separating themselves, and by attempting to grow up male by separating from whatever is perceived to be female and is embodied by their mothers and their mothers' lives. In this way separating, and growing up by separating, becomes a basic style or stance of maleness and of male life experience. The little boy resonates to the phrase "I can do it myself." Asking for help comes to be perceived as a sign of weakness. Depending upon relationships is perceived as "dependency" (or "apron strings"), and that means for many men that intimacy and the recognition of interdependency threaten their identities as males.

As psychologist Carol Gilligan has observed, in her book *In a Different Voice* (1982), these aspects of male experience have been assumed to be the psychological norm by theorists such as Freud, Jung, Piaget, Erickson, and others using terms such as "individuation," "self-reliance," "independence," "autonomy," and "maturing." Extrapolating from the male experience, human development is modeled as a movement from dependency (in relationship) to separation (rather than interdependency, which would be the female norm).

What do separated men do? They compete! It is as though in their aloneness they must constantly measure themselves against others, so they can constantly reassure themselves, in their separation, that they are good, better or even best!

THE SCHOOL AS A RACE COURSE

Now take that mind-set of separation and ask it to structure a classroom and an educational system—and you have just what we have today. Each child at each desk is running a lonely race from an early age, straining toward a future prize, gobbling up facts and figures and proficiencies so he (or she) can outperform all the fellow desk-runners. No communication from desk to desk ("talking") is allowed. The ethos is serious, the competition is assumed, the "play" of early childhood is obliterated, the wonderful diversity of human curiosity and talent and interest and personhood is trampled beneath the constant naming of the right answer or the correct way to do this or that, and all this is sealed as excellence, complete with grades, graduations and approval.

The Road Runner reigns supreme. The dutiful take up the imperative to race and start out upon an endless obstacle course that becomes a life of achievement, first in school, then college/professional school, and then career. The rebellious are labeled as dyslexic, disruptive, hyperactive, hard to teach, or simply dumb. It is hard not to take seriously Samuel Bowles and Herbert Gintis' accusation, in *Schooling in Capitalist America* (1976), that this schooling exists only to legitimate to those who learn to "run" that they deserve the spoils of an affluent material life-style, and to confirm for the rebellious that they, having "failed" at education, deserve to be poorly paid in uninteresting work in the middle or lower levels of our economic hierarchies.

What are we doing here to our future, to our children who are each born with a unique DNA that parallels the wondrous diversity of snowflakes? If God and creation and nature can affirm the diversity of each snowflake, why can't we? If the universe creates life by joining together, why do we never consider the possibility of "joining together" as a part of the educational life of the child?

Educational experiments that encourage cooperative diversity have a profound affect on participants. When the author and her husband were teaching at the MIT Sloan School of Management (1974–1976), they assisted a senior professor. As someone who was fundamentally a manager rather than an academic, Carroll Wilson was interested in problem-solving (which could be collaborative) rather than in assessing and rewarding individual performances. He had structured his academic courses into a very different experience for students. Students were asked to stop in the midst of their term-paper preparations and present a five-minute summary of their term paper to the seminar. They then received from their classmates five or ten minutes of *constructive* help such as "This bit of thinking which I know about might help you . . ." or "This book ties in with your argument" or "Your next question, then, might be . . ." Everyone was asked not to critique but to help, to assist, to lay out our own intellectual background so as to further one another's work.

The response of seminar participants was both interesting and startling. They thought the experience was wonderful. Many said they'd never had this sort of help from other students before, *never in their entire educational careers*. Others realized that they'd never tried to help, rather than critique, others. They had competed throughout their entire educations, and were just now "trying on" cooperation as an educational model. This seems particularly startling when we recognize that, in order to succeed later on in life, they will need to be able to collaborate as well as to compete. Although businesses compete with one another in the marketplace, it takes cooperation *within* a given corporation for the firm to be successful.

"SEPARATION" AS A CONDITION OF THOUGHT

We've been examining what separation and the ideal of autonomy, self-sufficiency, and independence have done, first to our classroom arrangements and second to our students. But let us turn now to what separation as a mind-set has meant to our thinking itself.

Let us begin by recognizing that reality and life come at us and are experienced by us as a continuity, all in one piece, so to speak. Look out your window. You see effortlessly interconnected in our natural world the fields of botany, zoology, biology, ecology, physics, chemistry, astronomy, astrophysics, and so on. Become introspective for a moment and look inside your own ongoing life. You will find, again effortlessly interconnected in reality, the fields of history, psychology, theology, ethics, philosophy, and so on.

Reality comes to us and we experience it as effortlessly integrated. But we have pursued a "divide-and-conquer" policy in education. You name it and we have a compartment for it, and usually a specialist to go with the compartment. This creates a kind of tunnel vision, someone has called it, where we each become experts on less and less.

Yes, the separated, isolated Road Runner has done to thinking what he has done to the arrangement of desks. All, all has been divided into pieces and tracks and lanes and fields and disciplines, the better to run and "master" it all. Just as we lost sight of the mystery and the wonder of each child's uniqueness, so we have lost sight of the mystery and the wonder of the world, which comes to us whole but varied, integrated and interconnected and interdependent. To become educated is almost to lose awareness of this wondrous wholeness because we are taught again and again to break a problem into its component parts to solve it, to study the bits and pieces of anything, assuming that they exist in isolation from their companions in time and space. Then we are surprised when the world falls to pieces at our feet, and we wonder why, and what it is we've done to it. "Whatever went wrong?"

The mind-set of the Separated Road Runner has made our science, our philosophy, our theology, and our psychology into cosmic stories of separation rather than connection. Mind and matter. Male and female. The observer and the observed. The subjective and the objective. The self and the other. Such dualisms abound and lie at the very foundations of our thought systems. To live by cosmic theories of separation when we are actually within an interconnected reality system is dangerous to the health and well-being of human society on this endangered planet.[3]

IS THERE ANOTHER WAY?

It is about this time that I begin to hear voices asking me, How would women do it differently? In your analysis, these voices say, you have laid on male consciousness the mentality of the Separated Road Runner which, you say, permeates our "pursuit" of knowledge. Even if all that you say is granted, the question remains, Would women do it any differently?

We know from the work of Carol Gilligan, Anne Wilson Schaef, and others[4] that women are more relational than men in the way they approach their lives. How would this more relational and contextual mode of living and thinking structure the educational system within which learning experiences take place? How would relationality and contextuality furnish and lay out the learning context (what we have called traditionally the classroom)? Would students work in groups? Would students compete? Could students be graded in comparison with each other? Would integrated studies—where, say, literature, theatre, art, architecture, religion, philosophy—were all studied together, become the norm instead of an occasional interdisciplinary experiment?

How, we would want to know, could learning take place through relationship, rather than through the top-down, empty-vessel, pour-in-the-knowledge-by-the-expert way we now structure learning?

These are questions that stagger an imagination steeped in "what is" and "what has been" within our educational systems. But turn your mind somewhat, and ask yourself how all that incredible learning of infancy and early childhood—before formal schooling—actually takes place. We are talking now about learning that is profoundly relational and contextual, in which not only language but a whole psyche takes its first shape in an individual, learning that is so rapid, so deep, so profound, and so embedded in the primary relationships of the family and its relationships with immediate neighbors and close family—and so totally unstructured by desk or lecture podium. Yes, we are talking about a starkly different learning experience and learning context than "what is" and "what has been" in our places of formal learning, "our schools."

ANOTHER WAY TO DO SCIENCE

So it's done differently in infancy and early childhood. Have we examples of another, more relational and contextual way of learning in adulthood? I think we do in Evelyn Fox Keller's book, *A Feeling for the Organism* (1983), which is the account of the life and scientific work (learning) of pioneer plant-geneticist Barbara McClintock. Evelyn Fox Keller is interested in "[w]hat enabled McClintock to see further and deeper into the mysteries of genetics than her colleagues."

> Her answer is simple. Over and over again, she tells us, one must have the time to look, the patience to "hear what the material has to say to you," the openness to "let it come to you." Above all, one must have "a feeling for the organism."
>
> One must understand "how it grows, understand its parts, understand when something is going wrong with it. [An organism] isn't just a piece of plastic, it's something that is constantly being affected by the environment, constantly showing attributes or disabilities in its growth. (p. 198)

What Barbara McClintock is describing is a starkly different kind of scientific "learning." We do not find here learning controlled by a previously formulated hypothesis, learning based upon standing apart and separate and viewing with so-called scientific objectivity and detachment. Instead, she is describing another sort of scientific learning, learning in which the learner becomes involved and takes the care and time to "hear" and from that "understand" what the material has to say to you.

> "No two plants are exactly alike. They're all different, and as a consequence, you have to know that difference," [McClintock] explains. "I start with the seedling, and I don't want to leave it. I don't feel I really know the story if I don't watch the plant all the way along. So I know every plant in the field. I know them intimately, and I find it a great pleasure to know them."
>
> ". . . I have learned so much about the corn plant that when I see things, I can interpret [them] right away." Both literally and figuratively, her "feeling for the organism" has extended her vision. (ibid.)

At another point Keller writes that, "Over the years, a special kind of sympathetic understanding grew in McClintock, heightening her powers of discernment, until finally, the objects of her study have become subjects in their own right; they claim from her a kind of attention that most of us experience only in relation to other persons" (ibid.). McClintock's research method is an example in adulthood of a very intense and scientifically sophisticated use of what I have here been calling "learning through relationship."

Perhaps we have difficulty imagining "learning through relationship" because we have not paid sufficient attention to outstanding women who know how to do it. Elizabeth Kübler Ross (1975) is another example of this approach to learning. She listened to her dying patients, and thus as a psychiatrist learned through this relationship the coping mechanisms and stages in the grieving process by which we humans mourn our passing from this mortal life.

Barbara McClintock, in her conversations with her biographer, also talks about her ability to draw upon ways of knowing which are out of the usual. "Somehow, she doesn't know how, [McClintock] has always had an 'exceedingly strong feeling' for the oneness of things: 'Basically, everything is one. There is no way in which you draw a line between things. What we [normally] do is to make these subdivisions, but they're not real. Our educational system is full of subdivisions that are artificial, that shouldn't be there . . .'" Her biographer continues: "The ultimate descriptive task, for both artists and scientists, is to 'ensoul' what one sees, to attribute to it the life one shares with it; one learns by identification (Keller, 1983, p. 204).

NEW GUIDING IMAGES

The Road Runner image has run out on us. In W. H. Auden's memorable phrase, "the Pilgrim Way has led to the abyss." And it is no wonder that it has. How could we not understand that seeing in three dimensions is only possible with two eyes, and that stereophonic sound requires two loudspeakers? In the mystery of evolution, along with sexual reproduction there has evolved a male and a female mode in our human species. Yet we have ignored and made invisible in the public realm that female mode.

What has happened is that for our shared public life and its institutions and culture, we have confused the male with the entire human species: when we've seen how men do or view something, we think we've seen how humans do or view it. We have lived only from that one male eye, that one male ear, that one male life experience, that one male imagination. This is what the author has written about elsewhere as a conceptual trap (Gray, 1982). To continue doing this is to career into our future like a racecar driver guiding a vehicle while keeping one eye firmly closed, one ear totally blocked, and the imagination locked upon competition, oblivious to hazards, and appearing to an outside viewer much like a kamikaze intent upon some inner goal even if it means his own destruction. The compulsiveness of this unresolved psychological dilemma in the males is evidenced by obliviousness. No amount of information about the ways these approaches contribute to world hunger, acid rain, or the threat of nuclear annihilation seem to have any force against it.

We are in need of a new metaphor, a new guiding image, from which to image not only a whole new way of *learning* but a more benign way of *living* as a human species upon this planet. One obviously and largely untapped resource is the "other" half of the human species, women, and the newly emerging sense by women not of just of themselves but of themselves *as women*. I believe it urgently behooves all of us, male and female, to bring to birth and tenderly nurture this emerging female sense of self, or female consciousness.[5]

If we but nurture this genuine emerging female consciousness, then out of that new conceptual and imagining "space" will come new guiding images, new metaphors. As in the experience of Barbara McClintock and Elisabeth Kübler-Ross, this emerging sense of the whole, and of the fundamental relationality of the different parts, suggests the possibility not only of different sorts of learning but different kinds of education. Can we imagine education which truly respects the human diversity of children? Or that perceives the wonder of existence whole rather than exploded into its parts? Or that nurtures a truly coed social construction of reality in our next generations?

I will end with one haunting question: Can the male of our species, so long accustomed to the male cultural dominance provided by patriarchy, accept the giver of new symbols, new metaphors, and new modes of viewing reality—if that giver is woman? Can the male give up his old monopoly on the role of giving such gifts to human culture and the human future? Can man share with woman the role of image-maker and image-shaper in the culture? Even beyond that, can man find in himself the open hand to receive a new image to complement his own, when the giver is The Other, woman? Can he do this, even if not just educational systems but his life and future on this endangered planet depends upon it?

It is a sobering question.

NOTES

1. This is spelled out at greater length by the author in *Patriarchy as a Conceptual Trap* (Wellesley, Mass.: Roundtable Press, 1982).
2. Nancy Chodorow, *The Reproduction of Mothering: Psycholoanalysis and the Sociology of Gender* (Berkeley and Los Angeles, Calif.: University of California Press, 1978). The pivotal role of the primary parent being mother is also central to the work of Dorothy Dinnerstein, *The Mermaid and the Minotaur: Sexual Arrangements and Human Malaise* (New York: Harper & Row, 1976).

3. See *Patriarchy as a Conceptual Trap*, pp. 120–125, for a fuller development of this point.

4. Gilligan, op cit. Anne Wilson Schaef, *Women's Reality: An Emerging Female System in the White Male Society* (Minneapolis, Minn.: Winston Press, 1981). See also Jean Baker Miller, *Toward a New Psychology of Women* (Boston: Beacon Press, 1976), and Lillian B. Rubin, *Intimate Strangers: Men and Women Together* (New York: Harper and Row, 1983). A rich and ongoing development of this relational psychology of women is taking place in the group of psychiatrists and clinical psychologists associated with Jean Baker Miller at the Stone Center at Wellesley College, Wellesley, Mass. Papers presented monthly are available as Working Papers either by subscription or individually.

5. I do not use here the word "feminine" but instead "female," for "the feminine" is a concept I consider a stereotypic projection of the dominant male psyche upon the-woman-as-other. As such, it says more about males' perception of women than it does about real females of our species.

REFERENCES

BERGER, PETER L., and LUCKMANN, THOMAS. *The Social Construction of Reality: A Treatise in the Sociology of Knowledge.* New York: Doubleday, 1966.

BOWLES, SAMUEL, and GINTIS, HERBERT. *Schooling in Capitalist America: Educational Reform and the Contradictions of Economic Life.* New York: Basic Books, 1976.

GILLIGAN, CAROL. *In a Different Voice: Psychological Theory and Women's Development.* Cambridge, Mass.: Harvard University Press, 1982.

KELLER, EVELYN FOX. *A Feeling for the Organism: The Life and Work of Barbara McClintock.* New York: W. H. Freeman, 1983.

KÜBLER-ROSS, ELISABETH. *Death: The Final Stage of Growth.* Englewood Cliffs, N.J.: Prentice-Hall, 1975.

24

Toward a New Concept of Career Development

CAROLE W. MINOR

Career development is an important issue to everyone in higher education. Underlying the purpose of developing individuals who are able to think critically, solve problems, be creative, lead others, and continue to grow intellectually after the end of their formal education is the goal of developing individuals who can fulfill their potential and become productive members of society. This implies, in the broadest sense, facilitating the capacity of individuals to make contributions through their chosen careers.

The idea of career *development* (an individual's growth via productive work accomplished through a series of choices and adjustments) as a broadening of the notion of career *choice* (a onetime event that produced a single occupation held for a lifetime) began to be discussed only as recently as the 1950s. Since then, many psychologists have incorporated the idea of the importance of work as a contributer to individual identity, building on Sigmund Freud's description of the healthy person as one who is able "to love and to work." Erik Erikson (1963) postulated that a major task of young adulthood is the formation of identity—which includes facing issues of life purpose, vocation, and occupation. James Marcia (1966) and Arthur Chickering (1969) each expanded on Erickson's ideas about identity formation, describing the processes by which it occurred. William

Perry (1970) developed a model of the cognitive development of college students that can be viewed as a context in which they make initial career field choices. One of the stages is commitment—to a philosophy, a life-style, a type of work. Donald Super (1957) proposed a model of career development through a series of hierarchical stages. This development occurred through a series of choices and adjustments as individuals sought to play roles they considered appropriate for themselves. David Tiedeman and Robert O'Hara (1963) described the mechanisms of differentiation and integration by which ego identity develops and stages through which individuals pass as they make initial and subsequent career decisions. Daniel Levinson (1978), Roger Gould (1978), and others have developed models of adult development that have a significant component of achievement of life satisfaction through work roles.

All of these models, however, were developed, and continue to be researched, primarily on men. The rationale has been that men have more predictable career patterns, or neater ones, or that most women don't have careers at all.

Two recent conceptual breakthroughs have stimulated thinking in a more inclusive way. In the career field, David Tiedeman and Anna Miller-Tiedeman (1984) have begun to discuss "life as career," the idea that career is much broader than paid employment or even other such roles as homemaking, student, or community involvement. Career, by their definition, is activity the individual finds productive or fulfilling. Each individual is responsible for building his or her life career according to individual needs. This would be finding some balance among work roles, family, social contributions, leisure and play, friendship, and so forth. In the developmental areas, Carol Gilligan (1982), in her research on moral development themes developed by Lawrence Kohlberg (whose research was also conducted on men), found that the women she studied spoke, as she titled her book, "in a different voice." While Kohlberg's model described development as passing from self-interest to adherence to abstract principles, Gilligan found women talking, for the most part, about relationships with other people. She found them moving from "selfishness" to "selflessness" to "interdependence." This difference in the moral development issues of men and women calls into question the applicability for women of *any* models developed on men. To encourage women's career development adequately it is essential to look at the developmental issues of women and to examine the social attitudes and conventions which affect women's choices as well as their experiences in the work world.

CAREER DEVELOPMENT ISSUES FOR WOMEN

Career Choice

The career development issues confronting students in higher education most often involve choices—initial occupational choice or choices enabling them to change an occupation or advance in a present one.

Three recent models of career choice contribute to our knowledge of how women make career decisions (Astin, 1984; Gottfredson, 1981; Hackett and Betz, 1981). Gail Hackett and Nancy Betz proposed a model of factors influencing career-related self-efficacy, how one views one's ability to do certain tasks and be successful in certain activities. They discussed three areas in which women are socialized to feel successful in different tasks than men. Young girls have more involvement in domestic and nurturing activities and less involvement in sports, mechanical activities, and other traditionally male activities. Thus, they feel successful at domestic and nurturing activities and less comfortable in most other activities. Young women have a predominance of role models in traditional roles and occupations. They do not have role models representing the full range of options. Thus, they have higher self-efficacy regarding traditional roles and occupations. Women also have a lack of encouragement, sometimes an active discouragement, for nontraditional roles and pursuits. This gives them a lower sense of self-efficacy toward a variety of nontraditional occupations. Implications of this model for redesigning women's experiences in higher education include (a) opportunity and encouragement to become involved in sports, student government, leadership, and other traditionally male-dominated activities; (b) exposure to female role models in a variety of fields: as faculty, staff, and administrators, and in occupations they may consider entering; and (c) recognition from faculty and encouragement to pursue fields of study in which they are capable.

Linda Gottfredson's model (1981) suggests that self-concept (defined as gender, social class, intelligence, interests, and values) in concert with occupational images (sextype, prestige level, and field) determine occupational preferences. These preferences, together with perceptions of job accessibility (opportunities and barriers), determine a range of acceptable occupational alternatives. This model highlights the significance of the sex-role socialization of the individual, the perceived sex type (appropriateness for one sex or the other) of the occupation, and the perceptions of opportunities or barriers to women or women's career choices. It specifies the role of feedback from the environment in the development of women's perceptions of themselves, of occupations, and of barriers or opportunities in the environment. The specific implications of this model include (a) socializing women to the wide range of options open to them, (b) providing role models to break down limiting notions of the sex type of occupations, and (c) changing women's perceptions of the barriers that face them in occupations just because they are women. These, of course, imply extensive discussion of these issues both in and out of the classroom.

Helen Astin (1984) proposed a model of career choice and work behavior that includes the influence of work motivation, sex-role socialization, and the structure of opportunity. Sex-role socialization takes place in play, in the family, at school, and at work. It interacts with the structure of opportunity, which includes the distribution of jobs, sex typing of jobs, discrimination, job requirements, the economy, family structure, and reproductive technology. This interaction is influenced by the three basic motivators for work (survival, enjoyment of the work, and a sense of contribution) to influence individual expectations, which influence career choice and work behavior. Implications of this model for the career development of women are (a) sex-role socialization needs to include achievement for women, (b) women need to perceive the structure of opportunity as open to them, and (c) women need to understand their own motivations for work. The implications of these three models for women's career development are summarized in Table 24.1.

We see in these three models that there are particular issues which are significant in the career development of women. One is the lower sense of self-efficacy many women have in areas not domestic or nurturing because of their sex-role socialization and their consequent lack of experience and/or experiences of success in traditionally male domains. Another is lack of exposure to role models of successful women in nontraditional occupations and the issues those women face in their careers. The third is the perception of barriers in the environment, such as societal sex typing of jobs as well as actual discrimination, which make it difficult for women to enter, or, more significantly, to be comfortable and/or advance in some occupations.

Access

Career issues facing women after choice can be described in terms of access, advancement, and balance. *Access* to most occupations had been restricted for women until the early 1970s. While many

TABLE 24.1 *Implications for Women's Career Development*

HACKETT & BETZ	GOTTFREDSON	ASTIN
1. Opportunity and encouragement to become involved in sports, student government, leadership, and other traditionally male-dominated activities.	1. Socializing women to the wide range of options open to them.	1. Socializing women at play, in the family, at school, and at work, that appropriate roles for women are equal to and not subservient to men.
2. Exposure to female role models in a variety of fields: as faculty, staff, and administrators and in occupations they may consider entering.	2. Providing role models to break down limiting notions of the sex type of occupations.	2. Changing the perceptions of structure of opportunity in terms of discrimination, job requirements, family structure.
3. Recognition from faculty and encouragement to pursue fields of study in which they are capable.	3. Changing women's perceptions of the barriers that face them in occupations just because they are women.	3. Assisting women in making informed decisions with information about the three work motivators: survival, enjoyment of work, and a sense of contribution.

more women are entering predominantly male occupations, vestiges of bias against women in these occupations remain in both men and women. Astin, Gottfredson, and Hackett, and Betz discussed how the activities and socialization of most women limit what options they consider for themselves. Hiring bias still exists. It is being supported now in part by a backlash against the young graduates of the 1970s who built competitive careers for themselves and found that they needed more time for relationships. Some of them are slowing down their careers to focus on relationships and/or children. Some companies view these women as having wasted the resources of the company and again are questioning the hiring of women for managerial positions. Certainly the companies in question had made little or no attempt to accommodate to the high value women place on relationships, expecting women to conform to the stereotypically male career pattern. While these problems remain, issues of *access* are certainly much less serious than they were in the early 1970s.

Advancement

Advancement, on the other hand, is a much more difficult issue for women today. For example, studies in business, academia, and science have shown that, while a much larger proportion of women have entered those areas since the early 1970s, the higher the position in the hierarchy, the lower the percentage of women in it. In addition, the higher position the greater the salary discrepancy between men and women. This is illustrated by the phenomenon that is being called "the glass ceiling." While women in business and other fields have succeeded in climbing the ranks of management, few have entered the top executive ranks. They get close enough to see the top, but do not advance because of an invisible barrier, "the glass ceiling." Speculation is that because these positions require "being like" those who are already top executives (who are men), women will have great difficulty breaking through the glass ceiling, no matter how closely they follow the male competitive model, just by virtue of being female, and therefore different.

Balance

Balance is a topic of current interest to women who have followed the male competitive model. More and more women have chosen since the early 1970s to achieve directly (Lipman-Blumen et al., 1983) in the arena of the workplace. Some of these women, after a number of years of nothing (or not much) but work in their lives, have felt the need for spending more time in relationships. This may mean finding an intimate partner with whom to share daily life, having children (or spending more time with ones they may already have), or developing a close circle of trusted friends with whom to share time and confidences, or it may simply mean making their families and/or friends a higher priority in their lives. It may also mean changing jobs and/or lowering advancement expectations at work (Cosell, 1985; Orsborn, 1986).

These models imply that it is important for women to receive from the academic environment reinforcement for their attempts to pursue nontraditional courses, majors, and occupations. This will help acquaint them with broader options now open to women. They also need to see role models of successful women in a variety of fields and to understand the issues they face and how they deal with those issues. It is also important that women, as well as men, have opportunities during their experience in higher education to reflect on their own skills, abilities, interests, values, and needs and to increase their ability to negotiate for what they want; to gain information about potential fields of study and occupations, their advantages and potential barriers or disadvantages to women; to have the opportunity to try some of these academic and occupational fields; to understand some future issues they may face in access, advancement, and balance; and to have help processing this information: synthesizing and making decisions.

The rest of this discussion presents some ways this could be done, and, in some cases, has been done in various higher education institutions.

FACILITATING CAREER DEVELOPMENT

As indicated above, a comprehensive program to facilitate the career development of women students would have several components. It would include reinforcement for being in higher education (acceptance, attention, and encouragement); the presentation of female role models, both as contributors to the discipline and as successful women in a wide range of fields and occupations; the development of an understanding of the issues women face in the workplace (access, advancement, and balance); the opportunity and stimuli to reflect on personal characteristics, interests, values, and goals and how they relate to occupations; opportunities to gain information about the wide range of occupational options available to them, and to try out on a low-risk basis some of these options; and assistance in processing all the information about themselves and opportunities to enable them to make decisions about their futures. These components are discussed in detail below.

Acceptance, Attention, and Encouragement

Issues involving classroom interactions are discussed in detail else-where in this volume. Since they are significant in individual career development, they are reviewed briefly here. Classroom interaction needs to be positive for women students. Women need to be called on for recitations; their ideas need to be taken seriously, even though they might be quite different from male or traditional ideas; and they need to be encouraged (behaviorists would say "reinforced") to be in college and to be in a wide variety of disciplines and courses. They need not to be demeaned, or told that they are silly or "Isn't that just like a woman!" All of these actions make young men fail to take women seriously and cause women to fail to take *themselves* se-riously. The California State University Women's Studies Program Committee has developed an excellent brochure that is designed to sensitize faculty to how they may be treating women and men dif-ferently in their classes.

The content presented in college classrooms needs to reflect the content and contributions of women. This is difficult to do because many times the contributions of women have been devalued and/or lost over time. At Northern Illinois University (as at many other col-leges and universities), the Women's Studies program sponsored sev-eral faculty colloquia, by departments, called "Women in the Curricu-lum." The director of the Women's Studies Program commissioned a bibliography for each department of contributions of women that could be highlighted in both introductory and advanced courses. Sev-eral faculty members who have worked in this area were brought in from other universities to lecture and interact with faculty. The two-day event for the faculty of each department was balanced be-tween lectures and interactions with faculty toward helping them know about and plan to include contributions of women. Such events provide support for those individual faculty members seeking (or needing) to make such changes, and help create a classroom and campus climate which is supportive of women.

Opportunities for Self-exploration

Opportunities for self-exploration for women students should be available in *all* areas of campus life. Not only should intellectual exploration be encouraged in the classroom, as has been discussed previously, but women students also should be encouraged to take diverse and challenging courses as part of their general education requirements. Women should also be welcomed and encouraged to participate in various social and special interest groups: the flying club, the ski club, intermural and intervarsity sports, the debate team, and others. It is from participation in a wide variety of curricular and noncurricular activities that women students will gain the experience that will enable them to be comfortable in intellectual and physically demanding activities. Facilitating career development for college students can begin with orientation. Acknowledgement of the importance of career issues to students can be highlighted by a discussion of career-related services, courses, and annual campus events. Some universities have orientation courses that have career development components. These courses assist students in identifying issues related to career decision-making, familiarizing themselves with campus services and programs that help with career decision-making and job-finding, and understanding the relationship between life and work and how decisions in one of these areas affects the other.

Opportunities for self-exploration can also be provided in discussions, support, or counseling groups for women interested in career issues. Special activities highlighting issues of women and career and dual career couples could be added to the groups frequently run by counseling centers and career planning and placement offices for individuals needing help with career planning. These groups usually begin by identifying the individual's view of self-strengths, skills, goals, interests, and values. They then attempt to identify possible occupations relating to those individual characteristics and assist the individuals in finding information about those possible occupations. Finally, the group members are taught decision-making processes and assisted in using the self and occupational information in decisions. In addition to these groups, special groups could be provided for exploration and support for returning women students (over the age of twenty-five, many over thirty-five). Other groups, composed of women, or men and women, could explore the changing roles of men and women at work and at home and the implications those changes have for their own lives. Such counseling and exploration groups are most appropriately led by trained counseling center staff, but may be held in settings such as residence halls, Greek houses, and women's centers.

Many colleges and universities have credit courses in career planning that follow the outline given above but include contextual information about work and society, specific assignments for self-exploration and occupational information-gathering, and the requirement to delineate logical next steps in students' career planning. Special issues of women and work, dual-career couples, and changing work and family roles of men and women can be included in such courses easily and appropriately. Catalyst, a nonprofit corporation dealing with the career issues of college-educated women, has developed a series of materials and activities which can be used in such courses or in the career planning groups previously mentioned to stimulate individual thinking about these issues.

Providing Role Models, Occupational Information, and Exploratory Experiences

Other ways academic departments can assist their women students are by providing female faculty members as role models for women and providing opportunities for successful women graduates, or others in related fields, to interact with women students.

Interacting with female faculty makes women students feel more accepted on campus—they have academic models with whom they can identify. They are also more likely to find a mentor, someone who takes a special interest in helping them prepare for careers, among the female faculty. Students need to see women faculty who are being successful in higher education. This means women who are advancing in the academic ranks and/or holding positions as administrators. Currently, more women are being hired as instructors and assistant professors, and for temporary positions. They are not moving up the ladder in as large percentages as men, however. In order to provide a more positive, encouraging climate for women students, institutions must provide a more positive, encouraging climate for women faculty.

It is also important that academic divisions provide opportunity for women students to interact with successful professional women. This can be done in a number of ways. The Louisiana State University Women's Studies Council has instituted an annual event that brings successful women in the community on campus to interact with faculty and students. These programs include panel discussions of issues facing women in that particular profession, an open discussion with students and faculty about issues identified, and a reception to allow for individual interactions. Other ways include (a) a series of brown-bag luncheon (or dinner) speakers who address opportunities and difficulties of women in specific occupations and

(b) class presentations by individuals working in a particular occupational field describing what that is like. In both cases at least half the speakers should be women. Organizations of students in specific majors, sororities, and other social or special interest organizations could have periodic lectures on issues of women in related occupations. Networks of successful women in the community or alumni could be created so that women students interested in related majors could contact them for interviews, shadowing experiences, or presentations to student groups.

In the Extern Program at Swarthmore College (Katz, 1972), alumni were recruited to volunteer to allow a student to spend a week "shadowing" them. Careful individual placements were made to ensure compatibility of students and alumnae. Students were able to get to know about the successful woman's job, her life-style, and the realities of her daily life. A program such as this would be invaluable to a student, not only for the information about the occupation but also for the intimate knowledge of the life and work issues faced by the professional woman. All of these activities, opportunities, and events should be well publicized to students and could be videotaped and placed in the Career Resource Center for later individual use.

A comprehensive and visible Career Resource Center (Minor, 1984) is essential for assisting both women and men students in considering the multiplicity of options available to them. This center would contain occupational information from the simplest occupational briefs and books to audio and video presentation, community referrals, and shadowing opportunities. It would be organized to facilitate the exploration of many occupations or fields and would be the site of some of the special events, lectures, and support groups previously described. Needs for information about opportunities for women and minority groups could be addressed through special collections, displays, and events. A videotaped collection of these events could be an invaluable resource to students who were unable to attend them but who might have an interest in the particular fields or topics discussed.

The logical culmination of these academic stimulations and self-exploration activities is the availability of opportunities for female (and male) students to work for a while in a job related to their academic majors. Many institutions have cooperative education or internship programs that provide the highest level of exploration and information: that of the individual actually working in an occupation. These experiences are designed, for the most part, so that the student spends one term or semester working (for credit as well as money) and the next on campus taking courses. This process may lengthen the individual's time before graduation, but it offers the twin advantages of earning money while in school and providing work experiences before graduation. Such experience is extremely attractive to many employers. It also gives the student the opportunity to try a job for a semester and, if it is not suitable, to try another one in the next cycle, without making a heavy commitment to a single occupation. It is particularly important for women students that their internship advisors or seminar instructors are educated about the issues women face in the workplace—from direct discrimination to more subtle issues of conflict between the traditionally male culture of the work world and women's values and expectations. In an atmosphere of intellectual and personal support, a student can practice grappling with such issues, trying out new behaviors, and altering her opinions and behaviors in the light of events, analysis, and personal convictions.

Enabling Opportunities for Women

Women students need assistance with gender-related academic, financial, and personal barriers that hamper their career development. Many women students, because of lack of interest or math anxiety, take the minimum requirements in mathematics, or none at all. In doing so they close themselves out of a great percentage of occupations. They need to be encouraged to continue their education in mathematics and encouraged and supported in the classroom also. Many universities now teach sections that are designated as "Mathematics for the Anxious."

A great number of women students are returning students, those who have "lived as adults" and have family, financial, and/or relationship responsibilities. Many of these students need special help, such as financial aid for part-time students or financial aid for the suddenly poor (divorced or unemployed). Financial aid eligibility is determined by the previous year's family income. For many women there may be no family and/or no income one year after having had one the previous year—and no help from the university. These women may also need on-campus child care, time management assistance, study skills help, and support from others who have been, or are, going through the same difficulties. Some of these women are almost immobilized with fear: fear of failure, fear of being noticed as out of the ordinary, fear of not being able to keep up academically, and fear of being alone through it all. These women need help through individual or group counseling. Others may be from ethnic backgrounds that do not support women being educated or independent. They too need counseling and/or support.

BEHAVIORAL AND ATTITUDINAL CHANGES NECESSARY

The academic changes and programmatic additions discussed above will require significant attitudinal and systemic changes in many higher educational institutions—beginning with presidents, provosts, student affairs vice-presidents, and deans. The first of those changes is *recognition of women's legitimacy in higher education and in the professional world* by male faculty. Many male faculty in senior positions came of age in the 1950s and took their faculty positions in the explosive expansion of higher education of the 1960s. They are supported at home by full-time homemakers, or at least women who, while working outside the home, make supporting their husbands' positions their highest priority. Many of these male faculty, and others, silently or perhaps vocally, feel that this supportive role is the only one appropriate for a woman. The policy decisions of these faculty in leadership positions and their day-to-day interactions with students do little to support and encourage women to excel and advance.

Increased knowledge by male and female faculty of the contributions of women to various disciplines and to scholarship is necessary in order for these contributions to be presented to students. His-story has indeed been recorded in many disciplines. Areas of scholarship and the arts contributed to primarily by women have often been taken as tangential or of less relevance because they were of primary interest to women. In addition, innumerable cases of a wife or junior colleague making a major or majority contribution to a work credited only to a male author make it difficult to know of many of their contributions.

Encouragement of women students by both male and female faculty is a must. Studies show a predominance of classroom interaction between teachers and male students begins in the elementary grades and continues through graduate school. Women students need to be attended to, at minimum, by equivalent classroom interaction.

Hiring and retention of female faculty to provide role models, support, and encouragement for women is necessary. While more women are being hired as instructors, lecturers and assistant professors, a smaller percentage are in the full-professor ranks than in the 1930s. Issues of why women leave higher education need to be explored. The short timeline of the "up-or-out" tenure process needs to be examined for potential flexibility for those women faculty who currently feel they must choose between having children and getting tenure.

Recognition by both academic and student affairs administrators of the need to provide appropriate stimulation, support, and role models for women students is needed. The programs described above will not have a significant effect on the career development of women in higher education if an isolated program or two is conducted in a few institutions. What is needed is comprehensive career development programming and curriculum infusion. *Faculty members need to be made aware of their importance in the career development of all their students and of the special needs of women students* for an environment that is encouraging, rather than discouraging, to achievement in their own style.

SUMMARY

Facilitating the career development of women students, traditional-aged, returning, of differing ethnic backgrounds or life-style preferences, should be a part of every institution of higher education. Women need to be engaged and encouraged in the classroom. They need interaction with successful role models in traditionally male as well as traditionally female occupations. They need opportunities and encouragement for nontraditional extracurricular activities, opportunities for self-exploration, and examination of issues of access and advancement in work and balance in work on other life roles. They need assistance with the internal and external barriers that threaten the development of their careers to their fullest potential.

A number of institutions provide components needed, but probably none is facilitating the career development of women students to the extent it could. In the past decade women's centers and women's studies programs have attempted to increase the visibility of and support to women on campus. Many institutions have developed special activities or programs such as those described above. It is important to remember, however, that a comprehensive program is necessary to:

1. provide reinforcement to women for being in higher education;
2. present female role models both as contributors to the disciplines and as successful in occupations;

3. present issues women face in the workplace;
4. provide the stimulus and support to examine personal values, needs, goals, and interests and relate those to occupations;
5. help students understand options open to them and to try out some of those; and
6. use all this information both to make career decisions and to continue to develop in their careers.

Of course, it is not possible to infuse such awareness into higher education in order to meet the needs of women students without affecting, and indeed improving, career development for men as well. Career development programs should facilitate the consideration of questions such as the following for both men and women: What is the relationship of work to paid employment? How are we to reconcile commitments to careers and career advancement with demands of intimacy, care, and responsibility in personal/family life? How can both men and women be responsible as professionals and as parents? How can the workplace be enriched by facilitating the diverse contributions of individual men and women from different backgrounds, ethnic groups and races? How can such diverse voices "hear" and learn from one another? How can the needs and priorities of the collective and the needs and values of the individual be reconciled?

To do so, higher education institutions must define it as their responsibility to equip students to make wise choices about work and about the complex interrelationships between their careers and other important areas of their lives. This means that such institutions cannot conceive of themselves as meeting their responsibility by simply facilitating, or matchmaking, the meeting of employer and prospective employee, as important as this traditional function is.

Rather, institutions of higher education must take responsibility not only for playing an important role in the education of students, but also for affecting the world of work. In training people for future employment, we are, in fact, affecting the shape of that world. Not to explicitly acknowledge and discuss the individual student's potential role in perpetuating or challenging, for example, inequality in the workplace is to reinforce the status quo and to discourage individuals from seeking answers to fundamental questions which will profoundly affect their daily lives.

For colleges and universities to accept this responsibility is in keeping with the finest ideals of academe—to question and to empower. It could also help remedy the problems experienced by women in the world of work and foster healthier communication and cooperation between men and women.

REFERENCES

Astin, H. S. "The Meaning of Work in Women's Lives: A Sociopsychological Model of Career Choice and Work Behavior." *The Counseling Psychologist* 12(1984), 117–126.

Chickering, A. *Education and Identity.* San Francisco: Jossey-Bass, 1979.

Cosell, H. *Woman on a Seesaw.* New York: Putnam, 1985.

Erikson, E. *Childhood and Society.* 2nd ed. New York: W. W. Norton, 1963.

Gilligan, C. *In a Different Voice: Psychological Theory and Women's Development.* Cambridge, Mass.: Harvard University Press, 1982.

Gottfredson, L. "Circumscription and Compromise: A Developmental Theory of Occupational Aspirations." *Journal of Counseling Psychology* 28(1981), 545–579.

Gould, R. *Transformations.* New York: Simon and Schuster, 1978.

Hackett, G., and Betz, N. E. "A Self-efficacy Approach to the Career Development of Women." *Journal of Vocational Behavior* 18(1981), 326–339.

Hymowitz, C. "Women on Fast Track Try to Keep Their Careers and Children Separate." *The Wall Street Journal,* September 19, 1984, pp. 1, 38.

Katz, J. K. "Swarthmore's Extern Program." *Journal of College Placement* 33(1972), 54–62.

Levinson, D., with Darrow, C. N., Klein, E. B., Levinson, M. H., and McKee, B. *The Season's of a Man's Life.* New York: Knopf, 1978.

Lipman-Blumen, J., Handley-Isaksen, A., and Leavitt, H. "Psychological and Sociological Approaches." In Spence, J. T., *Achievement and Achievement Motives.* San Francisco: W. H. Freeman, 1983.

Marcia, J. "Development and Validation of Ego-identity Status." *Journal of Personality and Social Psychology* 3(1966), 551–559.

Minor, C. "The Career Resource Center." In H. Burck and R. Reardon (eds.), *Career Development Intervention.* Springfield, Ill.: Charles C. Thomas, 1984, pp. 169–190.

Orsborn, C. *Enough Is Enough: Exploding the Myth of Having It All.* New York: Putnam, 1986.

Perry, W. *Forms of Intellectual and Ethical Development in the College Years: A Scheme.* New York: Holt, Rinehart, and Winston, 1970.

Super, D. *The Psychology of Careers.* New York: Harper and Row, 1957.

Tiedeman, D., and Miller-Tiedeman, A. "Career Decision-making: An Individualistic Perspective." In D. Brown and L. Brooks (eds.), *Career Choice and Development.* San Francisco: Jossey-Bass, 1984, pp. 281–310.

Tiedeman, D., and O'Hara, R. P. *Career Development: Choice and Adjustment.* New York: College Entrance Examination Board, Wall Street Journal, 1963.

PART FOUR

Transforming the Institution

Our society cannot afford to discriminate intellectually and emotionally between men and women. Nor can any society, from the most simple to the most complex. The demands of the time in which we live dictate that every person be given the opportunity to contribute to the full development of the human race. The world is too small, the problems are too complicated, the issues are too multifaceted, diverse, and overwhelming for men to solve or respond alone. Encouraging the full contribution of both sexes and all ethnic groups must be a major priority for today's colleges and universities for the major problems of our time to be solved.

Faced with the challenge of raising the far-reaching questions explored in Part III—about curriculum, pedagogy, academic services, and structures—even the most courageous and risk-taking educator is likely to feel somewhat daunted. And even though administrators may find these ideas stimulating and intellectually exciting, many of them may feel too pressed by more immediate issues such as enrollment, funding, or declining physical facilities. They may also believe that conservative faculties would never be willing to consider rethinking what they are currently doing.

Faculty members who wish to make major changes in what they do may fear or be reluctant to do so because they believe that administrators and other more powerful faculty will punish them for challenging the status quo when it is time for merit raises, promotion, tenure considerations, or even ongoing peer evaluation. Success, faculty tend to believe and their experience dictates, comes from making a recognized contribution to the dialogue current in their discipline; rarely does it come through fundamentally rethinking such questions as we have posed, and more rarely does it come from a serious reconsideration of what students need. Those faculty members who have begun to reconceptualize their disciplines to take account of the new scholarship are rewarded but in far different ways than their more mainstream peers.

Our students, too, may feel powerless to promote change, and also may believe that the way to succeed in the academic world of today is not to rock the boat. They may fear to move their emphasis away from good grades and positive letters of recommendation, lest they lose their competitive edge in admission to graduate and professional school and/or consideration for well-paying positions in their fields. Trustees, parents, and alumni may be disinclined to meddle in the academic affairs of an institution of higher learning because they do not feel qualified to do so, forgetting their own commitment to the power of inquiry.

In short, current academic culture and policies are not particularly hospitable to the consideration of any serious, major rethinking or reconceptualizing that would challenge current practice. Furthermore, since sexism and racism, for the most part, have become more subtle, much more serious rethinking is necessary to eradicate them. Therefore, only the most innovative and thoughtful universities and colleges will seem initially to be ready for the kind of serious reconceptualization advocated in this book. Yet, thoughtful people—be they faculty, administrators, students, parents, or trustees—who are aware of the profound changes going on in every area of our national life, know that we must ready our institutions for change.

We recognize that getting an institution, system, or organization to envision itself free from the confines of sex/gender bias is not an easy task, and it will not be accomplished overnight. The first step is to stop being satisfied with a slow, incremental process that reduces inequality somewhat and become committed to creating nondiscriminatory institutions that can genuinely learn from and facilitate difference as well as sameness. Accomplishing this end requires many different strategies and approaches. It combines practical, workable suggestions with historical, future-oriented explanations of the importance of addressing the role of women in the academy. This section is designed to put in motion a process that will sustain the necessary momentum for the changes we now perceive as well as those yet to be conceived.

Our suggestions for implementation are built on several basic principles which we think are essential to the change process:

1. *Every institution is a complex system.* Change can begin anywhere. For example, people often argue about whether change results from attitude or behavioral shifts. Actually, it can occur either way. Changing people's behavior—for example, requiring a department to hire and promote women—generally has the impact of changing attitudes as recalcitrant faculty are exposed to extremely competent and professional women peers and become accustomed to the idea through habituation. Education that seeks to change attitudes, such as workshops sensitizing faculty or others to particular behaviors that are generally seen as racist or sexist, often result in actual changes in those behaviors. Start wherever you can.

2. *It is easier to promote change when you are in a position of authority, but you can also initiate change without a recognized position.* If you have the skills of persuasion, the commitment to change, and the ability to build and use networks, you can initiate change. Change can begin anywhere, and virtually anyone can start the process. Indeed, even if you do not apparently already possess excellent communication and organizing skills, a commitment to making change, and acting on that commitment, will encourage you to develop the needed skills.

3. *No one has to lose.* Often men fear that the changes women want would result in women imposing their truths and models on men, analogous to the ways that male perspectives and standards have been inappropriately foisted on women. The paradigm shift described in this book, however, substitutes a world view of genuine pluralism—in which the needs of majority males would be as important as, but not more important than, those of majority females and minority females and males—for the current world view that allows one group to set the standards for all others. The goal, furthermore, is not a compromise which limits everyone a little, but a genuine pluralism, where it is possible for people to be fully themselves and still to be fully part of the system.

4. *Everyone has something to contribute.* The implication of this pluralistic approach is that no one can know the complete answer, but that everyone has part of the answer. This means that even serious and informed detractors contribute by raising hard questions that could be overlooked by more convinced advocates. No one can dictate what a genuinely pluralistic institution would look like. Everyone's views must be considered. The only enemies here are ignorance, denial, and inertia—the failure to see new truths, grapple with hard questions, and develop new and more adequate answers.

5. *Everyone does not have to believe the same thing in order to move ahead.* Because of our varied and pluralist backgrounds both culturally and socially, we have different views of the ways things should be and how our organizations should work. Just because common ground is difficult does not mean we should give up or be discouraged, but it does mean that we have to accept where people are and work with them. Part of designing systems that foster plurality must be recognizing our differences and providing for them while at the same time raising questions and being questioned. The end result could be an interactive dynamic system that provides for different beliefs, as long as those beliefs do not diminish others, and allows for people to participate as they feel comfortable to do so.

6. *Consensual, pluralistic change depends upon people's willingness, to use Socrates's words, to "know thyself."* This means that people must be willing to share what they know about their own aspirations, values, and commitments with other people. This atmosphere of candor and openness is diametrically opposed to ordinary "campus politics," in which some degree of duplicity and manipulation are normative. Such a change requires the creation of environments where people feel more safe to be honest and less reinforced in inauthenticity and shallow thinking. It can begin with a person or group of people who are willing to model this new behavior.

7. *Feelings as well as thoughts need to be respected in the process of change.* Since change is both exciting and unsettling for people, and since the degree to which people feel threatened and disoriented by change results from how much agency they feel or don't feel in its direction, the impact of changes needs to be considered and discussed publicly and explicitly. People's feelings as well as their thoughts need to be aired, and support systems should be developed to allow individuals to process the changes taking place and to feel supported in the process of personal growth and change.

8. *Change should begin where people are and proceed in as characteristic a way as possible for that institution.* Institutions are highly

individualized and have their own cultures. These cultures, procedures, and structures should be respected whenever it is possible to
do so. Although it is often necessary to create new structures, procedures, and to promote new attitudes and cultural values, as soon
as possible, new changes having to do with equity should be adopted
and become a normal part of the institution's ongoing processes.

9. *Confrontation is required to keep people thinking.* The "ostrich
syndrome" of putting one's head in the sand is a natural response
to change. People are even more likely to ignore data that suggest
the need for change when issues of gender and racial equity are
concerned. Usual responses include ignoring the data or segmenting
it off into special reports, policies, or programs, while "business as
usual" is the rule for the rest of the institution. Such habituated
responses will limit the change process severely unless a commitment
is made and ways found to continue to bring people back to serious
and informed thinking. Confrontation and persistence are important
tools for any change agent.

10. *A strategy, idea, or program does not have to be perfected
before the change process begins.* Often we believe that when making
change that our ideas must be thoroughly and perfectly developed in
order for them to be accepted. Sometimes it is important to get the
ideas out, take the criticisms, and make necessary alterations. This
process can help others to feel part of the change and improve the
product or outcome. It should be noted, however, that "doing one's
homework" on a change strategy is a crucial step not to be avoided.
Yet, not every "i" needs to be dotted, nor every "t" crossed, before we
start to work.

11. *It is important to start where you believe you can have an immediate and visible success.* Incremental change can be extremely
effective if it becomes cumulative. For example, if the faculty is not
prepared to undertake a full curriculum review, begin with something more modest that will enable learning through experience. You
might begin by hiring scholars who have focused on women and
women's issues, or negotiate for wherever you can start—even if it is
with one scholar for the current year. Another tactic is to take advantage of the most current campus issue. An example of a current issue
is sexual harassment. This is an excellent time to build campus-wide
educational programs in this area.

12. *A good track record for change can be built by starting in the
areas where people are most cooperative.* This may sound simplistic,
but it is actually a very important point that we sometimes overlook
in our zeal to be comprehensive or orderly. Making a careful assess-

ment of how people think and feel about initiating change may help to identify those people who are the most willing to assist in bringing about change.

13. *Believing that change is possible and that an individual can be a catalyst are essential ingredients for successful change.* The best strategies, the clearest guidelines, the most effective methods have in common believing that a revolution has been taking place in women's lives. The leadership of our institutions can no longer afford to argue with the changes that have happened in women's lives, nor can they any longer ignore the growing body of knowledge about women which must become known by an educated population. The best single factor in change is believing in and trying to understand how to address these issues. Admittedly, this is asking a great deal in this time of challenge to higher education on many fronts. The payoff, however, can be a new understanding of the possible solutions to the problems at hand and new resources to meet these new demands.

14. *Look for different kinds and levels of help from different people.* People vary in their receptivity to change, to particular types of change, in their perception of their own roles, and in the real and perceived power they hold. Some are comfortable with highly visible change strategies, others prefer to work behind the scenes. They also vary in terms of their awareness of women's concerns, in their degree of feminist consciousness, in their willingness to address equity issues individually or collectively. In planning the part of your change strategy which seeks help from others, try to use vocabulary and concepts which fit others' perceptions of their own roles. Not everyone can, or will want to, provide assistance of the same kind and degree. From some, you can't ask too much. From others, it would be shortsighted to ask for too little. Do not overassume or underassume. Start with where they are.

15. *Creating the atmosphere for and making profound change demands long-term commitment.* Many commissions on the status of women or similar task forces have been appointed on campuses throughout the country. Very often, their charge was to study the issues pertaining to women, make a report, and self-destruct. Experience to date tells us that colleges and universities need to make a much longer-term commitment to women and change institutions to meet their needs. Studies and reports are necessary parts of the process of change, but they are not sufficient. The last chapter of this book outlines some of the steps institutions need to take in order to initiate and sustain efforts to improve institutions for women.

In addition to the principles just discussed, we thought it would be useful to offer several models for social change in order to give readers ideas about ways to initiate change on their own campuses. These are not formal models of change, but are labels which we as practitioners in the field have given to various processes of change which we have observed over the years. Naturally, some are more effective than others. Some campuses exhibit a prevailing model which must be confronted or worked with in order to effect change; on other campuses, several models may be operating simultaneously in different parts of the institution. Here are our thoughts on models we have identified.

1. In the *Declaration Model*, the person in charge articulates the direction of desired change and proclaims that change will, in fact, occur. This leader also makes clear the anticipated results of resistance to such change. This model works well if the leader is respected and has a history of backing up words with action. However, no leader, no matter how admired by his or her constituency, can actually make people change except by firing them or driving them away. No one can actually *make* people change behavior. The leader can, however, lend the force of the institution's stature, resources, and culture to the change process and implement strategies that encourage people to change.

2. In the *Education Model*, either the designated leader or some other person or group selected, hired, or self-selected for the task inaugurates an educational initiative that gives involved constituencies and individuals information they need to form their own opinion about what actions should best be taken. Ideally, it will also include opportunities for individuals and groups to discuss their opinions and feelings and to move toward consensus. Any effective change process must include some educational elements.

3. In the *Crusade Model*, a person or group that is strongly committed to an idea identifies a goal, defines the opposition, and seeks to convert, silence, or defeat that opposition. While this approach—in its focus on overcoming the opposition—is in conflict with the principle of "no enemies," the energy of having a person or group absolutely committed to making change occur is critical to the success of the change process.

4. In the *Swiss-cheese Model*, the individual "finds a hole and keeps nibbling." Its essence is to find a place where it is possible to act out of one's new values and understanding immediately, with-

out requiring the rest of the institution to change. This is the social change model that has been most available to women and has been most evidenced in the past decade. While institutions as a whole have seemed conservative, individuals and individual programs have operated on very different principles. If enough people in an institution over a period of time adopt this approach, the configuration of the whole changes. Furthermore, the hold of the old paradigm on an institution is loosened as more and more people experiment with alternative ways of thinking and behaving. The holes created in the whole allow, literally, for more openness. Places where major institutional change happens rapidly have usually been prepared for such change by effective nibblers. (Note: The term "Swiss-cheese Model" of social change is attributed to Cynthia Secor.)

5. In the *Reflective Model,* a group or individual contemplates the change process through study and the process of reflection. It is like trying on costumes to see how you might act if under a different disguise. The validity of the reflective model seems to be in providing people with an almost totally painless way of imagining change. It requires a major commitment of time and creativity to keep the effort sustained long enough to convince people that what is contemplated might actually be tried.

6. In the *Democratic Model,* advocates are required to understand and use the political process to convince enough decision-makers so that when the vote is taken it will be in their favor. This, of course, can be a very useful change strategy. It can also be quite costly and offer setbacks that are difficult to overcome if, after great effort, the vote is lost. In the case of a narrow win, care must be taken to ensure the cooperation of the defeated minority or they may sabotage implementation of the new plan.

7. In the *Consensus Model,* elements of the other models just described play at least a small function. Education, dedication, reflection, working around the edges, taking straw votes—all these processes are necessary to the building of a consensus for change. Although it is probably the most thoroughly involving and initially the most time-consuming for the individuals involved, it no doubt brings about the most satisfactory change in the long run. It is the kind of change that has the most involvement, support, and commitment. Its drawbacks are time and, all too often, less change than the change-makers had envisioned. It also has little or no possibility of success unless some successes have occurred.

Finally, beyond the principles and models of change are processes of change. All the usual processes of the institutions can be utilized to promote equity: from faculty senate meetings, to curriculum committee meetings, to salary or tenure review. More fundamental, however, is the process of individuals talking to one another, in twos, threes, in small groups, and eventually in larger groups. Perhaps the single most effective process of the women' movement has been the phenomenon of consciousness-raising groups. Consciousness-raising is a process through which women learn to listen to themselves and others in new ways—by telling what they think and feel, sharing with each other how they see the world. Through this process, women begin freeing themselves from the confines of current, prevailing or dominant values which often did not speak to their individual needs.

In the late 1960s and the early 1970s women from all walks of life and in virtually every geographic area began to meet in small groups to talk about being women. What emerged was a shared perspective, a sense of commonality, which evidenced itself as a new and collective awareness of the discrepancy of individual women. The result was massive change, a change which is part of the "Feminist Enlightenment," named by sociologist Jessie Bernard, which has precipitated major changes in our culture, values, attitudes, roles, and institutions.

We believe that it is time for higher education not only to look at the implications of resulting changes in gender roles but also to undergo a second stage of consciousness-raising—this time involving both women and men. In the 1980s, individual change has surpassed changes in institutional structures, policies, and values not just for minority and majority women but also for minority and majority men. As in other times of major social change it is important to remember that our social institutions are built according to the assumptions and values of the old paradigm, and the rules of that old paradigm govern common discourse long after they have become anachronistic to many of the individuals involved. Conversely, many individuals may lag behind institutional change and continue to be resistant to relatively new ideas like affirmative action and women's studies. Part of the new pluralism we are discussing in this book, then, is the coexistence of people more happy with the old ways than the new together with people who have allowed themselves to be profoundly changed and influenced by the 1960s, 1970s, and 1980s. The result of any real, honest sharing—analogous to the women's consciousness raising discussed above—will likely be a dialectic process, the outcome of which reflects the best of old and new paradigm thinking. This synthesis, of course, provides the new foundation for further growth and change in our understanding of human liberation.

Changes are most effective when the processes used to promote it are consistent with desired goals. In this case, a pluralistic culture can be created by the very process used to promote it. The essays that follow explore the process of institutional change designed first to meet the needs of women, but in a way that also makes it possible to meet the needs of all the constituencies of the institution. Essays begin with a clear awareness of the current state of higher education to explore the structural, emotional, and intellectual changes that are necessary if both women and men are to be taken seriously by today's colleges and universities.

Mary P. Rowe, in "What Actually Works? The One-to-One Approach," issues a compelling invitation for each person to become involved in the recruitment, support, and promotion of women and minority men. She says, "Genuine *progress* is most likely to occur when Anglo males and others decide that they personally will make a difference. What is required, in fact, is that people decide they personally will do at least one thing each year to make a difference." Rowe provides us with very practical ideas about effective recruitment and retention programs built on a program of individual responsibility for an institution-wide goal to diversify the faculty, staff, and student population.

Karen Bogart, in "Toward Equity in Academe: An Overview of Strategies for Action," examines the conditions for change as well as a series of programs that have worked. They have worked because women, and some men, have listened well to what some women think and believe about the operation of the institution. These people have then gone on to design programs that enhance the roles of women students, faculty, and administrators. In this essay Bogart seeks to "assist administrators, faculty, and staff to accelerate the process of change toward equity in their own institutions by adapting the successful approaches of other institutions and by identifying and creating the critical conditions needed to make change efforts work."

Peggy Means McIntosh, in "Curricular Re-Vision: The New Knowledge for a New Age," paints a clear picture of the intellectually challenging task of thinking about, understanding, discovering, and fully incorporating into our knowledge base the new knowledge about women and women's lives. "Many faculty," says McIntosh, "seem, in fact, to go through a series of phases as they become involved in the study of women, first seeing women in terms of white Western men, then trying to see women diversely and on their own terms, and as a result reseeing women, men, and society. The work turns out to be conceptually far more difficult than originally anticipated."

Jessie Bernard, in "Educating the Majority: The Feminist Enlightenment," gives us the enormous benefit of her years of study and wisdom in describing and analyzing changes in attitude and roles for women since midcentury. The profound changes in the way women view themselves are leading to a different society and social order—not an age that discounts men, but rather an age that celebrates both men and women, minority and majority. According to Bernard, "when the story of this Feminist Enlightenment—including its raised consciousness, its defenses against societal attribution of inferiority, its activism—is fully told, it will surely demonstrate its significance as one of the great social movements of its time."

Our last chapter, "The New Agenda of Women for Higher Education," sets forth the next steps required to get closer to institutions that truly serve both men and women. This chapter forms the basis of the agenda that the Office of Women in Higher Education of the American Council on Education will encourage institutions to consider in order to bring about the kinds of transformations called for in this book. Your involvement in this process, whatever your status in relation to higher education, is important for its success now and in the future.

25

What Actually Works?
The One-to-One Approach

MARY P. ROWE

In the 1970s we tried hundreds of wonderful ideas to integrate academe. We tried to bring in minorities and women and permit them to thrive as well as do Anglo men (or, if possible, to permit them to do better, since many Anglo men do not thrive in academe either). All these ideas will not be discussed, though we tried hard with them.

This chapter is about five ideas that actually seem to work, especially when undertaken together. Each is necessary, but not sufficient, for women and minorities to thrive. Each depends on people and dealing with people, so the method is called the "one-to-one" method of progress. These five ideas are:

- commitment and action by the top administration;
- one-to-one recruitment of minorities and women;
- one-to-one mentoring;
- individual responsibility for networks; and
- a complaint system that works for individuals.

An extraordinary aspect of this set of ideas is that implementation requires no net financial cost to the institution.

COMMITMENT AND ACTION

If an institution is going to change, with respect to minorities and women, it will first be because of direct involvement in leadership on this issue by top administration. Of course, this *alone* is not enough. Even if the leadership truly wants involvement of women and minorities throughout the system, but nothing else is done, there will be only tokenism. A few women and minorities will appear, but basically the institution will not become fully hospitable to women and minorities. If, however, leadership is exerted, *and* the other four elements described here are in place, real change will take place. If the top administration does not lead, the other four elements will not succeed on their own in changing the institution. The other four elements may, over time, succeed in changing the top administration, either in the sense of changing minds or in the sense of a changeover in people. But committed top leadership is *essential*—necessary, although not sufficient—to the full and equitable participation of women and minorities in the life of a college or university.

What does a committed administration do? They talk and write about minorities and women, about diversity, about the excellent work of individual women and the honoring of an individual Black. They get to know professional women personally, at dinner, on planes, at squash, asking the questions that men have always wondered about: "Can women really be as good at math? Can men really care as well for babies?" They discuss with minority men and women the real and symbolic issues of importance to minorities and get to know these colleagues on a personal basis. Effective top administrators will listen and talk about issues of equal opportunity, in public, with ease, grace, and commitment. These activities and attitudes contribute to a public understanding that the senior administration is at ease with women and minorities, that they place the special issues of the participation of women and minorities high among issues of critical importance to the institution, and that they will hold all those who report to them accountable for affirmative action and equal opportunity.

Commitment from the leadership means that they will personally recruit and bring in an Hispanic male physician, a black female scientist, a top white female colleague in administration. They will personally serve as mentors, and will insist on mentoring and serious performance evaluation by their staffs. These senior administrators will support and encourage internal networks of women and minorities and will stay in touch with those networks. And they will establish and stand behind safe, fair, and accessible complaint systems.

The hallmark of the successful top administrator is joint "problem-solving" *with* minority women and men and majority women. The hallmark of the successful affirmative action activist is the same: joint problem-solving with the senior administration. "Us Against Them" is a terrible model, if progress is to occur and endure.

ONE-TO-ONE RECRUITMENT

All of the ordinary paraphernalia of affirmative action can only set a floor beneath abuse (below which the institution cannot sink). Genuine *progress* is most likely to occur when Anglo males and others decide that they personally will make a difference. What is required, in fact, is that people decide they personally will do at least one thing each year to make a difference. My ordinary request of anyone who "offers to help" is this: make sure that at least once a year you personally recruit one minority student, or one woman post-doctoral student, invite one Hispanic person to give a speech, or add one Asian woman to a committee, or recruit one Black and/or White woman faculty member. . . .

Almost everyone can "make a difference" each year. Administrators and faculty have the potential to make a difference within their own areas. Support staff can also be very effective recruiters of minority and female staff and students. Every academic institution can apply this recruitment plan: develop a plan to convince a set of people *personally* to recruit one woman, one minority man, in some way, every year. It is the sum of these "small" acts (one more White woman recruited to an athletic team, one minority male support person promoted, one Black woman guest lecturer brought to campus) that ultimately will change an institution.

Whether or not the institution is a top-ranked, elitist one or a lesser-known, the same process will work. The key is the building of a recruiting network and an ongoing search process. For example, each recruiter (faculty, staff, or administrator) should get to know *every* minority and female professional, of the appropriate type, that he or she meets while traveling and/or attending professional meetings. Each scientist should introduce herself/himself to women and minority men at professional conferences, on campus or industry visits, and in other similar situations. On visits away from home, each historian or English professor should make it a point to meet minority and women colleagues in the same field. These colleagues then become part of a personal recruiting network when a job opens up. These are the people one calls, one-to-one, when looking for candidates . . . and now this group includes women and minority men. . . .

One-to-one, steady-state recruitment has always been the mode for recruiting superstars. A department may "court" a top-ranked professional for several years. Exactly the same method works for minorities and women: "visiting" and guest invitations back and forth, meetings at conferences, discussions while serving together on national committees. It is this kind of contact that builds trust and convinces the desirable Hispanic or Asian or Black and/or woman to consider moving—even to an isolated college—or to consider recommending some other appropriate person. And it is this kind of continuous contact that persuades the host institutions (at low risk) that Ms. X or Mr. Y is the right person.

MENTORING

Good recruiters make good mentors. This is especially true when top administrators reward and compliment successful recruiting and mentoring, and especially true when the recruiters' pride is engaged in the success of their recruits.

For a mentoring system to succeed, it must apply to everyone in the institution, minority and nonminority, men and women, at every level. It should be integrated, if possible, with performance evaluation. It must be legitimated by top administrators or there will be tension about senior men mentoring junior women. There should, if possible, be choices for both mentors and mentees, in case individuals do not like each other or appreciate one another's work.

Many minorities and women prefer and need same-sex, same-race or ethnic mentors. Others prefer mentors of the gender and ethnic background who run the institution—typically Anglo males. An institution can provide both a same-sex, same-race "host" when the recruit first comes, and later a person of mutual choosing, whether the "host" or other.

I believe in highly individualized mentorships, with several mentors typically better than one. Black and white female professionals appear historically to have thrived with multiple mentors. This is especially helpful if one is in an isolated college, if one dislikes senior colleagues in one's department and the feeling is mutual, or if one is in a world-class institution and depends on worldwide referees for promotion. In short, a mentorship system should encourage multiple mentors—individually chosen and individually pursued.

The successful mentorship system depends on two elements: the expectation of senior colleagues that they will guide, coach and sponsor, and the expectation of junior people that they will personally expend whatever effort is necessary to find the guidance, coaching, and sponsorship they need. This system naturally works best when appropriate senior administrators thoughtfully and individually encourage both seniors and juniors to collaborate. This system can be implemented most effectively through personal encouragement, judicious matchmaking, and, especially, *by teaching each person that the responsibility is individually hers or his to make the mentoring work.*

NETWORKS

Networks are mentoring systems writ large. Minority and women's networks *will* exist wherever nontraditional people are in an institution. The question is whether they will be effective. Some are extremely effective.

Will the internal networks be positive and useful to its members, and to the institution? The answers depend on the degree to which individual senior administrators foster and stay in touch with the networks, and the degree to which individual network members take responsibility for forming, expanding, and maintaining both intragroup and external relationships. A networking system is, in short, like a mentoring system: it will work to the extent that individuals take personal responsibility for the painstaking, sometimes tedious, one-to-one relationships that make the structures effective.

It is particularly difficult to keep minority and women's networks healthy and effective because turnover is high, and because "all Blacks" and "all women" do not necessarily share anything beyond a skin color or a second X chromosome.

One effective mode is for administrators to foster connections between small groups of minorities and/or women who happen to share a common specific interest. For example, the women (and men) interested in day care, the secretaries worried about safety in Building X, the minorities interested in curriculum change—these are groups that have a substantial interest in getting together and doing what amounts to an enormous amount of free work for themselves and their institutions.

Self-formed or institution-facilitated, responsible interest groups can be supported in two ways. Some administrator (perhaps an ombudsperson) should take responsibility for being sure each group is working in a problem-solving mode with the line administrators appropriate to their interests. Each small interest group can be asked to nominate a representative to an institution-wide Women's Advisory Board or Minority Interest Committee that meets regularly with senior administrators. In one model, each self-formed, specific interest group nominates one member who is then appointed by the President to a Presidential Advisory Committee.

This model builds on the real interests motivating women and minorities, guarantees that the networks surface genuine issues continuously, and provides upward feedback to the President, as well as collegial support among the network members. No one will be "left out" because an infinite number of responsible networks can self-form as new ethnic and other groups appear.

COMPLAINT SYSTEMS

Women and minorities (and other people) face problems within institutions: overt discrimination, subtle discrimination, red tape, plain human meanness. If nontraditional people, especially, are to survive, there *must* be individualized responses to individual needs and complaints. If institutions are to change, there must be upward feedback in addition to that which can be provided by mentoring and network systems.

A complaint system must be just that: a *system* of complaint-handling functions, both informal and formal. Most people just think of formal grievance procedures; this is not enough. However, there is a paradox here. Unless an institution has a fair, accessible, formal complaint-and-appeal structure for grievances, the rest of a complaint system (the informal part) will not work. But if the whole complaint system works well, with both informal and formal channels and functions, then the formal channel(s) will be used very rarely, and most problems will be solved in an informal mode.

The following functions must be present in a complaint system, especially if it is to work well for women and minorities:

DEALING WITH FEELINGS.   Dealing with traditional, white, male institutions brings rage, grief, and bewilderment on occasion to everyone, and especially to minorities and women. Having a problem often engenders such strong emotions that an individual cannot think through any responsible and effective response. A good complaint system must have people highly skilled at dealing with feelings.

Sometimes this is in fact all that is needed. Every experienced complaint handler has the odd experience of having someone blow up and/or weep for hours in the office, only to report back on the next day that "everything now seems much better."

At other times, it is critical to help someone with a problem express feelings (for days or weeks or months) before a proper plan of action can be undertaken. Since this appears especially to be true for sexual and racial harassment, it is vital to the progress of equal opportunity that there be complaint handlers to support peoples' feelings and understand the pressures of bringing complaints.

GIVING AND RECEIVING DATA ON A ONE-TO-ONE BASIS.   Frequently people do not even know the name of their college president, much less how the college determines salary equity, promotions, transfers, or benefits. It is therefore very important that complaint handlers give out information and make referrals on a one-to-one basis, at the time and in the fashion needed by a complainant. This may, again, be all that is needed to help someone understand that a specific troubling or puzzling event actually follows a customary rule or practice that is in fact not discriminatory. Or that the complainant can easily learn how to deal with the appropriate administrator directly.

At other times, learning how the system is supposed to work illuminates that the individual *was* improperly treated. Or the complaint handler may learn how a good rule is being wrongly applied in a way that should be changed. Or the complaint handler may discover that no relevant policy exists, though it should, as for example, was common before the days of sexual harassment policies.

COUNSELING AND PROBLEM-SOLVING, TO HELP THE COMPLAINANT HELP HERSELF OR HIMSELF.   Some complaint handlers are either too eager to take over someone else's complaint or are eager to forget or ignore it. The skilled counselor will help a visitor develop, explore, and role-play options, then support her/him in choosing an option, and then will follow up to see it worked. Most women and minorities as well as Anglo males prefer to "own" their complaints and deal on their own with their difficulties, if effective options to do so can be developed and pursued. It is essential, therefore, that a complaint system have counselors who are effective at helping people help themselves.

These first three functions must be available on a confidential basis and should be available from impartial persons. Usually this will mean the availability of a college or university ombudsperson in addition to student, employee and medical counselors. It also will help enormously if there are women and minorities available as counselors and ombudspersons, since the credibility of a complaint system is its chief asset.

SHUTTLE DIPLOMACY. Sometimes a complainant will ask for a go-between. This is especially true if one or more parties need to save face or deal with emotions before a good solution can be found.

MEDIATION. Sometimes a complainant will choose the option of meeting with the other side together with a third party complaint-handler. Like shuttle diplomacy, this usually happens on an informal basis. However, the settlements of shuttle diplomacy and mediation may be made formal.

INVESTIGATION. Investigation of a complaint can be formal or informal, with or without recommendations to an adjudicator—for example, to a disciplinary committee or line administrator. All four of these investigatory options should be available within a complaint system.

ADJUDICATION—FORMAL COMPLAINT-AND-APPEAL GRIEVANCE PROCEDURES. Sometimes a complainant will ask to bring a formal complaint for formal review and decision-making. This process must be perceived as accessible and fair, for minorities and women as well as for white men. (There are a number of useful publications available on this topic.)

UPWARD FEEDBACK. Possibly the most important function of a complaint system is that it be able to receive information that will foster timely change in the institution. Are policies unintelligible or outdated? Have new problems arisen? A healthy institution is constantly changing in response to new needs and data—and in response to new diversity in its population.

These last five functions require impartial or at least fair complaint handlers. Except for formal adjudication, which is almost never the province of an ombudsperson, it may help to provide ombudspeople or "internal mediators" in addition to other staff and line administrators. In a college that is too small for a full-time ombudsperson, impartial third parties may be provided by designating certain college personnel as available mediators. If this plan is followed, the "internal mediators" should be given a common charge and common training.

The one-to-one method of progress is built on the idea that institutional progress is the sum of the individual successes of individual people. Goals and timetables are only numbers. Women and minority are individuals. No two are alike and each must thrive in his or her own unique terms in order to thrive at all; each needs personal attention and each will have her or his own voice.

This point of view gives hope to the individual woman, minority or majority, who wishes herself to make a difference. She need not wait for others to initiate change or for the institution to change. One woman can seek to make contact with the college president. One woman can start a network. One woman can herself recruit minorities and women, and seek to encourage others to do the same. It takes just one to start talking about mentoring, to mentor, and to seek mentors. It takes only one woman to analyze her institutional complaint system and to ask for improvements if needed. One woman as an ombudsperson, operating formally or informally, can help individual people as well as the system to change. (She is moreover likely to save much more money than she costs.)

Successful diversity benefits everyone. The successful change agent will exemplify this point of view, problem-solving *with* her male and female colleagues, rather than taking issue against them. This is perhaps most easily done by an ombudsperson. But it can be done by anyone. And this particular set of ideas requires no net financial cost to the institution.

26

Toward Equity in Academe:
An Overview of Strategies for Action

KAREN BOGART

Women and men continue to have very different experiences on college and university campuses, although they study and work side by side. Women students continue to be counseled into traditional courses of study and careers associated with low status and low pay. They study a male-centered Eurocentric curriculum taught by faculty, men and women, who often unconsciously exhibit subtle forms of discrimination both in and out of the classroom. Some experience sexual harassment, ranging from the use of sexual humor and innuendoes to physical threats and sexual assault.

Women faculty continue to be few in number and concentrated in nontenurable and nontenured appointments (as instructors, lecturers, and assistant professors) while men dominate the tenure track and tenured positions. Women administrators hold, for the most part, junior and midlevel appointments. The exclusion of women from faculty and administrative posts not only means a loss of talent to academic institutions but also a denial of opportunities for students, male and female, to interact with women role models.

And yet, positive change has taken place on college and university campuses—in response to the women's movement, the passage of Title IX of the Education Amendments of 1972 plus other relevant laws, and the ensuing efforts to promote educational equity in the schools. Women today constitute the majority of undergraduate students in colleges and universities, many studying on a part-time and reentry basis. They earn half the bachelor's and master's degrees awarded each year as well as 27.5 percent of the professional degrees and 32 percent of the doctoral degrees (National Center for Education Statistics, 1986). Between 1971 and 1980, women increased by more than 25 percent in numbers earning bachelor's degrees, by more than 60 percent in numbers earning master's degrees, and by more than 100 percent in numbers earning doctoral degrees. Most impressive of all, they increased by 550 percent in numbers earning professional degrees (National Center for Education Statistics, 1980).

Additionally, more women than ever before are earning degrees in male-dominated occupational fields (defined by the National Center for Education Statistics as fields in which men earned more than 90 percent of all degrees awarded in 1971). By 1979, women accounted for more than 20 percent of all bachelor's degrees awarded in such traditionally masculine fields as business and management, computer and information sciences, and the physical sciences. They also accounted for nearly 20 percent of the master's degrees awarded in these fields and more than 10 percent of the doctoral degrees. These figures represent increases of 100 percent and more since 1971 in the number of women earning degrees in these male-dominated occupations (National Center for Education Statistics, 1980). Changes in the aspirations and achievements of women in postsecondary education cannot be disputed. At the same time, it is important to be aware that most degrees earned by women continue to be concentrated in the disciplines they have traditionally dominated.

Change has not been limited to increases in the number of women earning advanced degrees. Institutional change is also apparent. A small but increasing number of institutions are integrating scholarship on and by women into the curriculum of higher education. Overt forms of discrimination in education and employment have largely disappeared, in part thanks to the monitoring of efforts to enforce Title IX in colleges and universities by the Project on the Status and Education of Women at the Association of American Colleges and many other groups concerned with equity for women in higher education. Subtle and sometimes not so subtle forms of discrimination still remain. A number of institutions are making special efforts to hire, tenure, and promote women faculty. The number of women college presidents has increased from about 150 in the mid-1970s to more than 300 today, in part as a result of the activities of the Office of Women at the American Council of Education to promote women into positions of leadership through the ACE National Indentification Program for the Advancement of Women in Higher Education (Shavlik & Touchton, 1984). Women are also increasingly moving into administration, aided by the training programs of the Higher Education Resource Services, with branches at the University of Denver, the University of Utah, and Wellesley College, and by opportunities provided by the Bryn Mawr Summer Institute for Women in Higher Education Administration.

The lessons learned by those who have worked to promote educational equity in colleges and universities have demonstrated that change is slow, but that it can and does happen. Colleges and universities have introduced programs and policies that promote sex equity for women students, faculty, administrators, and staff. A number are exemplary in the range and variety of approaches they offer to meet the multiple needs of the women who study and work in academic institutions. Increasingly, academic institutions are integrating equity planning into their institutional mission. They are conducting institutional studies of the needs of women and minorities, strengthening existing approaches to address identified needs, and introducing new ones.

This chapter examines efforts to achieve sex equity in academe in terms of the conditions needed for change efforts to succeed, the strategies that can be used to develop these conditions, and specific examples of programs and policies that promote equity in academic institutions. Its objectives are to assist administrators, faculty, and staff to accelerate the process of change toward equity in their own institutions by adapting the successful approaches of other institutions and by identifying and creating the critical conditions needed to make change efforts work.

The primary data source for the observations that follow is an empirical study of programs and policies in progress in colleges and universities across the country that address specific needs of women in the academic community, conducted with a grant from Carnegie Corporation of New York. This study involved interviews with program directors; review of supporting materials such as reports and publications; and survey by mail of administrators, faculty, students, and others familiar with each program. The publication produced by the study, *Toward Equity: An Action Manual for Women in Academe* (Bogart, 1984), includes an examination of the ABCs or dos and don'ts of change by thirteen change agents who have succeeded in promoting change in postsecondary education; a comparative examination of seven institutions featured for the range and variety of programs they offer to address the multiple needs of women in academe; and abstracts of approximately one hundred fifty programs and policies that address specific needs of women and are adaptable by other institutions.

INDENTIFYING THE CRITICAL CONDITIONS FOR CHANGE

How does the introduction of programs and policies that promote equity for women and minorities become possible in an academic institution? Clearly, sex equity does not require particular demographic characteristics, since institutions identified as most successful in promoting change are noteworthy for their differences. A study of *Everywoman's Guide to Colleges and Universities* (Howe, Howard, and Strauss, 1982), which rated nearly six hundred academic institutions in terms of their programs and environments for women, suggests that women's colleges and coeducational institutions that were at one time normal schools providing teacher training to women students have the advantage, but other institutions were rated as highly. The institutions featured in *Toward Equity: An Action Manual for Women in Academe* (Bogart, 1984) illustrate the diversity: Hunter College of the City University of New York, Denison University, Towson State University, the University of Delaware, the Massachusetts Institute of Technology, Wellesley College, and Spelman College vary considerably in demographic attributes.

At the same time, these institutions are similar. They share the recognition that:

- programs and policies that promote equity are an investment in excellence in postsecondary education;
- multiple and mutually enhancing programs and policies are required to achieve sex equity;
- women students, faculty, administrators, professional and support staff all continue to have equity needs. Women of color, older women, and disabled women have special needs that require programs developed especially for them;
- the programs and policies that benefit women also benefit men; and
- change is a slow complex process that requires long-term planning and management.

A number of conditions present in these institutions also appear to have helped make it possible for them to respond in the ways in which they have to the needs of women and minorities. These include:

- *Strong institutional leadership.* Most importantly, the chief executive officer has exercised leadership in promoting sex equity, by initiating programs and policies and/or by responding positively to equity needs brought to his/her attention;
- *The presence on campus of one or more women who are catalysts for change.* At each institution, there has been one or a few women administrators who has served as a catalyst for change, motivating and mobilizing others, creating the critical mass of support needed throughout the institution for change efforts to succeed;
- *Networks.* Women administrators, faculty, staff and students are organized at each institution as both formal committees and informal networks that identify problems, set priorities, develop action agendas, and put new programs into place;
- *An overall plan.* Each institution appears to have developed an overall strategic plan (with specific programs and policies representing the components of this plan) for institutional change that recognizes that the investment in programs and policies that promote equity is an investment in excellence in postsecondary education.

DEVELOPING THE CRITICAL CONDITIONS

If one objective in examining exemplary institutions is to identify the conditions that help promote sex equity in academe, another is to help others develop these conditions. There are a number of possible approaches that can complement each other: learning from the experiences of others who have succeeded in promoting change in postsecondary education; conducting institutional studies to identify and prioritize needs and to establish tangible and specific objectives for achieving change; seeking assistance from national resources and programs, such as those of the Project on the Status and Education of Women at the Association of American Colleges, the Office of Women in Higher Education at the American Council on Education, and the offices of the Higher Education Resource Services, with branches at the University of Denver, Wellesley College, and the University of Utah. Each approach is discussed briefly in turn.

Benefit from the experience of others.

A number of educators who have succeeded in introducing change to improve the status of women in postsecondary institutions were asked to describe their own dos and don'ts or ABCs of change in essays contributed to *Toward Equity: An Action Manual for Women in Academe*. They call attention to specific actions that can be taken to obtain support from senior institutional leadership, to identify women and men who can serve as catalysts for mobilizing others, to develop networks and to establish an overall plan. A sample of their comments illustrates that their experiences have many common elements:

How does change begin?

> Individual trustees, students, faculty, support staff, legislators, administrators and community leaders have a responsibility for institutions of higher education. It is in the individual acceptance of responsibility that change begins. (Cynthia Secor, Director, Higher Education Resource Services/Mid America, University of Denver)

At the same time, change does not appear to be achieved by any one individual alone. Team efforts are critical.

> One woman is never a critical mass. One needs to work with other women and men. (Mary P. Rowe, Special Assistant to the President, Massachusetts Institute of Technology)

> If those working for equity for women on campus coordinate their efforts, develop an effective communication network, and learn to be politically smart, they can make significant progress. (Sara Coulter, Professor of English, Towson State University)

> Do not hesitate to build on existing attitudes, interests and points of view. Work with those who are with you, even though they may not know they are going to be your allies. (Louis Brakeman, former Provost, Denison University)

> Seek out support groups and supportive individuals on and off campus. (Anne T. Truax, Director, Minnesota Women's Center, University of Minnesota)

> New networks typically designate their purposes as support of colleagues and provision of programming to increase individual skills. As networks mature, they frequently add an advocacy component to their goals to address issues of concern for women on campus. The shift from a focus exclusively on the individual to analysis of group concerns reflects a growing sense of group trust, power and esteem. (Carolyn Taylor and

Mary Gustafson, Higher Education Resources Services/West, University of Utah)

Become knowledgeable about women's issues, about a particular need and the solution that can address it, and about the formal rules and informal procedures that should be followed to introduce a new program or policy.

Know as much as you can about the history of women's issues and progress on (and off) your campus and others; what factors in and outside that academy helped shape that history, and how have they changed? Then, describe your undertaking in a way that places it in its moment. (Elaine Reuben, Elaine Reuben Associates, Washington, D.C.)

Know the rules and the politics under which the "customer" has to work, such as university formal and informal policies and applicable laws. (Mae R. Carter, former Director, Office of Women's Affairs, University of Delaware)

We are all familiar with catalysts for change in higher education. . . . They have an understanding of relevant data and have developed a believable plan of action which can be considered for long term implementation. (Carol Stoel, former Associate Provost for Educational Services, Hood College, and Deputy Director, Fund for the Improvement of Postsecondary Education)

Be positive.

Expecting the best from everyone isn't a bad place to start. If you are disappointed, reevaluate the situation and work to change one thing, one person, one issue at a time. (Donna Shavlik, Director, Office of Women in Higher Education, American Council on Education)

Try never to speak ill of anyone. People change faster if one comments on things that go well. (Mary P. Rowe)

Maintain your sense of humor and of porportion. (Anne T. Truax)

Work hard to make others "look good." We try to make it a positive experience for people and offices who work with us. We all want to "look good." (Mae R. Carter)

Continue to try.

Unless institutions take an active role in helping achieve equity, men and women on campus, although studying or working side by side will have very different experiences on campus. (Bernice Resnick Sandler, Director, Project on the Status and Education of Women, Association of American Colleges)

If all the alternatives are bad, try to find another alternative. (Mary P. Rowe)

One thing I have learned is that change takes place slowly, but with consistent, constant and low-key pressure, change can and does happen. (Mae R. Carter)

Meritocracy and egalitarianism are not contradictory and do not require compromise. (Margaret B. Wilkerson, Professor of Afro-American History, University of California, Berkeley)

Considering the basic conservativism of institutions and those who carve their careers within them, a 50-50 chance is the best one can expect. Change is incremental; it occurs only slowly, is subject to constant setbacks, and needs infinite patience. It also needs energy and stamina. New participants must be recruited for the effort to sustain it. (Dorothy O. Helly, Associate Professor of History, Hunter College, City University of New York)

Conduct institutional studies to identify and place needs in order of priority and to develop tangible and specific objectives for addressing them.

A number of self-assessment tools and procedures can be used to help promote institutional change. The *Institutional Self-study Guide on Sex Equity for Postsecondary Educational Institutions* (Bogart et al., 1981) was developed, with grants from Carnegie Corporation of New York and the Fund for the Improvement of Postsecondary Education, to facilitate voluntary institutional change to improve the status of women students, faculty, administrators, staff, and the social-educational climate. Based on an empirical study that involved interviews with more than two hundred observers knowledgeable about the treatment of women in higher education, this self-assessment tool probes a broad range of practices, both subtle and overt, individual and institutional, with and without legal implication, that should be considered when evaluating an institutional response to questions of sex equity. The self-study guide is now in use in hundreds of institutions throughout the country. This response illustrates the receptivity of the postsecondary community to voluntary efforts to promote institutional change, the withdrawal of federal funds and efforts to enforce legislation to achieve sex equity in education notwithstanding.

Everywoman's Guide to Colleges and Universities (Howe, Howard, and Strauss, 1982), which profiles approximately six hundred institutions with emphasis on programs and facilities for women students, can also be used to promote voluntary institutional change. Three equity indicators and a ten-page questionnaire together provide the basis for each institution's profile. By assembling enrollment, faculty, and degree information needed for the indicators, and completing the questionnaire, an institution can compare its environment for women students with those of others. The self-study required by the regional accrediting associations can also be used effectively to raise questions and develop plans regarding equity for women and minorities.

Seek assistance from national resources and programs.

Administrators and faculty seeking to improve the status of women can seek assistance from a variety of national resources that disseminate information; conduct workshops, minicourses, and conferences; provide telephone information and referral; and offer on-site assistance. The Project on the Status and Education of Women of the Association of American Colleges monitors federal legislation and policies affecting women in higher education, develops materials that identify issues and provide numerous recommendation for overcoming barriers to equity for women in higher education, and publishes a quarterly newsletter, *On Campus with Women*. The Office of Women in Higher Education, American Council on Education, conducts a National Identification Program (NIP) that promotes women for positions of senior leadership in colleges and universities. ACE National Forums, conducted by the NIP, bring together established and emerging education leaders to discuss critical issues related to leadership and management in higher education. The forums are invitational and include women who are ready for college or university presidencies, in addition to men and women who already serve as chief executive officers. As a part of the NIP, the Office of Women also conducts the Focus on Minority Women's Advancement (FMWA). The primary objectives of the FMWA are more fully to involve minority women—Black, Hispanic, Asian Pacific, and American Indian—in the ongoing National Identification Program, thereby providing them with the means to be identified to one another and to powerful allies who can help them achieve equality of opportunity in administration ranks. The Higher Education Resource Services, with branches at the University of Denver, Wellesley College, and the University of Utah, also facilitate the professional development of women in higher education and their advancement into positions of authority and responsibility. Women seeking to advance in administration can also take advantage of the programs offered by these groups including the Bryn Mawr Summer Institute for Women in Higher Education Administration and the Wellesley Management Institute for Women.

As women are empowered by being promoted into positions of senior leadership, they can take an active role in integrating equity concerns into the basic mission of their institution.

PROGRAMS AND POLICIES THAT PROMOTE EQUITY FOR WOMEN IN ACADEME: SOME ILLUSTRATIVE EXAMPLES

The programs and policies described in *Toward Equity: An Action Manual for Women in Academe*, highlighted by those briefly discussed below, were identified through contacts with members of the higher education community; through reviews of projects funded by the Fund for the Improvement of Postsecondary Education, the Women's Educational Equity Act Program, the National Institute of Education and other federal and foundation sources; and through the responses of program directors to published announcements of the project inviting postsecondary institutions to submit examples of programs and policies considered exemplary.

These activities called attention to more than one thousand programs and policies introduced to promote equity for women between the mid-1970s and the present. Some no longer function. At the same time, the number and diversity of programs identified seem to justify optimism about what can be done, often with a limited budget, to address specific needs of women in academe. The development of *Toward Equity* had begun with the expectation that it would be difficult, if not impossible, to identify as many as one hundred exemplary programs and policies. Instead, it was difficult to narrow the choice of programs for the book to approximately one hundred fifty different approaches. The programs included in the handbook, and the subset illustrated in this essay, are a sample of the best activities promoting sex equity for students, faculty, administrators, professional and support staff, and improving the social-educational climate. Some excellent approaches were not identified in time to be included.

Programs for Students

Women may now constitute the majority of students in colleges and universities, but the curriculum of higher education continues to be male-centered. Courses and programs in women's studies often offer students their only opportunity to study the new scholarship on and by women in all academic areas. Change, however, is in progress. A small but increasing number of institutions, private and public, large and small, coeducational and women's colleges, are now conducting programs to encourage faculty to integrate the new scholarship on and by women into traditional academic disciplines.

The Wellesley College Center for Research on Women, a leader in curriculum integration efforts, has conducted a national program offering fellowship support to five scholars a year to work at the Wellesley Center and address questions of how the scope, content, and methodology of their disciplines would have to change to reflect the fact that women are half the population. This program provides consultants to colleges and universities that are initiating curriculum integration projects. The University of Maine at Orono has conducted a curriculum integration project that involves both UMO and seven other cooperating institutions in New England. Faculty development programs are in process at the University of Arizona, Montana State University, Towson State University, and Hunter College. Women's colleges are also actively involved, including Wheaton College, Spelman College, and Smith College.

Programs at different campuses vary, although the intended outcome is the same, offering other institutions interested in adapting their approaches to a wide variety of choices. At UMO, for example, faculty participants have been volunteers who work in female/male teams in a department to analyze a course and develop bibliographies, revised syllabi, and so forth. Faculty members use the materials they develop in their own courses, share their materials with others, write and report, and present within their department or college and in at least one university-wide symposium. The program at the University of Arizona has been directed to tenured faculty, including many department heads, who teach core courses in the humanities and social sciences and participate by invitation. The focus of the program is a seminar in which faculty read material on women's studies and integrate the material into academic curricula. Hunter College has invited one member of every department that offers an undergraduate major to spend a semester in a workshop to revise the introductory level course in the department. Participating faculty are released from teaching one course during the semester. Whereas most institutions take the approach of directly encouraging faculty to integrate content on women into academic courses and indirectly into research, Smith College has conducted a program in which faculty integrate the study of women into research and translate their research findings into the academic curriculum.

A different but related approach to broadening the educational experiences of students has occurred at Denison University, which requires that every student, male and female, take at least one course in Women's Studies or Minority Studies. The Women's Studies Librarian-at-Large at the University of Wisconsin System offers one more approach, providing a range of publications and services for both Women's Studies and other programs at all campuses within the University System.

Postsecondary institutions are also making a variety of efforts to increase educational opportunities for women students in science, mathematics, engineering, business, and computer and information sciences. Purdue University and the University of Arizona, for example, conduct programs for women in engineering that recruit young women high school students, retain them by offering social support and role models, and prepare them for a transition to employment or graduate work. Visiting women professionals in nontraditional careers have served as role models to women students at Denison University. Role models are also an important component of the Women in Science Program at the University of Michigan, and of the Pre-Freshman Summer Science Enrichment Program and the Health Careers Program for Women College Students at Spelman College. The Science Anxiety Clinic at Loyola University of Chicago, the Center for Mathematical Literacy at San Francisco State University, and courses in nonthreatening mathematics offered by numerous institutions help women and men students overcome avoidances of mathematics, sciences and technology.

Student development is also promoted through opportunities to win prizes and awards, establish mentor relationships with women or men professionals, and receive leadership training through participation in student government, the student newspaper, and other organizations. In these areas as in others, the opportunities for women have been fewer than those for men. Denison University awards an annual Women's Studies Prize. The University of Delaware hosts an annual Women of Promise Dinner at which tenured women faculty recognize outstanding women students. It also recognizes reentry women with an annual award. The University of Kansas honors women students, faculty, and staff annually and elects outstanding professional women to a women's Hall of Fame. The University of Delaware and the University of Akron offer low-cost leadership training programs for women students. Access, Inc., a nonprofit organization, has developed a model leadership training program for Hispanic women students.

Programs for Faculty, Administrators, Professional and Support Staff

To address inequities in the employment of women faculty, administrators, professional and support staff, an increasing number of colleges and universities are making efforts to hire, tenure and promote women and to establish salary equity. For example, to detect inequities in hiring for administrative, faculty and staff positions, Wellesley College, Hunter College, and Rutgers University collect, analyze, and report annual data in which all full-time positions and hires are compared with national availability. These reports not only call attention to departments with records of underutilization of minorities and women but, additionally, departments may be reviewed and permitted to hire only after demonstrating that they have established applicant pools that reflect national availability. These colleges and universities exemplify the principles intended by the concept of affirmative action and legally that should be followed by all institutions considered federal contractors.

A variety of programs promote the professional development of women and help to increase their chances for promotion and/or tenure. The University of Delaware provides funds for departments to bring women scholars to the campus. Visiting scholars provide opportunities for professional interaction for women faculty in isolated departments, help male faculty interact with recognized women experts, and encourage departments to identify and hire women. They also serve as role models for students. The University of Delaware and the University of California at Berkeley have conducted promotion and tenure workshops for women faculty (men may also attend) who often do not have as easy access as their male counterparts to the informal channels of communication through which information about the promotion process is ordinarily exchanged. Hunter College has initiated a program to humanize the personnel system of the university. This program promotes the upward mobility of secretarial and clerical staff, the majority of whom are minorities and women. Components include an employee assistance program that offers a range of social services for employees with special concern for the needs of working women and ethnic/racial minority populations and a career mobility program that provides training in data processing and computer programming. The University of Maryland is also engaged in efforts to improve career mobility for secretarial and clerical staff.

An increasing number of institutions share a commitment to

salary equity but use different procedures to identify and correct possible inequities. For example, Hood College publishes a salary analysis each year showing distributions by rank and sex for assistant, associate, and full professors. Published information also includes the annual rank adjustment, merit, additional adjustments (promotion or elimination of inequities), and the total percentage increase for the rank. The analysis, originally initiated by the president, is coordinated by the provost. Southern Methodist University has used a regression analysis to determine the variables that carry the most weight in determining men's salary, such as credentials, productivity, and the entrance rate for the department. Then characteristics of individual women faculty are inserted into the estimating equation for men to obtain the salary that a person with those characteristics would be expected to achieve. Possible salary inequities are adjusted by the provost. At the University of Maryland, committees have been established at each divisional level (social sciences, humanities, and so forth) that review salaries in all departments within the division and are in a position to deal with particular cases. Adjustments are made from departmental and divisional funds.

Programs Affecting the Social-Educational Climate

Women students and faculty study and work within a social-educational climate that subtly continues to discriminate against them, even as overt forms of discrimination are being addressed. Subtle forms of discrimination can be described as "microinequities," or inequities that when taken singly seem so insignificant that they may not be identified, much less protested. At the same time, taken together they constitute formidable barriers to equal opportunities for women (Rowe, 1977).

"The Classroom Climate: A Chilly One for Women?", published by the Project on the Status and Education of Women (PSEW) (Hall and Sandler, 1982), identifies differential behaviors, on the part of both male and female faculty, that discriminate against women students overtly and covertly and offers over one hundred recommendations for change. This report has produced numerous responses from postsecondary institutions seeking to address the problems it identifies, including specialized campus dissemination efforts, workshops, lectures, research projects, and surveys. PSEW has also published a report on "Selected Activities Using 'The Campus Climate: A Chilly One for Women?", a report on out-of-classroom forms of differential treatment of women and men, and in 1986 *The Campus Climate Revisited: Chilly for Women Faculty, Administrators, and Graduate Students.*

Another easily adaptable program, developed by the University of Delaware, helps administrators and others involved in hiring, evaluating, and recruiting faculty, students, and staff to understand perceptual bias and its negative effect on judgments about women. This informal approach brings a small number of administrators at the same level (peers) together for a discussion of research on perceptual bias. A nonthreatening compilation of the research, summarized in a pamphlet called *Seeing and Evaluating People* (Geis, Carter, and Butler, 1982) is used as a basis for discussion. A longer version is available for those wanting more detail on the research studies. Highly respected senior faculty and administrators serve as facilitators for these discussions.

These programs represent only a sample of many approaches now in progress to address not only the issues cited but a variety of others, including admissions, financial aid, continuing education, counseling, support services, sexual harassment, and others. All have the support of one or more senior administrators at their institutions. A number, although by no means all, are initiated and conducted by Commissions or Committees on the Status of Women, with the approval and support of the president or chancellor. Commissions on the status of women offer an especially effective approach to identifying needs and for developing and setting programs in motion to meet them.

None of the programs described have required the infusion of massive amounts of money, thus illustrating how cost-effective approaches to promote equity for women can be and serving to remind us that lack of dollars is often used as an excuse for inaction.

SUMMARY

There are many institutional types and needs and hence many paths to equity. No institution is expected to find all approaches helpful, since not all may be congruent with its mission, or viewed as increasing educational equity for that institution, or as financially feasible. At the same time, it is hoped that this process of change toward equity in their own institutions, by adapting the successful approaches of other institutions and by identifying and developing the critical conditions needed to make change efforts work, will succeed.

REFERENCES

BOGART, K. et al. *Institutional Self-Study Guide on Sex Equity for Postsecondary Educational Institutions.* Washington, D.C.: Project on the Status and Education of Women, Association of American Colleges, 1981.

BOGART, K. *Toward Equity: An Action Manual for Women in Academe.* Washington, D.C.: Project on the Status and Education of Women, Association of American Colleges, 1984.

GEIS, F., CARTER, M., and BUTLER, D. *Seeing and Evaluating People.* Newark, Del.: University of Delaware, 1982.

HALL, R., SANDLER, B. *The Classroom Climate: A Chilly One for Women?* Washington, D.C.: Project on the Status and Education of Women, Association of American Colleges, 1982.

HOWE, F., HOWARD, S., and STRAUSS, M. J. *Everywoman's Guide to Colleges and Universities.* Old Westbury, N.Y.: The Feminist Press, 1982.

NATIONAL CENTER FOR EDUCATION STATISTICS. *Earned Degrees, Conferred, 1979–1980.* Washington, D.C.: National Center for Education Statistics, 1980.

——. *Degree Awards to Women: 1979 Update.* Washington, D.C.: National Center for Education Statistics, 1981a.

——. *Digest of Education Statistics, 1981.* Washington, D.C.: National Center for Education Statistics, 1981b.

——. *The Condition of Education: A Statistical Report.* Washington, D.C.: National Center for Education Statistics, 1981c.

——. *Digest of Educational Statistics, 1985–86.* Washington, D.C.: Center for Education Statistics, 1986.

ROWE, M. "The Saturn's Ring Phenomenon: Micro-inequities and Unequal Opportunity in the American Economy." In P. Bourne and V. Parness (eds.), *Proceedings of the NSJ Conference on Women's Leadership and Authority.* Santa Cruz, Calif.: University of California, 1977.

SANDLER, B., and HALL, R. *The Campus Climate Revisited: Chilly for Women Faculty, Administrators, and Graduate Students.* Washington, D.C.: Project on the Status and Education of Women, Association of American Colleges, 1986.

SHAVLIK, D., and TOUCHTON, J. "Toward a New Era of Leadership: The National Identification Program." In Tinsley, A., Secor, C., and Kaplan, S. (eds.), *Women in Higher Education Administration.* Washington, D.C.: Jossey-Bass, 1984.

27

Curricular Re-Vision:
The New Knowledge for a New Age

PEGGY MEANS McINTOSH

Serious discussion of educating the majority allows us to celebrate not one but two cultural shifts. A majority of Americans of all ethnic and racial groups now have some chance at higher education, and within higher education women have now become the majority within the student population as they are in the population at large. Work, struggle, legislative mandate, and unanswerable demonstrations of ability have won significant access to education for previously excluded groups.

The work toward equal access goes on, but now we must give concentrated attention to the content of the curriculum. For access to education does not ensure educational equity. Access to a sexist and racist curriculum is not sex or race equity. Women, now the numerical majority in college as in U.S. society, still learn from the curriculum that they are a marginal majority. Students who are told they have equal access to higher education sit in classes that day in and day out deliver the message that white Anglo-European males are more real than anyone else. Such courses do not give all students equal access to a sense of identity. They teach students to defer to white Western male authority and thus subtly persuade our future voters, policymakers, parents, and teachers to keep cultural and political power in the hands of those who currently have most of it.

Curricular shifts toward inclusiveness have a long but hidden history, marked by occasional lurches toward democratic rethinking despite resistances and conceptual challenges. The development of women's studies since the early 1970s is a dramatic curricular achievement that would be very hard to wipe out entirely. There are now more than five hundred women's studies programs in the United States, almost half of them offering a major in women's studies as well as elective work. There are more than fifty Centers for Research on Women. The publications emanating from teaching, scholarship, and research on women are astonishing in their volume. Beyond its informational content, the work points to reconceptualizations of knowledge itself, of education, and of societal structures.

Further institutionalization of women's studies is our best present hope for meaningful education of women as well as men, for it is the only area of the curriculum in which women's existence is fully registered, a *thoroughgoing* methodological awareness is encouraged, and there is an attempt to develop frameworks that get beyond implicit metaphors of conflict and conquest for life and learning. Women's studies provides a systematic way to critique our present systems and clarify the ways these systems operate to exclude many people or underreward many of the most constructive functions of human personality and society. The cultural pluralism represented on our campuses today cries out for new and innovative thinking about pluralistic pedagogy and inclusive politics in the classroom. In addition, the violence of individuals and institutions calls for citizens educated to think about life not simply in terms of winning and losing, but in terms of working for the decent survival of all. The classroom is the place to prepare women and men students for the complexity of roles they must play in our society and the world in a nuclear age. To date women's studies, more than any other field, has worked toward systemic visions of our problems and has given permission to students to try to conceptualize a world in which all human beings might survive with dignity.

Such an understanding of women's studies is rare in teachers and administrators, most of whom have seen the area as simply one more narrowly specialized curricular development. We who care about educating the majority will need to continue to make the case for women's studies on our university and college campuses, despite the misunderstandings and antidemocratic reactions which are inevitable. An argument for women's studies based on the ideal of curricular justice does not serve us well, since institutions of higher education have never been particularly concerned with justice. We will do better to argue first on the academy's own grounds, that a curriculum that lacks women's studies suffers from gross scholarly inaccuracy. Likewise, a curriculum for future citizens and voters is dysfunctional if it teaches students to overlook half the population of the nation and the world. Further, a university cannot claim to benefit students' development if its curriculum jeopardizes the mental health of half the students by implying they are not fully real, while inflating the egos of ther other half by implying that they are larger than life. Moreover, universities that claim to give students a sense of tradition and history, but fail to teach about women, men of color, working-class people, or daily maintenance of society and psyche, serve to keep the majority of students from a sense that they have been part of history and that it is they who will help to create the future. Finally, we need to urge the university to rethink its work, since education in this troubled age can help us with our problems only if it involves development of many capacities beyond competition and what is called rational analysis.

We who care about educating the majority will need to continue to argue for women's studies as a source of new information and new perspectives which will benefit people of both sexes and of all cultural and racial groups. Far from being the exclusive study of a narrow interest group, women's studies is centered in the experience of the majority and committed to the healthier development of all our political and social institutions as well as our individual female and male psyches in all of their affective and cognitive capacities. Far from being an isolated undertaking, of interest only to women, women's studies promises to alter teaching, thinking, and the role of feeling in every one of the academic fields. Since this author's work has centered on the usefulness of feminist materials and perspectives for changing the rest of the curriculum, her contribution here centers on implications of women's studies for other disciplines and for administrators as they consider how best to use their resources to educate the majority.

It is now clear that research on women—the study not only of the women we are allowed to call "notable" but of women as half the world's population—poses questions for scholars and teachers in each of the academic disciplines. As we came to see the comparative absence of women's experience from the account of reality passed on to students by our present curriculum, we began to ask questions that would help us, as scholars, to fill in the overlooked record of the "other" half of the human race. In the Mellon National Faculty Development Program that this author directed at the Wellesley College Center for Research on Women from 1979 to 1985, faculty from many fields were encouraged to focus on two key framing questions. First, what is the basic content, scope, and methodology of my discipline? Second, how would my discipline need to change in order to reflect the fact that women are half of the world's population and have had half of the world's lived experience?

The initial answers vary from discipline to discipline and thus appear at first to reinforce our sense of the differences between disciplines. But in the end, the answers lead us to perceive that some of the boundaries between disciplines result from the same tendency to compartmentalize that has kept women's experience from being construed as a part of social reality in the first place. Therefore, research on women has come to pose a challenge not only to the epistemological ground rules within disciplines, but also to the very distancing between disciplines, and between people, which our present modes of finding and passing on knowledge enforce and reinforce.

The traditional humanities curriculum has stressed the public sphere: laws, wars, cultural change, public events, individual accomplishment, conflict, and the activity of "the makers and shapers of civilization," or of those who have survived fairly well within cultural systems. But society has been held together by groups of people who are not distinguished by public achievement, public power, or recognized cultural innovation—those who have made and mended the personal and social fabric, living outside of most scholars' fields of vision. The valuable work that such people have done has included taking care of people and systems and maintaining reproduction and production. Many have barely survived; some have prospered; all have lived within worlds we were taught to overlook, those "lower worlds" including that of "women's work." The richness and complexity of their lives, the concerns of their existences, their particular textures of "achievement" and "genius" have yet to be recognized within our academic disciplines or explored for the development of our students' humanity.

If we balance the curriculum, we would diminish the emphasis on those who attained power, "importance," or "excellence" as we have been taught to define them. We would increase the attention given to those women and men, previously invisible in the curriculum, whose lives are equally important, interesting, and revealing for us to study, if we are claiming to "know" about human life and history. We would also increase attention to the functions of personality and society which have provided our daily material and relational matrices.

If transformed, the field of religion would become less centered on theology and public institutions and would suggest the *effects* of religious belief or observance on the daily lives of ordinary people. Intellectual history would balance attention to the thought of recognized individuals and "movements" with the study of platitudes, truisms, and the belief systems that permeate "ordinary" lives. Such givens may not have the cerebral clarity of thought displayed by the thinkers whom we are told shaped intellectual history, and to study them well requires more intellectual rigor than most scholars have realized. History itself, if it reflected the fact that women are half the world's population, would concern itself less with laws and wars and more with the social fabric of most people's lives. A course called "History of France" that omitted women would have to change its name. Historians would attempt to answer more questions like "What was it like to live, to be a human being, especially a woman, in given ages of the world's history, and in a variety of statuses, places, and cultural contexts?" Historians who feel these questions are pointless are those who have not done or studied the research. For richness emerges with the answers. Although women's studies scholars sometimes ask, "What was it like for those at the bottom?" they also begin to doubt whether what we defined as "top" and "bottom" are in fact so high and low, and to ask who wrote those definitions, and whom the definitions serve.

The study of music, art, and architecture is transformed if one goes beyond those works that were made for public use, display, or performance and were supported by aristocratic or institutional patrons. One begins to study quilts, breadloaf shapes, clothing, pots, or songs and dances that people who had no musical literacy or training took for granted. One studies what music meant to audiences as well as to composers. Architecture becomes less the study of the architect's place in a tradition of designers and more the study of human arrangements of space and effects of spaces on those who inhabit them—the effects on daily lives of buildings, pavements, and kitchens. One looks at the same time for the influence that women did have in shaping or resisting their environments and in bringing about architectural and environmental change; we learn what they cared about in their surroundings.

Economics, changed to reflect the fact that women are half the world's population, would put more emphasis on unpaid labor. To consider unpaid, unsought labor as a central part of the economic picture would truly transform economics. In political science, the meaning of "politics" needs to be extended to cover private relationships that do involve power but which are not often acknowledged by scholars in political science: the politics of neighborhoods, of schools, of curricula, of families, of bedrooms, of classes, of races, ethnic, and religious groups outside of public institutions, and of all people who are given responsibility without corresponding authority. To see personal relations as having political dimensions is both to make women visible and to reconstrue "politics."

A freshman English curriculum reflecting the fact that women have been half of the world's population may now recognize writing in many modes rather than simply stressing the art of rhetoric, a genre derived from the Greek conventions of persuasion in which one male leader aimed to persuade a group of listeners of his point of view. Women, like most people we do not often study, have chiefly used language to make connections between people, to elicit information, and to carry on daily work. Teachers are beginning to devise ways to give academic credit for forms of communication that do not lend themselves to the argumentative monologue of the expository essay. In literature itself, we need far more descriptive work on writing by women and unread men. Critics are asking how it happens that the genres most used by women—for example, in the United States, the journal, diary, letter, and the short story—are considered marginal or subliterary. Or how thousands of novels by nineteenth-century women have disappeared from accounts of America's literary history. (Editor's note: For examples in science, see Harris et al. in Part Three.)

One moves from simple answers to complex answers in addressing the question "How would my discipline need to change in order to reflect the fact that women are half the world's population?" In general, the simple answer involves getting the "women's sphere" added to the subject matter of the discipline. But it is now clear that the discipline itself is not simply enlarged but also challenged in its essential terminology and methodology by the addition. Research on women calls into question Matthew Arnold's conviction that one cultural group can simply identify for all "the best that has been thought and said in the world." Research on women both challenges the definition of "best" and asks who defined what is best, whom the definitions benefited most, and why the student must be called upon to look "up" rather than "down," *around*, and *within* in being taught about the world. Hierarchies and canon-making in the academy were corollary to hierarchies and cannon-making in social life, and so it is not a surprise that a thorough study of women also makes visible many men who were not previously featured in the curriculum. In fact, about nine tenths of the world's population suddenly becomes visible when one takes the emphasis off the public lives of white Western men, who are seen as cultural leaders, and includes those who for reasons of sex, race, class, nationality, or religious background were defined as "other" and therefore lesser. One sees that the record of knowledge was not only incomplete but that it was also *incorrect*, and that its errors perpetuated the past balances of power in our societies. In the words of Marilyn Schuster of Smith College, "At first, you study women to fill in the gaps. But then you see that the gaps were there for a reason." Our curriculum and our other societal structures were products of the same social and political construction of reality. So we begin to see, for example, that most affective functions of men's lives were left out of the record, as were most women's activities; this double suppression perpetuates a particular identification of masculinity with cognitive control. The omission, then, has political consequences.

The new scholarship on women has unearthed such tremendous amounts of material that this development of new knowledge cannot be seen merely as a fad. It promises to widen the account of reality that institutions of higher learning pass on to their students, to broaden or challenge the definitions of the "best that has been taught and said [and done] in the world," and to increase students' awareness of the world in which they live. The traditional curriculum was designed for the education of white male Western leaders in a time of Western dominance and economic expansion. A revised curriculum would give both our male students and our female majority a better preparation for a world in which non-Western people of color are the world's majority. The life of Western dominance and expansion should no longer be taken for granted, and the caretaking roles assigned previously to women and other lower-status people are needed on a global scale for human survival.

How can our educational institutions work toward an inclusive curriculum that recognizes and better educates students for a world of interdependence and survival rather than violence in the service of winning? Faculty can do much of the work, and students' interest and gratitude fuels the effort, but support from administrators is essential to the development of inclusive curriculum in all of its forms. In colleges and universities to date, a strong women's studies program with a budget for administration, instruction, and programming has been the most effective starting point, for as indicated here, women's studies is the field that has showed the most coherent concern about inclusive educational content, methods, and ideals. We need far more tenured positions in women's studies. Women's studies programs will continue to be necessary and desirable even if all of the other departments work to bring women and undervalued human capacities into the curriculum, just as English departments will continue to be necessary even if they persuade all other departments to work on the problems of students' writing and reading. Women's studies is the center and source of most of the new interdisciplinary insights that inclusive curriculum projects rely on, and in a number of colleges where inclusive curriculum change projects were undertaken without a women's studies program, a program was eventually developed in response to the need for a theoretical, interdisciplinary, and coherent base to aid the work. Faculty development has been a critical component of many women's studies programs. We need college administrations to fund such activity and fully support and reward the participation of all faculty in bringing their knowledge, awareness, and aims for education in line with our needs in the late twentieth century.

For the faculty members doing the work, women's studies is both difficult and gratifying. Administrators will help most if they fund women's studies faculty adequately for their complex interdisciplinary tasks and recognize the degree of effort and innovation involved in keeping up with a tremendously burgeoning interdisciplinary field. With regard to carrying work into other disciplines, administrators will be able to help most if they understand how much emotional and intellectual growth is necessary in all faculty members as they face new scholarship on women and new feminist perspectives on society and learning. New work on women is not simply summer reading. It challenges the intellect and puts stress on the belief systems of the teacher. On the basis of work with college and school teachers on curriculum change over the last decade, here are some of the elements of those stresses and challenges in the faculty development process.

When facing this new scholarship for the first time, most white faculty members of both sexes receive bad blows to the ego. As professors, most of us had learned to think of ourselves as fairly intelligent, fair-minded, knowledgeable, on guard against being politically manipulated, and unique or at least free to be unique in our styles of teaching.

The now-massive new scholarship on women implies that we were not so intelligent or fair-minded if we never learned about women and never noticed the omission, and not so knowledgeable if we knew nothing of the lives or perspectives of the world's majority. We were not only manipulated but were manipulating others in passing on, under the illusion of objectivity, bodies of knowledge that kept most "lower-caste" people's lives and perceptions invisible.

It is hard for us as white teachers, who considered ourselves part of the solution to societal problems of class, race, and sex, to realize that we have instead been part of the problem, insofar as we have been competent teachers of a defective curriculum. Finally, it is a blow to the ego to realize that one's teaching and scholarship were not special but at best merely average, following traditional lines of exclusion and incomplete generalization.

First encounters with work from women's studies, then, tend to undermine the sense of professorial self in the experienced college teacher. If he or she can get past the first natural defensive emotions, a process of intellectual and personal development is set in motion that, when fostered, eventually reinstates and renews the sense of professional self on a far firmer grounding than before. That is, one feels truly more intelligent, more fair-minded, more knowledgeable than before, more alert to manipulation and more innovative in one's research and teaching.

But this process of intellectual and emotional development is full of challenges. Most faculty need the support of administrators and colleagues to face the undertaking. Faculty who thought that women's studies was about women's "contributions" or "achievements" learn that, more importantly, it asks who defined contributions and achievements in ways that leave out the lives of most people of the world, including most men. Those who thought it was only about women's "issues" find instead that it is about women's whole existences seen in all of their complex contents.

Those who thought that women's studies was an optional "approach" contributing a new set of data to existing tables learn that it does not merely add new materials and perspectives to the existing bodies of knowledge; it critiques those bodies of knowledge and their unacknowledged political underpinnings. Finally, newcomers to women's studies scholarship learn that it is not the study of a few white women. It aspires to be the multiracial and cross-cultural study of women as half of any population, and at its best it embodies a new aspiration for methodological, emotional, and intellectual awareness in all of the liberal arts disciplines. But one does not learn all of these things at once.

Many faculty seem, in fact, to go through a series of phases as they become involved in the study of women, first seeing women in terms of white Western men, then trying to see women diversely and on their own terms, and as a result reseeing women, men, and society. The work turns out to be conceptually far more difficult than originally anticipated. I attribute the difficulties in part to encountering worlds for which one has not been given names or concepts. We have plenty of words, for example, surrounding the human capacity for competition that has been identified in the West with white males, and has been overrewarded in them, and overdeveloped also in all of our psychological structures, institutions, and learning systems. But we have few words and concepts for the equally important human capacity for collaboration that has been, I think, projected onto women and lower caste males, and then underrewarded and undervalidated in them as in all of our psyches, institutions, and learning systems. Traditional curricula give us models and vocabulary for the vertical ladder-climbing processes in all of the discourses of arts and sciences. Winning and losing are familiar and, sadly, accepted givens. We have not yet fully developed the vocabulary we need to give attention to and validation for the lateral and sustaining functions, and to teach students of both sexes how to develop in themselves both the competitive and the collaborative human skills.

Like other colleagues who have done faculty development work in women's studies, this author has noticed some recurring patterns of changed consciousness and curricula as traditionally trained faculty approach the study of women. I see interactive phases of personal and curricular change occurring in both individuals and courses specifically in conjunction with raised consciousness about vertical and lateral elements in the psyche and the society. Within the development of history courses, for example, this author names Phase I: Womanless History; followed by Phase II: Women *in* History, as exceptions. Next comes the issues-oriented Phase III: Women as a Problem, Anomaly, Absence, or Victim in History. Then comes a radical turn into the study of women's lives on their own terms—Phase IV: Women's Lives *As* History, which reaches toward Phase V: History Redefined and Reconstructed to Include Us All, which this author sees as a one hundred-year project.

Phase II courses bring in a few famous or notorious women, but do not challenge the traditional outlines and winner-focused definitions of those who "made" history. In Phase II, one teaches about heroines, exceptional or elite women, who are seen to have climbed above their group. In Phase III, Issues History, one studies women (or lower-caste men) as victims, as deprived or defective variants of more powerful Anglo-European men, as losers, as "have-nots," or as protesters, with "issues." Women can at least be seen in a systemic context, since class, race, and gender are seen as interlocking political phenomena by faculty who have gotten beyond Phase II. But it is insulting to any individual or cultural group to be defined as having only what this author would call a "deficit identity." We will never make "ordinary" people's experience seem either real or valid if our teaching and research still rest on the categories of analysis which were derived from the experience of those who had the most power, and who saw themselves as the chief models.

In Phase IV, the categories for analysis shift. The faculty member begins to realize that since women have had half of the world's experience, we need to ask what that experience has been and to consider it as half of history. Phase IV takes a positive look at women and at our strategies for coping or thriving, and for maintaining life; it looks also at the lives of many of those men, equally overlooked in the curriculum, who were likewise doing the work on which human survival has depended. It often focuses on *lateral functions of personality and society* more than on discrete individuals or groups of either sex. Phase IV is racially inclusive, multifaceted, and filled with rich variety; it suggests and validates plural versions of reality. It brings in all kinds of evidence and source material that academic people are not in the habit of using. It examines and tries to name the communicative, relational, passionate affiliations and affections. Faculty doing Phase IV work often feel by turns unprofessional and truly engaged in genuine research and teaching for the first time. The teacher becomes less of an expert, the student more of a resource; both can bring the authority of their own (avowedly limited) experience to the alert, empathetic study of diverse phenomenona.

We need to move beyond Phase IV, since women and little-studied functions of men's lives are not all of history. Phase V will help students to have that "doubled vision" which the late historian Joan Kelly described: the sense that we are both part of and alien to the dominant culture, the dominant version of history. And when history is seen as a series of constructs to begin with, students are then empowered and invited to create more usable and inclusive constructs that validate a wider sample of life and help us to recognize the human talent for identification and caretaking which is currently projected onto and demanded of too small a group. Phase IV consciousness is still rare in individuals and in institutions. This author thinks Phase V history will be one hundred years in the making, if we live that long. Meanwhile, Phase I versions of history, of politics, of welfare, and of leadership endanger us all.

The Phase I syllabus in every discipline is very exclusive. Phase IV and V syllabi are very inclusive. Individuals and consciousnesses and causes do not exist fixedly in given phases, but show points of dynamic interaction among several of the phases, if the teacher or researcher is conscious of the many forms of the problem of curricular politics. But often superficial curriculum change gets arrested in Phases II and III. The study of women only as exceptions or as victims perpetuates misogyny, so it is important to move individual faculty and their courses through discussion of "role models" or struggles for women's rights to acknowledge also the truly interdisciplinary and genuinely new human-centered scholarship of Phase IV, and to imagine the reconstructed knowledge of Phase V.

How can administrators help? As has been indicated, strong women's studies programs are the best starting point, because at present they have the most inclusively humanistic aims. Reeducating faculty in traditional disciplines is an essential step. Deans can make a real difference not only by strengthening women's studies programs, but also by providing released time, money, colleagueship, and incentives for faculty to retrain themselves to teach about women. They benefit from each other's help as they begin the disconcerting work of reading voluminous scholarship on women and understudied men, seeing from new angles, seeing the present curriculum as a social and political construction, and at least recognizing if not yet correcting exclusive habits of thinking, reading, teaching, and doing research which pervade the traditional academy.

Administrators and tenure and promotion committees together can provide the most important incentives by gradually instituting policies that reward faculty who incorporate the scholarship on women into their teaching, and thereby avoid passing onto students versions of reality which are obsolete. A faculty member who, in 1988, is still wholly incompetent in scholarship on women is a poor candidate for several decades of tenure.

Finally, administrators can insist that discussions of general education include consideration of women's studies. Since women now constitute the majority in college populations as in the population at large, further exclusion of women from the "core" will eventually have to be seen as conscious misogyny on the part of faculty committees. The time is past for the objection that women's studies is political. All curricula are political. A curriculum that leaves women out is highly politicized. Which *forms* of curricular politics the colleges and universities choose now is the question.

An inclusive curriculum stands to benefit, and to change, men as well as women. In the light of our global emergencies, one hopes that the colleges and universities will elect to develop inclusive versions of reality rather than standing by the old exclusive ones. It has become clear that our collective human survival depends on different processes, in women's and especially in men's minds, from the ones we have set in motion in the past. No investment in faculty and curriculum that colleges and universities can now make bears more importantly than women's studies on human futures, individual, and collective.

28

Educating the Majority:

The Feminist Enlightenment

JESSIE BERNARD

THE NEED FOR ENLIGHTENMENT: THE CURRICULUM OF INFERIORITY

> Male rationality has judged women's mental abilities—as well as their physical abilities—inferior; why emulate it? (Young-Bruehl, 1987, p. 211)

> Since the early 1970s, research has documented the ways in which . . . history and psychology, literature and the fine arts, sociology and biology are biased according to sex . . . They exclude women from their subject matter, distort the female according to the male image of her, and deny value to characteristics the society considers feminine (Jane Martin, quoted ibid.)

> One persistent question has stimulated research . . . throughout this century: why have women's achievements failed to match those of men? why are there so few outstanding female artists, scientists, or statesmen? (Tyler, 1968, p. 208)

It was against a background of such female denigration in the 1960s that the necessity for a Feminist Enlightenment became clear to a cohort of feminists and the crucial importance of its success widely recognized. Their new, modern, late twentieth-century feminism was different from any of the historical ones, different from the feminism of the suffrage movement, different from the feminism that rested its case only on the issue of the victimization of women. In these traditional feminisms the vocabulary, the conceptualizations, and the perspectives were still those of the male world. This one sought—with a new vocabulary, new conceptualizations, new perspectives—not to destroy the male achievements in knowledge but to correct and augment them.

The Feminist Enlightenment is in process now. This essay explores the need for this period in human history and discusses some of its dimensions. Before we can truly educate anyone—and especially women—there must be present a conviction on their part that they are capable of learning and worthy of it. We cannot, unfortunately, take it for granted that all the women who come to our colleges and universities—even those who succeed in them—have this self-confidence, this belief in their intellectual talents. The opposite belief—in the intellectual inferiority of women—has been a persistent theme running through human history in the West and, as Pearson, Shavlik, and Touchton remind us, "the conventional wisdom" has taught us that "learning was too strenuous for women" (unpublished paper, 1987). In brief, one of the first steps in the education of women had to be emphasis on the development of a positive self-image, to show them, one way or another, that their own experiences were as valid as those of men, to free women's minds from the crippling acceptance of their imputed inferiority. To convince them that they had as much right to define the human situation as men did, that they did not have to accept the male definition of everything, that as human beings—diverse, heterogeneous, variegated—they were deserving in their own right, that they did not have to be like men to be worthy. As individuals there would perhaps always be women who, for one reason or another, lacked a positive self-image, but hopefully not because they lacked maleness. Freed from the limits imposed on them by their low self-image, there was no way of knowing what as yet uncultivated strengths women could contribute to the human enterprise. Recognizing the need for this knowledge and learning how to achieve and disseminate it were among the goals of the movement here referred to as The Feminist Enlightenment. It was unique, sui generis. Women had participated in other enlightenments, specifically in the French Enlightenment of the late eighteenth century, and their contribution had not been trivial (Beard, 1946; Lougee, 1976). But those enlightenments had been male-oriented, based on male issues and perspectives. The women were performing in a male system, seeking, as in the French Enlightenment, to introduce civility into human intercourse (Beard, 1946, p. 323). Fraternity, not Humanity, was its motto.

AN ANCIENT AND MANY-FACETED CURRICULUM

There is a long history of attitudes and behaviors that have had the result, if not necessarily the intent, of convincing females of their inferiority to males, especially in the important intellectual qualities that really counted. In biblical times a female had about three fifths the value of a male. Riane Eisler has reminded us of the violent behavior sanctioned toward daughters in the Old Testament without any thought of its horror for the victimized women (1987, pp. 97–101). DeMause tells about infanticide in Rome and in the Middle Ages, in which girls more often than boys were likely to be selected for such sacrifice. Thus Hilarion, in a letter to his wife: "If, as may well happen, you give birth to a child, if it is a boy let it live; if it is a girl, expose it." The effect could hardly be avoided of convincing little girls of their relative worthlessness. Even today, when there is only enough money for one child in a family to go to college, in most cases the daughter's education is likely to be sacrificed rather than the son's. This is, to be sure, a logical marketing decision, because his education will pay off better than hers in the job market, where an enormous body of research has documented the status inferiority of women.

The mass media have taught the same lesson. Thus, a study of the themes and characters on prime-time television since the mid-1950s—including 620 episodes and 7,000 characters from 20 different series—reported the general inferiority of women they reflected. Women rated "a clear second to men" (Lighter et al., 1986). They were less in evidence, less likely to be mature adults, less well educated, held lower-status jobs, and "in many ways were portrayed as the weaker sex." Before 1965, more than a fifth of the episodes had rejected the feminist position. Since then, however—the date of the beginning of the Feminist Enlightenment—not a single episode had made fun of the idea of sexual equality. After 1965, characters who did laugh at women's abilities were invariably put down by the script. In brief, television was sending mixed signals. Although writers and producers might have thought of themselves as progressive on feminist issues, the invisible paradigms were still at work in the assumptions that shaped their female characterizations. The authors of this study conclude: "to the men behind the tube, women are still the second sex."

Other mass media have also put women down. In 1945, *Life* magazine was calling women "simply ridiculous" (Beard, 1946, p. 18). Comic strips have also been insulting to women. Thus, an outraged reader complained to the editor about one such strip, which was "no more than incessant repetition of sexist comments employing the cliché figures of trapped husband and brainless wife ... The cartoonist's assumption ... seemed to be that the reader is another male and will ... enjoy being reminded of women's superficiality, irrational needs and inability to function as adults" (*The Washington Post*, August 23, 1986). She protested this strip especially and reminded the editor of his responsibility to oncoming generations, who should not be encouraged to perpetuate these sexist anachronisms.

Nor, finally, has academia escaped the downputting practices vis-à-vis women. For until one has examined them in some detail, it is surprising to find how inimical to women they can be. One of the earliest cases of downputting behavior toward women in academia was reported by Radcliffe women, behavior that I later called the "stag effect." It was "a complex of exclusionary customs, practices, attitudes, conventions and other social forms which protected male turf from the intrusion of women" (Bernard, 1976, p. 23). They were, for example, not invited to scientific meetings, professional clubs, and stag dinners and were thus deprived of the helpful "easy social contacts ... of learned societies" (Bernard, 1964, p. 303). When invited, they were ignored in their professional societies, "made to feel not quite 'acceptable' and rather 'de trop' " (ibid., p. 302). More than a decade later, "women in graduate and professional schools were subject not only to these negative kinds of behavior [—exclusion or ignorance—] but also to more positive kinds as well." That is, they were not only avoided by many professors but also positively disparaged by them (Bernard, 1976, p. 25). Elizabeth Minnich in this volume illustrates more current examples. She describes, for example, an archetypical curriculum committee that challenges proposals for women's studies courses, implying that they are not quite worthy of a place in the curriculum, as, in fact, they would be a lowering or watering down of the university's academic standards.

It is surprising how old-fashioned thinking of this kind— untouched by the Feminist Enlightenment—seems today. For example, there is a distinguished professor in a great university, with an international reputation, writing about the classical theories in the discipline that he has loved and taught for almost a third of a century. His book deals with ambiguities of language and experience and different ways of dealing with them, including trying to avoid them, which he does not favor. There is no mention or even reference to one of the basic ambiguities in his own discipline. Does Man or Mankind include women? If so, do females appear in all the paradigms as males? or as pseudo males? Do all the generalizations and insights about males apply equally and identically to females? Whose voice is telling us all this about Men? or Mankind? Mary Beard was already discussing the anomalies involved in gender terminology decades ago (1946). And Minnich reviews the Broverman et al. study that illustrates the ambiguities. In one study, for example, subjects identified "normal" humans with "normal" men, leaving, she notes, the option for a woman of being a "normal" woman and thus an "abnormal" human or a "normal" human being and hence an "abnormal" woman.

It is not only the absence of women in the course content that is downputting; so also may be the wrong kind of attention paid to them. Some examples of such downputting take the form of embarrassing women by telling "biological" jokes in class; being called "hen medics"; hearing at a conference in 1972 that "women can't think analytically"; in 1973, "small but significant insults at Yale"; in 1973 that the professor says he has no use for women in meteorology; in 1975, that "frankly, we have too many women students in this department already." And, finally, the assignment of the solo woman in a laboratory group to the role of "deviant."

For, not only is it the classroom that is chilly for women in academia (Hall and Sandler, 1982). So also, apparently, is the laboratory. Thus in one mixed-sex experiment it was reported that "All the women studied expressed feelings of depression and frustration. Three considered themselves to be casualties of the experience. And whereas some of the men had experienced personal growth, among the women, growth was slowed down rather than enhanced and self-esteem [was] lowered" (Bernard, 1974, pp. 27–28). Understandably, the dropout rate for women was high because of less encouragement. Self-images suffered, and so did performance. More than among men, these women "come to feel they do not have the ability to finish and even more of them find emotional strain a threat to completion of the degree program" (Bernard, 1974, p. 28). It is surprising that, made to feel unwelcome, more women students did not report emotional strain as a barrier (ibid., p. 27).

A review of the situation in the mid-1970s had concluded that the situation for women in academia was not good for the self-image of women so essential for success in that ambience:

> The research literature . . . documents in painful detail just how the self-image of women—superior to men because they are a more highly selected population—is damaged as a result of their [academic] experi-

ence. The recipe is simple. Take a cohort of women graduate students and deny them intellectual support from professors and peers, make belittling comments about them—"hen medic," "women's lib freak"—and slowly but surely their self-image, their self-concept, their self-confidence will shrink. If they do not drop out, at least they will learn their place. Even the most elite—women in the disciplines dominated by men—lower their sights . . . They settle for less than their abilities would qualify them for. (ibid., p. 28)

So ancient and so widespread are the male practices of putting women down that Daniel Freedman, a psychologist, suggests a genetic interpretation to explain the success so many cultures have had in lowering female self feeling:

It may well be . . . that males everywhere tend to demean women, belittle their accomplishments, and in the vernacular . . . "put them down." I have not heard of a culture in which the males do not engage in this chauvinistic sport, although cultures certainly vary with regard to womens' rights. (Freedman, 1979, p. 62)

He also believes women collude with their downputters, in effect, "blaming the victim." "Women are more often than not willing to go along with this strategy, agreeing to hold in abeyance the anger that would appear to be inevitable." He reviews a body of experimental research that seemed to him to confirm his conclusion. In one study, even those females selected as participants—because of their known, tested superiority to their matched male partners—assumed an inferior status vis-à-vis the males.

But, objects one professor, that is all over. The putdowns of the past no longer exist. That was 1979. Still, only half a decade later, a report on "Barriers to Equality in Academia" from MIT found that *plus ça change, plus c'est la meme chose:*

. . . The computer science environment . . . is perceived as "particularly harsh for women." It focuses on those subtle types of behavior, which, while perhaps not intended to be discriminatory, undermine the professional image of women, both in their own eyes and in those of their colleagues. Any one incident may appear trivial when viewed in isolation. However, "when women experience such incidents daily, the overall effect of the environment is much greater than the sum of the individual incidents." (*Association of Women in Science,* 1984)

Five recommendations were included in response to this charge: (a) there should be no personal remarks not suitable for men as well as women; (b) stereotypical assumptions about women's roles and values were to be avoided; (c) women should be included in informal interactions among students; (d) questions from women should be dealt with in the same way as questions from men were dealt with; and (e) it should be assumed that women were as capable of completing research tasks as men were. The response from male students was favorable; they had learned from the study to see male gender-based biases and prejudices more clearly. This was enlightenment of the first order, hopefully for the professor as much as for the students.

After the painful enlightenment shed on the subtle aspects of the female inferiority curriculum, eliminating the more blatant ways of teaching women their inferiority became relatively easy. Admission quotas, higher admission requirements, documented discrimination—in financial assistance, hiring, promotion, tenure, health care, housing, salary—could be fairly well dealt with by administrative reforms:

> The development of women's studies programs, transformations of the curriculum projects, affirmative action, implementation policies for Title IX, and creation of support services such as campus women's centers means that a substantial amount of practical wisdom is now available. Educators have become sensitized to the need for such programs and are now interested in learning how to do the job of educating women in a competent, intelligent, and effective way. (Pearson et al., 1986)

So far so good. But it is far too early to conclude that the job is finished, that at last we know how to educate the majority. For studies still indicate that the present record of higher education, in spite of some significant efforts, is not yet particularly good. Female students, on the whole, still experience a loss of personal and career confidence over the period they spend in higher education, even when they make very high grades. For men, the reverse is true (Elkhawas, 1980). Still remaining on the agenda are ways to recognize and counter subtle teaching of the damaging inferiority lesson, ways less amenable to straightforward legal and administrative solutions, obstacles that in fact are still only in the process of being specified, defined, and researched. Feminist enlightenment is still called for.

Similar refrains were echoing and reechoing around the world. In Japan, for example, the first step in educating women was coming to be recognized as freeing them from the status of being "the second sex," as developing self-confidence; in Sweden, it was viewed as helping returnees regain self-confidence lost in periods of time away from school; in India, the task was to help women acquire self-respect and self-confidence; and everywhere, to overcome the devastating impact of a downputting ambience ("Alternatives Within," 1986, pp. 27 ff.). Clearly some vital ingredient was missing in the efforts to upgrade the education of women. The research already available suggested that one of the first steps in educating this majority may have to do precisely with overcoming the poor self-image inculcated in women almost universally.

Before leaving the topic of the potentially destructive emotional consequences of poor self-images among women in academia, two addenda dealing with nonacademic aspects are relevant here, one negative and one positive. The first deals with a strange set of symptoms in their patients that psychotherapists began to report in the 1970s. One such therapist had found in both her research and practice "men and women who have every reason to be on top of the world" who were nevertheless "miserable because in their [own] eyes they never measure up. They believe they are never as bright or as talented or as sharp as others in their fields. They believe their success has come from every reason in the world except the real one: [that] they . . . [really did have] the ability and the brains" (Clance, 1985). The author labeled this set of symptoms "The Imposter Phenomenon." Men as well as women were vulnerable to it, but the cases presented were mostly of women. These "imposters" had two faces, one with a confident smile, a look of authority, and self-assurance; but underneath this mask the face looked anxious, scared, tired, with even a touch of panic. Analysis of the personal histories of many of these cases showed development factors to be common, especially in family relations. But even with ideal family and school histories, the very ambience of our society toward women had assumed female inferiority; the invisible paradigms showed through.

The other addendum indicates how serious the matter of poor self-esteem has become, not only in academia but also throughout our society. On the basis of a considerable cache of research it has, in fact, become a political issue. California is a case in point. In 1984 the first so-called self-esteem bill died in the State Senate; the next year it was vetoed. The current version had strong bipartisan support, and it passed. The bill established a Task Force to Promote Self-esteem and Personal and Social Responsibility. Applicants for membership on a twenty-five-member fact-finding task force included educators, therapists, correctional workers, ministers, and retirees. The whole idea seemed hilarious to some people, including the popular cartoonist G. B. Trudeau, who made it the topic of a series of comic strips that week. Still, the simple political act of recognizing a relationship between self-esteem and personal and social responsibility and trying to improve it was a first step in the right direction.

THE FEMINIST ENLIGHTENMENT

Enlighten. To illuminate, to instruct, to inform, to impart knowledge, wisdom. (*Oxford English Dictionary*, 3rd ed.)

Withdrawing Consent to the Curriculum of Inferiority

The Feminist Enlightenment is sometimes referred to as a revolution (Hite, 1987). It is true that its effect may have been revolutionary, but it was not directed so much at the political overthrow of governments as at the liberating of the human mind. If it is true that knowledge is power, it is a special kind of knowledge, the kind that challenges an old consensus based, as most knowledge to date is, on the male perspective alone. In the last analysis, power in a democratic society rests on the consent of the governed, that is, on a consensus. If women no longer give consent to the male definitions of any and every situation, if they no longer concede to males exclusively the right to define or to name, that constitutes a kind of revolution in and of itself. The women of the Feminist Enlightenment are claiming that right for women, the right, that is, to define and name at least their own experiences, their own grievances and, in due course, their strengths.

The times seemed to be auspicious. So far as we know now, there had never been a time when so many members of the female half of the human species were achieving control of reproduction, becoming literate, even educated—albeit in the male tradition—and, perhaps even more significant, achieving the intellectual ability to challenge a status quo. Any event that involved half the human species, as this one did, had to be taken seriously, and its participants understood.

Some of these women were members of the Kennedy-appointed Commission on the Status of Women (1960), who were becoming angry at the slow progress it was making toward women's political and social equality (Carden, 1974, p. 31). Others, The Women's Liberation Group, were young activists of the New Left, some of whom had been members of Students for a Democratic Society (SDS), and they were angry at the "New Left Males' refusal to treat seriously their complaints about being treated as inferior" (ibid., p. 32). The thinking of the Commission on the Status of Women was in the long tradition of women's rights, based on political and economic issues. The thinking of the members of the liberation groups was far more radical. Most of the participants in both groups were middle class, mainly white, mainly well-educated, and cosmopolitan. They were spectacularly brilliant, avant-garde, widely diverse in geographic distribution, in education, in occupation, in race, in class, in ideology. Many were to become solid researchers, serious writers, subtle analysts. They gave theoretical and research substance to Betty Friedan's feminine mystique. True, some may have been pranksters. They threatened to burn bras at a beauty contest. None ever did. Still, the epithet "bra burner" became a part of the language, serving the need of hostile critics to express their anger at such unwomanly behavior. Nevertheless, despite such hostility, little by little it became clear that these women were changing a lot of minds, that a great deal formerly invisible was becoming visible. Nothing remained sacred, nothing inviolable, nothing that could not be said or told. A whole fabric that had hidden the darker corners of women's lives was torn asunder. All aspects of the relations between men and women in whatever roles—political, economic, academic, family, even sexual—came under scrutiny. They had been well trained for activism.

In the 1960s and early 1970s women had been members of the SDS and, along with college men, were learning the skills and the vocabulary of civil rights activism and of antiwar demonstrations. They had envied the protesting men, who had draft registration cards to burn before the television cameras. They had identified with all the liberating movements, felt themselves to be as much a part of them as were the men they were working with. When goals were achieved—civil rights legislation for blacks won, and the war over—and new paths being planned to carry on, the women learned, much to their shocked amazement, that their male co-members did not accept them as equals. After participating as equals with males in a decade of activism, they did not relish being ousted from sharing the prestigious work of developing strategies for reform—or revolution, as the case might be—and being asked, instead, to do menial, female-type chores—typing, copying, serving coffee—which were uninfluential, even downputting. Now they seemed suddenly to be discovering the sexism the men felt toward them, the same men for whom racial equality had been such a taken-for-granted goal of activism.

A digression is called for here to conclude the story of the relations between the leftist women and SDS. The New Left had begun in 1962 with a manifesto, the so-called Port Huron Statement, which was followed by sit-in protests against segregation, by antiwar marches, and by urban antipoverty campaigns. In 1961 the SDS had 575 members; in 1965, 10,000. By 1970 "it had all but disintegrated into windy Marxism and nihilistic violence" (Lehman, 1987).

Among the several errors to which their demise was due was

the downgrading of women, which proved to be the most expensive error possible at this time and place. When women had spoken at an SDS national convention in 1965, their remarks were received with ridicule. The next year, when the women asked for "a plank supporting women's liberation, they were 'pelted with tomatoes and thrown out of the convention.' A year later, in 1967, at the New Left 'National Conference for New Politics,' the issue was treated more gingerly though still unsympathetically . . . During the next year most of the New Left men disregarded the women's movement growing within their ranks—but many of the women did not. Gradually they began to take sides on the issues. Some identified themselves as primarily feminists; others as primarily members of the New Left" (ibid., pp. 60–61). Many of the women left the male-run organization and organized their own meetings. Of those who remained with the male group, some achieved positions of leadership, but it was not in any sense leadership in behalf of women. Some became part of the fatal criminal sector that brought death and imprisonment. One was killed in an ad hoc bomb factory in the basement of a New York building. One of the leaders of the SDS, Tom Hayden, summarized its history in 1977 as follows: "We ended a war, toppled two Presidents, desegregated the South . . . How could we accomplish so much and have so little in the end?" (ibid.).

A not-impossible reply might well be their stupid way of dealing with their women members. After participating as equals in a decade of activism these bright, energetic, committed women did not relish such downgrading. For some it produced an epiphany that removed blinders from their eyes. They now could see what the structure of sexism was, the "invisible paradigms" that shaped it, the infrastructure, in brief, that had been so long in place that it had become normative, invisible (Schuster and Van Dyne, 1984). It was an enlightenment whose time had come. In due course, these women were organizing their own separate liberation groups. By 1968 there were such groups in five different cities, and the number was growing. They practiced what they could salvage from what they had been taught by their professors. They learned that much of it either ignored what they themselves knew about the world women inhabited or assumed it was the same as the one men inhabited. They wrote and debated. They were among the first modern educators of the majority. A great many of their efforts were directed toward their own education. They were beginning to see a great deal about their own lives as women that no one had taught them. In the so-called consciousness-raising groups they were beginning to learn from one another what the lives of women were like. Teaching one another, discovering, verbalizing, analyzing. Doing research. Creating whole new areas of human knowledge, both in and beyond academia. And most of all, they were becoming aware of the curriculum that had meant profound ignorance about their own lives, their dependence on male-created knowledge, and the gender bias in knowledge that had all but strained women out of human history.

This new, this modern, this late twentieth-century feminism was different from the historical ones, different from the feminism of the suffrage movement, different from the feminism that rested its case only on the issue of the victimization of women. In these traditional feminisms the vocabulary and the conceptualizations and the perspectives were still those of the male world. This one—with a new vocabulary, new conceptualizations, new perspectives—sought not to destroy the male achievements in knowledge but to correct and augment them.

Goals and Hopes for Feminist Enlightenment

The Feminist Enlightenment may be defined in terms of the several statements of its goals and hopes as registered in the early issues of the numerous feminist journals established in the early 1970s. There were fifty such journals in the United States by the 1980s. Along with floods of papers, pamphlets, reports, newsletters circulating among seemingly insatiable readers, these journals were powerful tools for disseminating the new feminism. They varied among themselves and early on stated their several positions on key feminist issues.

Here, for example is the story of one of the first that appeared in 1968. Other examples follow which demonstrate the scope and depth and the common themes of the material produced.

> The reactions to our first journal (un-titled, unstructured, without page numbers or table of contents or date of publication or copyright, and barely escaping total anonymity) have been many and varied. The most consistent criticism from those who enjoyed the journal was that we provided no structure, no solutions. They say that although we identified a whole array of problems and feelings which touched them acutely, they felt somewhat lost as to what could be done in their day-to-day lives. The very layout of our first journal should indicate the degree of our own dilemma. We simply knew that we had to begin somewhere, and at least to speak out. So our first action was to publish a journal.
>
> We all felt strongly that our movement must be grassroots, and emerge from the truth of our suffering. We wanted to set an example of what could be done. None of us was a professional editor, nor did any

of us have experience in organizing and fund-raising. Movement people were hostile to our ideas and plans, so we had no access to their experience and knowledge and machinery. Our own interests and occupations were varied enormously—nurse's aide, poet and mother, student, welfare mother, bio-chemist, teacher, computer programmer, former prostitute. But we did it: we produced a journal. (*No More Fun and Games*, 1969, p. 4)

Three years later marked the emergence of *Feminist Studies*, founded "for the purpose of encouraging analytic responses to feminist issues and analyses that open new areas of feminist research and critique" (*Feminist Studies*, 1972, p. 1). In their statement of purpose the editors expressed their commitment "to providing a forum for feminist analysis, debate and exchange," with the approach and conclusions of any given article "not necessarily reflect(ing) the opinions of the editors" (p. 1). Many of the succeeding issues were edited by university women.

Another significant journal begun in 1972 was *Women's Studies*, founded "to provide a forum to discuss and explore the implications of feminism for scholarship and art, to chronicle changing consciousness, and finally to help to create a more equalitarian society" (Martin, 1972, pp. 1–2). In the opening issue editor Wendy Martin wrote in her editorial, "Why Women's Studies?":

artistic and cultural values as well as the social and economic structure of patriarchal societies ensure male dominance by inculcating the myth of female inferiority. Since the university mirrors larger social structures, teaching and scholarship often reinforce male dominance, and academic disciplines such as history, literary criticism, psychology, political science and even anthropology, sociology and biology become bastions of male supremacy. Although sexism in academia is often unconscious, it is important to understand that the university, along with other major institutions, is often hostile to women.

In spite of, or perhaps, because of, this hostility, feminist thought and scholarship are rapidly advancing. The conviction that men and women should have equal political, economic, and social rights, which constitutes the core of feminism, makes it obvious that extensive research into past beliefs and practices as well as considerable rethinking of our present values is necessary in order to reverse the effects of male chauvinism and the internalization of patriarchal values by women. (Martin, 1972, p. 1)

The year 1974 saw the emergence of *Quest, A Feminist Quarterly*, described by the editors as follows:

Quest, a feminist quarterly is seeking long-term, in-depth feminist political analysis and ideological development. *Quest* is not an end in itself, but a process leading to new directions for the women's movement possibly including such concrete forms as regional or national conferences, a national organization or a political party. We, the editors, are all women who have been in the movement for several years and have reached a point where each answer leads us to more questions. We have been through various ideological and activist metamorphosis and end up feeling that our overall perspective is still not adequate. Where has the struggle brought us? Closer to real economic, political, and social power for women? Closer to an end of the exploitation of and violence against women? Closer to self-determination for all women? We do not have all the answers ourselves and expect that feminists across the country and the world will contribute to this process of seeking. (*Quest*, 1974, inside front cover)

In 1976 another journal, *Women's Agenda*, was launched, giving voice to women's growing sense of themselves and their increasing courage to speak out on their own issues, needs, and concerns. The first women's editorial in this journal, "A Women's Voice," was eloquent:

A national women's voice is in the making. It is the voice of women who are able and willing to act upon the major social issues of our times. It speaks for women who are concerned about reforms that will affect not only themselves but all members of the society. It has become a catalytic force for social change on the broadest scale. This powerful new voice directly confronts the old myths that women are divided and that the goals of the women's movement are supported by a small minority. The creation of this voice was made possible by the hard work of feminists who, over the years, raised the consciousness of this nation to the inequities of pervasive sexism. The creation of this new voice was made necessary by this nation's lack of commitment to humanism.

This voice represents women who reside in every region of the country and who are of diverse cultural, religious, ethnic and economic backgrounds. Our diversity is our strength, but only as long as we listen closely to each other and share our information. The purpose of *Women's Agenda* is to keep alive the dialogue within this greatly expanded women's movement by facilitating the interchange of information and ideas. Our publication is for the women—more and more every day—who have stepped down from their pedestals and are getting together to plan their own agendas for action. (*Women's Agenda*, 1976, p. 2)

The year 1976 also marked the beginning of another significant academic journal, the *Psychology of Women Quarterly*. In her opening editorial Georgia Babladelis wrote:

Recently concerned critics have pointed out that... most of our information about behavior is based on the study of men only. Once more scientists are responding effectively and a new literature on the psychology of women is emerging. A paramount purpose of this journal is to make that literature readily available. In the publication of this journal there is the intent to redress past shortcomings by filling the gaps in our understanding of women's behavior. It is time to ask hard questions about establishing facts and to explore new questions and find new facts . . .

We are opposed to sexism in content and language and aim to become an educative force in that regard. . . We are committed to investigations of the *psychology* of women. (Babladelis, 1976, pp. 3–4)

Another illustration of a feminist journal formed in the early years of the women's movement is *Chrysalis,* launched in 1977. As described by its editors:

Chrysalis A magazine of women's culture. . . takes its form and content from the women's movement itself. Feminism is not a monolithic movement, but rather includes the experiences, values, priorities, agendas of women of all lifestyles, ages, and cultural and economic backgrounds. Women building practical alternatives to patriarchal institutions, women developing new theories and feminist perspectives on events and ideas, women expressing their visions in verbal or visual art forms—women's culture includes all of this, and *Chrysalis* exists to give expression to the spectrum of opinion and creativity that originates in this diversity. (*Chrysalis,* 1977, p. 3)

In the 1976 issue of *Signs,* Catharine R. Stimpson, Joan N. Burstyn, Donna S. Stanton, and Sandra L. Whistler wrote in their editorial:

Journals should have an animating purpose. For *Signs: Journal of Women in Culture and Society* that purpose is to publish the new scholarship about women from both the United States and other countries. The form the work will take may be reports of original research, contemplative essays, or a synthesis of report and essay . . . Like any decent scholarship, the study of women must avoid the luxury of narcissism. It must be neither limited nor self-reflexive. It is a means to the end of the accurate understanding of men and women, of sex and gender, of large patterns of human behavior, institutions, ideologies, and art . . . The consciousness of such scholarship respects many of the concepts, tools, and techniques of modern study. It uses them to compensate for old intellectual evasions and errors, to amass fresh data, and to generate new concepts, tools, and techniques. It also tends to question the social, political, economic, cultural, and psychological arrangements that have governed relations between females and males, that have defined femininity and masculinity. It even suspects that those arrangements have been a source of the errors that must be corrected. Scholarship should map the consequences of specific actions. Its discoveries and conclusions should then be used to improve the material conditions of the lives of women. (Stimpson et al., 1976, pp. v, vii)

Four years later, in Volume 6, Number 2, Winter 1980, in the last issue of the Stimpson editorial term, the following update occurred: "Before and during the years that we were developing *Signs*, the new scholarship about women itself changed. It started with the urgent need to document women's sufferings, their invisibility and subordination. There was disagreement about the universality of women's secondary status, but not about its existence ... Intelligence and passion have helped to map ... this female world and in the process, the notion of woman herself has become less passive, more active; more that of a primary force than of the marginal flesh" (p. 188).

Psychological and Structural Routes to Enlightenment

The term "enlightenment" may refer both to the collective process by which knowledge is generated and spread or to the personal psychological process by which individuals experience the insights available from the knowledge. Over time, historically, a wide variety of ideas and emotions and philosophies and beliefs have given rise to such collective enlightenments, some of which have been spread by the sword; or, in some cases, by inquisitions; in others, by dedicated missionaries; by crusades; by slow invasion. Students of collective behavior have proposed a number of models applicable to such enlightenments: Allport's J-curve, for example, or the diffusionist model used by anthropologists, or Lipman-Blumen's crisis model. All might be applied to the spread of The Feminist Enlightenment.

From the personal rather than the collective perspective, enlightenment might take the form of sudden individual conversions by simple exposure to feminist principles, in which, with no particular response pro or con, there takes place within the individual a sudden epiphany, like the classic example of Saul on the road to Damascus (*The Holy Bible*, Acts, 20). Or, not quite so spectacularly, the "click" described by Jane O'Reilly (1972). Or a "moment of truth" occurs as among members of a Tanzanian women's group as they recognized their common grievances (Bernard, 1987). To some, enlightenment comes despite resistance; even, in some cases, because of it. Sometimes, that is, the resister objecting to the feminist message finds unexpectedly that she has actually assimilated the new point of view. She has changed. With little awareness of the process, she has found that what she had once rejected has become matter of fact for her. Why had it ever seemed outré?

One of the answers lay in the new consciousness she had experienced in these groups, groups that came in time to be called "consciousness-raising groups."

The Consciousness-raising Route to Enlightenment

By the late 1960s enough experience in groups had been garnered that participants could analyze and specify useful procedures to be followed in organizing and leading them. Personal recognition and testimony were to be highlighted. There should be "on-going consciousness expansion . . . [by] going around the room with key questions on key topics; speaking out one's experience at random; cross-examination by members of the group; relating and generalizing individual testimony." (Sarachild, in Morgan, 1970 pp. xxiii–xxiv). There should be help in overcoming repressions and delusions. One should understand the reasons for repressing one's own consciousness. One should overcome fear or despair for the future. One should analyze valid and invalid fears. One should dare to share one's experiences with the group. And understand and develop radical feminist theory. And, "using the above techniques, to begin to understand our oppression." There should be at least monthly meetings and, from time to time, conferences as well. By 1970 there were such groups "in every major city in the United States, and in many cities of secondary and tertiary size. Large cities like New York, Chicago, or Los Angeles tended to have between 50 to 200 groups" (Sarachild, in Morgan, 1970, p. xxv). New York had over two hundred. There were such groups in universities, high schools, and among older women, as well as in at least a dozen foreign countries. Experiences in these groups had a galvanizing, electrifying impact on many women. Nothing looked the same after such consciousness-raising. Indeed, one of the most powerful ways to become aware of the enlightenment proved to be through consciousness-raising groups. By the 1970s, meetings occurred almost everywhere, now here, now there, similar and different in details but overall essentially identical whether in the United States, Tanzania, or Colombia.

The feminism articulated in consciousness-raising groups provided a powerful curriculum, an education not generally recognized in formal pedagogy. In Colombia the women discovered that they often did not even have the words to express themselves. They found, as Mary Beard had found in 1946, that they had no language to suit their needs. Beard had shown that in English "man" and "mankind" often buried human beings who were not men. In the same way women in Colombia found that they used a language that could not describe even half of who they were, and therefore language became an expression of their alienation. They had to employ the masculine form when referring to both sexes, a situation that only reinforced the—to them inappropriate—male view of the world (Velez Saldarriaga, 1986, p. 8). Consciousness-raising groups helped to overcome these difficulties. Understandably, therefore:

> Consciousness-raising groups have played a central role in the women's movement as women have struggled to identify and take action against their oppression. Because women are so often divided and isolated, it is necessary first for women to look at the ways that everyday life and thought are controlled by patriarchal values and structures, and the ways our personal lives reveal the underlying oppression of women. Left political movements rarely look at how consciousness develops. Women took the radical step of educating themselves by focusing on the personal and developing a political analysis of women's oppression through an awareness of women's own experiences . . . Consciousness-raising . . . groups were a means of support and empowerment, and a crucial part of women's discovery of their common bonds and experiences. ("Alternatives Within," 1986, p. 8)

Little by little, step by step, experimentally and falteringly, groups of women came to understand the processes of consciousness-raising, the joy but also the pain it involved, the successes but also the failures. And, in the end, that the price—joy or pain—had to be paid:

> To rethink one's personal history collectively, to talk about what happens inside ourselves—our anguish, happiness, dreams, hopes, fears, fantasies and ghosts—is a revolutionary act of rebirth and transformation. The way I see it, this process is the only thing that can make real changes. It is necessary to go through consciousness raising, where we can untangle our alienation, where we can say the unsaid, and where, in struggling with the dialectic between the personal and the political, we can rescue ourselves from the anguish and loneliness that has been our personal history. (Velez Saldarriaga, 1986, p. 9)

Upon achieving a feminist consciousness, women discovered their alienation, their cultural and historical marginalization, their lack of sense of self and even of language with which to verbalize these insights. So the elation did not last forever.

The process of consciousness-raising was not necessarily, or even usually, pleasant for all women. They joined groups for the opportunity they offered to talk out role-related problems in their lives. The fortunate ones succeeded in achieving a new perspective on these problems and on their identity as women. The common experience was to question, rethink, and revise the models of female gender one had been taught to follow. After participating in consciousness-raising sessions everything one read, saw, or heard took on a wholly new meaning. Films, books, plays became revelations of the way roles were programmed to fit the status quo. Every conversation with men took on a new light. "The role-playing and unnaturalness of one's own actions are revealed. It is like being reborn" (Sarachild, in Morgan, 1970, p. xxiii). Upon achieving a feminist consciousness, women discovered their alienation, their cultural and historical marginalization, their lack of a sense of self and even of a language with which to verbalize these insights.

In the case of some women, the original exhilaration soon receded. Frustration, anger, depression took its place; they could not always count on group support. Groups began to split. The result often was demoralizing for those too new to the movement to have achieved a firm feminist consciousness.

For them and for others not yet committed but sorely tempted to succumb to the lure of feminism and for others, like them teetering on the brink of commitment, there was soon help in the form of ways to resist such defection. It was a kind of preemptive enlightenment to forestall it. It met and demolished the tempting antifeminist arguments. It specified the errors in thinking that had to be corrected. Or prevented from arising, in the first place, such errors as: "Anti-womanism, Glorification of the Oppressor, Excusing or Feeling Sorry for the Oppressor, Romantic Fantasies, 'An Adequate Personal Solution,' Self-cultivation, Rugged Individualism, Self-blame, Ultra-militancy, etc." (Sarachild, in Morgan, 1970, p. xxiii). Not necessarily easy. Still, many minds were saved from defection.

The Women's Studies Route to Enlightenment

One of the major routes to the Feminist Enlightenment was by way of the formidable research creativity that produced whole libraries of knowledge about female history and achievements and an astonishing growth of women's studies courses to disseminate it. Familiarity with this knowledge became a sine qua non of the education of the majority, not only in our society but elsewhere as well. This applied to the education of men as well as of women. It is interesting to note how truncated and quaintly old-fashioned the research and thinking of many distinguished male scholars and students in the social and behavioral sciences appears when they omit this new knowledge.

This enrichment of the traditional curriculum was only the most recent of many such changes in the original colonial male model of higher education in the United States, designed as a training ground for ministers. It had seemed for decades to be immune to challenge. By the nineteenth century, however, it had become clear that changes were having to be accepted. Little by little curricula had to add science to courses on the Evidences of Christianity. By the end of the nineteenth century traditional government courses, based primarily on exegesis of documents, had become political science and included voting behavior and political parties as legitimate topics; political economy became economics, in which even labor unions were a relevant concern. It was now, similarly, becoming obvious that women could no longer be omitted from the curriculum. If anything, one might say that the call for courses dealing with women had been rather slow in coming.

Once the Feminist Enlightenment had made this need incontrovertible, the growth in women's studies courses in the United States was phenomenal, increasing from fewer than twenty in 1969–1970 to thirty-thousand in 1986. And of the more than five-hundred-fifty programs of women's studies, almost half offered majors in the field. More and more students—male as well as female—were having their eyes opened, blinders removed, and being educated for a new reality.

Not that there was no resistance. In Japan, for example, Treece tells us:

> Activist women complain that academic Women's Studies bring about little real change, and it is true that on college campuses political issues such as peace, equal pay and women's employment are rarely taken seriously. I think there is a gap between university Women's Studies and grassroots women's activism, and more of a dialogue between the two is necessary. (1986, p. 28)

But some argued that the purpose of women's studies was not primarily one of activism, or even of education. It was, rather, one of consciousness-raising. And even of subversion. Consciousness of both men and women should be raised to such a level that "women need no longer be regarded as the 'second sex.' " Special courses should help students to question traditional roles, "and to value and develop women's abilities and confidence." And then, the ultimate dream:

My hope is that fifty years from now—or 100 or 200 years from now—
there will no longer be a need for Women's Studies courses because all
classes will naturally be taught from the perspective that women and
men are equal in talent, ability, and in their contribution to society and
to history. (Treece, 1986, p. 28)

One ought to be able to close this discussion with this idealistic peroration, surely a feminist one. But if there were some students who criticized women's studies because they did not promote activism, there were others who objected to the whole subject
of women in any course. Thus, Beth Hartung reported "resistance
among students in incorporating research data on women into college courses." She noted that "the mere mention in class of a problem
that is unique to women often is construed by many students as an
attack on males" (Bose et al., 1987, p. 34). Hartung reminds us that
many students were born in the mid-to-late 1960s and could therefore not even remember a time when women were not at least visible. She continues: "Related to resistance to feminist scholarship is
the anger and confrontation that result from awakening female students to feminist issues. Male students also grow angry when confronted with the essential fact of their privilege as males" (Bose et
al., 1987, p. 35). In such a chilly atmosphere, it is not surprising that
students conclude that it is all right to trivialize women's issues. At another campus, SUNY Albany, the hostile male comments during class
discussion evoked defensive solidarity among women. How much
learning took place might therefore be equivocal.

But there were pedagogical possibilities available. Janet Lee at
Mankato State University, for example, used activism itself as an
agent of change among her students, including involvement in community organizations such as rape crisis centers, shelters for battered
women, and nuclear disarmament groups (Bose et al., 1987, p. 34).
Such activism contributes to change in selves, in relationships, and
ultimately in society, along with the acquisition of theoretical and
research tools.

In Canada, M. L. Girou-Swiderski, Coordinator of the Women's
Studies Program at the University of Ottawa, saw three alternatives
for the future of women's studies: persistence along with the present
curricula; infiltration of parallel disciplines; or making up for past
deficits in human knowledge by way of a wider multidimensional
approach. The first, even if established, might not be able to persist
without considerable support; the second might lead to absorption
or cooption by other disciplines. The author's preferred future called
for the third or multidisciplinary approach with appropriate new

methods. In her view what was needed, in fact, were wholly new disciplines, new in content, methodology, and teaching.

> The classical methods of the disciplines are unable to do justice to the new themes and subjects introduced by Women's Studies. The framework itself, based on chopping up reality into various disciplines, is revealed as useless.... Our task ... involves not just rethinking reality ... but also making space not only for the intellect, but for the engagement of the whole person—intellect and emotions together. (Girou-Swiderski, 1986, p. 28)

Girou-Swiderski is under no illusion with respect to the problems she is confronting. Surely, the understatement of the year was her conclusion that "numerous ambiguities appear in the attempt to integrate feminist perspectives into the structure of formal educational institutions" (ibid.).

Feminist Activism via the Project Route

Some activists expressed their feminism and zeal for spreading it by carrying on projects varying from publishing books and periodicals to operating centers for rape victims, homeless women, abused women, or victims of domestic violence. Some nonactivist but supportive feminists expressed their vicarious feminism merely with their checkbooks. And—though they did not all necessarily agree on all the details of all the messages—teachers, writers, speakers, consultants, advisers, and counselors brought the message in person to the general public, to the corporations, to the legislatures. And there were the academic research-oriented feminists who expressed their feminism in the questions they selected for study. There were also the feminists who did not read widely but who somehow or other got the message and passed it on. There were, for example, the women who did not like the way things were being run in their neighborhoods, the women who had to work in the mines to support their families and fight for the right to do so, the women who did not need a lecture on feminism to know that they needed protection against rape, battering in the home, harassment on the job. Other kinds of projects involved other kinds of women. They did not have to burn bras but only threaten to do so to get on the evening television news. They did not have to invade editorial offices of women's magazines to reach the media directly. They became skilled in street theatre. And some who were more leftist than feminist left the women's groups, joined the male groups, and learned the deadly skills of guns and bombs.

Some of the projects—like, for example, street theatre—involved behavior so startling and messages so far out that the media found them irresistible. Indeed, Carden (1974) states that the movement had, in effect, been created by the media but that "in another sense the mass media were only the means whereby an already established movement was suddenly brought to the attention of large numbers of people" (p. 33). All too often, however, the penchant of the media for sensational reporting may have influenced the form and direction of the movement (ibid., p. 33).

How successful were the media and all these projects for the dissemination of feminist issues? In some respects, remarkably so. Thus the survey referred to earlier, of prime-time television themes over a thirty-year period, found that a third of the major themes had to do with women's rights and sexual equality. In 1965–1966 a "new woman" appeared in the media, independent and competent. (Nevertheless, with all her strengths, she was always "a clear second to man." Shadows of the inferiority curriculum still lurked in the background). Of fifty-four cases in which women's rights or sexual equality were addressed, most—almost three fourths (71 percent)—came out foursquare for women's rights. And progress did seem to be taking place. Thus, before 1965, fewer than one fourth (22 percent) of the episodes had reflected a feminist position. After that, not even one derided the idea of sexual equality (Lighter et al., 1986).

Resistance to Feminist Enlightenment

Not everyone welcomed or was even susceptible to the knowledge created by the Feminist Enlightenment. The rejection, resistance, or fear almost intrinsic to enlightenments were not absent in the case of this one. And there was no lack of male—and female—support for such resistance and rejection. So, astoundingly successful as it was in many ways, it was a costly success for many of its participants in terms of rejection by staunch upholders of the status quo.

So powerful was the paradigm for suitable behavior for women that even merely pointing out the exploitation or oppression of women elicited charges that they were man-haters, rejected by males, hostile. And those who went beyond verbal charges of sexism were laughable freaks. When they protested against male downputting they were attacked as complaining, whining bitches. Just recognizing discrimination was a rebellious, hostile act, and calling it "oppression" or "exploitation" added insult to injury. Just critically verbalizing the proper mien for women—"suffer and be still" was scandalous. These were not women as the public had always known women to be. They did not come with myrrh and incense.

Some men attempted a humorous—allegedly "sympathetic"— approach to the feminist assault. Thus "a light-hearted love letter to Women's Liberation" explored "the spectrum of Women's issues" with, allegedly, a "witty and sympathetic eye" and invited the reader to . . . "have a look. The laugh's on us" (publicity release for book by Mort Gerberg, 1971). From the back cover:

> Right On, Sister! is a wry-eyed, lighthearted look behind the scenes of the Women's Liberation Movement. If you don't understand what they want. . . . If you think they have it too good. . . . If you think their place is in the kitchen. . . . Well, man—or woman—the Women's Lib hasn't reached you yet! But Mort Gerberg's cartoons and rhymes offer you enlightenment with a smile. Here's fun for all sexes—and you don't have to be liberated to like a laugh!

Some quotations from this "love letter":

> "Why can't you just nag me the way you used to!" (Husband reclining in armchair as wife lectures to him on women's lib, p. 92)

> "Listen, unless we get that equal-pay-for-equal work thing settled, I don't *want* her to grow up to be president." (wife folding diapers to father playing with infant, p. 93)

> "You never heard of a lady guru? That just goes to show how unenlightened you are." (women sitting on high mountain, to traveler passing by, p. 84)

> "You and Dr. Whitehead also share a common ideology—you're both male chauvinist pigs" (hostess introducing two guests, p. 85)

> "You will meet a beautiful, dark-haired girl from Women's Liberation who will tell you to go to hell." (fortune-teller to male customer, p. 83)

There were daily pronouncements in the press that such foolishness could not last; young women would repudiate it; it was just a passing fad; it was certainly not to be taken seriously. Women who did take it seriously were ridiculed as mere publicity seekers. Bra burners. Man haters. Rejected by men. Street-theatre buffs. The behavior of some of them was too shocking to be taken seriously. These rabid rabble-rousers who seized microphones and invaded editorial offices of women's magazines could only be attention-seeking brats. The press reported the end of the movement regularly.

Not everyone took the matter all that seriously. Why should anyone take it so seriously, some objected. At worst, it was just a matter of bad manners. Men "did not really mean to exclude women, put them down, slight them, denigrate them" (Bernard, 1976, p. 31). Women should have more of a sense of humor about all this. Not be so sensitive about it. Boys will be boys, after all. Women should just grin and bear it (ibid., p. 31). If it did not have such serious consequences for women it might have seemed funnier than it did.

At the other end of the scale was the response of another writer to the women engaged in the Feminist Enlightenment. Feminism had replaced the nineteenth-century, admittedly saccharine idealization, of women and domesticity and substituted a woman who was "hateful and angry" (Gilder, 1973):

> The average American woman who looks into the media—that vivid trick mirror of her society—finds a cluster of negative images. Gloria Steinem has memorably declared her, in essence, a "prostitute." Germaine Greer thinks she is "a female eunuch," not even being paid . . . Betty Friedan envisages woman as a vain gull of male exploitation, frittering away her talents in boredom and drudgery. Ellen Peck sees her remorselessly trapped by babies . . . The beat goes on. John and Yoko scream, "Woman is the Nigger of the World". . . . Esther Vilar, supposedly anti-feminist, finds the average woman a "parasite." Greer, in debate with her, shrewdly agrees . . . [But she] puts it more intricately: Women are sick, but only when the society deems them healthy, or when they are dull and happy and important . . . A thousand writers find them hopeless puppets of Madison Avenue, hapless victims of sexism, reluctant prisoners of suburbia. And many of these negatives, widely propogated by the media, influence the self-image of millions of women. (Gilder, 1973, pp. 240–241)

This hard-faced and hard-hearted feminism opposed anything that interfered with a woman's goals. It was anti-family. As well as anti-men.

Such an ideology told women how foolish they were to be so exploited as to be wives and mothers, how they did not need to take such treatment, how they were as good if not better than any man.

Other opponents were less choleric in their attacks. They viewed the Feminist Enlightenment as a minor event, a passing phase, a deviant blip on the screen of history, not important enough to be taken seriously. Like the lamenting Anglo-Saxon poet Deor, they consoled themselves with the belief that, just as other similar misfortunes had been "o'er passed," so also would this one be. It was contrary to feminine human nature. It did not have to be actively fought. It would pass of its own irrelevance. Women would themselves soon recognize this irrelevance. Indeed, this wish was often father to the thought. Until well into the 1980s, almost weekly some pundit reassured us that feminism was fast departing the scene. Periodically the press reported that now, having had their little fling, women were leaving their "women's lib" feminism and returning to their senses; young women were no longer seeking "liberation." In fact, "feminism had become a dirty word" (*The New York Times*, October 17, 1982).

WHITHER BOUND?

Actually, when the story of this Feminist Enlightenment—including its raised consciousness, its defenses against societal attribution of inferiority, its activism—is fully told, it will surely demonstrate its significance as one of the great social movements of its time. The French Enlightenment might well have lost its historical identity if scholars had not recognized its significance so that by 1865 it was included in English dictionaries (*Oxford English Dictionary*, 3rd ed., 1952). The Feminist Enlightenment will, I am sure, not have to wait that long for such scholarly recognition. Thus, while proponents of received mainstream wisdom were complaining of intellectual "fatigue," the torch of the Feminist Enlightenment was being fueled by a seemingly unending stream of books, articles, research monographs, polemics, and essays, and thus adding handsomely to human knowledge, especially to the long neglected knowledge of women and their world.

No movement dealing with half the human species can be cavalierly written off as a passing fad, like a showing of a Parisian couturiere. Most assuredly not this one, as the authors of this book make clear. This epic deals not with arms and the man but with women and their words. Books continue to flow from the presses with astonishing speed; periodicals multiply; meeting follows meeting; conference follows conference where ideas are generated and transmitted. And, hopefully, all these will continue from here on out. If our colleges and universities can accept responsibility for fostering the powerful lessons of the Feminist Enlightenment and encouraging those who are keeping it alive, then women will be valued equally with men for their potential contribution to society. In the last chapter of this book, the editors have set forth an agenda that will help institutions of higher education accomplish these goals. Then the education of the majority truly will be in good hands.

REFERENCES

"Alternatives Within." *Connexions*, No. 21, Summer 1986.
Association of Women in Science. Editorial. *Newsletter of the Association of Women in Science*, Washington, D.C., December–January, 1984.

BABLADELIS, GEORGIA. Editorial. *Psychology of Women Quarterly*, Vol. 1, No. 1, 1976.

BASHOR, MARY. Letter to the Editor. *The Washington Post*, August 23, 1986.

BEARD, MARY. *Women as Force in History*. New York: Macmillan, 1946.

BERNARD, JESSIE. *Academic Women*. University Park: Pennsylvania State University Press, 1964.

──────. "Where Are We Now? Some Thoughts on the Current Scene." *Psychology of Women Quarterly*, Vol. 1, No. 1, Fall 1976, 21–37.

──────. "Change and Stability in Sex Role Norms and Behavior." *Journal of Social Issues*, Vol. 32, No. 3, pp. 27–28.

──────. *The Female World*. New York: Free Press, 1981.

──────. *The Female World from a Global Perspective*. Bloomington: Indiana University Press, 1987.

──────. *The Feminist Enlightenment*. In process.

BOSE, CHRISTINE, HARTUNG, BETH, and LEE, JANET. "Issues in Feminist Pedagogy." *SWS Network*, Vol. 4, No. 1, January 1987.

CARDEN, KAREN LOCKWOOD. *The New Feminist Movement*. New York: Russell Sage, 1974.

"Chapel Hill's Coeds." Editorial. *The Washington Post*, January 31, 1987.

Chrysalis, Vol. 1, No. 1, 1977.

CLANCE, PAULINE ROSE. *The Imposter Phenomenon*. New York: Bantam, 1985.

EL KHAWAS, ELAINE. "Sex Differences in Academic Development." In Leland, Carole, et al., *Men and Women Learning Together: A Study of College Students in the Late 70s, Report of the Brown Project*. Providence, Rhode Island: Brown University, 1980, pp. 1–42.

EISLER, RIANE. *The Chalice and the Blade*. San Francisco: Harper and Row, 1987.

Feminist Studies, Vol. 1, No. 1, 1976.

FLEMING, JACQUELINE. "Top Schools Pose Problems for Blacks." *The Washington Post*, September 13, 1986.

──────. *Blacks in College*. San Francisco: Jossey-Bass, 1984.

FREEDMAN, DANIEL. *Human Sociobiology: A Holistic Approach*. New York: Free Press, 1979.

FRIEDAN, BETTY. *The Feminine Mystique*. New York: Norton, 1963.

GERBERG, MORT. *Right On, Sister!* New York: Grosset and Dunlap, 1971.

GILDER, GEORGE. *Sexual Suicide*. Chicago: Quadrangle–New York Times, 1973, pp. 240–241.

GIROU-SWIDERSKI, M. L. "Alternatives Within." *Connexions*, No. 21, Summer 1986, p. 26.

HALL, ROBERTA M., with BERNICE SANDLER. *The Classroom Climate: A Chilly Climate for Women*. Washington: Association of American Colleges, 1982.

HARVEY, JOAN C., with CYNTHIA KATZ. *If I'm So Successful, Why Do I Feel a Fake? The Imposter Phenomenon*. New York: Pocket Books, 1985.

HITE, SHERE. *Women and Love: A Cultural Revolution in Progress*. Knopf, 1987.

HOGAN, MARY ANN. "California's Head of Esteem." *The Washington Post*, February 9, 1987.

440   Transforming the Institution

LEHMAN, DAVID. "Radical Cheek." *Newsweek*, July 13, 1987.

LIGHTER, S. ROBERT, LIGHTER, LINDA S., and ROTHMAN, STANLEY. "From Lucy to Lacey: TV's Dream Girls." *Public Opinion*, September–October, 1986.

LOUGEE, CAROLYN C. *Le Paradis des Femmes: Women, Salons, and Social Stratification in 17th Century France.* Princeton: Princeton University Press, 1976.

MARTIN, WENDY. "Why Women's Studies?" *Women's Studies*, 1972.

MILLER, JAMES. *Democracy in the Streets.* New York: Simon and Schuster, 1987.

MORGAN, ROBIN. *Sisterhood Is Powerful.* New York: Vantage, 1970.

No More Fun and Games, A Journal of Female Liberation, No. 2, including a report on issue No. 1 (1968), February 1969.

The New York Times, October 17, 1982.

O'REILLY, JANE. "Click!" *Ms.*, Preview Issue, Spring 1972.

Oxford English Dictionary, 3d ed. New York: Oxford University Press, 1952.

PEARSON, CAROL S., SHAVLIK, DONNA L., and TOUCHTON, JUDITH G. Unpublished paper 1986.

Quest, A Feminist Quarterly, Summer 1974.

ROGERS, E. M. *Diffusion of Innovation.* New York: Free Press, 1962.

SCHUSTER, MARILYN, and VAN DYNE, SUSAN. "Placing Women in the Liberal Arts Curriculum. *Harvard Educational Review*, No. 4, Vol. 54, November 1984, pp. 413–428.

STIMPSON, CATHARINE. "The Idea of Women's Studies: An Assessment." Manuscript, 1986.

————, BURSTYN, JOAN M., STANTON, DONNA S., and WHISTLER, SANDRA L. Editorial. *Signs: Journal of Women in Culture and Society*, Vol. 1, No. 3, pt. 2, 1976.

TREECE, KATHRYN TIETZ. "Alternatives Within." *Connexions*, No. 21. Summer 1986, p. 28.

TRIEBWASSER, WILMA, and MANDULA, BARBARA. "Identifying and Countering Discriminatory Behavior." *Association of Women in Science.* Vol. 12, No. 6, December–January, 1984.

TRUDEAU, G. B. "Doonesbury." *The Washington Post*, February 9, 1987.

TYLER, LEONA B. "Sex Differences." *International Encyclopedia of the Social Sciences.* Vol. 7. New York: Macmillan, 1968.

VELEZ SALDARRIAGA, MARTA, CECELIA. "Letting Go of Silence." *Connexions*, No. 21, Summer 1986.

The Washington Post, August 23, 1986.

Women's Agenda, Vol. 1, No. 1, 1976.

YOUNG-BRUEHL, ELIZABETH. "The Education of Women as Philosophers." *Signs*, Vol. 12, No. 2, Winter 1987.

29

The New Agenda of Women for Higher Education

DONNA L. SHAVLIK, JUDITH G. TOUCHTON, AND CAROL S. PEARSON

The status of women in our society has changed profoundly over the last two decades. The fundamental nature of the changes is inescapable. Women are a majority of all students in higher education. The numbers of women in the paid work force have vastly increased. Women are present to some degree in virtually every occupational field. They are an influential force in the electorate. They are recognized and courted as powerful consumers. They have introduced new vocabulary and concepts to everyday life. And they have caused society to question traditional notions about sex roles and cultural expectations.

Even with these changes, however, women still do not share an equal role in charting the future of our country and in shaping foreign policy. They do not serve in significant numbers in top federal, state, and local policymaking roles. Nor do they head major corporations, or lead more than 10 percent of our colleges and universities. Thoughtful men and women concerned with the status and influence of women have spent many hours engaged in research, identification of strategies, or in discussions designed to encourage women and to help them appreciate their own worth and value. These collective efforts have led to significant changes and much has been accomplished. What has not been done, however, is to consider the *context* in which change occurs. There has not been sufficient change within institutional structures to encourage, support, and maintain women's new roles or the new roles that are emerging for men.

As a society we have a collective value system, or set of assumptions, that still supports traditional roles for men and women. For the most part this value system views women who achieve in nontraditional ways as extraordinary performers, as exceptions to the rule. Perhaps the reason so many women feel like "superwomen" is that the role is expected of them! Most women executives, for example, are expected to perform as professionals *as well as* chief caretakers in the family, as statespersons or politicians *and* primary parent, as chief executives *and* nurturers. Complaints by women about the difficulty of multiple roles are often met with a "you chose it" response, implying that they could elect to play one role *or* the other, and that individual women are the ones who have to pay the price if they dare to choose both. It is important to note that most minority women have been expected to play and, in fact, have positively played both roles for years.

Rarely, if ever, are men required to make a similar choice, between career and home. Rarer still are questions asked about how our social systems could be changed or redesigned to accommodate families: children, women, and men together. Structures and systems supporting multiple roles for men as well as women could redress imbalances and enable women to make a fuller contribution to the total society. The prevailing values in our country support structures and systems that prevent us from discovering and implementing changes that could solidify new roles for women and for men. It is time to attend to these values, and there is no better place to start than with the education system.

Higher education influences current leaders and prepares future ones. It is imperative, therefore, that careful examination of these values and the resulting assumptions governing the behavior of women and men in society occupy a central place in higher education's comprehensive planning efforts. The intent of this chapter is to call attention to the fact that the agenda for women in society and in higher education has not been met. Indeed, in some important ways, it has not been allowed to develop. Some people with vision have been asking some of the same questions about higher education's response to women for decades. Where is the flexibility that responds to women's lives? Where is the information about women and their lives? What is the purpose of higher education for women? It is time for a "new agenda" for women in higher education that incorporates these and other questions. The ultimate goals of this agenda are to recognize the importance of change in both individual and institutional response and to resolve the questions of full and equitable participation of women in higher education.

From the earliest recorded history of higher education for women, there has been recognition that women had special "needs." Often, these so-called needs were not defined as just different; the women with these different needs were defined as deficient in comparison to men. Unfortunately, little has changed. Because of the prevalence of this deficiency assumption in defining women's needs it remains difficult to place women's special concerns and issues high on the institutional priority list. As a result, it is also difficult for women themselves to speak up for and attend to their own needs. It is even more difficult for women to develop their own visions for the future. Nonetheless, many women and some men have dedicated much of their academic lives to the pursuit of a new vantage point—one from which to view higher education and its potential for reflecting a new social order where women as well as men are valued for all they bring to the human condition.

The women's movement on college campuses was born out of the rich heritage of the national women's movement for personal and civil rights. Both were fueled by and intermingled with the civil rights struggles of minority women and men. In fact, minority women who have been in the middle of both movements—and not always by choice—often have served to bridge the gaps between groups working to build a more equitable society.

As we strive for a new vision for our institutions, we seek value-added change where we all learn to value more than one world view. Every institution in higher education must enhance the worth of each person by recognizing his or her talents, history, and cultural heritage, and by encouraging a celebration of diversity born out of fuller knowledge of the world.

WHY NOW?

The New Agenda of Women for Higher Education articulates what we hear women asking of higher education and what we believe to be higher education's responsibility to them. Women are calling for institutions to recognize their worth fully and to stop assuming that knowledge about men and men's lives necessarily speaks to women and their lives. They are calling for institutions to start systematically educating women for leadership in society. And they are calling for institutions to stop expecting them to give up their own strengths as women to become part of the male system.

Now is the time for our colleges and universities to become responsive to the values, ideas, beliefs, talents, hopes, dreams, and visions of women. The reasons are many. There are three primary ones.

- Our global society is facing problems of potentially cata-strophic proportions. We need the best and brightest minds to attend to these problems. Women constitute half of the hu-man resources available. They have the potential of providing at least half the answers.
- Higher education has a special responsibility to be a progres-sive, enlightening social force. This is our heritage, and this is our role. We should be a model for others to emulate. How can we expect society to do what we cannot do for ourselves?
- Theory, knowledge, and practice have been developed by and about women to help us rethink our institutional priorities, plans, and programs, and reshape the process. It is intellectually irresponsible not to use this new body of knowledge and grasp its implications for all our institutions.

A CALL FOR ACTION

Higher education can be a model for addressing the larger questions facing women's participation in society. For this reason, the American Council on Education's Commission on Women in Higher Education and Office of Women in Higher Education present the following Na-tional Agenda to address the future of women in the academy. This agenda is offered to every campus in the hope that the work of the last few years focusing on equity will not be forgotten, discounted, or trivialized. Further, it is offered to assist our colleges and universities in transforming their institutions into ones that truly value diversity, reflect this value in their policies and practices, and promote the full participation of each person based on her or his individual merits.

The Commission is calling for each campus to attend to the following major recommendations in order to maintain a focus on the importance of women's role in the future of higher education and, thus, their future in our society.

Each recommendation should be looked upon as a concept to be taken seriously, and then reshaped according to institutional culture and ethos. Many colleges and universities, especially some of the women's colleges and the community colleges, have instituted programs to address some of the issues we suggest need attention. If an existing program, practice, or policy can be adopted to meet the criteria implied by these suggestions, then that might be an appropriate way to respond. We are not eager to proliferate more bureaucracy. Rather, we are interested in making the institution work in the interest of women and, thereby, improving it for all.

We do not underestimate the magnitude of the task of reshaping our institutions. The shelves of the Office of Women in Higher Education are replete with reports by colleges and universities on the status of women in their institutions. Most of them were prepared in the early 1970s under the impetus of federal laws and executive orders. The reports cover everything from salary inequities to differences in the support of women's and men's athletics. What is devastating about these reports is that the information has not produced the permanent changes necessary for women to be considered as valuable as men. Of course, there have been some improvements. There are more women faculty than a decade ago. On some campuses, salaries are more equitable, there are more women administrators, there are more women in top sports competition, and, of course, women constitute more than half of the total undergraduate enrollment in higher education. Nonetheless, women are still second-class citizens on our college campuses—unrepresented in the curriculum, often put down in the classroom, and underrepresented in the major leadership roles in higher education.

It is no longer enough to make simple adjustments in our institutions to accommodate women. The recommendations we call for are designed to mobilize the entire campus community to rethink the way the campus functions relative to women. This process demands time, effort, and commitment. Some of the recommendations presented here may sound very familiar, some may seem very routine, and some are very new. All are important to the rethinking process. They must be reshaped and remolded to suit a particular campus. Most important, they should be enhanced by the experiences of those who choose to take up the challenge for their individual campuses. To these people we issue this call to action.

1. Seek a strong commitment from the leadership of the institution to understanding and addressing the concerns of women students, faculty, staff, and administrators

Having the understanding, support, and encouragement of the institutional leadership, particularly the president, is extremely important. The president, along with the governing board, sets the tone for the institution and establishes the institutional agenda. The agenda called for by the Commission requires the full participation of the board and the president to be completely successful. Planning can be undertaken and work can be done without these essential players, but eventually they must be part of the process, preferably, the initiators.

2. Correct inequities in hiring, promotion, tenure, and salary of women faculty, administrators, and staff

Serious inequities remain in the hiring, promotion, tenure, and salary of women faculty and in the hiring, promotion, and salary of women administrators and staff. Although women students constitute 52 percent of all students today, women faculty comprise only 27 percent of total faculty and only 10 percent of all full professors. Women presidents constitute only 10 percent of all college and university presidents, with about 8 percent women of color. Salary disparities remain in faculty and administrative positions nationwide, despite attempts at some institutions to achieve equity. While disparities are greatest at more senior levels, they continue to exist at entry levels as well.

These inequities need to be addressed and corrective action taken on every campus. Efforts need to be intensified to bring more women into faculty, administrative, and other influential roles. The reasons for this are more than parity and equal opportunity. Women's perspectives and contributions are needed at all levels and in every arena. Students deserve to see numerous women, including women of color, who have achieved, not just a few. The behavior attitudes, and styles of one group—currently, majority males—should not dominate higher education as a whole. Men and women, in all their diversity, need to be working together and learning from one another, providing new approaches to assist us in moving into a new age.

Implied in these recommendations is a new understanding of access. In the 1970s the concept of access applied mostly to entrance into the academy. Majority women have achieved this level of access, although women and men of color have not. Neither majority women nor minority men and women, however, have achieved full access to the arenas that position them for leadership, or to leadership positions themselves. As we approach the 1990s our new definition of access should include access in every arena to every level, including the top. We cannot allow the struggle to blind us to the goal.

Accomplishing these goals will take effort on everyone's part, with specific roles for administrators on campus, including department chairs. Many resources and guidelines on policies and actions to achieve equity in recruitment, retention, promotion, and salary are available. Experience suggests that there is not so much a shortage of ideas as determination to apply them. Most important is personal and institutional commitment, and the belief that it can be done.

3. Provide a supportive campus climate for women

Despite all the gains that have been made, sex discrimination in higher education is a reality. It is pervasive and exists in some form in all institutions. It is, on the whole, less overt than in previous years. Many of the remaining vestiges of sexism fall into the category of covert and sometimes unintentional discrimination against women. Whether overt or subtle, intentional or unintentional, its cumulative effects can be damaging to individuals, to the learning process, and to institutions.

Campus climate issues must be made a high priority in the classroom, the extracurricular program, and the larger community. Campus climate in this context refers to those aspects of the institutional atmosphere and environment that foster or impede women's personal, academic, and professional development. Campus climate issues include a wide range of individual behaviors and attitudes as well as institution-wide policies and practices, formal and informal, that reflect differential treatment of women because of sex. With respect to students, climate issues include classroom and out-of-classroom experiences that affect the learning process (see Hall and Sandler, 1982; 1984). Regarding faculty and administrators, climate issues center on their professional experiences, characterized by subtle social and professional barriers that communicate to women that they are not quite first-class citizens in the academic community (see Sandler and Hall, 1986).

Educational programs designed to help faculty, students, administrators, and staff recognize the micro-inequities that contribute to a generally unfavorable climate are important. The term "micro-inequities," first described by Mary Rowe (Rowe, 1977; see also Sandler and Hall, 1986), refers collectively to ways in which individuals are either singled out, overlooked, ignored, or otherwise discounted on the basis of unchangeable characteristics such as sex, race, ethnicity, handicap, or age. Such behaviors are often so small that they go unnoticed when they occur, but they have a cumulative impact. Becoming aware of such behaviors can be useful to students in preparing for a lifetime of men and women working and living together. A Women's Center or other place where women can congregate to gain support and check out their perceptions during the change process is important. Creation of a Center for the Exploration of Community and Personal Relationships (see discussion below) may also be helpful to men and women in dealing with these changes. A campus-based group focusing on women should collect data on the particular issues facing the campus, analyze them, and plan programs to address them.

4. Make a permanent institutional commitment to women's studies

The discovery and, in some cases, the rediscovery of knowledge about women has not only brought new perspectives to women's lives, but it has also uncovered whole new scholarly dilemmas. What has yet to happen on all of our campuses is the transformation of knowledge and, therefore, of the curriculum demanded by this explosion of new information and by challenges to conventional ways of thinking and knowing. Women's studies, the new scholarship on women, or transformation of the curriculum projects—the names vary according to campus and culture—should be goals of the faculty and academic administration on every campus. Recognizing, supporting, and encouraging this new knowledge is of critical importance to the advancement of knowledge and culture. We have an intellectual as well as a moral obligation to be actively engaged in this process. For this process to be fully responsive to all students it must be interactive with efforts to incorporate knowledge and research on and by minority women and men. Further, it must address pedagogical and classroom climate issues related to the diverse learning needs and preferences of men and women, different ethnic groups, and individuals with differing learning styles. Then, and only then, will the institution be on track in learning to appreciate and foster diversity, and in appropriately preparing tomorrow's leadership.

We recommend that each campus have both a women's studies program and a transformation of the curriculum project that includes women and minority women and men. Both help an institution not only incorporate new research, but examine current theories and methodologies for hidden gender and racial bias that may limit or invalidate their usefulness. The program clearly informs the integration or transformation project. The interaction between the two creates an important dynamic that is necessary to sustain energy for the massive changes called for by new knowledge. Strong institutional priority should be reflected in level of funding and faculty/administrative support.

5. Review all policies for effect on majority women and minority women and men

Policies that have been set in place to correct inequities in the system—such as salary equity reviews, sexual harrassment, grievance procedures, eligibility to be principal investigator in research studies, equal opportunity for women in sport, search procedures for all position levels, including students, faculty, and administration, and so forth—should be reviewed and, possibly, revitalized. Key questions to ask include: What was the intent of the policy? What has been the result? What was the impact on majority women and minority women and men? What policies now need to be established? What impact do you want them to have? How will you assess effectiveness? What will be the review mechanism? Responses should be incorporated in the planning process and new policies established to correct the inequities. All institutional policies should be reviewed periodically to assess whether there is a differential negative impact on majority women and minority women and men, and if corrective action should be taken.

6. Integrate impact studies into the planning process

Many institutions—especially those taking seriously their need to prepare for the future—are going through a long-range planning process. We are concerned with planning, too, and especially with the impact of that planning on majority women and minority women and men. We applaud planning and propose a new component—that at each stage of the planning process the question of *impact on minority/majority women and minority men* be asked. For example, one response to the call for quality in higher education was to raise board score requirements, implying that better quality education would result. Instead, if examined for impact, it might have helped people see that raising entrance requirements is no guarantee that education will be of higher quality. In this case, the quality of education may well remain unchanged, and one impact is that fewer people may have access to it.

If an institution decides to build up its minority enrollment, it needs to ask several questions: What assumption are we making about minorities relative to this institution? What values do we hold that we may need to examine? What are our motivations, e.g., why do we want them here? What adaptations do we need to make institutions more hospitable and help students succeed? What adaptations do we expect the students to make to the institutions? What will be the impact of expected changes on minority students? majority students? faculty? staff? administrators?

Are we aware of the "unofficial requirements" affecting admission and retention, such as assuming that students can make classes at times convenient to faculty, or that they can handle sexist or racist treatment without being demoralized? In recruiting and admitting women faculty and graduate students, are there institutional cultures that are opening their doors without accommodating to women's needs and respecting the concerns raised that differ from those typically raised by men? Is there justification, other than tradition and custom, for not adjusting tenure clocks for pregnancy? In recruiting women administrators, are there institutional policies and culture that mandate, by the power of assumption, traditional sex roles? For example, does the search for a "presidential couple" (or other senior administrative post) overlook excellent candidates, male or female, who are single? These are just some of the questions that are helpful to raise as institutions develop plans for their futures.

7. Give specific attention to sexual harassment

Even though there are several suggestions that lend themselves to examination of this topic, we felt it deserved special mention. Whether incidents of sexual harassment are simply being reported more now than ever before or whether such incidents are on the rise, the devastating effects on the academic and personal lives of students, as well as some faculty and staff, can be tragic.

The educational mission of college or university is to foster an open learning and working environment. Implicit is our ethical obligation to provide an environment that is free from sexual harassment and from the fear that it may occur. Each institution is legally as well as morally obligated to develop policies, procedures, and programs that protect students and employees from sexual harassment and to establish an environment in which such unacceptable behavior will not be tolerated.

An effective campus program on sexual harassment has at least these five elements: (a) a basic definition of what constitutes sexual harassment; (b) a strong policy stating clearly that sexual harassment will not be tolerated; (c) effective communication channels for informing students, faculty, staff, and administrators of the campus policy against sexual harassment; (d) educational programs designed to help all members of the community recognize and discourage sexual harassment; and (e) an accessible, effective, and timely grievance procedure. Alternative methods of initiating complaints and a procedure to insure the rights of all parties are protected as much as possible should be provided (see Sexual Harassment on Campus, 1986).

8. Prepare an annual status report

Institutions should prepare an annual status report on women for the total campus community, including the governing board. This report should be comprehensive and include issues of importance to all women on campus—data on women (majority/minority) administrators, faculty, students, and support staff. Minimally, this report should cover recruiting at all levels, salaries reported by position and compared with men, promotion and tenure decisions by sex (as well as race, ethnicity, age, and handicap), impact studies of new policies on women, continuing problem areas (e.g., salaries), and numbers at every level. It is often useful to focus on a particular aspect each year in addition to the baseline functions of the report.

There are many models for such reporting (see also Bogart et al., 1981; Sandler and Hall, 1986). Time and effort are required for such a report. Sufficient resources, therefore, should be allocated to insure its quality and accuracy. The report should be presented to the entire community. Every group, from governing board members through students, should have an opportunity to discuss openly the issues raised and to develop action plans for eliminating problems.

9. Initiate a campus values inventory

The norms, customs, and beliefs we live by constitute a complex web of interconnections and assumptions we call values. Much of what we value in higher education is either stated in broad, generalized terms or assumed. We should not be surprised, therefore, that questioning these assumptions or making them explicit is an anxiety-producing process. Nonetheless, those who have been excluded or undervalued by these assumed values must persist in attempts to examine and call into question the very values that continue to support their exclusion.

Nearly twenty-three years ago the Civil Rights Act was passed and fifteen years ago major legislation was enacted to protect the rights of women. (The rights of handicapped persons and older persons came later.) These were crucial steps and they have produced dramatic changes in individual as well as institutional behaviors. Now it is time to focus attention on those more fundamental questions of value that continue to prevent the full inclusion of women, minority and majority, and minority men in our total educational system and in society.

For these reasons we recommend that campuses undertake an institutional values inventory that could help clarify what the institution really prizes. The Office of Women in Higher Education plans to work with the Society for Values in Higher Education to expand on their current values assessment tool to include a next stage—to help institutions assess how these values affect their goals for improving the status of majority women and minority women and men.

This process of institutional values clarification holds potential benefits for majority men students as well as for the institution itself. It also serves as a way to validate and encourage majority women and minority men and women. Some majority males are also adversely affected by those aspects of the system that have a negative impact on minorities and women. Institutions that address these values will be enhanced because of their responsiveness and claimed responsibility to their students.

10. Develop an institution-wide concern for children and families

Lately, there has been much said about families and children. Discussions about how families do not spend time together, how the traditional family is "breaking up," how hard being single parents can be, what to think about new configurations of families, are common. We believe that issues of caring for and about children are central to creating a more caring, humane, and effective society. Colleges and universities should begin, if they have not already done so, to think about policies, procedures, and programs that support and encourage families in the broadest sense. Such an approach would include the development of maternity/paternity leave, "stop the clock" tenure policies for childbearing time, and providing childcare that is safe, of high quality, convenient, and affordable.

Since one of our goals is to help our institutions become more humane places, looking at issues for families and childcare is essential. These policies and actions could take many forms, from assistance for parents in caring for children to actually providing a childcare center on campus. Most important is that colleges and universities have an opportunity to take the leadership in seeing that children and, therefore, families become a high priority for our society.

11. Appreciate the value of diversity

Learning to respect diversity, and recognizing that doing so will not be an easy task, are helpful steps in the process of understanding both the need and direction of change. The momentum to perpetuate the prevailing norms is very strong in most institutional settings, so developing a new mind set to appreciate what diversity means takes commitment and perseverance. In a society that values individual performance and achievement as much as ours, understanding diversity can be a real challenge. The struggle to comprehend diversity is in the best tradition of the liberal arts and the scientific method of inquiry, combining what we know from past experience and tradition with a quest to understand what we do not know or understand. Valuing diversity means that there is more than one right way to do things, that there is more than one way to think, feel, believe, and act—that there is more than one world view. To appreciate diversity is to know its richness and to realize that it does not mean second class, decrease in excellence, or change for the sake of change.

The concept of diversity must be remembered when designing curriculum, appointing search committees, planning cultural programs and ceremonies, selecting faculty and campus leaders, recognizing accomplishments, building new programs, determining admissions policies, and thinking about future directions of the institution. It is also important to the design of strategies for institutional assessment. Institutions need means to assess their ability to develop the full potential of women as well as men and minority as well as majority group members. Just as every major shift in values has wrought dramatic change, so, too, could the true celebration of diversity bring new vigor to our institutions. Diversity holds the potential for discovery, innovation, enlightenment, and solutions to the complex problem of how to share this planet.

12. Make leadership development and commitment to fostering women's leadership joint priorities

Institutions must commit to identify, encourage, and develop women and men, minority and majority, who have the potential for making a difference. This suggestion sounds so simple that one might miss its vital significance and fail to create a plan for implementation. Despite extensive discussion on the topic of leadership in recent years, not much has changed. Clark Kerr (1984) discusses the importance to higher education of cultivating its own leaders. Now, more than ever, he believes, these leaders must be sensitive to the feelings, thoughts, and cultures of new and continually emerging constituencies. Planning for the development of talent at every level of the institution should be a major priority.

Institutional leaders also must specifically commit to the identification, encouragement, and development of women leaders. Existing programs to identify and develop new leaders have shown that there are talented women ready and able to become major forces in higher education. (Such programs include the ACE Fellows Program, ACE National Identification Program for the Advancement of Women in Higher Education [ACE/NIP], Higher Education Resource Services [HERS] regional programs, and the Leaders for the Eighties Program of the American Association of Women in Community and Junior Colleges.) What is needed is a commitment to these talented women and the assurance that institutions are ready to consider and hire them.

13. Establish or reaffirm the commitment to a Commission on Women

To help envision, implement, and monitor these recommendations we suggest that each campus establish or reaffirm its commitment to a Commission on Women. The role of a Commission on Women is to identify concerns and issues, coordinate efforts to improve the campus for women, target specific issues to be addressed and monitor their progress, and report to the president and the governing board. Members of the commission should include men as well as women, both minority and majority. The successful commission will have the full and enthusiastic backing of the president and the cooperation and support of those already active on behalf of women's concerns on campus. The appointed chair should be a respected leader with status and support. It is not expected that the institution can be sufficiently influenced by the commission in one, two, or even five years. It is important that the institution have a standing commitment to the commission or other appropriately constituted group.

14. Appoint a high-level person whose formal responsibilities include advocacy for women on campus

Advocacy for women needs to be part of the formal institutional structure. It is not sufficient to make the monitoring of policies and programs the responsibility of volunteers and task forces that come and go, or to assign total responsibility to the human relations office or affirmative action officer. All of these offices have important roles to play, as do other administrators, including department chairs, but someone needs to be concerned with the totality of the institution and its response to women (majority/minority). The importance of a paid person assigned to do so should not be dismissed.

The person designated to have this responsibility could be a senior administrator or faculty member. Whatever her (or possibly his) role, the person should be a highly respected member of the academic community. The appointment should convey the importance of this person—through title, salary, reporting relationship, and/or released time for this role—to the chief executive officer and to the institution as a whole. The designated person should be given staff and funding to do the job well.

There are many possible ways of implementing this suggestion and each campus must decide what will work best for it. Some existing models include an Associate Provost for Women's Affairs, a Special Assistant to the President with institutionwide responsibility for women's equity and concerns, and an Office of Women's Affairs. It is important for the designated person and/or office to work closely with other formal and informal groups concerned with women's issues on campus. The office also could enhance the role of the Commission on Women by providing staff support to it. It also is important to note that a similar role must be constructed to support minority concerns on campus. These two people working in tandem would benefit majority students, both women and men, as well as minority students, both women and men.

15. Create a center for the exploration of community and personal relationships

Our final recommendation is a very new idea offered for consideration. Over the years, individual and group counseling has played a very important role in the lives of students and, on some campuses, faculty and staff. With the advent of new or different expectations for the ways that men and women work and live together, students, faculty, and staff now need individual and group attention to work through these issues. Massive changes in societal gender roles have implications for education that are at least as profound as the technological revolution. Most campuses have established computer centers to help computerize their campuses. This requires providing technical skill; teaching faculty, staff, and students new attitudes while also establishing competence in a new area; and overcoming predictable fear and resistence to change. Most also have counseling centers that provide individual and group counseling for students and, on some campuses, faculty and staff. It could be useful to provide, through a center or program, comprehensive services including educational programs; opportunities to discuss feelings, attitudes, and values regarding new demands for equity between the sexes; and settings that make it comfortable for faculty, staff, and students to raise questions about their own and each others' expectations about what constitutes appropriate behavior in this changing world.

Unintentional behavior that devalues women's contributions and their self-worth in the classroom, feelings about the intent and quality of women's scholarship, and assumptions about women interested in nontraditional careers or, conversely, men interested in nontraditional careers, take valuable time away from the seriousness of the academic enterprise. Active attention to these problems is urgently needed. Nonetheless, active pursuit of these questions is critical to effective education. Creation of a center or program where these kinds of problems could be addressed in a variety of ways could serve as a powerful catalyst for the examination of both institutional and personal values. It could, in essence, provide education on how to respect and know oneself and others, an essential tool for today's educated person.

CONCLUSION

There are no cookbooks, prescriptions, or magic formulas for the changes that must occur. If there were, we would have used them already. There are some checklists, there are a few models for change, there is an enormous body of knowledge that needs to be integrated. There are women leaders and thinkers in every facet of the areas mentioned in this chapter and in the book of which it is a part. And there is real and latent desire for the kinds of change discussed in this paper.

What is essential is to recognize that each person has a role to play, and that collectively we can reshape and redirect our institutions. We need to be aware of the complexity and difficulty of the concepts that require understanding, the values that will be challenged, and the problems that will be encountered. We need to be prepared for the time it will take, but delay no longer. Then, and only then, will we be able to move this agenda and, concomitantly, our institutions and our society to bring women into their rightful place in the world.

REFERENCES

BOGART, KAREN, et al. *Institutional Self-Study Guide on Sex Equity for Postsecondary Educational Institutions.* Washington, D.C.: Project on the Status and Education of Women, Association of American Colleges, 1981

HALL, ROBERTA M., and SANDLER, BERNICE R. *The Classroom Climate: A Chilly One for Women?* Washington, D.C.: Project on the status and Education of Women, Association of American Colleges, 1982.

————. *Out of the Classroom: A Chilly Climate for Women?* Washington, D.C.: Project on the Status and Education of Women, Association of American Colleges, 1984.

KERR, CLARK. *Presidents Make a Difference: Strengthening Presidential Leadership in Colleges and Universities.* A Report of the Commission on Strengthening Presidential Leadership. Washington, D.C.: Association of Governing Boards, 1984.

ROWE, MARY P. "The Saturn's Rings Phenomenon: Micro-Inequities and Unequal Opportunity in American Economy." In Patricia Bourne and Velma Parness, eds., *Proceedings* of the National Science Foundation's Conference on Women's Leadership and Authority. Santa Cruz, Calif.: University of California, 1977.

SANDLER, BERNICE R. and HALL, ROBERTA M. *The Campus Climate Revisited: Chilly for Women Faculty, Administrators, and Graduate Students.* Washington, D.C.: Project on the Status and Education of Women, Association of American Colleges, 1986.

Sexual Harassment on Campus: Suggestions for Reviewing Campus Policy and Educational Programs. Washington, D.C.: American Council on Education, 1986.

Contributors

DIANNE ANDREWS is currently Associate Producer for a public television documentary on energy conservation. She has broad experience in environmental education, including work with *Environment* magazine, the Center for the Biology of Natural Systems at Washington University, and the Wilderness Society. She has a teaching credential for secondary schools and an abiding interest in women's studies and educational policy.

PATRICIA BELL-SCOTT is Associate Professor, The School of Family Studies, University of Connecticut, Storrs; co-editor of *All the Women Are White, All the Blacks Are Men, But Some of Us Are Brave* (Feminist Press, 1982); and founding co-editor of *SAGE: A Scholarly Journal on Black Women.* She is nationally known for her leadership and advocacy of minority women and her scholarship on Black women.

JESSIE BERNARD is a distinguished scholar, author, and sociologist. She taught for many years at Pennsylvania State University and retired from academia with the status of Research Scholar Honoris Causa. She has written numerous articles and more than a dozen books, the most recent of which are *The Female World* (1981) and *The Female World from a Global Perspective* (1987). Other books by her include *Self Portrait of a Family,* based on thirty years of correspondence with her three children; *Women, Wives, Mothers; The Future of Motherhood; The Future of Marriage;* and *Women and the Public Interest.*

KAREN BOGART is President of the MAFERR Foundation, Inc., which conducts research on sex roles and seeks to improve the status of women and men in the family, education, employment, and health care. She also co-directs Consultants for Design and Analysis, a social and behavioral research firm located in Great Falls, Virginia. Her publications include the *Institutional Self-Study Guide on Sex Equity for Postsecondary Educational Institutions* and *Toward Equity: An Action Manual for Women in Academe.*

MARILYN J. BOXER is Dean of the College of Arts and Letters and Professor of Women's Studies at San Diego State University. She is co-author and editor of *Connecting Spheres: Women in the Western World, 1500 to the Present* (Oxford University Press, 1987). She has written on French women's history and on women's studies, including the essay "For and About Women: The Theory and Practice of Women's Studies in the United States" in *SIGNS: A Journal of Women in Society and Culture.*

CAROLYN DESJARDINS is Director of the National Institute for Leadership Development, Maricopa County Community Colleges, in Phoenix, Arizona. She is a nationally known lecturer and workshop leader on women's issues—leadership, adult development, and college reentry. She recently spent a semester at Carol Gilligan's center at Harvard and also lectures on Gilligan's work.

YVONNE DUFFY is author of *All Things Are Possible*, a study of the life-styles of women with physical disabilities. A widely acknowledged expert on the sexuality and self-esteem of women with disabilities, she speaks frequently at conferences and workshops across the country. When not traveling, she makes her home in Ann Arbor, Michigan, where she writes a local newspaper column and participates in politics and community activities.

ROBBI FERRON is Director of the Office of Affirmative Action at the University of Kansas. She is Lakota Rosebud Sioux whose activities include having served as a homemaker, parent, artist, teacher, counselor, tribal court judge, and higher education administrator. She has a strong record in volunteer activities at the local, state, and national level. She is an attorney.

FAITH GABELNICK is Director of the Honors College, Western Michigan University. She previously served as Associate Director of the Honors Program and as affiliate faculty member in Women's Studies and in Family and Community Development at the University of Maryland. She has received postdoctoral training in group process, psychology of women, and analytic psychology. Her major work has involved presentations, conferences, and consultations in organizational dynamics, intellectual development, and classroom teaching strategies.

JANE S. GOULD is former Director of Career Services at Barnard College from 1965 to 1972. She was founder and the first permanent director of the Barnard Women's Center from 1972 to 1983. Since retiring from Barnard, her activities have included participating as a member of Women's Studies International in the United Nations End of the Decade Women's Forum in Nairobi in 1985 and as a member of a Russell Sage Foundation Task Force on the Project on Women in Higher Education.

ELIZABETH DODSON GRAY is Co-director of the Bolton Institute for a Sustainable Future in Wellesley, Massachusetts, as well as coordinator of the Theological Opportunities Program at Harvard Divinity School. She has taught at MIT's Sloan School of Management, Williams College, and Boston College. She combines environmental and futurist concerns with Christian ethics and theology, using her own feminist adaptation of insights drawn from the sociology of knowledge. She is the author of *Green Paradise Lost* (1979) and *Patriarchy as a Conceptual Trap* (1982).

BEVERLY GUY-SHEFTALL is Director of the Women's Research and Resource Center and Associate Professor of English at Spelman College. She is co-editor of *Sturdy Black Bridges: Visions of Black Women in Literature* (Doubleday, 1979); founding co-editor of *SAGE: A Scholarly Journal on Black Women;* and author of *Spelman: A Centennial Celebration* (Delmar, 1981). She serves on the Executive Board of the National Council for Research on Women and is a widely recognized scholar on Black women.

ANNE L. HAFNER is a statistician at the Center for Education Statistics in Washington, D.C. She formerly was a research analyst at the Higher Education Research Institute at UCLA. She served as founding editor-in-chief of the *UCLA Journal of Education.* Her current areas of research include construct validation, cross-national comparison of teaching methods, test bias, and higher education issues.

JUDITH HARRIS is Associate Professor at the University of Colorado Museum. She is a vertebrate paleontologist who has studied the evolution of African ecosystems and fish systematics. In addition to her paleontological teaching, she has taught a course in Women and Science for the last three years and is currently working on a book that explores our concepts of form, time, space, and evaluation through history.

MARY M. LEONARD is Staff Psychologist at the Counseling Center and Associate Professor in the Counseling and Personnel Services program, College of Education, University of Maryland. Her research interests include leadership development and empowerment of women, examining the perceptions of differential treatment of students on college campuses, and the role of denial in the perception of sexism. She developed the Campus Environment Survey, an instrument which examines campus and classroom climate. She is a nationally recognized speaker and consultant on these topics.

ABIGAIL MCCARTHY is currently President of Herald Communications, Ltd. She is the author of the critically acclaimed memoir, *Private Faces/Public Places*, of three novels (*Circles, A Washington Story*, and *One Woman Lost*), and other works. She lectures frequently on college and university campuses and is known for her work in ecumenical activities, her concern with women's equality and interracial justice, and her dedication to her four children. She has received many honors and awards.

PEGGY MEANS MCINTOSH is Associate Director of the Wellesley College Center for Research on Women. She directs several faculty development programs and has consulted widely with college, university, and secondary-school faculty interested in integrating materials and perspectives from women's studies into their curricula. She is co-founder of the Rocky Mountain Women's Institute and a contributing editor of the *Women's Studies Quarterly*. She and Elizabeth Minnich are co-authoring a guidebook on implications of women's studies for humanities disciplines.

TONI A. H. MCNARON is Professor and Director of Undergraduate Studies in English at the University of Minnesota. She also teaches regularly in Women's Studies and has edited two books (one on incest and one on the sister bond). Her current research includes revising her autobiography (*Magnolias for Whites Only*) and writing a book about Virginia Woolf's primary relationships with the many women who sustained her.

SARA E. MELÉNDEZ is Director of the Special Minority Initiatives and Associate Director of the Office of Minority Concerns of the American Council on Education. She is the past president of the National Association for Bilingual Education, and she currently serves as an

Overseer of the Wellesley College Center for Research on Women. She is co-author, with Alba Ambert, of *Bilingual Education: A Sourcebook* (Teachers College Press, 1987). She has written numerous articles and spoken about minorities and women in higher education and bilingual education at meetings and conferences around the United States.

CAROLE W. MINOR is Associate Professor and Chair of the Counselor Education Faculty at Northern Illinois University, DeKalb, Illinois. She has written articles and book chapters on career resource centers and career theory and co-produced a videotape, "New Faces at Work," about men and women in nontraditional occupations. Her recent research interests include factors influencing the career decisions of women in traditional and nontraditional occupations. She is a member of the Board of Directors of the National Career Development Association.

ELIZABETH KAMARCK MINNICH is a faculty member of The Union Graduate School and Coordinator of its graduate Women's Studies program. She is a nationally known consultant and writer on the theory and practice of curriculum transformation projects, working with a feminist critique of the liberal arts as preparation for the inclusion of women's studies materials.

L. LEOTUS MORRISON is Associate Director of Athletics at James Madison University in Harrisonburg, Virginia. She was Past President of the Association for Intercollegiate Athletics for Women, the National Association for Girls and Women in Sport, and served on the U.S. Olympic Committee for eight years. She is an expert on athletics, especially the development and administration of sport programs for women, and has been a speaker and official delegate to numerous national and international conferences, including a UNESCO Conference on Sport and Physical Education and the First Pan-American Conference on Women in Sport.

JEAN F. O'BARR is Director of Women's Studies at Duke University and the Editor of *Signs: Journal of Women in Culture and Society*. A political scientist, she has written in the area of language and politics, Third World women, and women and education. For eleven years she served as the Director of Continuing Education at Duke, developing programs for adult women and men to return to school, to pursue leisure interests, and to make effective use of their retirement opportunities.

CAROL S. PEARSON is President of Meristem, a center for professional development and personal growth that offers consulting and educational services in areas such as curriculum development, teaching and learning, learning assessment, team-building, and leadership development. Former academic dean at Goucher College and director of Women's Studies at the University of Maryland, she is the author of numerous articles and three books: *The Hero Within: Six Archetypes We Live By* (1986); *The Female Hero in American and British Literature* (1981) (with Katherine Pope); and *Who Am I This Time? Female Portraits in American and British Literature* (1976) (also with Katherine Pope).

JANICE PETROVICH is Director of the ASPIRA Institute for Policy Research at the ASPIRA National Office in Washington, D.C. She is founder of the Center for Research and Documentation on Women (Centro de Investigacion y Documentacion de la Mujer—CIDOM) at Inter American University of Puerto Rico and has spoken, written, and conducted research on Puerto Rican women and sex equity.

MARY P. ROWE is Special Assistant to the President of Massachusetts Institute of Technology. She has served in that position, as a full-time ombudsman, since 1973. She is also Adjunct Professor of Management at the Sloan School of Management. She is an editor of *Negotiation Journal*, past president of the Corporate Ombudsman Association, was a founding Board member of *Sojourner*, and is Secretary on the Board of the Bay State Skills Corporation. She has spoken and published widely on subtle discrimination, day care, harassment, complaint systems, and other problems of women and minorities in the workplace.

DONNA L. SHAVLIK is Director of the Office of Women in Higher Education of the American Council on Education. An expert of women's advancement in higher education, she is founder of ACE's National Identification Program for the Advancement of Women in Higher Education. She has written about and consulted widely on issues affecting women in higher education for over fifteen years. With Judith G. Touchton, she is currently working on a study of women college presidents and on the first *ACE Fact Book on Women in Higher Education.*

CAROLYN M. SHREWSBURY is Professor of Political Science at Mankato State University in Minnesota. She previously chaired the Women's Studies Department at that university and has written and spoken widely on topics related to feminist pedagogy and feminist leadership issues. She was the recipient of a Chancellor's Fellowship funded by the Bush Foundation.

BRENDA ALPERT SIGALL is a clinical psychologist at the University of Maryland Counseling Center and in private practice. She has been appointed to the Maryland Governor's Task Force on Eating Disorders and does extensive speaking, program design, training, and consultation on role conflict, leadership, and eating disorders.

JOANN SILVERSTEIN has been Assistant Professor in Civil, Environmental, and Architectural Engineering at the University of Colorado since 1982. Since 1982 she has worked professionally in environmental engineering, specifically in water and waste treatment. She has been especially concerned with increasing the presence of women in engineering. 75 percent of her graduate students are women.

BARRIE THORNE is Professor of Sociology at Michigan State University, where she also teaches in the Women's Studies Program. She is former chair of the Section on Sex and Gender, and of the Committee on the Status of Women, of the American Sociological Association. She co-edited *Language, Gender and Society* (1983) and *Rethinking the Family: Some Feminist Questions* (1982), and is currently writing an ethnography of gender arrangements among elementary school children.

M. ELIZABETH TIDBALL is Professor of Physiology at the George Washington University Medical Center. Widely published and honored both as scientist and educator, her research of the past few decades has utilized an interdisciplinary approach to characterize collegiate environments most conducive to the development of women and men who subsequently attain outstanding intellectual or career accomplishments. She has served as a member of and consultant to a number of college governing boards, on the editorial boards of several scholarly journals, and on innumerable national commissions and committees.

TIN-MALA is Project Director for Asian American Enterprises: "An Educational Equity Blueprint for Asian American Students," funded by the Women's Educational Equity Act program, U.S. Department of Education. She is an outspoken advocate for Asian-Americans, with a long-standing commitment to women's issues and, more recently, to student's concerns. In 1985–1986 Tin-Mala conceived and directed the WEEA project "From the Curriculum to the Mainstream," through which pilot courses on Asian-American women were conducted at leading universities nationwide.

JUDITH G. TOUCHTON is Deputy Director of the Office of Women in Higher Education and Director of the Senior Executive Leadership Service of the American Council on Education. She has written and spoken widely on topics related to the status of women in higher education, career development of academic women, sex equity, administrative searches, and professional development of women and men in the academy. With Donna L. Shavlik, she is currently completing a study of women college presidents and preparing the first *ACE Fact Book on Women in Higher Education.*

MARGARET B. WILKERSON is a professor in the Department of Afro-American Studies at the University of California at Berkeley. She is former Director of the Center for the Study, Education and Advancement of Women at Berkeley and has written on topics related to equity, affirmative action, and educational leadership. A nationally known theatre educator, she is the author of *9 Plays by Black Women*, the first anthology of its kind, and is currently writing a literary biography of Lorraine Hansberry.

JOANNE SANAE YAMAUCHI is Professor of Communication, American University, Washington, D.C. Her research, teaching, and consulting interests include interpersonal communication management in organizational, intercultural, Asian-American, women's, and human-computer contexts. She has integrated her research and teaching through conducting applied communications management workshops for all of the major national Asian-American associations and all major federal government agencies.

Resource List

WOMEN'S ORGANIZATIONS

AMERICAN ASSOCIATION FOR THE ADVANCEMENT OF SCIENCE (AAAS)
Office of Opportunities in Science
1333 H Street, N.W.
Washington, D.C. 20005
202/326-6670

Sponsors a LINKAGES project for community organizations to promote the involvement of women, minorities, and the disabled in science, engineering, technology, and math.

AMERICAN ASSOCIATION OF WOMEN IN COMMUNITY AND JUNIOR COLLEGES
American Association of Community and Junior Colleges
1 Dupont Circle, N.W., Suite 410
Washington, D.C. 20036
202/293-7050
Dr. Jacquelyn M. Belcher, President
Address: Vice President for Instruction, Lane Community College, 4000 East 30th Avenue, Eugene, OR 97405 (503-747-4501)

Organization working for the concerns of women in community colleges. Represents its members on a regional and state basis. Benefits include a quarterly newsletter, a job bank, and a variety of professional development activities for women in two-year colleges at the local, state, and regional levels. Sponsors "Leaders for the Eighties" project, a project to identify and train women administrators for senior positions in community colleges.

ASSOCIATION OF BLACK WOMEN IN HIGHER EDUCATION
c/o United Negro College Fund
500 East 62nd Street
New York, NY 10021
212/326-1239
Lea E. Williams, Edd., President

Network of black women administrators from the MidAtlantic region. Association publishes a quarterly newsletter highlighting topics of interests to black women administrators and sponsors an annual conference addressing issues of concern to black women.

**HIGHER EDUCATION RESOURCE SERVICES (HERS) -
NEW ENGLAND**
Wellesley College
Cheever House
Wellesley, MA 02181
617/235-0320 ext. 2529
Cynthia Secor, Director

Sponsors the Management Institute for Women in Higher Education, an integrated seminar series offering women administrators and faculty professional management training. Institute held in five weekends during academic year, at Wellesley College.

**HIGHER EDUCATION RESOURCE SERVICES (HERS) -
MID AMERICA**
University of Denver
Colorado Women's College Campus
Denver, CO 80220
303/871-6866
Cynthia Secor, Director

Sponsors professional development activities designed to improve the status of women in higher education.

**HIGHER EDUCATION RESOURCE SERVICES (HERS) -
WEST**
University of Utah
293 Olpin Union Building
Salt Lake City, UT 84112
801/581-3745
Shauna Adix, Director

Provides professional development opportunities to enhance the visibility and upward mobility of women in all areas of higher education. Sponsors annual four-day Summer Institute. Serves primarily the Inter-mountain west states.

HERS SUMMER INSTITUTE FOR WOMEN IN HIGHER EDUCATION ADMINISTRATION
Bryn Mawr College
Bryn Mawr, PA 19010
215/645-6161
Cynthia Secor, Co-Director
Margaret Healy, Co-Director

Residential program on the Bryn Mawr College campus offering women faculty and administrators intensive training in educational administration and management skills.

MEXICAN AMERICAN WOMEN'S NATIONAL ASSOCIATION
1201 16th Street, N.W.
Suite 420
Washington, D.C. 20036
202/822-7888
Veronica Collazo, President

Concerned with the status of women of Mexican American descent. Provides a national forum for Mexican American women in various political, educational, and professional fields. Offers information on scholarships and sponsors an annual conference.

NATIONAL ASSOCIATION FOR GIRLS AND WOMEN IN SPORT
1900 Association Drive
Reston, VA 22091
703/476-3450
Sue G. Mottinger, Executive Director

Devoted to providing opportunities for girls and women in sport related disciplines and careers. Mission is to serve as the primary organization under an educational aegis for professional development of girls and women as sport leaders and to advocate programs of sports and physical activity for all females. Members include professionals involved in teaching, coaching or officiating sports, athletic administration and athletic training, club sports, and intramurals.

NATIONAL ASSOCIATION FOR WOMEN DEANS, ADMINISTRATORS, AND COUNSELORS
1325 18th Street, N.W.
Suite 210
Washington, D.C. 20006
202/659-9330
Patricia Rueckel, Executive Director

National professional organization providing information and support for women educators. Engages in a variety of activities designed to encourage

professional growth and renewal of its members. Sponsors annual conference, numerous publications, including bibliographies on women in higher
educations. Publications list available upon request.

NATIONAL COUNCIL FOR RESEARCH ON WOMEN
Sara Delano Roosevelt Memorial House
47-49 East 65th Street
New York, NY 10021
212/570-5003
Mariam Chamberlin, President
Mary Ellen Capek, Executive Secretary

An independent association of established centers and organizations which
provide institutional resources for feminist research, policy analysis, and
educational programs. Institutional membership.

NATIONAL IDENTIFICATION PROGRAM (ACE/NIP)
Office of Women in Higher Education
American Council on Education
1 Dupont Circle, N.W., Suite 887
Washington, D.C. 20036
202/939-9390
Donna Shavlik, Director

Program through which ACE's Office of Women in Higher Education addresses its primary goal of advancing talented women in the administration
of colleges and universities. At both state and national levels, the aim is to
develop and strengthen a series of overlapping networks which offer opportunities for linkages between and among women administrators and other
prominent educational leaders.

NATIONAL INSTITUTE FOR WOMEN OF COLOR (NIWC)
P. O. Box 50583
Washington, D.C. 20004
202/291-6615
Sharon Parker, Chair, Board of Directors

The National Institute for Women of Color, founded in 1981, is a nonprofit
organization created to enhance the strengths of diversity and to promote
educational and economic equity for women of color (Hispanic, Black, Asian
American, Pacific Islander, American Indian, Alaskan Native.)

NATIONAL NETWORK OF HISPANIC WOMEN
12021 Wilshire Boulevard
Suite 353
Los Angeles, CA 90025
213/938-6176
Celia Torres, Chair

Resource and dissemination project linking Hispanic women in business, higher education, and civic affairs. Concerned with issues related to education, employment, leadership development, and advancement of Hispanic women and girls.

NATIONAL WOMEN'S STUDIES ASSOCIATION
Art-Sociology Building, Room 3311E
University of Maryland
College Park, MD 20742
301/454-3757
Caryn McTighe Musil, Director

Founded to promote the educational, political, and professional development of women's studies and feminist education. Members include individuals, academic and community based programs and projects, women's centers, and groups interested in feminist education at every level and in every setting.

NORTH AMERICAN INDIAN WOMEN'S ASSOCIATION
202/534-7107

Dedicated to the personal and intellectual development and the social support and nurturance of Native American women, and to the preservation of the various native cultures of the women. Through its programs and conferences NAIWA serves the needs of individual women and girls as well as the different tribes.

ORGANIZATION FOR PAN ASIAN WOMEN
P. O. Box 39128
Washington, D.C. 20016
202/659-9370
June Inuzuka, President

Pan Asian is the oldest public policy organization representing the concerns and perspectives of Asian and Pacific Islander women in the nation's capitol. With its unique multi ethnic focus, it seeks to insure the full participation of Asian Pacific American women in all aspects of American society, especially in those areas where women have been traditionally excluded or underrepresented.

THE PROJECT ON THE STATUS AND EDUCATION OF WOMEN
Association of American Colleges
1818 R Street, N.W.
Washington, D.C. 20009
202/387-1300
Bernice R. Sandler, Director

Provides information concerning women students, faculty, and administrators and works with institutions, government agencies, and other associations and programs relating to women in higher education. Develops and distributes materials which identify and highlight institutional and federal policies as well as other issues affecting women's status on campus. Publishes *On Campus With Women*, a newsletter to which individuals may subscribe.

PUBLICATIONS

American Council on Education, *The Fact Book on Higher Education.* New York: ACE/Macmillan, 1986–87. Updated biennially.
  Includes population and demographic statistics, higher education institutional characteristics, faculty characteristics, earned degree data, enrollment data, and financial statistics.
American Council on Education. *Minorities in Higher Education: Annual Status Report.* Office on Minority Concerns, American Council on Education, One Dupont Circle, Suite 800, Washington, D.C., 20036.
  Provides an overview of the condition of education for Asians, Blacks, Chicanos, Native Americans, and Puerto Ricans. Includes statistical and narrative summaries. Updated annually.
Bogart, Karen, ed. *Institutional Self-Study Guide on Sex Equity for Postsecondary Educational Institutions,* 1981. Sponsored by the American Institutes for Research. 5 booklets. Available from the Association of American Colleges, Project on the Status and Education of Women, 1818 R Street, N.W., Washington, D.C., 20009.
  Guide designed to facilitate voluntary institutional change and enhance sex equity in education and employment. Includes easy-to-read checklists accompanied by suggestions for possible actions or responses.
Center for Educational Statistics, U. S. Department of Education. *Digest of Educational Statistics, 1987.* Updated annually. Washington, D.C.: Government Printing Office.
Geis, F. L., Carter, Mae R., and Butler, D. J. *Seeing and Evaluating People.* University of Delaware, Newark, DE, 1982.
  A summary of scientific research on perception and perceptual bias. Examines the role of stereotypes in perception and evaluation and suggests ways to counteract perceptual bias and invisible discrimination. Research report (84 pages) or summary (20 pages) available upon request from the Office of Women's Affairs, University of Delaware, DE 19711.
Hall, Roberta M., and Sandler, Bernice R. *The Classroom Climate: A Chilly One for Women?* Association of American Colleges, Project on the Status and Education of Women, 1818 R Street, N.W., Washington, D.C., 20009, 1982.
Hall, Roberta M., and Sandler, Bernice R. *Out of the Classroom: A Chilly Climate for Women?* Association of American Colleges, Project on the Status and Education of Women, 1818 R Street, N.W., Washington, D.C., 20009, 1984.

Hall, Roberta M., and Sandler, Bernice R. *The Campus Climate Revisited: Chilly for Women Faculty, Administrators, and Graduate Students*. Association of American Colleges, Project on the Status and Education of Women, 1818 R Street, N.W., Washington, D.C., 20009, 1986.

Howe, Florence, Howard, Suzanne, and Strauss, Mary J.B., eds. *Everywoman's Guide to Colleges and Universities*. Old Westbury, NY: The Feminist Press, 1982.

Minority Women's Organizations and Programs: A Partial Annotated List. Association of American Colleges, Project on the Status and Education of Women, 1818 R Street, N.W., Washington, D.C., 1984.

On Campus with Women. Published quarterly. Washington, D.C.: Association of American Colleges, Project on the Status and Education of Women, 1818 R Street, N.W., Washington, D.C., 20009.

Rix, Sara E., ed. *The American Woman, 1987–88: A Report in Depth*. Prepared for the Women's Research and Education Institute of the Congressional Caucus for Women's Issues. New York: W.W. Norton, 1987.

SAGE: A Scholarly Journal on Black Women. Published quarterly. Atlanta: SAGE Women's Educational Press, P. O. Box 42741, Atlanta, GA, 30311.

Schmitz, Betty. *Integrating Women's Studies into the Curriculum*. Old Westbury, NY: The Feminist Press, 1985.

"Sexual Harassment on Campus: Suggestions for Reviewing Campus Policy and Educational Programs." American Council on Education, One Dupont Circle, Suite 800, Washington, D.C., 20036. 1986.

Shavlik, Donna L., and Touchton, Judith G. *Women Chief Executive Officers in Colleges and Universities*. Summary table prepared annually by the Office of Women in Higher Education, American Council on Education, One Dupont Circle, Washington, D.C., 20036.

Journal of Women in Culture and Society. Published quarterly. Chicago: University of Chicago Press, 5801 Ellis Avenue, Chicago, IL, 60637.

A journal of women in culture and society, offering research papers in many academic fields. Contains essays, short stories, and articles.

Vetter, Betty M., and Babco, Eleanor L. *Professional Women and Minorities*. Commission on Professionals in Science and Technology, 1500 Massachusetts Ave., N.W., Suite 831, Washington, D.C., 20005.

Provides comprehensive coverage of the academic workforce with emphasis on faculty by discipline. Contains data on participation and availability of women and/or minorities in those professions generally requiring formal education to the baccalaureate degree as a minimum.

Women's Studies Quarterly. 311 East 94th Street, New York, NY 10128.

SELECTED SOURCES OF NATIONAL DATA ON GIRLS AND WOMEN IN EDUCATION

Education Information Office, Office of Educational Research and Improvement, U. S. Department of Education, Washington, D.C., 20208. Tel: 800-424-1616; local 626-9854.

Women's Bureau, Department of Labor, 200 Constitution Avenue, N.W., Room 3309, Washington, D.C., 20210. Tel: 202-523-6627.

Bureau of Labor Statistics, U. S. Department of Labor, 441 G Street, N.W., Room 2486, Washington, D.C., 20212. Tel: 202-523-1944.

Education and Social Stratification Branch, Population Division, U. S. Census Bureau, Washington, D.C., 20233. Tel: 202-763-1154.

National Commission on Professionals in Science and Technology, 1500 Massachusetts Avenue, N.W., Washington, D.C., 20005. Tel: 202-223-6995.

National Science Foundation, 1800 G Street, N.W., Washington, D.C., 20550. Tel: 202-357-7734.

INDEX

INDEX

A

Acosta, R. Vivian, 259
Adams, Abigail, 284
Adams, John, 177, 283–284
Adams, Mischa, 321
Adamsky, Cathryn, 312
Adelman, Mala B., 64
Adelson, Joseph, 162
Administrators, 5, 11
Admissions, 4, 66, 70
Advancement, 351
Advocacy for women, 455–456
Affirmative action, 4, 52, 151
Age Discrimination in
    Employment Act of 1967, 4
Agnes Scott College, 213
Agonito, Rosemary, 300
Agor, Weston H., 326
Alcoholism, American Indian
    women and, 87
Aldrich, Michelle, 295
*All the Women Are White, All the
    Blacks Are Men, But Some of
    Us Are Brave* (Hull, Smith, and
    Bell-Scott), 206
Allen, M., 43
Alper, T.G., 237
Alternative institutions, 150
Alumnae, 12
    of Catholic women's colleges,
        180
    women's centers and, 227–228
    of women's colleges, 166–167
Ambitions and Realizations
    (McLaren), 94
American Association for Health,
    Physical Education and
    Recreation (AAHPER), 254
American Council on Education,
    71

Commission on Women in
    Higher Education, 97, 444
National Identification Program
    for the Advancement of
    Women in Higher Education,
    151, 385–386, 392
Office of Women in Higher
    Education, 150–151, 158, 373,
    388, 392, 444
American Indian women, 21,
    80–89
    acculturation of, 81
    activism and, 85–86
    alcoholism and, 87
    diversity of, 80–82
    educational funding and, 82–84
    enrollment statistics, 34
    right-brain dominance and,
        84–85
    women's movement and, 87–88
American Psychological
    Association, Committee on
    Black Women's Concerns, 207
Anderson, Richard E., 168
Andrews, Dianne, 6, 294–310
Androcentrism, 300–301
Angelou, Maya, 214
Annual status report, 451
Anthony, Susan, 284
Arkoff, A., 73
Arnold, Matthew, 405
Asian/Pacific American Concerns
    Staff, 76
Asian Pacific American women,
    20–21, 69–79
    current educational initiatives
        and, 74–75
    enrollment statistics, 34
    implications for institutional
        change and, 75–77
    value orientations, 72–74

(Continued from front flap)

Practical as well as scholarly, **Educating the Majority** emphasizes both essential theoretical foundations and concrete examples and recommendations about what can be done to remedy current problems. The contributions offer fresh insights and workable models for effective change. This volume will encourage dialogue and further study that will advance research and practice in this critical area of higher education, and empower educators to make changes that will benefit women specifically and higher education generally. The book is intellectually stimulating, exciting reading for all college and university presidents, deans, chancellors, chairpersons, faculty members, trustees, administrators, policymakers, and students.

About the editors
Carol S. Pearson is President, Meristem, in University Park, Maryland. **Donna L. Shavlik** and **Judith G. Touchton** are, respectively, Director and Deputy Director of the Office of Women in Higher Education, American Council on Education.